Cities in Transition

Cities in Transition focuses on the sustainability transitions initiated in 40 European cities. The book presents the incredible wealth of insights gathered through hundreds of interviews and questionnaires. Four key domains – local energy systems, local green spaces, local water systems and local labour markets – have been the focus of the field research investigating local potentials for social innovation and new forms of civil society self-organisation. Examining the potential of new organisational frameworks like cooperatives, multistakeholder constructions, local–regional partnerships and networks for the success of such transitions, this book presents the key ingredients of a sustainable urban community as a viable concept to address current global financial, environmental and social challenges.

Crucial reading for academics and practitioners of urban planning and sustainability in Europe, *Cities in Transition* is an innovative roadmap for sustainability in changing cities.

Thomas Sauer is Professor of Economics at the Jena University of Applied Sciences (EAH), Department of Business Administration. His key qualifications as a researcher are urban and regional economics and the analysis of collective decision-making. He is member of several international economic associations like the International Society for Ecological Economics.

Susanne Elsen has worked as Professor of Sociology and Social Development at the Free University of Bolzano since 2010. She is Vice Dean for research and Director of the Faculty of Education's PhD Programme. Her main research topics are social innovation, local development and community economy, sustainability and post-growth society.

Cristina Garzillo is coordinator for Governance and Social Innovation at ICLEI – Local Governments for Sustainability. Previously contract professor at the University of Parma, she is recognised for her expertise in local sustainability processes, integrated management and governance, and her publications in the field of local sustainability, knowledge brokerage and transition.

"This is an unusual book: no cheap language on green growth, no moral appeals as to what should be done for a sustainability transition. Instead: serious comparative analysis for forty cities in Europe, based on careful theoretical reasoning in the tradition of Ostrom and focussing on the conditions of self-organization of civil society."
—Marina Fischer-Kowalski, Institute for Social Ecology Vienna

"*Cities in Transition* provides a rich and innovative inventory of the decision making and organization of urban sustainable transitions. By empirically identifying the potentials of new urban organizational frameworks, the authors demonstrate the key ingredients to a successful transition towards sustainable urban prosperity."
—Wiltrud Terlau, Bonn-Rhein-Sieg University of Applied Sciences

"The literature on urban bottom-up solutions to counter climate change and other environmental problems is quickly growing. This contribution is particularly attractive because of its systematic approach covering water through energy to green spaces and even local labour markets. The thorough empirical basis, involving a careful selection of relevant city case studies and their comparison, means a great step forward in comparison with previous studies. The book moreover provides an ambitious theoretical synthesis of recent thinking on such diverse issues as a multi-level sustainability transition, Ostrom's management approach to common pool resources, and the revived debate on growth-versus-the-environment."
—Jeroen van den Bergh, Universitat Autònoma de Barcelona

"This book advances the concept of urban commons by invigorating the role they play in urban sustainability transitions. With a fresh look on the institutional configurations in cities and how they challenge political processes and governance architectures, the book opens a new theoretical pathway of urban studies for sustainability."
—Niki Frantzeskaki, Erasmus University Rotterdam

Cities in Transition

Social innovation for Europe's urban sustainability

Edited by Thomas Sauer,
Susanne Elsen and
Cristina Garzillo

LONDON AND NEW YORK

First published 2016
by Routledge
2 Park Square, Milton Park, Abingdon, Oxon OX14 4RN

and by Routledge
711 Third Avenue, New York, NY 10017

Routledge is an imprint of the Taylor & Francis Group, an informa business

© 2016 Thomas Sauer, Susanne Elsen and Cristina Garzillo

The right of Thomas Sauer, Susanne Elsen and Cristina Garzillo to be identified as the authors of the editorial material, and of the authors for their individual chapters, has been asserted in accordance with sections 77 and 78 of the Copyright, Designs and Patents Act 1988.

All rights reserved. No part of this book may be reprinted or reproduced or utilised in any form or by any electronic, mechanical, or other means, now known or hereafter invented, including photocopying and recording, or in any information storage or retrieval system, without permission in writing from the publishers.

Trademark notice: Product or corporate names may be trademarks or registered trademarks, and are used only for identification and explanation without intent to infringe.

British Library Cataloguing-in-Publication Data
A catalogue record for this book is available from the British Library

Library of Congress Cataloging-in-Publication Data
Names: Sauer, Thomas, 1958– editor. | Elsen, Susanne, editor. | Garzillo, Cristina, editor.
Title: Cities in transition : social innovation for Europe's urban sustainability / edited by Thomas Sauer, Susanne Elsen, and Cristina Garzillo.
Other titles: Cities in transition (Routledge)
Description: Abingdon, Oxon ; New York, NY : Routledge, 2016. | Includes bibliographical references.
Identifiers: LCCN 2015035162| ISBN 9781138923843 (hardback) | ISBN 9781138923874 (pbk.) | ISBN 9781315684765 (ebook)
Subjects: LCSH: Regional planning—Environmental aspects—Europe. | Sustainable urban development—Europe. | Environmental policy—Europe. | Urban policy—Environmental aspects—Europe.
Classification: LCC HT395.E82 C57 2016 | DDC 307.1/216094—dc23
LC record available at http://lccn.loc.gov/2015035162

ISBN: 978-1-138-92384-3 (hbk)
ISBN: 978-1-138-92387-4 (pbk)
ISBN: 978-1-315-68476-5 (ebk)

Typeset in Bembo
by Apex CoVantage, LLC
Printed in Great Britain by Ashford Colour Press Ltd

Contents

List of figures	viii
List of tables	x
Abbreviations	xii
Notes on contributors	xiv
Preface	xvi

1 Urban prosperity without growth: the role of actors and social innovation   1

THOMAS SAUER

    1.1 Sustainability needs transition 1
    1.2 New seeds of sustainable prosperity 5
    1.3 The European Cities of Tomorrow: an urban commons focus 8
    1.4 Structure of the book 11

2 Selecting forty cities   13

YANNICK KALFF AND THOMAS SAUER

    2.1 Methodological approach 13
    2.2 Criteria for the country and city selection 16
    2.3 Methods and methodological reflections 33

3 Patterns of change: a general model of socio-ecological transition   39

THOMAS SAUER

    3.1 An institutional focus for transition analysis 39
    3.2 General model of socio-ecological transition 44

4 Socio-ecological transitions in the energy system: the local government view   59

YANNICK KALFF

    4.1 The role of the energy resource system in sustainability transition 59
    4.2 Self-organisation capabilities and sustainability transitions 61

4.3 Actors, factors, and lessons learned 71
4.4 Norm adoption and local decision-making autonomy 80
4.5 Discussion of the findings 88

5 Socio-ecological transitions in the green spaces resource system 93
JUDITH SCHICKLINSKI

5.1 The role of the green spaces resource system in sustainability transition 93
5.2 Self-organisation capabilities and sustainability transitions 94
5.3 Actors, factors, and lessons learnt 109
5.4 Norm adoption and local decision-making autonomy 116
5.5 Discussion of the findings 122

6 Socio-ecological transitions in the water system 125
STEPHANIE BARNEBECK

6.1 The role of the water resource system in sustainability transition 125
6.2 Self-organisation capabilities and sustainability transitions 127
6.3 Actors, factors, and lessons learned 138
6.4 Norm adoption and local decision-making autonomy 146
6.5 Discussion of the findings 154

7 The governance of regional labour market policies 158
PETER HUBER

7.1 Trends in regional labour market governance: an overview 158
7.2 Stylised facts of local labour market governance in the EU 160
7.3 Conceptual framework and hypotheses 170
7.4 Results from forty European cities 174
7.5 Summary and policy conclusions 188

8 Institutional diversity 192
STEPHANIE BARNEBECK, YANNICK KALFF AND THOMAS SAUER

8.1 Urban resources: energy, green spaces, and water 192
8.2 Labour markets: respecting spatial dimensions 199
8.3 Institutional diversity in a socio-ecological transition 203

9 Governing the multilevel transition 204
CRISTINA GARZILLO AND STEFAN KUHN

9.1 Governance and local transitions 204
9.2 Governing sustainable cities 205
9.3 The governance of transitions 209
9.4 Key issues of urban transition governance 212
9.5 Outlook 219

10 Mobilising the citizens for the socio-ecological transition 221
SUSANNE ELSEN AND JUDITH SCHICKLINSKI

10.1 Social innovation and the significance of civil society actors for socio-ecological transitions 221
10.2 Self-organisation and the 'third sector' 224
10.3 Reflexive localisation, democratisation, and polycentric governance 227
10.4 Interactive community governance 230
10.5 Civic economies: new alternative urban spaces 232
10.6 Obstacles to and basic conditions for citizen participation and self-organisation 235
10.7 Cooperative knowledge production for active citizenship and social innovation 236
10.8 Conclusion 238

11 Cities as places of a new, shared prosperity 239
THOMAS SAUER, SUSANNE ELSEN AND CRISTINA GARZILLO

11.1 Laboratories for new ways of producing, distributing, and consuming goods 239
11.2 Cities as laboratories of sustainability transition 241
11.3 Solving the trade-off between complexity and participation 242
11.4 Stepping stones towards urban sustainability transitions 243

References 253
Index 271

Figures

1-1	Decomposition of the change in total global CO2 emissions from fossil fuel combustion	2
1-2	At-risk-of-poverty rate by degree of urbanisation, 2012	7
2-1	Sample creation process	17
2-2	Map of 40 selected cities	27
3-1	Eight rungs on a Ladder of Citizen Participation	42
3-2	Micro-situational and broader context variables of social dilemmas affecting the levels of trust and cooperation	47
3-3	Action situations embedded in broader socio-ecological systems	48
3-4	Rules as exogenous variables directly affecting the elements of an action situation	51
3-5	Socio-ecological systems transition model as a sequence of norm set adoption	57
3-6	Research questions derived from the SES transition model	58
4-1	Differences in sustainability perception according to European region	63
4-2	Anticipated challenges to the availability of affordable energy	65
4-3	Leadership shown by local actors in developing local renewable energy	67
4-4	Leadership in improving energy efficiency and developing renewable energy locally	68
4-5	Cooperation and conflicts	70
4-6	Cooperation and conflicts II	70
4-7	Influence on the local energy mix	72
4-8	Influences on the energy consumption in the past ten years	75
4-9	Difficulties to agree on local energy strategy	77
4-10	Agreement with governance principles for the local energy system	81
4-11	Agreement with governance principles for the local energy system	82
4-12	Local decision-making autonomy for different sectors	85
4-13	Local decision-making autonomy for different regions	88
5-1	Regional differences in assessing the status of green spaces	95
5-2	Regional differences for civil society involvement in green spaces governance	101
5-3	Regional differences in the contribution of the nonprofit sector to green spaces	101
5-4	Regional differences in citizens' motivations for self-organisation in green spaces management	105

5-5	Regional differences in actors showing concrete leadership (reputation and capability) in green spaces management	110
5-6	Sector differences on statements on privatisation	114
5-7	Sector differences in agreeing with statements on norms governing the local green space policy	117
5-8	Regional differences in the relevance of different government levels in ensuring the availability of green spaces	121
6-1	Challenges for the water provision until 2030	130
6-2	Leadership of civil society organisations (in terms of reputation and capability) in ensuring the quality and availability of drinking water	134
6-3	Statements on norms of trust	136
6-4	Leadership (in terms of reputation and capability) in ensuring the quality and availability of drinking water	138
6-5	Priorities for ensuring or improving the quality of drinking water by 2030	140
6-6	Priorities for ensuring the availability of drinking water by 2030	141
6-7	Aspects that determine the level of water consumption	142
6-8	Common understanding regarding a joint strategy for drinking water provision	144
6-9	Status of privatisation	145
6-10	Agreement on governance principles regarding the local water provision system	147
6-11	Agreement on governance principles regarding the local water provision system (regional differences I)	148
6-12	Agreement on governance principles regarding the local water provision system (regional differences II)	149
6-13	Effectiveness of sanctions	150
6-14	Statements on public support and the issue of privatisation	152
6-15	Statements on local decision-making autonomy	154
7-1	Stakeholders involved in PES decision-making by city size and region (share of positive answers)	165
7-2	Change in the importance of stakeholders since 2007	166
7-3	Share of PES organisations with target groups and change of importance in these target groups	167
7-4	Share of PES organisations with sector strategies and change of importance in these sector strategies	168
7-5	Importance and change of importance in objectives of Pact/LEIs	169
7-6	Share of Pact/LEIs with sector strategies and change of importance in these sector strategies	170
7-7	Conceptual framework of the study on labour markets	171
9-1	Interrelations among the three sustainability pillars	207

Tables

2-1	Country selection per European region	16
2-2	Population, GDP per capita and number of selected cities per country in 2013	18
2-3	Characteristics of welfare regimes	19
2-4	Typologies of state structure	21
2-5	Draft typology of territorial governmental systems in the EU27+2 countries	21
2-6	Local government systems	23
2-7	Urban Audit indicators included in evaluation of data availability	24
2-8	Cities selected	28
2-9	Realised results for data inquiry	30
2-10	List of actors	31
3-1	IAP2/TEPSIE spectrum of public participation	43
3-2	Four types of goods	44
3-3	Variables that affect the likelihood of self-organisation	49
3-4	Variables influencing trust and the solution of social dilemmas	50
3-5	Interactions between micro-situational and socio-ecological context variables with rules governing transitional action situations	52
4-1	Importance of sustainability issues (scaled from 0: none to 4: very high)	62
5-1	Influences on civil society groups' existence in green spaces	108
6-1	Influences on the leadership of civil society organisations in the water system	137
7-1	Sample structure by city size, European region, territory serviced, and age and function of Pact/LEIs	161
7-2	Indicators for autonomy of regional PES organisations	164
7-3	Regression results for the number of stakeholders involved in a PES organisation	175
7-4	Regression results for the probability of a stakeholder to be involved in a PES organisation	177
7-5	Determinants of share of target groups and sector strategies followed by PES organisations and change in importance of target groups and sector strategies	180
7-6	Logit regression results for probability to observe a Pact/LEI in a region	183

7-7	Correlation of Pact/LEI functions and partnership size with regional and PES characteristics	185
7-8	Correlates of the share of target groups and sector strategies followed and the share of target groups and sector strategies with a change in importance since 2008	186
11-1	Findings and recommended stepping stones	244

Abbreviations

CO_2	Carbon dioxide
Coef.	Coefficient
DISCUS	Developing Institutional and Social Capacities for Urban Sustainability
ECO	Related ecosystems
EU	European Union
EU 13	Newer members of the European Union with the enlargements in 2004, 2007 and 2013
EU 15	Members of the European Union prior to the eastward enlargement in 2004
EU 28	Members of the European Union from 1 July 2013
EU 28 + 2	EU 28, Switzerland and Turkey
GDP	Gross domestic product
GS	Governance system
Gt	Gigatons
I	Interactions
IAD	Institutional Analysis and Development
IAP2	International Association for Public Participation
ICT	Information and communication technologies
ISCED	International Standard Classification of Education
LEI	Local Employment Initiative
MICV	Micro-situational context variable(s)
NACE	Statistical Classification of Economic Activities in the European Community
NGO	Nongovernmental organisation
NPO	nonprofit organisation
NUTS	Nomenclature of Territorial Units for Statistics
O	Outcomes
Obs.	Observations
Pact	Territorial Employment Pact
Pact/LEI	Territorial Employment Pact or Local Employment Initiative
PER.KA	Periastikes Kallirgies
PES	Public Employment Services
RE	Renewable Energies
ROCSET	The Role of Cities in the Socio-Ecological Transition of Europe

RS	Resource system
RU	Resource units
S	Variables of the social, economic, and political settings
SECV	Socio-ecologic context variable(s)
SES	Socio-ecological system
SET	Socio-ecological transition
Std. Dev.	Standard Deviation
Std. Err.	Standard Error
TEP	Territorial employments pacts
TEPSIE	Theoretical, Empirical and Policy Foundations for Social Innovation in Europe
U	Users
UN	United Nations
WBGU	German Advisory Council on Global Change
WWWforEurope	Welfare, Wealth, and Work for Europe
★	significance level 10%
★★	significance level 5%
★★★	significance level 1%

Notes on contributors

Stephanie Barnebeck has worked as research assistant at the Jena University of Applied Sciences since 2014. She studied Business and Economics at the Friedrich-Schiller-University of Jena and gained experience as Marketing Manager. Her special interests are questionnaire survey, quantitative data analysis and civil society's scope in socio-ecological transition.
Current affiliation: Jena University of Applied Sciences (EAH Jena), Germany

Susanne Elsen has worked as Professor of Sociology and Social Development at the Free University of Bolzano since 2010. She is Vice Dean for research and Director of the Faculty of Education's PhD Programme. Her main research topics are social innovation, local development and community economy, sustainability and post-growth society.
Current affiliation: Free University of Bolzano, Italy

Cristina Garzillo is coordinator for Governance and Social Innovation at ICLEI – Local Governments for Sustainability. Previously contract professor at the University of Parma, she is recognised for her expertise in local sustainability processes, integrated management and governance and her publications in the field of local sustainability, knowledge brokerage and transition.
Current affiliation: ICLEI – Local Governments for Sustainability, Germany

Peter Huber has been affiliated with the Structural Change and Regional Development research area at the Austrian Institute of Economic Research (WIFO) since 1998. From 2012 until 2015, he was Deputy Director of the WIFO. His foci are regional labour markets, the spatial effects of integration and regional business cycles and growth factors.

Yannick Kalff has worked as research assistant at the Jena University of Applied Sciences since 2014. He studied sociology at the Ludwig-Maximilians-University Munich and is a PhD student at the Friedrich-Schiller-University Jena. His special interests are the sociology of work, the sociology of organisations, self-organisation of civil society and qualitative data analysis.
Current affiliation: Jena University of Applied Sciences (EAH Jena), Germany

Stefan Kuhn is Deputy Regional Director for Europe at ICLEI – Local Governments for Sustainability, leading the network's activities in urban governance and social

innovation in Europe. An urban geographer with further studies in the economy, social sciences and educational sciences, he develops and supervises international projects and strategies around sustainable urban development.
Current affiliation: ICLEI – Local Governments for Sustainability, Germany

Thomas Sauer is Professor of Economics at the Jena University of Applied Sciences (EAH), Department of Business Administration. His key qualifications as a researcher are urban and regional economics and the analysis of collective decision-making. He is member of several international economic associations like the International Society for Ecological Economics.
Current affiliation: Jena University of Applied Sciences (EAH Jena), Germany

Judith Schicklinski has worked as research assistant at the Free University of Bolzano since 2013. She studied pedagogy, languages, and European politics and is a PhD candidate at the Free University of Bolzano. Her special interest is civil society's role in the socio-ecological transition and in urban green spaces governance.
Current affiliation: Free University of Bolzano, Italy

Preface

This book presents the key results of the Role of Cities in the Socio-Ecological Transition (ROCSET) project. ROCSET was part of the wider Welfare, Wealth, Work for Europe research project (WWWforEurope, www.forEurope.eu). In this context, ROCSET contributes to a better understanding of the regional and local dimensions of a new European path to socio-ecological transition with a particular focus on European cities.

The overarching question for the WWWforEurope project was

> *What kind of new European growth and development strategy is necessary and feasible, enabling a socio-ecological transition to high levels of employment, well-being of its citizens, social inclusion, resilience of ecological systems and a significant contribution to the global common goods like climate stability?*

With robust research as a foundation, the ultimate impact of the project is to contribute to a change of the actual course of economic policy in the direction of a socio-ecological transition.

A new growth model for Europe needs to have a stronger participation of civil society actors and bottom-up approaches. Although this is uncontroversial, there is a lack of research identifying the exact nature of the links between regional policy implementation and national and regional institutions. This applies in particular when potential differences in these links across policy fields are considered. The lack leaves policy makers rather unprepared in designing appropriate policies in this respect. ROCSET aims at filling this gap from an urban perspective and showing the special relevance of civil society engagement in socio-ecological transition.

The WWWforEurope project started in April 2012 as a four-year research project funded by the European Commission. We acknowledge the masterly coordination of the consortium of 34 partners from 12 European countries by WIFO, the Austrian Institute for Economic Research in Vienna, under the auspices of the WIFO president Karl Aiginger and his team. The WWWforEurope project has received funding from the European Union's 7th Framework Programme for research, technological development and demonstration under grant agreement no. 290647.

This book never could have been completed successfully without the extensive work, cooperation, aid, and help of a great number of people. Thus, we want to acknowledge the efforts of all members of the project team, Adrien Labaeye, Benjamin Gloy, Enkeleda Kadriu, Kira Reich, Judith Schicklinski, Nadine Marmai, Stephanie Barnebeck and Yannick Kalff.

The careful and enthusiastic field research of Aleksandra Marta Duda, Alina Brasoveanu, Dalia Campoccia, Etrit Shkreli, Hana Belohoubkova, Isabel Fernández de la Fuente, Joakim Toll, Judith Schicklinski, Júlia Colomer Matutano, Juliette Muguet-Guenot, Lea K. Baumbach, Michael Bockhorni, Mikaela Lise Vasström, Renaud Hourcade, Vasileios Latinos and Vildan Aydin delivered the data and transcripts we relied on in our analysis of the case studies.

Johanna Hopp from the Jena University of Applied Sciences (EAH Jena) supported the project team throughout the whole research with valuable advice on the topic of water systems. We would particularly like to thank the WWWforEurope project office team at WIFO for their steady support and assistance.

Jena, Bolzano, Freiburg, 1 September 2015
Thomas Sauer, Susanne Elsen, Cristina Garzillo

Chapter 1

Urban prosperity without growth
The role of actors and social innovation

Thomas Sauer

1.1 Sustainability needs transition

Since the 1992 Earth Summit in Rio de Janeiro, the concept of sustainable development has become more and more mainstream in global political thinking. The most prominent, and at the same time very general, definition of sustainable development was developed by the Brundtland Commission, formally known as the World Commission on Environment and Development (The World Commission on Environment and Development 1987). It considers sustainable development as development to meet present needs without compromising future generations' ability to meet their own needs. The United Nations is currently preparing a 'Post-2015 Agenda', breaking down the overall idea into a set of measurable sustainable development goals for the period up to 2030 – succeeding the current Goals of the Millennium Declaration of 2000 (UN 2014a) and the Kyoto Protocol on reducing worldwide greenhouse gas emissions as well. Both are in urgent need of a binding follow-up.

Confronting the slow progress in realising past sustainability commitments, the question arises whether becoming mainstream will be enough to stop the ongoing human-inflicted contribution to global warming and loss of biodiversity. The answer to this question is probably negative. However, in the community of concerned scientists, a major paradigm shift is underway. It is a shift from the early 'Limits to Growth' debates of the 1970s, which were referring mostly to assumed trends of human overpopulation, towards a debate recognising the implications of core planetary boundaries (Johan Rockström et al. 2009). Their trespassing would cause an irreversible loss of human control capacities on the endangered global resource systems. If this trespassing is caused by humans, it is realistic that the geologic era of the Holocene already passed into a new period to be labelled as the Anthropocene (Jan Zalasiewicz et al. 2012). Considering the current geologic epoch as Anthropocene implies admitting the outstanding human responsibility for a resilient future of the earth system.

Since the early 1990s, economic sciences have debated on two main alternatives for optimal policies for the stabilisation of the climate processes: pricing the greenhouse gas emission via carbon taxes or constraining the eligible quantities of greenhouse gas emissions. The latter option presupposes that the markets would find the appropriate prices for the emission certificates, derived from such greenhouse gas emission control rates (William D. Nordhaus 1994). Both policy strategies are intended to internalise the "greatest externality ever" (Hans-Werner Sinn 2007) by giving greenhouse gas emissions a price in order to reduce the demand for it and to cover the social costs of such global overuse of the atmosphere. Despite some successes (Mikael S. Andersen 2010), only some of the EU countries introduced carbon taxes while the EU as a whole opted for an Emission Trading System, which is currently under reform after delivering some disappointing results in the first two phases (European Commission 2013b). Nevertheless, the problem appears more profound than simply choosing between two different ways of internalising the externalities of global market activities by international agreements or optimising emission trading schemes.

What if the United Nations takes the already agreed 2°C goals seriously as the limit for acceptable global warming in the twenty-first century? To meet this target, the world would have to reduce its CO2 emissions by at least 41 per cent up to 72 per cent in the four decades between 2010 and 2050 (IPCC 2014). Keeping in line with this goal would imply an annual reduction of CO2 emissions of at least 1.1 per cent in the world average until 2050. But, hoping this reduction could be led by a significant reduction of carbon energy intensity alone is misleading, as experience shows: The carbon intensity of economic growth, measured as CO2 emissions per $1 GDP, decreased by only 1.2 per cent per year as an average for the two decades from 1990 to 2010 (UN 2014a). Thus, by this strategy alone, the average country would have had a maximum eligible growth corridor of 0.1 per cent per year (1.2 per cent annual reduction of carbon intensity minus 1.1 per cent annual CO2 reduction). Given that this low average speed of carbon intensity reduction would be representative for all countries – and lasts until 2050 – there would be no room for GDP growth on the global scale.

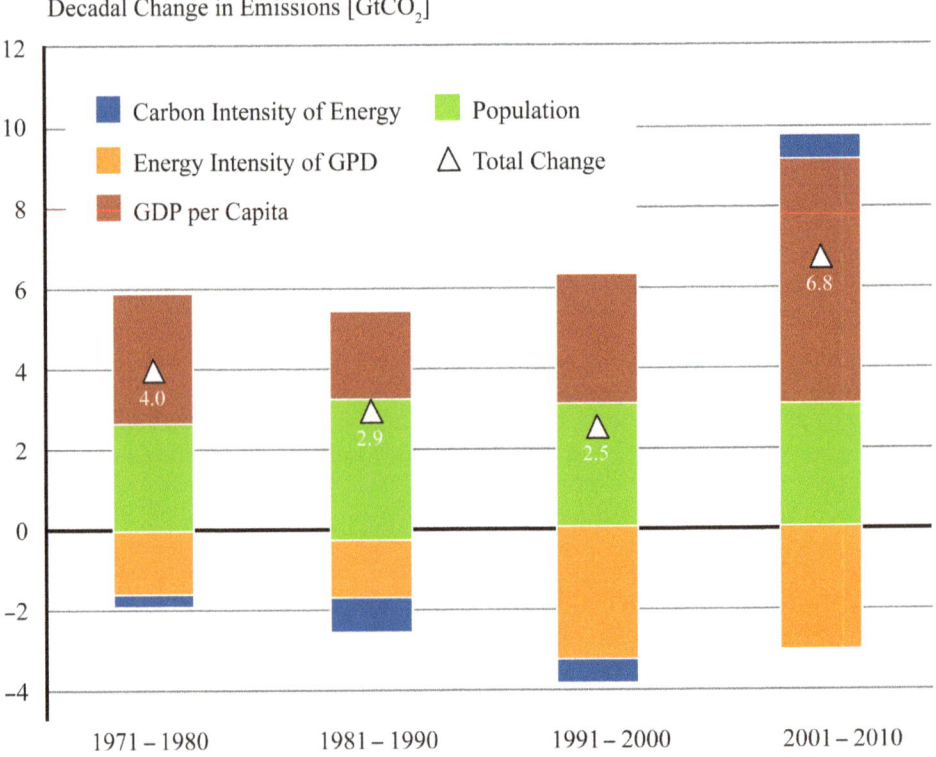

Figure 1-1 Decomposition of the change in total global CO2 emissions from fossil fuel combustion

Nevertheless, as Figure 1-1 reveals, the real development is even worse: The decreasing energy intensity of income per capita alone could have contributed significantly to the reduction of CO2 emissions over the last four decades – if neither world population nor world GDP had grown during the same time. Obviously, this was not the case: Growing world population induced a decadal CO2 emission increase of around 3 gigatons (Gt) of CO2 since the 1980s. Moreover, the CO2 emission growth induced by GDP growth per capita even accelerated, particularly in the first decade of the twenty-first century. In this time period, the high growth rates of world GDP coincided with an accelerated growth of world CO2 emissions up to a maximum of an additional 6.8 Gt and with a sudden increase of carbon intensity of energy after three decades of decrease. There is obviously no turnaround in the direction of shrinking global CO2 emissions in sight, despite the 1997 Kyoto Protocol and a series of high-ranking international climate conferences since the early 1990s.

A decoupling strategy, aimed at decreasing the energy intensity of GDP, is widely considered as the most helpful factor for a transition towards a climate-neutral regime. However, this kind of strategy delivers nowhere near enough reductions of greenhouse gases. The slowest factor for climate relief is probably population growth, because this variable entails long time lags and can hardly be influenced by demographic policies, at least in the time period available to stop global warming. Therefore, climate policies could focus on per capita income growth and the growth of carbon intensity of energy. However, the latter, carbon intensity, is probably a variable dependent on the former, the growth rates of GDP per capita. In the decade with the lowest growth rates of GDP (the 1980s), the most significant decline of carbon intensity was observed. In contrast, the extraordinarily high GDP per capita growth rates of the 2000s coincided with the strongest increase of carbon intensity in the same decade.

This is bad news for the hope that high GDP growth rates of the emerging markets in Asia and elsewhere would automatically induce a kind of ecological leapfrogging through the high investment rates of these countries. Despite the significant investments in renewable energy technologies, the proportion of investments in conventional fossil-fuel-consuming technologies appeared to be even higher there. Thus, the global GDP growth rate remains without doubt the critical variable for reducing emissions of CO2 and other greenhouse gases to a level consistent with the internationally agreed 2°C ceiling of global warming in the twenty-first century. The same is probably true as well for the overall planetary boundaries, like biodiversity loss, caused by human economic activities (Rockström et al. 2009). To conclude, market income growth, measured as GDP per capita, is the most severe risk for the resilience of key global resource systems.

A central question arises: Are the problems of global warming and of violating the overall planetary boundaries unsolvable social dilemmas in economic reality? Not at all, if the economic sciences would shift their focus from internalising the externalities towards the search for a more comprehensive economic approach regarding the governance of commons and the resilience of resource systems. The term socio-ecological transition (SET) concerns the shift of socio-ecological systems from one state to another. This implies that transitions are always directed towards something like a new equilibrium, a new regime, or a certain benchmark like 'strong sustainability'. Thus, new institutional arrangements beyond the simple market–government dichotomy are needed to enhance human prosperity without overstretching earth's capacities to recover. Such a transition towards a regime of strong sustainability presupposes the transition of the economic system towards a higher degree of institutional diversity. This would enable experiments with new forms of economic governance, which could be independent of the ever-growing consumption of natural resources.

Institutional diversification implies by definition, not only the emergence of new institutional arrangements, but the persistence of incumbent institutions as well. This raises the particularly important question of how an economy in transition towards a growth regime capable of safeguarding the resilience of ecological resource systems would affect the institutional settings constituting labour markets. They have to cope with any change in an economic and societal system that is induced by a socio-ecological transition. Since any governance mode, by policies or self-organisation, that relies on a reduction of CO_2 or, in a broader sense, on a sustainable paradigm affects economic competitiveness, unemployment disparities are unequally hit by sustainability policies. A perspective has to be taken to make the efficiency of labour market policies visible and especially show how this institutional setting is altered and governed by policies. After all, all markets are dependent on coherent governmental intervention. Nonetheless, the perspective shifts from an overarching to a contextual one that differentiates structural features of the individual regions.

So there are strong reasons to look at such processes of institutional diversification and change, taking the multilevel character of governance of the global commons into account at the same time:

> [W]hile many of the effects of climate change are global, the causes of climate change are the actions undertaken by the individuals, families, firms, and actors at a much smaller scale. . . . To solve climate change in the long run, the day-to-day activities of individuals, families, firms, communities, and governments at multiple levels – particularly those in the more developed world – will need to change substantially.
> (Elinor Ostrom 2009, 4)

For research strategies regarding such social dilemmas, this entails a significant shift of perspective towards the behaviour of individuals and groups managing critical resource systems on a local scale.

For climate-neutral policies – as well as those regarding ecological resilience – the option to choose a bottom-up approach would skip any excuse for persistent inaction:

> [C]ontinuing to wait may defeat the possibilities of significant adaptions and mitigations in time to prevent tragic disasters. . . . [W]ithout numerous innovative technological and institutional efforts at multiple scales, we may not even begin to learn which combined sets of actions are the most effective in reducing the long-term threat of massive climate change.
> (Ostrom 2009, 4)

Thus, for solving social dilemmas at the global level, it is crucial to understand and to change the determinants of human economic behaviour at the local level in its relation to the socio-ecological context first. Local cooperation produces a wide variety of social innovations that are adapted to the local context they concern (Geoff Mulgan et al. 2007; James A. Phills, Jr., Kriss Deiglmeier, and Dale T. Miller 2008; Hans-Werner Franz, Josef Hochgerner, and Jürgen Howaldt 2012; Andreas Reinstaller 2013; Harald A. Mieg and Klaus Töpfer 2013). "Social innovations are new solutions (products, services, models, markets, processes etc.) that simultaneously meet a social need (more effectively than existing solutions) and lead to new or improved capabilities and relationships and better use of assets and resources" (Anna Davies and Julie Simon 2013, 5). This book focusses on social innovations in three urban resource systems (energy, green spaces, and water), as well as regarding the local labour markets of 40 European cities.

1.2 New seeds of sustainable prosperity

At the very heart of our understanding of whether our market-based economies have to grow, notwithstanding the resilience of ecological resource systems, is the concept of capital. It entails a range of important questions, such as: Is it sensible to assume a general ability to substitute natural capital by human-made capital, or is such substitutability constrained by planetary boundaries as sketched above? Is economic capital by definition forced to grow – as it is expressed with the concept of capital accumulation? Moreover, what is actually assumed as growing when economists are talking about capital accumulation?

The latter question was already put by Gabriel de Tarde in his "Psychologie économique" of 1902:

> In my view, there are two elements to be distinguished in the notion of capital: first, essential, necessary capital: that is, all of the ruling inventions, the primary sources of all current wealth; second, auxiliary, more or less useful capital: the products which, born from these inventions, help, through the means of these new services, to create other products. These two elements are different in more or less the same way as, in a plant seed, the germ is different from those little supplies of nutrients which envelope it and which we call cotyledons. Cotyledons are not indispensable; there are plants that reproduce without them. They are very useful. The difficulty is not in noticing them, when the seed is opened, for they are relatively large. The tiny germ is hidden by them.
> (Tarde 1902, 229, as translated in Bruno Latour and Vincent A. Lépinay 2009, 49–50)

Tarde defines *necessary capital* as the capability to innovate processes as well as products – already before Joseph A. Schumpeter published his "Theory of Economic Development" in 1911. Like a *germ*, it is the source of all current wealth. In contrast to that, Tarde compares *auxiliary capital* with cotyledons: These are useful suppliers of nutrients for seeds, but they are not necessary to reproduce these seeds. Because cotyledons are relatively large compared to germs, the germs are often hidden by them. This metaphor ends up in a comparison between economists and botanists: "The economists who saw capital as solely in the saving and accumulation of earlier products are like botanists who would view a seed as being entirely made up of cotyledons" (Tarde 1902, 229, as translated in Latour and Lépinay 2009, 50).

As in the days of Tarde, most of the economists today are still focusing on the 'more of the same' concept of capital as the wealth-enhancing approach, still mixing up the saving and accumulation of earlier products with real generation of wealth. In contrast to that, a modern concept of capital should start with Tarde's idea of emphasising the capability to innovate and to learn as its core characteristics and to discard income growth as its key property. This could free the mind of economists and enable them to search for new institutional arrangements.

What is needed is an economic system that would be able to cope with growth rates of market income, which are safeguarding the resilience of local ecological resource systems as well as the global ecological system within their planetary boundaries. It is obvious that there exist neither ready-made blueprints nor panaceas for such a sustainable economic system. If anything, market income growth appears to be deeply entrenched in the contemporary market-based economies. Thomas Piketty (2014) observes a strong long-term tendency for the rate of return on capital to be even greater than the rate of overall economic growth. This is feasible only at the cost of labour income and results in a concentration of wealth – as well as of economic and political power – in the hands of a few. Otherwise, modern welfare states are heavily dependent on taxing value-added and market incomes for financing their comprehensive tasks in stabilising the economy and for compensating the majority of the electorate for the most severe consequences of the unequal distribution of wealth and income. Finally, yet importantly, modern labour markets are dependent on economic growth for keeping employment rates stable or even increasing them. Thus, this profound entrenchment of the pursuit for economic growth in the institutional setting of current market economies is not easily resolved. However, there appears to be no other way to keep human development inside the crash barriers of planetary boundaries. This affects labour market policies as well, following the argument in this section. Instead of widespread distribution of employment, labour markets as institutions pronounce the more locally rooted microbalance of social inequality in the form of unemployment disparities.

Therefore, we face the task of finding new institutional arrangements ensuring human well-being and the resilience of ecological resource systems at the same time. For labour markets, the task is very similar: Instead of finding distinctive new institutional settings, it is urgent to find structural improvements to the existing exchange mechanisms. This means that policies need to be analysed, and it needs to be scrutinised which goals are necessary for the altering of functions. Thus, the question arises of where to find such new institutional arrangements – which would follow a strategy generating prosperity without growth (Peter A. Victor 2008; Tim Jackson 2009) or "Green Agrowth" (Jeroen van den Bergh and Giorgios Kallis 2012; Jeroen van den Bergh 2015). It is extremely likely that neither the profit-driven business sector nor the tax-revenue-dependent government sector would emerge as home of such growth-ignoring new institutions, even if it were possible to shift governance revenues towards a more tax-independent financing by profits of state and private enterprises. If this is true, it makes sense to direct the focus of inquiry towards a third sector of not-for-profit economic activities born in the civil society (Adalbert Evers and Jean-Louis Laville 2004; Frank Moulaert and Oana Ailenei 2005; Stephen P. Osborne 2008). This third sector is probably the home of new institutional arrangements like cooperatives, multistakeholder constructions, local–regional partnerships, and networks. It can provide an organisational frame for sustainable development on the local and regional level. These arrangements could also be considered as laboratories for new forms of a more sustainable way to produce and consume and to coordinate these activities beyond the traditional market–government dichotomy. The perspective taken in this research tries to explore the potential of a third option *beyond* this dichotomy and open up the discursive closure that only allows for the two poles of resource governance in society. This includes research into the institutions governing the labour markets as the foremost mechanism of social integration. Their reliance on economic growth puts them potentially in contradiction to the necessities of a socio-ecological transition. This is reinforced by the fact that the efficiency in which economic growth is producing new jobs has been declining for the last few decades.

Unfortunately, this third sector is not well defined. At least there exist no comparable international statistics for the exact scope of this sector – simply because of not being in the central focus of interest of public policy and economic sciences, yet. Furthermore, because the third sector is somehow a residual of the formal market and government-driven economies, it includes rather heterogeneous forms of economic activities. These consist of the cooperative movement and the social and solidarity economy (Moulaert and Ailenei 2005; Jenna Allard, Carl Davidson, and Julie Matthaei 2008; Emily Kawano, Thomas N. Masterson, and Jonathan Teller-Elsberg 2009; Bénédicte Fortenau et al. 2010; RIPESS 2013; UNRISD 2013). Further, there are some overlaps with definitions of the charity and voluntary sectors as used in the UK or US, and with the more radical concept of a community economy (J.K. Gibson-Graham 1996). Thus, to avoid premature reduction and to capture as many aspects as possible, we define the third sector as the sector of not-for-profit enterprises or the civil society sector, located beyond the business and government sector.

This civil society sector embraces a multitude of initiatives, institutional arrangements, and experiments with the microeconomics of a growth-independent economy. To name a few: An exhibition in the Architekturzentrum Wien in 2012 impressively showed the long history of hands-on urbanism like community gardening and urban agriculture. These initiatives served not only as reactions to crisis situations, avoiding famine, and solving supply bottlenecks in urban areas but also as experimental laboratories for an alternative economy on urban green spaces (Elke Krasny 2012). Another important civil society

Figure 1-2 At-risk-of-poverty rate by degree of urbanisation, 2012

movement is formed by the renewable energy source cooperatives, which try to intervene in the transition of the European energy systems towards a low- or even zero-carbon regime. They organise on the local, national, and European level as well (REScoop.EU 2013). The European civil society campaign for a 'Right to Water' collected 1,884,790 signatures in EU countries for the first successful European Citizen's Initiative, urging that water supply and the management of water resources should not be subject to internal market rules and that water services are excluded from liberalisation (Louisa Parks 2014). Another movement that regained momentum as opposition to the neoliberal way of urbanism is the "Right to the City" (Henri Lefebvre 1990, 1996; Mark Purcell 2003; David Harvey 2008, 2012). Ultimately, all of these movements could agree with the insistence that the key resource systems such as green spaces, energy, climate, and water should be regarded as commons (Elinor Ostrom 1990; The Ecologist 1994; Ostrom 2009; David Bollier and Silke Helfrich 2012; Silke Helfrich 2012), and not as traded goods.

1.3 The European Cities of Tomorrow: an urban commons focus

In the late 1990s, the European Union started a process to formulate its own European urban agenda (Stephanie Barnebeck and Yannick Kalff 2015). This process has now reached the stage of 'Cities of Tomorrow reflection process', embracing ten main urban challenges in four categories: smart growth, green growth, inclusive growth, and transversal challenges. Summarising the European Commission (2014a):

- Smart growth deals with an envisaged transition towards a knowledge society and the development of an economic and financial city resilience.
- Inclusive growth aims to counter social and spatial segregation or polarisation, integrating newcomers like migrants, and the reaction to demographic challenges.
- Transversal challenges focus on the cities' attractiveness and territorial coherence and cohesion.
- Green growth challenges are about achieving greater energy and resource efficiency, and the sustainable management of natural resources like water, waste, air, soil, and land.

In addition, it reflects the acceleration of the transition towards a sustainable city, "given the inherent inertia of infrastructure provision" (European Commission 2014a), like housing, transport, water, and energy systems.

This book presents research results on such 'green growth challenges', particularly on the management of natural resources like water, soil, and land, as well as on the transition of the water and energy systems towards a regime of strong sustainability. That is not because of an obviously misleading assumption that social inclusion would not interfere with the sustainable management of natural resources and infrastructure provision. However, it is because the focus of one part of this inquiry is laid on the potential of new institutional arrangements for the socio-ecological transition of urban common-pool resources like green spaces, water, and energy. Above that, the research considers the ongoing dynamics that labour markets in the European Union are confronted with – sometimes in a direct relation to programmes and strategies that foster a socio-ecological transition and react to persisting moments of economic crisis. The transition of existing institutional settings like markets is an important issue as well.

"Cities are where the opportunities and threats to sustainable development come together" (European Commission 2014c, 1). This quote nicely summarises why the focus of this research is laid on the role of cities in the European socio-ecological transition towards strong sustainability, in short, the European sustainability transition. Cities are defined according to European conventions as urban centres of 50,000 inhabitants or more, while towns and suburbs have the majority of their population in an urban cluster of 5,000 up to 49,999 inhabitants, and rural areas are defined as the residual of these two categories. According to this classification more than 200 million people are living in a total of 811 European cities, around 159 million in towns and suburbs and a remainder of 154 million in rural areas (European Commission 2014a, 11).

Figure 1-2 reveals an interesting aspect of European urbanisation processes. While the EU-28 average shows only insignificant differences between the at-risk-of-poverty rate in cities on the one hand and towns, suburbs, and rural areas on the other, there are huge differences between the more and less advanced EU countries. In more advanced EU countries like Sweden, France, Luxemburg, The Netherlands, United Kingdom, Denmark, Germany, Belgium, and Austria, the poor are more likely to be living in the cities than in more dispersed or rural areas. The picture in the remaining EU countries – most extreme in low-income EU countries like Bulgaria and Romania – is the direct opposite: The risk of poverty here is significantly higher in rural areas, towns, and suburbs than in cities. This could be seen as a relevant hint at the role of urbanisation processes on the one hand and at the role of the agricultural sector on the other as important elements of the specific national welfare regimes.

What is at stake here is the role of common-pool resources in the urban sustainability transition. We selected two natural resource systems and one hybrid resource system for our inquiry into the role of the third sector in this transition, understood here as the transition of socio-ecological systems (Ralf Schüle 2007; Michael McGinnis and Elinor Ostrom 2010; Oran R. Young 2012). In this kind of transition, social heterogeneity and inequality are relevant again. If only a few participants benefit, it is probably difficult to come to an agreement on the contribution of such key resources to the overall provision of the population. This is particularly true if no possibility exists to agree on an equal distribution of costs and benefits. Heterogeneity in the access to and dependence on common-pool resources expresses differences in the distribution of power resources. Small subgroups of users could try to capture bigger parts of the resources and to block the access for other members of the community (Amy R. Poteete, Marco A. Janssen, and Elinor Ostrom 2010, 231). Mancur Olson (2000) developed for such kind of rent-seeking behaviour the term stationary bandits. Such stationary bandits might be very powerful in influencing the direction and speed of socio-ecological transitions and even in the position to block them totally. Therefore, the focus on social inequality and heterogeneity has to play an essential role for any relevant transition research.

Access to clean drinking water plays a key role in any human settlement decisions, especially regarding urbanisation processes (William A. Blomquist, Edella Schlager, and Tanya Heikkila 2004; Audun Sandberg 2008; Edella Schlager and William A. Blomquist 2008; Gabriel Weber and Ignasi Puig-Ventosa 2013; European Environment Agency 2014; Parks 2014). Water basins are very early topics for the research on the boundaries and sustainability of common-pool resources as well as on institutional change and institutional failure regarding their governance (Ostrom 1990). Only in some research on common-pool resources is water already considered as urban commons (Geeta Lakshmi 2011). Despite this, at least since the European Citizen's Initiative, water could also be considered an urban common-pool resource (Elinor Ostrom, Roger B. Parks, and Gordon P. Whitaker 1978; European Environment Agency 2014; Parks 2014). The rights on water are frequently closely connected with the property rights on land and soil. Private property rights on land repeatedly entail the right to benefit from the water sources on this land as well. On the other hand, there are rapid and complex urbanisation processes, in most cases reliant on the public infrastructures for water provision, and in this sense they are really services of general economic interest.

Green spaces appear to be a paradox in urban areas, as the degree of urbanisation is regularly measured in terms of density, that is the population living on a defined area. In this sense, places appear to be more urbanised if they possess less green spaces. However, this is only part of the story: One of the first demands of the emerging civil society in Europe was to open up the formerly closed castle-gardens for the public and the idea of urban allotment gardens arose out of serious food supply problems during rapid urbanisation processes and wars in Europe and the US. Nowadays we find a worldwide movement for urban agriculture, in more and less advanced countries all the same (Krasny 2012; Stephan Barthel, John Parker, and Henrik Ernstson 2013).

Considering the urban energy systems, we assume that the decarbonisation of the energy system has significant spatial implications. Such kind of energy transition in urban areas, decentralising the production of renewable energy as well, could reunite the local production and consumption of electric power. The technological shift from fossil fuels to renewable energies provides a new opportunity for such a spatial recoupling of energy transformation and energy consumption. If the proportion of renewable energy harvesting in overall energy provision increases, and if the chosen path of renewable energy technology development is in favour of miniaturised and decentralised energy generation, the ratio of energy transformation to its total final consumption inside the city limits should increase. As a result, the boundaries of the energy system on the one hand and the governance systems on the other hand could be more equivalent on the local level and enhance the involvement of urban and regional actors in the governance of the energy system.

Furthermore, such a spatial recoupling of energy transformation and energy consumption on the local level could be an opportunity to increase the role of nonprofit activities in the third sector. If new actors were to appear in this civil society sector, this could be seen as a Great Transformation underway (Karl Polanyi 1944; WBGU 2011). The initial points of the study on regional labour market policies are the huge regional unemployment rate disparities in the EU and the fact that previous studies have – depending on the authors – emphasised two very different potential explanations for these. Some analysts have blamed rigid national labour market institutions that would impede regional mobility and regional labour market flexibility in the EU.

Finally, yet importantly, the role of labour markets 'at risk of poverty' is a central one. As it has been pointed out, the specific divergences between well-developed and less-developed countries is striking. It shows that further disparities in unemployment across regions may foster the risk not on a national level but on a more substantial level. There is a specific trade-off between the sustainable organisation of urban common-pool resources and the overall well-being of the citizens in structurally weak regions. Therefore, the two goals might be incompatible as long as they are not considered as a central mechanism in the socio-ecological transition. This is the main reason this study explores self-organisation strategies for urban common-pool resources and the transformation of labour markets via policy developments. Institutional diversity here becomes a multifaceted term that not only entails 'new' institutional settings but also alters common ones, and not only one type of (new) institutions but a plural – diverse – set of policies according to their efficiency in the structuring of fields of action.

This research focuses on the regional and local dimensions of the new European path to socio-ecological transition. Its central assumption is that any strategy developed to enhance socio-ecological transition is unlikely to yield strong results unless the resources of regional and local actors are mobilised and the complex interactions between central policy initiatives and their regional or local implementation are taken into account. A new development path for Europe therefore also needs to be underpinned by regional, spatial, and local policies.[1] It also requires the development of institutional arrangements beyond the simple market–government dichotomy that ensure human well-being and the resilience of the ecological resource system.

As evidenced by the repeated reference to the role of regional and local actors in contributing EU policy initiatives (e.g. the Lisbon Agenda and the current EU 2020 strategies), this statement is uncontroversial both in the academic and the public debate. There is, however, a lack of research identifying the exact nature of the links between regional policy implementation and national and regional institutions as well as institutional development. Thus, recent studies (Carlos Tapia et al. 2013) document the vast heterogeneity in terms of progress in socio-ecological transition in European regions. They conclude that differences in the quality of governance are an important factor in explaining this heterogeneity. These studies, however, remain unclear what 'good governance' for socio-ecological transition entails. This leaves policymakers rather unprepared in designing appropriate policies.

This implies a set of overall research interests the study tries to address by means of several research objectives. These aims can be formulated as a set of theses:

1. EU-wide, national, and regional policies interact with the implementation and outcomes of the envisaged socio-ecological transition on the local and regional level.
2. Different tiers of governance take different roles in the process. These are perceived differently on each level. The evaluation of the potency of the actors creates different possibilities of agency.
3. The so-called third sector takes a special responsibility in the ongoing transition. Its potential lies in the overcoming of the traditional market–state dichotomy and the forming of productive alliances on different levels of society.
4. New institutional settings interact with existing governance structures and produce social innovation, either by conflict or by cooperation. The results can be traced to policy development and especially to the development of socio-ecological transition policies.

This research tries to evaluate how coherent different approaches to a socio-ecological transition in the European Union are and can be. It sheds light on these new institutional settings and their dynamics.

1.4 Structure of the book

This study and the argumentation are structured in the following way: Chapter 2 presents the research design, which generated the data for the study. It presents the sampling strategy as well as methodological reflections, methods used, and difficulties faced in the process.

Chapter 3 develops the theoretical framework of urban resource commons. The concept of self-organised resource systems in urban contexts is rooted in the works of Elinor Ostrom and are extended by own assumptions. The chapter sets the theoretical context for chapters 4 to 6, which discuss the empirical findings of the three resource systems – energy, green spaces, and water – and the capability to self-organise in the cities. Chapter 7 considers labour markets and shows how spatial attributes are integrated into the function of the institutions. The chapter adds an institutional setting for market-based mechanisms and shows how European and national policies have effects on it, whether they are place-based or place-blind. Chapter 8 sums up the results of this first part and discusses institutional diversification in the two empirical fields of urban resources and labour markets.

Chapter 9 leaves the local level and shows how socio-ecological transitions affect several levels and how they are entangled. Chapter 10 sheds light on the part of the civil society in socio-ecological transitions. The potentials of an active public sphere are discussed and focus the difficulties that civil societies face. Chapter 11 contextualises our insights in the ongoing discourse on growth and degrowth and brings up the concept of prosperity. Stepping stones towards urban sustainability transitions will be outlined.

Note

1 This book discusses respective policies for resource and labour market governance. A central policy development process for urban areas and urban sustainability, the Urban Agenda and sustainability strategies tied to it, are discussed in Stephanie Barnebeck and Yannick Kalff (2015).

Chapter 2

Selecting forty cities

Yannick Kalff and Thomas Sauer[1]

This chapter outlines the research design and reflects the empirical data sampling and inquiry process. In brief, the structure follows three sections: 1) The methodological approach describes the analytical framework and research methods used, as well as the material generated in the field phase. 2) Following this, the chapter discusses the first instance of the strategic sampling procedure on the national and regional level. Further, on the bottom level, the second instance of selecting actors that were to fill out questionnaires and were engaged in face-to-face interviews is described. 3) Methodological reflections complete this chapter by assessing the challenges and pitfalls on handling poor data availability in the city selection process as well as by providing a critical assessment of the applied sampling strategy and research methods for data inquiry.

A mix of quantitative and qualitative methods appears to be appropriate for the research strategy chosen. This mix could provide at least an insight into normative shifts that are leading to institutional changes. A comparative research design enables the identification of specific institutional settings, external to the urban action area. Thus, the research design presented in this chapter considers the following variables:

- In demographic and economic terms, the size and growth rates of the country where the city is located regarding population and total GDP
- In geographic and cultural terms regarding its location in Northern, Southern, Eastern, or Western Europe
- Regarding the national government structure as defining the degree of administrative decentralisation and the degrees of local decision-making autonomy
- Regarding the welfare regime of the nation where the city is located as a determinant for the type and degree of heterogeneity of local user groups relevant for the governance of urban common-pool resources.

2.1 Methodological approach

This study will rely on triangulation (Alan Bryman and Emma Bell 2011, 397–98), combining methods by using both quantitative and qualitative data collection. Triangulation allows for a better understanding and sharper display of research results by getting a fix on the research objective from several positions (Uwe Flick 2011, 179–95). Triangulating the results provides excellent insight into the material from different angles. Individual shortcomings of each research methodology and method are complemented by the focus of the other methods. This cannot simply be realised by 'adding' the one to the other, so the several distinct features, pros, and cons have to be reflected and adjusted (Bryman and Bell 2011, 619–22). For the quantitative data analysis, the study relies mainly on primary data of a survey, undertaken in the field phase, supplemented with secondary data. The qualitative data analysis bases on primary data in the form of expert interviews. The used research methods have to be deducted from the methodology of the study to fit the research interest and the research questions accordingly. Therefore, this section begins with an outline of the Institutional Analysis and Development framework as the foundation of an applicable methodology.

2.1.1 The Institutional Analysis and Development (IAD) framework

Based on the Institutional Analysis and Development (IAD) framework – developed by Elinor Ostrom and continuously sharpened by her and other researchers over the past years – the research undertakes a structural analysis and focuses on institutional settings. Ostrom and others draw upon a linguistic approach towards a syntax, constituting rules (Elinor Ostrom 2005, 139–52), an elaborated "Grammar of Institutions" (Ostrom 2005, 137). It allows us to assess institutional diversity beyond markets or governmental organisations. The basic outlines for the theoretical approach of this study as well as additions and further enhancements of the IAD framework are discussed in chapter 3.

The approach towards socio-ecological transitions in urban contexts used in this research is extended by several aspects that surpass the theoretical approach laid out by Ostrom and others. First, it is an attempt to apply the works of Ostrom and others who demonstrated its explanatory power for rural resource systems to urban contexts. By focusing on self-organisation capabilities, we believe to have a more directed approach to resource governance in the action arenas of local resource systems – cities – towards a sustainable and resilient treatment at our hands. Self-organising capabilities can under certain circumstances prove themselves to be important transition drivers and integrate into recent discussions and socio-political movements that claim a "Right to the City" (Harvey 2008); forces that cannot be neglected.

The number of 40 selected cities as well as the treatment of these cities could be referred to as a case study. Nonetheless, the foundation of analysis is not the individual city but – more aggregated – the constitution of transition processes in three distinct resource systems – energy, water, and green spaces – and local labour market institutions with a regional clustering of Europe (cf. Table 2-1). The research design evaluates the role of cities in socio-ecological transition, where cities are the spatial delimiting factor and the transitions are the phenomena. Taking into account that each city is highly individual, the research reconstructs a contrasting picture of transition processes. Case study designs provide single outcomes that are not generalisable. This is not a flaw but a trait:

> In social case work we do not gather data in order to compare, classify, and analyze with a view to formulating general principles. We gather the data case by case in order to make a separate, differential diagnosis, with little or no regard for comparison, classification, and scientific generalization. The diagnosis is made with a view to putting treatment into operation in this particular case.
> (Pauline Young 1939, 235–36, in John Gerring 2007, 190)

The research design here provides the insights into the transition processes of single resource systems and above that for differential diagnosis of certain individual and contextualised aspects. Although Poteete, Janssen, and Ostrom (2010) for example base their work on detailed case studies of single local entities, this research will not make use of such an approach. Moreover, the basal research interest will be a regional understanding and comparison of sustainability in socio-ecological transitions. Reasons for this are found in a practical aspect. Forty case studies are difficult to handle; above this, the material necessary for in-depth case studies is complex and manifold, and thus the inquiry, too, is complex and time-consuming (e.g. ethnographic research, interviews, document analysis, and so on, although not all sources have to be served for a coherent study; cf. Robert K. Yin 2003, 86, Figure 4.1). In terms of content, institutional *diversity* is of more importance for the research than detailed individual case studies to point out the individual case structures. Yet, as John Gerring puts it: "The product of a good case study is *insight*" (Gerring 2007, 7) and the insights this research targets are the special features of socio-ecological transitions of different resource systems and institutions. The entity of the city is not the first point of interest but the details of the transitions across several cases. This includes contradicting and sometimes ambiguous results and furthermore an inherently problematic definition of 'cases' as entities of research. A "[c]ase connotes a spatially delimited phenomenon (a unit) observed at a single point in time or over some period of time" (Gerring 2007, 19). This, however, does not add much to a robust definition and is open to interpretation.

2.1.2 Experts and expert knowledge

The empirical data was mainly collected through expert interviews and questionnaires. Key actors in the chosen cities were selected as experts (Alexander Bogner, Beate Littig, and Wolfgang Menz 2009). Their central positions in city politics and administration, in the business sector, and in civil society grant insights into the dense sociopolitical field of ecological transitions and its challenges (for a detailed list of actors, cf. Table 2-10). Thus, they have the possibility and the aims to influence local sustainability transitions to a certain degree and, above all, to have a certain degree of knowledge and experience of or with the field as well as motivation to get involved in transition processes. The interviewees are at the heart of these discussions and interactions, and they are involved in the topics on a daily basis. Therefore, their knowledge and experience is *expert knowledge*. This knowledge can open up and clarify the (pre)conditions of socio-ecological transition dynamics and the possibilities for self-organising capabilities. Generally, the status of an expert in expert interviews refers to a special insight into practices, dynamics, and so on that the researcher is interested in. Socio-ecological transition as a topic for political decisions, administrative work, civil society commitment, and so on can best be narrated by persons that actively hold adequate positions and work with these topics (Beate Littig 2011). The method of expert interviews relies on the special status of the expert's knowledge: To gain insight into the field, the researcher needs the expert to explain to him what the important aspects are, to point out the relations and the history. Different actors mean different versions of the local narrations (at best). All experts' narrations have to be taken for granted by the researcher. A critical contestation can only occur in contrast to other experts' narrations. In contrast to an in-depth analysis, the statements of the interviewees are used to illuminate a local arena which is unknown to the researcher, while in-depth analysis tries to reconstruct subconscious patterns of the interviewee. Therefore, inquiring into in-depth structures of the individual statements aims at completely different results. Moreover, it would be a violation of ethical conduct in social research resulting from a misinformation of the interviewees on how their statements are used (Clifford G. Christians 2005, 144–45). In short, expert interviews are a suitable method for research that 'does not know' what is going on and needs an explanation of local practices, constellations, and dynamics for assessing the local socio-ecological transition towards sustainability in the city.

2.2 Criteria for the country and city selection

This section illustrates the process of the country and city sampling (see Figure 2-1). A random sample on city basis is not applicable because the goals of the study are an equal representation of the European population. Random selections of a number as small as 40 cities can over- or underrepresent certain areas, regions, or countries. Thus, the selection process bases on a theoretical sampling that reflects populace and economic growth to generate a sample that describes the socio-structural texture of the EU. General selection criteria for the cities (and regions) were defined, following a qualitative sampling strategy with prescribed selection criteria (Jennifer Mason 2002; Jane Ritchie, Jane Lewis, and Gillian Elam 2003). The sampling process is thus not randomised nor is it comparable to a theoretical sampling that emerges from the research process (e.g. in grounded theory).

The sample was generated in two steps. In a first approach, 40 cities in 14 countries were selected. For the second selection step, field researchers on site identified the specific actors for enquiry. Special 'keyholders', selected beforehand, supported them locally. These keyholders were contact persons of the local administration, recognised by ICLEI – Local Governments for Sustainability, who had a special overview of the city's relations and relevant characters.

2.2.1 Country selection

In preparation of the city selection process and in order to facilitate the coordination of the field research, several countries that are representative of all European regions and of the institutional diversity governing urban development in Europe were identified. An average of two to three cities per country results in about 14 countries for selection. This allows at least two cities per country to be contrasted according to criteria that are discussed in detail below.

Table 2-1 Country selection per European region

Region	Country
Eastern Europe	Poland, Czech Republic, Romania
Northern Europe	Denmark, Sweden, United Kingdom
Southern Europe	Greece, Italy, Spain, Turkey (Istanbul)
Western Europe	Austria, Germany, Switzerland, France

Source: UN classification in major area and region in the world (UN 2010)

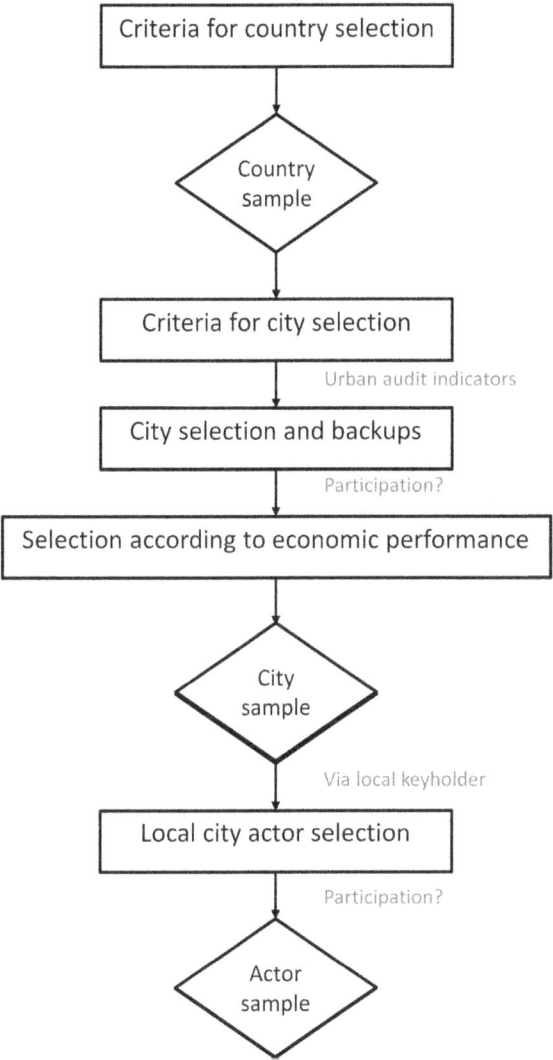

Figure 2-1 Sample creation process

The following subsections present the refined features for a strategic sampling used in this research and try to distinguish European countries according to their GDP and population shares as well as welfare state regimes and administrative features. Weighting according to regional representation was the foremost criterion to select a country sample.

Regional representation

In a first step, 14 countries were chosen in order to represent first all main regions of Europe (according to the UN classification in major areas and regions in the world (cf.

Table 2-1); second a significant proportion of the European population (cf. Table 2-2); and third a complete range of development levels in terms of income per capita. Two non-EU countries have been included: Switzerland was selected due to its unique experience with local autonomy and self-administration and because of its environmental policy programme, "2000-Watt-Society strategy" (2000-Watt Gesellschaft n. a.; Lukas Gutzwiller 2006). The UN classification (2010) also refers to the *geographical* region of Europe, thus including Switzerland although it is not part of the European Union. Turkey was selected although considered as 'Western Asia' according to the UN (2010). Nonetheless, in the case of the city of Istanbul, it is debatable that it – geographically – is still part of the European continent. Furthermore, because of the extraordinary dynamism of the Istanbul urban area and Turkey's long-term involvement with the EU as a major accession candidate, its selection can be justified.[2] These non-EU cities bring additional and contrasting insights into the understanding of socio-ecological transition at the urban level in the future EU as well.

Table 2-2 shows that the country selection achieved a fair representation in terms of population (around 85 per cent of the overall population) and income level. Therefore, the aim of choosing a representative selection with 40 cities in 14 countries is realised. In this form of strategic sampling, the explanatory power of the results can be ensured to a certain degree, one that outmatches a mere random sampling on country and/or city level.

Table 2-2 Population, GDP per capita and number of selected cities per country in 2013

Country	Population in 1,000	Share EU 28	Share 28+2	GDP/Capita (Idx)	Cities
EU 28 + 2	589,397.0		100.0 %		
EU 28	505,730.5	100.0 %	85.8 %	100	
Germany	80,523.7	15.9 %	13.7 %	122	5
Turkey	75,627.4		12.8 %	53	1
France	65,633.2	13.0 %	11.1 %	107	4
UK	63,888.0	12.6 %	10.8 %	109	4
Italy	59,685.2	11.8 %	10.1 %	99	4
Spain	46,704.3	9.2 %	7.9 %	94	4
Poland	38,533.3	7.6 %	6.5 %	67	3
Romania	20,057.5	4.0 %	3.4 %	55	3
Greece	11,062.5	2.2 %	1.9 %	73	2
Czech Republic	10,516.1	2.1 %	1.8 %	82	2
Sweden	9,555.9	1.9 %	1.6 %	127	2
Austria	8,451.9	1.7 %	1.4 %	128	2
Switzerland	8,039.1		1.4 %	163	2
Denmark	5,602.6	1.1 %	1.0 %	124	2
Total Sample		83.1 %	85.5 %		40

Source: Eurostat (2013b), Eurostat (2014) sorted by population (abs.)

Welfare regimes

It can be argued that several different details and aspects of government, state, and social welfare institutions influence the involvement of actors with sustainability issues on a city level. These can stretch from affecting the rights and means to organise grassroots or bottom-up initiatives to the sphere of influence cities, regional governments, or national governments have on certain issues and legislative frames. Also governmental organisation – on all levels – is affected by differing administrative structures and bureaucratic procedures as well as by the political agenda shaping for instance welfare, environmental, and economic policies.

Drawing on our regional preselection, these countries could be characterised as diverse institutional taxonomies according to national welfare regimes, the degree of administrative decentralisation, or styles of local government. According to Anthony S. Kasozi (2004, 1), "the taxonomy ... draws on existing accepted definitions providing categorizing criteria to address these definitional ambiguities" and further "the taxonomy should enable easier differentiation of institutions from related aspects" (Kasozi 2004, 14). The argumentation for a differentiated institutional approach is very much taken from *neo-institutionalism*, and it accounts on varying backgrounds and the processes of isomorphism in institutional settings (Paul J. DiMaggio and Walter W. Powell 1983). It can be extended by cultural aspects on differing institutional settings, origins, and materialisations (Stewart R. Clegg 1990).

The concept of (national) welfare regimes was developed by Gøsta Esping-Andersen (1990) to characterise three distinct kinds of welfare state capitalisms by considering their degrees of de-commodification and the dominant locus of solidarity. The concept of de-commodification reflects the granting of social rights: "If social rights are given the legal and practical status of property rights, if they are inviolable, and if they are granted on the basis of citizenship rather than performance, they will entail a de-commodification of the status of individuals *vis-à-vis* the market" (Esping-Andersen 1990, 21). This means that de-commodification allows for a life and for survival far from market logic, for example by granting welfare services and the like. Table 2-3 lists the three distinct types Esping-Andersen elaborated: liberal, social democratic, and conservative. These reductions show the relations between family, market, and state and the dominant mode of solidarity of the welfare state. These result in varying degrees of de-commodification.

Table 2-3 Characteristics of welfare regimes

	Liberal	*Social democratic*	*Conservative*
Dominant mode of solidarity	Individual	Universal	Kinship Corporatism
Dominant locus of solidarity	Market	State	Family
Degree of decommodification	Minimal	Maximum	High (for male breadwinner)
Modal examples	USA	Sweden	Germany
Assignment of country sample	Czech Republic, Poland, Romania, Turkey, United Kingdom	Denmark, Sweden	Austria, France, Germany, Greece, Italy, Spain, Switzerland

Source: Adapted from Esping-Andersen (1999); additional sources: Arin (2002), Kolberg and Esping-Andersen (1992)

Eastern European and Mediterranean countries are not initially represented in Esping-Andersen's typology of welfare regimes. However, later he described the specific situation in countries like Italy, Spain, and Greece with their dominant locus of solidarity in "familialism" (Gøsta Esping-Andersen 1999, 45) – but not as an addition to his initial typology. Similarly, Wil Arts and John Gelissen (2002) discuss the addition of a fourth category "Mediterranean countries" (Italy and Spain) to Esping-Andersen's three categories, extending his ideal types in response to several critiques. Arts and Gelissen (2002, 142–46) sum up the discussion of several authors arguing that Mediterranean states represent an additional prototype that cannot be subsumed as a subcategory under the existing three worlds. Thus, there appears to be an essential need for additions to the three ideal types and several authors urge to fill the gap against Esping-Andersen's objection.

Gøsta Esping-Andersen (1996) rejected the idea of a 'new' postcommunist type of welfare state in Central Eastern Europe, instead suggesting that the differences between these countries and his proposed three welfare types were only of a transitional nature. Eastern European states were subsumed under the existing labels, mainly under the liberal label. Yet, H.J. Menno Fenger (2007) identifies six different types of welfare regimes as a result of a hierarchical cluster analysis. His categorisation complements Esping-Andersen's 'three worlds'. Czech Republic and Poland correspond to a postcommunist European type of welfare regime, and Romania is considered as a developing welfare regime (Fenger 2007, 27–28; Zsuzsa Ferge 2008). Two intermediate forms complement the existing three distinct types. Esping-Andersen's adherence to three types of regimes neglects experienced transitions towards postcommunist societies. These countries have doubtlessly undergone profound structural changes as well as systemic and institutional transformations. More broadly, it denies an existing diversity in Eastern European welfare state developments (Dorothee Bohle and Béla Greskovits 2007; Jolanta Aidukaite 2011; Dragos Adascalitei 2012). Yet, this 'inflation' of welfare regimes would obviously not comply with Esping-Andersen's criteria of "explanatory parsimony" (Esping-Andersen 1999, 90) that should better be traded in for individual case comparisons. Additionally, he rejected the further adding of an "Antipodean Fourth World" (Esping-Andersen 1999, 89–92), including the Mediterranean, relying on familialism, and East Asia, relying on a unique form of capitalistic economy and an "either unique or hybrid" mix of "conservative and liberal elements" of a welfare state (Esping-Andersen 1999, 91).[3] The reason for this lies in the lack of a yet "distinct logic per se" (Esping-Andersen 1999, 92); these forms are only variations of Esping-Andersen's existing three distinctions. With regard to de-commodification, if taken as a central analytical concept for Esping-Andersen's welfare regimes, indeed it can be argued for a model that represents his initial three logics. Nonetheless several distinct influences on welfare state regimes can be pointed out that come from cultural or religious trajectories (Wim van Oorschot, Michael Opielka, and Birgit Pfau-Effinger 2008). Thus, keeping one's eyes peeled for cultural, structural, and institutional differences of Eastern and Southern European countries yields insights that also have to be reflected in the sampling.

Table 2-3 refers to Esping-Andersen's initial categorisation and depicts his initial typology. It is extended by an assignment of the sampled countries to the three pillars. Switzerland and Turkey have also been categorised based on works by Tülay Arin (2002) as well as Jon E. Kolberg and Gøsta Esping-Andersen (1992).

Degrees of administrative decentralisation

The governmental structure of a state strongly influences policy implications and decision taking. Generally, the aspect of centralisation and decentralisation touches the judicial aspects of governments and nations. Especially in constitutional questions and the representation of the people, differences are assessable and with them differences in legal and constitutional frameworks that influence possibilities of direct action on several levels of governance. According to ESPON (2005), four typologies of state structure were defined as in Table 2-4. The new EU member states of Czech Republic, Poland, and Romania were not included because of the early stage of the analysis. Iván Tosics (2011) provides a typology of territorial government systems in EU countries. It describes and analyses the formal vertical/multilevel government structures in the EU-27 countries in terms of unitary and federal structure, including the new member states. Here the unitary states are classified into five subcategories including the new member states (cf. Table 2-5). Markus Boeckenfoerde, Philipp Dann, and Verena Wiesner (2007) distinguish between unitary and federal states and define a unitary state as "a state or country which is generally governed as one single unit" (Boeckenfoerde, Dann, and Wiesner 2007, 6).

Table 2-4 Typologies of state structure

Type of state	Modal examples
Unitary states	Greece
Decentralised unitary states	Denmark, Sweden
Regionalised unitary states	France, Italy, Spain, United Kingdom
Federal states	Austria, Germany, Switzerland

Source: ESPON (2005, 285)

Table 2-5 Draft typology of territorial governmental systems in the EU27+2 countries

Government structure	EU-15 and European Free Trade Area (EFTA) countries	New member states
1 Classical unitary countries	Greece Ireland Luxembourg	
2 Centralised unitary countries with strong, but nonintegrated, local authority level	Portugal	Bulgaria Malta Czech Republic Hungary Romania Slovakia Cyprus
3 Centralised unitary countries with strong, integrated local authority level	Denmark Finland The Netherlands Sweden Norway	Estonia Latvia Lithuania Slovenia

(Continued)

Table 2-5 (Continued)

Government structure	EU-15 and European Free Trade Area (EFTA) countries	New member states
4 Centralised unitary countries with strong local and regional level	France United Kingdom	Poland
5 Regionalised countries	Italy Spain	
6 Federal states	Austria Belgium Germany Switzerland	

Source: Adapted from Iván Tosics and Joe Ravetz (2011, 81)

Especially when contrasting centralised versus decentralised states, the differences in autonomy become obvious. While the main selection criteria for the sample was the regional weighted distribution and an orientation on the proportion of GDP per capita and population, the degree of decentralisation is a further detail for governmental and administrative influences on local-level environmental policies. For example, Greece is considered a unitary state, although it can be argued that especially administrative reforms decentralised the state, government, and administration. These reforms were initiated due to financial and economic crises that especially struck Greece in 2009 and 2010 but still are not established entirely (Dimitrios S. Goulas and Georgia N. Kontogeorga 2013; Eleni Sofianou et al. 2014).

Napoleonic systems of local government

Jeffrey M. Sellers and Anders Lidström identify four categories of local government systems according to local capacities and the type of supra-local supervision (cf. Table 2-6). In their taxonomy, systems of local governments that rely on administrative centralisation but are "politically decentralized" are labelled as "Napoleonic" (Sellers and Lidström 2007, 615). A common characteristic is that "many countries under the influence of the Napoleonic tradition have territorial offices of administrative supervision over local government that corresponds fully or partly to the French prefect" (Sellers and Lidström 2007, 619). They conclude that "[t]raditional institutional distinctions between federal and unitary states, or even many general analyses of centralisation and decentralisation at higher echelons of states, fail to capture this crucial local dimension of the state" (Sellers and Lidström 2007, 626). Under "this crucial local dimension", the authors see local governments as a precondition for the possibility (and lasting success) of Scandinavian welfare policies. Overall, they assess that there is a trend for focusing on local-level governance and especially capable forms of local-level organising. Yet, the field lacks a concrete and extended classification of different types. Although the authors only refer to social democratic welfare regimes, Sellers and Lidström argue for a "close relation between decentralisation to local government and the character of the welfare state itself" (Sellers and Lidström 2007, 610). For this research, the correlation between degree of decentralisation and welfare state is an important aspect.

Table 2-6 Local government systems

Type of system	Modal examples
Northern European	Denmark, Sweden
Central European	Austria, Germany, Switzerland
Napoleonic	France, Italy, Greece, Spain
British	United Kingdom

Source: Anders Lidström (2003), as cited in Sellers and Lidström (2007, 614)

Other concepts

Of course, other typologies and comparisons of government structures, welfare regimes, and economies exist.[4] Their understanding of institutions comes very close to this research's definition. Hall and Soskice are following Douglass C. North (1990, 3) and "define institutions as a set of rules, formal or informal, that actors generally follow, whether for normative, cognitive, or material reasons, and organizations as durable entities with formally recognized members, whose rules also contribute to the institutions of the political economy" (Peter A. Hall and David Soskice 2001, 9). Bruno Amable uses a definition of 'institution' that comes even closer to the one used by Ostrom (2005): "Institutions will be defined as a set of rules that structure social interactions in particular ways" (Bruno Amable 2003, 36).

These approaches are also focusing on different institutional settings for a capitalistic system of economy. They include more or less comparable aspects and try to argue for historical and institutional path dependencies in the development of national governance differences. Overall, they all rely on comparative positions, as is also the goal of this research endeavour. There can be crossing lines as well as distant vanishing points that these frames, as well as the one proposed here, share. Therefore, this literature on 'varieties of capitalism' could deliver valuable background to our institutional comparison on local common-pool resource governance, but would distract our attention too far from our focus on socio-ecological systems – at least for the moment.

The use of the chosen typologies clearly shows that the country selection is representative of European countries in regards to the criteria of local government, welfare, and decentralisation. Thus, the country selection provides a representative sample of the EU in terms of population, regional and income distribution as well as institutional classifications.

2.2.2 City selection

Prior to going to the field, a city selection was done. It followed several criteria to achieve as objective a selection as possible. This meant the sample should be representable by key figures that displayed economic performance and success as well as decline. In addition, a specific sample had to be set that allowed for 'backup cities', if a chosen municipality declined its cooperation or showed no interest in the research endeavour, to ensure 40 cities as well as structural adequacy.

In order to support the city selection process, a list of indicators from the Urban Audit database (now named City statistics) in Eurostat was taken into account to evaluate data

Table 2-7 Urban Audit indicators included in evaluation of data availability

	Variables			
Demographics	DE1001V: Total resident population			
Economy	EC2031V: Gross domestic product per inhabitant in PPS of Nomenclature of Territorial Units for Statistics (NUTS) 3 region			
Social indicators	SA1001V: Number of dwellings	EC3055V: Total number of households with less than 60% of the national median disposable annual household income	TE2031V: Number of residents (aged 15–64) with International Standard Classification of Education (ISCED) level 5 or 6 as the highest level of education	IT1005V: Percentage of households with Internet access at home
Employment	EC1001V: Total economically active population	EC1010V: Residents unemployed	EC1012V: Female residents unemployed	EC2012V: Employment (Jobs) in public administration, health, education, other (Nomenclature générale des activités économiques dans les Communautés Européennes [NACE] Rev. 1: L-P)
Pollution/air quality	EN2002V: Summer smog: number of days ozone (O3) concentrations exceed 120 micrograms/m³	EN2003V: Number of hours per year that nitrogen dioxide (NO2) concentrations exceed 200 micrograms/m³	EN2005V: Number of days particulate matter (PM10) concentrations exceed 50 micrograms/m³	

Water	EN3003V: Total consumption of water	EN3011V: Percentage of the urban waste water load (in population equivalents) treated according to the applicable standard	
Waste	EN4001V: Annual amount of solid waste (domestic and commercial)	EN4004V: Annual amount of solid waste (domestic and commercial) that is recycled	
Land use	EN5012V: Green space area	EN5016V: Land used for agricultural purposes	EN5024V: Land used for commercial activities (industry, trade, offices)	EN5004V: Land area in housing/ residential use
Transport	TT1010V: Percentage of journeys to work by public transport (rail, metro, bus, tram)	TT1007V: Percentage of journeys to work by bicycle	TT1008V: Percentage of journeys to work by foot	TT1012V: Percentage of journeys to work by car or motorcycle

Source: Eurostat (2004)

availability (cf. Table 2-7). This preselection was extracted from cities included in the Urban Audit database hosted by Eurostat, as it is the most comprehensive database on European cities currently available. Indeed, it is of crucial importance that a certain amount of data is available for cities included in the final selection. In this spirit, and before proceeding to the preselection, a filter was applied excluding cities that were judged to have poor data availability. In order to assess the availability of data for the cities selected in the case studies series, a set of 26 indicators of Urban Audit were considered. It provided the research team with an overview of data availability. With the insight it was decided to define poor data availability based only on the assessment of data available under 12 environmental indicators (indicator code starting with EN). Concretely, for each country, the availability of environmental data was assessed and defined as poor when demonstrating a significant lack in availability of recent data (2007–2012) compared to other cities of the same country. As a result, from 275 cities represented in the Urban Audit, 89 cities were excluded from the sample for showing poor data availability. In the end, 186 cities remained for preselection.

This secondary quantitative data analysis delivers additional data to the quantitative data gathered by the field researchers. To define the number of cities for each country, the following strategy was applied. First, the population size of the countries was compared. In order to achieve significant and comparable results, it is reasonable to aim at a proportional distribution of the number of cities for each country. That means a country with a bigger population is represented by a larger number of cities than a country with a smaller population. Nevertheless, for each country at least two cities were selected. An exception is Turkey, where only one city was chosen. It was handled this way according to the argumentation that led to including Turkey in the country sample: Istanbul – it can be argued – is geographically situated at least partly in continental Europe. Table 2-2 shows the population size and the number of cities in the individual countries selected.

Further, it was important to contact key actors in cities that could provide information and confirm a possible participation of the city, a phase carrying a high level of uncertainty depending on the willingness of the local actors. Therefore, in order to ensure a final number of 40 city cases, a larger preselection of 80 cities was made, which was reduced to 40 after establishing positive contacts to the cities.

To proceed to the preselection of cities for each country, a fair representation of the full range of possible city developments within the country is desired. To fulfil this condition, the preselection of case studies per country was performed according to the following procedure: The first city was the one with the highest GDP growth rate in the country (GDP data is at NUT3 level). The second was the city with the lowest GDP growth compared to the national average. The third – if available – city was the one closest to the national average, making sure average cities are represented. This sequence was repeated until the necessary number of cities was reached. In the special case of Switzerland, there is currently no GDP data available at NUT3/city level. Consequently, GDP was substituted in the selection procedure by population data, still reflecting a trend of city development. Refer to Table 2-8 for an overview of the selected (and finally successfully enlisted) 40 cities for the research project (see also Figure 2-2). This procedure rules out subjective patterns in the selection of the cities, basing it on comparable and assessable parameters. The sample depicts manifold directions in which European cities (and among them three that could be classified as 'megacities': London, Paris, Istanbul) are developing and in addition shows the structural diversity of successful and less successful developments. Although

Figure 2-2 Map of 40 selected cities

these traits do have diverse structural, institutional, or other reasons, according to key figures, it allows individual and contrasting statements to be assessed for environmental policies and influences on them.

2.2.3 Identifying and interviewing fifteen key local actors

After country and city selection, the third sampling level gathered at the actor level. Identifying and approaching actors for the interviews had to follow predefined selection criteria to assess a comparable sample across all cities.

The final research was conducted 'on site' by 15 external field researchers who were fluent in English and native speakers of the language of the country to be field researched.

Table 2-8 Cities selected

Country	City	Avg. annual GDP growth	Performance avg. pop growth/avg. GDP growth	Regarded time span
Austria	Innsbruck	3.84	C/C	1996–2007
	Linz	3.86	B/C	1996–2007
Czech Republic	Jihlava	4.93	B/C	1996–2007
	Prague	7.31	A/A	1996–2007
Denmark	Aalborg	5.32	C/C	2005–2007
	Copenhagen	1.81	A/B	2005–2007
France	Nice	4.62	B/A	1996–2007
	Paris	3.94	B/C	1996–2007
	Rennes	4.51	A/A	1996–2007
	Strasbourg	3.08	B/B	1996–2007
Germany	Dortmund	3.85	S/C	1996–2007
	Freiburg	2.55	A/B	1996–2007
	Kiel	2.60	A/B	1996–2007
	Potsdam	3.96	A/C	1996–2007
	Saarbrücken	4.05	S/A	1996–2007
Greece	Larissa	3.92	A/B	1996–2007
	Thessaloniki	2.62	S/B	1996–2007
Italy	Milan	2.59	S/B	1996–2007
	Naples	3.13	S/C	1996–2007
	Rome	3.03	S/C	1996–2007
	Trieste	4.33	S/A	1996–2007
Poland	Cracow	7.80	S/A	2001–2007
	Lodz	6.56	S/C	2001–2007
	Lublin	4.76	S/B	2001–2007
Romania	Giurgiu	5.63	S/B	2001–2007
	Sibiu	12.74	S/A	2001–2007
	Timisoara	13.67	S/A	2001–2007
Spain	Barcelona	5.44	B/C	1996–2007
	Bilbao	6.81	B/A	1996–2007
	Madrid	5.66	B/C	1996–2007
	Valencia	5.78	B/C	1996–2007
Sweden	Goteborg	4.62	A/C	1996–2007
	Umea	4.20	A/C	1996–2007

Country	City	Avg. annual GDP growth	Performance avg. pop growth/avg. GDP growth	Regarded time span
Switzerland	Lugano	1.08	A/–	1990–2008
	St. Gallen	–0.08	S/–	1990–2008
Turkey	Istanbul	N/A	A/–	
United Kingdom	Birmingham	4.46	S/C	1996–2007
	Glasgow	5.45	S/A	1996–2007
	Leeds	4.54	B/C	1996–2007
	London	5.45	A/A	1996–2007

Note: A: Overperformer, B: Underperformer, C: Close to average, S: Shrinking City (where population growth is considered); values for Switzerland reflect average population growth

Source: Urban Audit Database

The goal was to perform adequate research in every country of the first level of research, so the questionnaire and interview guide had to be translated into the local language. Interviews were conducted in the local language.

Organising interviews

The process of data inquiry from quantitative questionnaires and qualitative interviews was organised and supported by ICLEI and included the identification and selection of relevant local actors. The researchers were provided with a field handbook describing the main goals of the research and the selection criteria for the local actors. In June 2013, before the field phase commenced, an initial briefing meeting was held in Berlin with the field researchers due to the complex nature of both quantitative and qualitative data gathering (Sue Arthur and James Nazroo 2003, 133–36). The field researchers were given clear guidance and templates to assist them in carrying out the interviews and in collecting the data. The event was also an opportunity to listen to and exchange on any potential concerns or difficulties that researchers felt could arise. After the field phase was finished, a debriefing meeting took place, again in Berlin, in December 2013. This meeting provided an opportunity for the field researchers to give feedback to the project consortium on the knowledge and information they had gathered while visiting the cities and conducting the desk research.

While organising the interviews, the interviewers worked autonomously and coordinated with the keyholder within the local government. The keyholders were involved at an early stage to discuss the research aims and objectives and to explain in detail what was required in terms of identifying people for the interviews and questionnaires.

Regular reporting and continuous communication with the ICLEI team were considered of utmost importance, especially when problems emerged locally. Despite the huge amount of data, there were no problems in the process. The conducted inquiries were done in face-to-face situations to ensure a quick response and to assist the respondents while filling in the questionnaires to ensure they understood the questions. The quite

Table 2-9 Realised results for data inquiry

Type	Planned	Realised	Challenges
Qualitative interviews	160	155 (96.88%)	Lacking cooperation and political issues
Quantitative inquiries (energy, green spaces, water)	480	453 (94.4%)	Standard issues with nonresponse, complex questionnaire and time issues
Quantitative inquiries (labour market)	80	66 (82.5%)	Problems with identification of Pact/LEIs; absence of Pact/LEIs in some cities

complex questionnaires for the three different resource systems (energy, water, and green spaces) and the labour market questionnaire took about one hour to be completed. Before entering the field phase, it was pretested and refined accordingly. In some cases, due to the limited time of the actor and the complex nature of the questionnaire, it was only handed over and then sent back to the interviewer. This was an alternative procedure but opened possibilities for nonresponse. Especially interviewing the actor *and* having the questionnaire completed was in some cases time-consuming and collided with the actors' schedules. All in all the field researchers realised a very good return rate with both the questionnaires and the qualitative expert interviews (cf. Table 2-9).

Selection of the actors

Before arranging the face-to-face interviews, every field researcher was required to identify relevant local actors in each city they were responsible for. In total, the field researcher had to prepare a tentative list of 15 potential interviewees that followed the guidelines that were set up preceding the field phase and communicated in the previous briefing that prepared for the outlines and needs of the strategic sampling process (Mason 2002, 123–27). ICLEI approved these lists and advised and organised the field phase and the researcher deployments. To help in the identification of the local actors, the keyholder in each city was available to advise and to support. They provided orientation in the cities and established contacts if necessary. Once the tentative actors list had been approved, the field research commenced.

The interviewed individuals were important key actors in the local arena for environmental and sustainability or labour market issues. The selection of actors was done according to the thematic focuses in the research, namely, energy, water, green spaces as well as labour markets. For this purpose, actors active in the field with expertise and knowledge were potential interviewees and were recruited from representatives of local politics, local government and administration, but also from the business sector as well as from leaders of civil society or from bottom-up initiatives and NGOs in the field of socio-environmental issues. A list of positions of actors in each city is displayed in Table 2-10. Distributing the different types of questionnaires was realised via a simple segregation: While actor 1 was only interviewed, actors 2, 3, and 4 were interviewed and filled in questionnaires, and actors 5 to 15 only filled in questionnaires. Actor 2 always filled in a questionnaire on energy; actors 3 and 4 filled in questionnaires according to the city's dominant focus (water or green spaces). Qualitative expert interviews implicitly followed the same selection criteria although the field handbook or the initial briefings did not implicate this. This leaves the research with a certain constraint: The energy sector does not include interviews from civil society actors (actor 4) and only very few business actors (actor 3). This leads to difficulties in the qualitative analysis and interpretation of self-organisation capabilities. Since only political and administrative actors were interviewed on energy – and almost none from business or civil society – the results remain a bit one-dimensional. In reverse, this also applies to water system and green spaces, where almost no political and administrative actors have been interviewed but predominantly actors from business and civil society.

Table 2-10 List of actors

Actor	Profession	Conducted inquiry
1	Politician with a particular interest in sustainability (mayor for smaller cities).	Semi-structured interview only
2	Head of environmental/sustainability department (or other department dealing with environmental issues or sustainability).	Questionnaire on energy; semi-structured interview
3	A representative of the private sector with particular relevance to the issue of sustainability. This could be from the local chamber of commerce of a major business in the city.	Questionnaire chosen from water or green spaces; semi-structured interview
4	A civil society representative (or leader of bottom-up initiatives, NGO, etc.).	Questionnaire chosen from water or green spaces; semi-structured interview
5	Director/manager of energy provision company.	Questionnaire on energy
6	A civil society representative (or leader of bottom-up initiatives, NGO, etc.).	Questionnaire on energy
7	Representative of the private sector with particular relevance to the issue of energy (local chamber of commerce, energy-intensive industry, local private energy producers, etc.).	Questionnaire on energy
8	Director/manager of water provision company (water expert).	Questionnaire on water
9	A civil society representative (or leader of bottom-up initiatives, NGO, etc.).	Questionnaire on water
10	Where water is provided by a private company a representative of that company, otherwise a representative of a business that has a significant impact on water resources such as industries or large-scale farming.	Questionnaire on water

(Continued)

Table 2-10 (Continued)

Actor	Profession	Conducted inquiry
11	Director/manager of urban planning department (or department in charge of green spaces).	Questionnaire on green spaces
12	A civil society representative (or leader of bottom-up initiatives, NGO, etc.).	Questionnaire on green spaces
13	A representative of the private sector with particular relevance to the issue of green spaces (forest owners, park manager, local chamber of commerce, etc.).	Questionnaire on green spaces
14	Manager/expert at the Public Employment Service (PES) organisation responsible for the city.	Questionnaire on labour markets, face-to-face interview
15	Manager/expert for one of the Local Employment Initiatives (LEI) or Territorial Employment Pacts (TEP) operating in the city (if no such initiative exists this interview does not have to be done).	Questionnaire on labour markets, face-to-face interview

For labour markets, the following process of interviewing was conducted: The field researchers were asked to interview one person from the management of the regional Public Employment Services (PES) and one person from the management of one Territorial Employment Pact or Local Employment Initiative (Pact/LEI) operating on the city territory. In many countries, the territories are serviced by different PES tiers that do not correspond to the administrative city limits. Since interviewing multiple tiers of the PES was not feasible on account of financial and time constraints, interviewers were asked to interview the lowest tier level of this organisation operating on the territory of the city they were researching, irrespective of whether this level of organisation was also responsible for other regions or not.[5] The second type of actor interviewed were representatives of Local Employment Initiatives or Territorial Employment Pacts. From the literature, it is known that these organisations are extremely diverse in their organisation and objectives and often hard to identify for an outsider (Michael Geddes 1998; Frank Pyke 1998; Anita Buchegger-Traxler, Martin Roggenkamp, and Elke Scheffelt 2003; Ida Regalia 2008). Additionally, a comprehensive interviewing of *all* initiatives in the city was not feasible, so only one initiative operating in each of the cities was interviewed. To select this initiative, the field researchers asked the interviewed PES representatives for a suggestion and, if such a suggestion could not be obtained, interviewed a randomly selected initiative.[6] Field researchers, however, were told that in some cities no Pact/LEIs might exist. In this case, they were instructed to conduct no interviews with Pact/LEIs.

The overall character of the sample for questionnaires on urban resource systems represents the following features: Approximately 75 per cent are male, the overall age ranging from 23 to 83 years, 48 years on average. More than 75 per cent completed a second cycle at university (master's degree or equivalent). Of these 75 per cent, 14 per cent have a doctorate. The majority (60 per cent) is involved with sustainability as a central part of their job; 28 per cent, as a secondary part. Fifteen per cent are involved in their free time. It can be assessed that the selected and questioned actors are experts in their field(s). Furthermore, there is a gender bias that might come from the higher academic qualifications and the overall age of the sample as a mirror of social and societal state. The labour markets sample consists of 42 per cent male candidates. The age ranges from 32 to 60 years with an average of 48 years. These differences in the age span are not surprising, as only persons of working age could be respondents to the labour market questionnaire.

2.3 Methods and methodological reflections

This section reflects the sampling strategy and the research methods used. It tries to point out shortcomings of the research design and to delimit the range of possible research results. Since the research design in itself is very complex, there is an essential need to have a self-reflective approach towards the process and to keep the limitations in mind when approaching the material for interpretation. Many different aspects produce hard-to-control effects on the research, the inquiry, and the data. Not all can be assessed at this point, but the most important ones will be pointed out.

2.3.1 Quantitative data

The field researchers collected quantitative data with five different questionnaires (cf. Table 2-10 for an overview of questionnaires and actors). As described earlier, in each city, 15 actors in the fields of energy, water, green spaces, and labour markets were identified. Each actor apart from actor 1 filled in one questionnaire, depending on the personal area of expertise. In sum, we expected 480 questionnaires on the three resource systems – an average of 160 each on energy, water, and green spaces – and 80 questionnaires on labour markets.

In the end, 518 questionnaires were completed (151 energy, 167 green spaces, 135 water, and 65 labour market). These split into the three sectors as follows: 135 from government, 166 from business, and 152 from civil society experts for the resource system (total: 453). For labour markets, 40 were from PES organisations and 26 from Pact/LEIs. Of the completed questionnaires in 40 cities within the four regions, 23 per cent are from Eastern Europe, 17 per cent Northern Europe, 28 per cent Southern Europe, and 33 per cent Western Europe. As the questionnaires on labour markets differed from the ones on the resource systems, methods of analysis differed as well.

The questionnaires on energy, green spaces, and water contained about 35 questions. These questionnaires covered topics such as the understanding of urban sustainability, the state of the city's resource system, challenges, actors, objectives, distribution of costs and benefits, learning due to prior experience and networking, norm-adoption, and institutional diversity. The questionnaires were analysed jointly for the first two sections, which covered questions about socio-demographic data and the experts' understanding of urban sustainability and socio-ecological transition. Chapters 4–7 focused individually on the specific resource systems and were therefore analysed separately.

For data analysis, the software solution STATA was used (Version 13), allowing for all state-of-the-art statistical analysis instruments. Initially a descriptive analysis of the research questions was performed. Differences between the answers of the regional clusters (north, south, east, and west) and the sectors (business, government, and civil society) were analysed alongside the seven research questions outlined in chapter 3. Afterwards, a regression analysis was performed with identified factors influencing *self-organisation capabilities* to uncover relationships between local preconditions and the emergence of new institutional arrangements. On the whole, a five-stage scale measured answers, so measures for ordinal-scaled variables were used for the analysis. The differences between groups of respondents were analysed with the Kruskal-Wallis equality-of-populations rank test. It tests the hypothesis that several samples are from the same population (David Sheskin 2000, 595–609). Three different significance levels were observed and marked ($\star$ $\alpha = 0.1$; $\star\star$ $\alpha = 0.05$; $\star\star\star$ $\alpha = 0.01$). The regression was performed as ordered logistic regression, controlling for the cities and the sectors (J. Scott Long and Jeremy Freese 2006, 188–93).

The first labour markets questionnaire contained 23 questions structured into 5 blocks and was given to representatives of PES organisations. These representatives were asked questions on autonomy, objective structure, and target groups of their organisations as well as on the major changes that occurred with respect to these dimensions since 2008. Furthermore, following the differences between PES organisations and Pact/LEIs, the Pact/LEI questionnaire differed from that for PES organisations. In particular, literature suggests that Pact/LEIs often draw their partnership from among regional and local organisations and operate on a rather informal basis (Mark Shucksmith 2000; ECOTEC 2002; Peter Huber 2005; Raymond Saller 2005; Cristina Martinez-Fernandez et al. 2011). The questionnaire was shorter with only three blocks of questions. The respondents were presented a different list of potential partner institutions, which put substantially more emphasis on regional partners. They were also asked to differentiate between formal partners (i.e. those involved because of a formal pact agreement) and informal partners (i.e. those considered partners for other reasons).

The set of questions used to determine the autonomy of the PES included asking whether the PES was an independent organisation or part of a ministry and for the share of the autonomously decided budget, but also whether the PES had responsibilities with respect to a list of 21 tasks, which, following Francesca Froy and Sylvain Guère (2009), were grouped into 6 groups of competencies related to designing programmes, allocating budgets, defining target groups, monitoring and evaluating results, administrative competencies, and competences in outsourcing. The objectives of the PES, by contrast, were elicited by a block of questions on whether the specific target group (among 21 listed) was a priority of the PES and whether the organisation followed specific strategies with respect to 10 listed fields of economic activities of particular relevance in urban labour market contexts. In addition, PES representatives were also asked to pick, from a list of 19 types of actors, which of these were considered stakeholders in their organisation. Finally, they were asked whether there had been any changes in autonomy, the importance of target groups, sector strategies, and stakeholders since 2008.

2.3.2 Qualitative data

Interviews on energy, green spaces and water were conducted following a semi-structured topic guide.[7] This guide provides an interview structure that makes the interviews easier to compare, and it served as a reminder that no essential questions were forgotten (Arthur and Nazroo 2003, 115–26). The answers depict the object in the view of the specific actor, which exactly means that things might be denoted differently or even contradictory, marking a problematic discourse (e.g. different views of a business representative and the member of an ecological NGO). The interview situation is effective to foster reflection of the actors so they can give elaborated statements and assessments. This produces reflections and thus insights into the inner structure of socio-ecological transitions. For the interviewees, it offered an opportunity to reflect the picture of the local transition.

Initially, 160 interviews were planned – 4 per city; 155 interviews were realised. The interview length stretched from 18 to 118 minutes with an average duration of 55 minutes. One-hour face-to-face talks had very good results and promised differentiated and considerable statements of the interviewed. In addition, the time corresponds with a specific time slot that the interviewees were able to allocate in an otherwise tight schedule. Native speakers conducted all interviews in the local language, transcribed them, and translated them into English (on the translation process cf. section 2.3.4). The analysis and interpretation process made use of computer-assisted qualitative data analysis software, especially MaxQDA (Version 11). The project was set up as a team project to allow easy cooperation and work division. In a first step, the interview transcripts were proofread for corrections and layout issues and to gain insight into their content. Second, the initial coding process commenced, using Elinor Ostrom's *second tier variable system* (Elinor Ostrom 2007; Poteete, Janssen, and Ostrom 2010; Thomas Sauer 2012) as a starting point. The given code system was refined and differentiated with our own codes, generated in an open coding process, yet remaining within Ostrom's system. The third step aggregated the coded passages according to the several research questions. By paraphrasing the retrieved coded segments for each research question, keywords and 'headlines' were generated and allowed for thematic comparison (also with the results of the quantitative research). This led to the fifth step through the empirical interpretation with focus on the determination of the self-organisation capabilities in the three resource systems: energy, water, and green spaces.

2.3.3 Additional field research resources

In addition to quantitative questionnaires and qualitative expert interviews, each field researcher had to provide a general city case study report and a personal field report. The first one served as an overview of the situation in the city and was composed as a desk research task profiting from the insights gained through the field research. By assessing documents, webpages, and the like, the researchers provided a document stating the public self-display and discourse of each city, along with a critical inquiry into the topics and discussions that were under local debate. The goal was to identify key issues in each of the resource systems and was supported by the interviewed key actors. Further, it was possible to get a neutral overview of local challenges and transition factors in contrast to the assessments made by the interviewees and, above all, provided context knowledge. Initial desk research before the interview phase served the same purpose: finding suitable interviewees as well as gaining context and background knowledge for the interview situations and refinements for potential questions during the interviews.

The latter – the personal field report – served as a possible way to reflect on the field phase, identifying and contacting interviewees and providing feedback on the field inquiry. Generally, this document provided details on contacting keyholders and potential interviewees and feedback for the research team on the questionnaire and the semi-structured topic guide for the interviews. When planning a sample with 40 cities, nothing ever runs as planned. So, the personal reports also served as a possible way to examine nonresponsive actors and possible local structural problems (e.g. missing actors), as well as to give a flavour of what was happening in the city, but which might not be reflected in the data.

While the personal reports will not be published (due to confidentially issues), the city case study report is available via online download (Cristina Garzillo and Peter Ulrich 2015). Its content adds to the empirical work of the research and sustains the interpretation of the material.

2.3.4 Methodological reflections

This study used a qualitative sampling strategy as depicted in section 2.2. A first important aspect related to sampling is the ability to generalise results. Because a random sample has not been conducted – as it is required for any form of inductive statistics – it cannot be assumed that the findings of this research can be generalised in a statistically correct way. The shape and details of our sample did not allow for an easily accessible and randomly drawn sample (cf. section 2.2). This mainly comes from the fact that this research design is aimed at surveying members of institutions (e.g. politics, governments, parties, administration, NGOs). They cannot be randomly selected from a city. Nonetheless, there are possible ways to achieve a certain degree of generalisability, rooted mainly in qualitative methodology (Jane Lewis and Jane Ritchie 2003).

Every research design has its assets and drawbacks. The reflections on the methodology and methods used try to evaluate possible strengths of the set as well as potential drawbacks and shortcomings. First, a mixed methods approach that combines quantitative and qualitative analysis is a good starting point to provide differentiated insights into the research field.

Reflecting the qualitative research methods used, the topic guide structured the interview. It assesses transition locally and the state of the local resource system, lessons learnt and policy implications as well as transition factors and challenges. The latter two can be considered as perpendicular to the assessments of the local state of the system. This is sustained by the expert interview as a device to encourage actors to engage in self-reflection on the local transition, which likely produces expounding problems in the field. In addition, interviewer effects cannot be excluded. Qualitative research is affected broadly by a complex set of uncontrollable influences on the interview situation. The field researcher's context is essential in the interview situation: personal qualification, knowledge or lack of knowledge of the field, appearance, and interaction (verbal, nonverbal) with the interviewee affect the situation. These cannot be controlled by the research team but only by the individual researchers themselves. Thus, adequate and dedicated personnel with an understanding of and qualifications for qualitative research were hired.

Another aspect was the 'quality' of the chosen experts. Subsection 2.2.3 described a brief structure of the selected sample that allows for an attribution as 'experts'. In general, every chosen actor had to fill in a questionnaire. Only the political actors (a1) were not given questionnaires. Concerning the qualitative interview partners, there was a question in the interview guide that served as an entry to the more elaborate topics: It addressed the actor's personal involvement in sustainability topics and the personal motivation to grapple with these issues. All interviewees could state their own affiliations with the topic as well as their own involvement through their positions. Hence, the questioned persons are experts in their fields and are able to contribute insights of value. This shows that the initial identification process of the field researchers to preselect relevant persons that have expertise and information in the field of sustainability was successful.

On the level of methodology, the procedure of data interpretation has to be addressed. For the qualitative data, several methodological approaches can be considered. Usually, expert interviews are interpreted by means of content analysis. Another way could have been grounded theory, but it was not a goal of the inquiry to generate theory (first of all the grounded theory would have required an open approach to the field and one to multiple returns to the field to retrieve refined information). In addition, the information gained from the experts is used as insight into local proceedings, processes, and *their* knowledge of the system and used to explain to the researcher the mechanisms at work in the field. Assessing the expert's knowledge means taking it seriously, as an access to social reality. A content analysis focuses the surface of this knowledge not of the underlying structures producing or limiting this knowledge and therefore is most applicable.

Another critical aspect for the research was that all data was gathered locally in the country's language (Katharina Inhetveen 2012). Thus, it was important that the questionnaires and transcripts were translated. Whilst the transferring of the quantitative data might not have posed a severe difficulty, the translations of the transcripts were a more complex task. For quantitative analysis, a problem can be recognised in the fact that questionnaires were translated from English to the local language, which could shift sense and understanding that led to violations of quality criteria for research (objectivity, reliability, and validity). In the process of data interpretation, complex questions tended to have not been treated equally in translation and/or handling and thus could not be handled accordingly in the data analysis. The translation of the expert interviews in contrast produced less grave problems, as in expert interviews, which should give an insight into the fields of the actors, only the concrete meaningful and semantic relations are important on the surface. In-depth interviews cannot be treated the same way because the translation process would have destroyed the in-depth meaning. In addition, the transcription process sufficed on a plain level that 'flattened' spoken language (e.g. by erasing all filler words like 'eem' or 'uhm' and erasing repetitions). The translation only concerned the written account as the interview itself took place in the country's language by native speakers and was then transcribed in the original language and lastly translated.

Despite the described (potential) problems with translating questionnaires and/or interviews, the process was considered more accurate than conducting all research in English. Especially comprehensibility of both questionnaires and interviews was extended since the capability of understanding and answering questions in English cannot be assessed and might have been less detailed. Nonetheless, the research team proofread the initial translations to check for any deviations from the original sense.

Notes

1 Kindly supported by *Adrien Labaeye, Benjamin Gloy, Enkeleda Kadriu, Kira Reich, Peter Huber,* and *Stephanie Barnebeck.*
2 The latter point was valid before the Gezi Park protests in 2013. In the aftermath of the governmental dealings with the protests, EU negotiations and talks with Turkey about joining the EU have come to a halt.
3 A more detailed elaboration on the East Asia welfare state with special focus on Japan can be found in Gøsta Esping-Andersen (1997).

4 Basically, their notion of institutions also shares common roots with works on neo-institutionalism (cf. Paul J. DiMaggio and Walter W. Powell 1983).
5 We decided for these lowest-tier organisations even though this implies sampling organisations that service a larger or a smaller territory than the administrative city limits of the respective city level. This guarantees the best possible comparability between different PES organisations. However, and this will also become apparent below, even the lowest tier PES in most regions operates on a regional scale exceeding administrative city limits. This can be justified by the openness of urban labour markets, which often necessitates a close coordination of urban labour market policies with the suburban regions surrounding the city (OECD 2009b), but also clearly documents the complicated position of cities when attempting to have their specific labour market problems considered in designing regional labour market policies.
6 By referring field researchers to the advice of an expert institution such as the PES, we hoped to get a sample of initiatives that are rather highly esteemed and both well known and functioning in the respective regions. One disadvantage of eliciting interview suggestions in this way is that the regional PES may have been more likely to mention initiatives in which it had a strong role.
7 Qualitative data is used for the research on urban resource systems only. The research on labour markets queried actors in the 40 cities with a structured questionnaire and closed questions.

Chapter 3

Patterns of change
A general model of socio-ecological transition

Thomas Sauer

We hypothesise that favourable institutional conditions, such as decision-making autonomy and social equality, which allow and support new institutional arrangements, make self-organised and cooperative forms of management of common-pool resources in the urban resource systems more likely. This book explores these conditions systematically in the context of socio-ecological transitions with a special focus on the overarching research question: What is the transformative role of institutional diversification and innovation in the governance of core urban common-pool resources? This research question also implies the aim to find out how the governance of common-pool resources in the three core resource systems – energy, green spaces, and water – in cities could be improved to better contribute to a transition to sustainable development. The theoretical frame developed in this chapter will be used in chapters 4 to 6 to analyse the cities' resource governance.

3.1 An institutional focus for transition analysis

In this chapter, a new approach for sustainability transition analysis will be developed. In the entire book, the term 'transition' will be used in the sense of 'sustainability transition', if not specified otherwise. Sustainability transition is the pursued process of an accelerated changeover towards strong sustainability and therefore goes beyond incremental sustainable development. The term 'analysis' stresses the intention to avoid an approach that would be normative and managerial beforehand. The aim is to develop an approach enabling the analysis and understanding of the normative dynamics in times of transition in whichever direction. This aim is based on several assumptions. First, it makes sense to distinguish between the concepts of transition and transformation: Transitions may happen on a well-defined institutional basis, while transformations entail changes of the institutional basis itself. Therefore, sustainability transitions may entail shifts from one regime to another – without reflecting the underlying institutional setting. For example, the term 'green economy' frequently refers to a green market economy without questioning the superiority of market instruments for such greening of the economy. This might be a short-sighted view if these market instruments do not abandon striving for economic growth and respect the planetary boundaries of the Anthropocene instead. Second, a broader approach to sustainability transitions is needed to bring the possible institutional change itself into the focus of inquiry and the resource systems which are key for such socio-ecological transitions towards strong sustainability as well. The transitions of the individual resource systems will have spillover effects; we therefore also argue for 'the socio-ecological transition', since the change of a single part affects the entire system.

Thus, a framework is required that allows two things: (1) to treat social and ecological systems in almost equal depth and (2) to analyse the feedbacks between the resource conditions and the rules determining the harvesting rates of the resource. Aiming to identify the institutional changes required for improving the conditions of a more sustainable way to produce and consume inevitably directs the analytical focus on the determinants of these harvesting rules. These rules are the key interfaces between societal and ecological systems. Thus, it is crucial to compare the ecological impact of the rule sets available and to analyse the factors determining the evolution of these rule sets of human resource governance at the same time.

For the development of such a framework that is capable of assessing the transformative potential of diverse institutional settings concerning their sustainability characteristics, an outstanding starting point exists: This is the *tragedy of the commons*, telling a widespread story about the overgrazing of pastures jointly belonging to the inhabitants of a village. It raises the question whether human communities are able to manage such territories jointly in a way that there would be enough fodder for their cattle in the future as well. Here we have as a metaphor the key problem of global sustainability: How to organise our economic activities in a way compliant with the future needs of the human community, namely, respecting the planetary boundaries and the resilience of the ecological systems surrounding us. Solving such social dilemmas by choosing the appropriate institutional settings is obviously crucial for the sustainable governance of such common-pool resources, like pastures, lakes, groundwater basins, fisheries, forests, and other ecological resource systems. Therefore, we proceed in sketching the consequences of introducing the concept of common-pool resources in a typology of goods: This step implies the diversification of the institutional settings available for the sustainable governance of resources. If institutional settings diversify, they could be reselected in a way that improves the sustainability of resource governance significantly. This leads us to the question what innovative role could be assigned to self-organised forms of resource governance by civil sector actors on the local level.

3.1.1 Self-organised governance of common-pool resources

In standard textbooks for a long time, it was taken for granted what Garret Hardin proclaimed in his seminal publication of 1968: "Freedom in a commons brings ruin to all" (Garrett Hardin 1968, 1244). Thus, selling these commons as private property or keeping them in public property but allocating the right to use them appeared to him as the only reasonable solution to avoid such ruin. That is what Harding labelled – with reference to William Forster Lloyd 1833) – as the "tragedy of the commons": The inter-temporal problem of securing for the future the fodder of the cattle on common rural ground was transferred by both of them to the feeding of humans in the face of an expected overpopulation. In the meantime, modern game theory has well explored that this class of social dilemmas builds on further assumptions, namely, (1) complete and common information, (2) independent and simultaneous decisions, (3) no communication, and (4) no central authority. "When these assumptions are made for a game that is not repeated, or is finitely repeated, the theoretical prediction derived from noncooperative game theory is unambiguous – zero cooperation" (Ostrom 2009, 6).

In contrast to this, many field studies have found that "local groups of resource users ... have managed to create viable institutional arrangements for coping with common-pool resource problems" (Ostrom 2005, 221). Thus, it is very promising to explore such self-organised resource-governance systems at the local level. A special focus on the characteristics of these institutional arrangements could help to understand better their role in safeguarding the resilience of the ecological resource system under scrutiny. In a next step, one could try to apply these hopefully new insights to scale up to superior governance levels.

Institutions are defined in this study as "the prescriptions that humans use to organize all forms of repetitive and structured interactions . . . at all scales" (Ostrom 2005, 3). From this point of view, institutions are the "underlying rules of the game" (North 1990, 4–5). Regarding self-organisation, it makes sense to refer to the following description as a starting point: "Self-organized resource-governance systems . . . may be special districts, private associations, or parts of a local government. These are nested in several levels of general purpose governments that also provide civil, equity, as well as criminal courts" (Ostrom 2005, 283). Such resource-governance systems may be run by civil cooperatives in the energy and housing sectors, or by community groups caring for local green spaces, or nongovernmental organisations intervening in the management of water or other ecological resource systems, or nonprofit organisations managing urban farming initiatives.

Here an important distinction between participation and self-organisation has to be made, according to the locus of initiative-taking. In the case of participation, initiative-taking exclusively lies with public authorities, whereas in the case of self-organisation it rests with "members of civic society or business, indifferent to public policy objectives" (Beitske Boostra and Luuk Boelens 2011, 109). In contrast to Boostra and Boelens (2011), independence of public policy objectives is taken here as the better wording (compared to indifference): Independence of civil society actors could be supportive, indifferent, or conflictive regarding public policy objectives and be an important source for the revision of such objectives.

Participation can precede self-organisation, yet it is not a prerequisite for it, but self-organisation can emerge independently of existing participation options. According to another definition, self-organisation "comprises all forms of self-organized measures that do not necessarily have to emerge out of a participatory development process but that can be initiated from the beginning by citizens" (Michael T. Wright, Hella von Unger, and Martina Block 2010, 45, own translation). Similarly, it designates "initiatives that originate in civil society from autonomous community-based networks of citizens, who are part of the urban system but independent of government procedures" (Boostra and Boelens 2011, 113). Whereas participation

> refers to goals set by government bodies on which citizens can exert influence through procedures set by these government regimes themselves, . . . self-organisation stands for the actual motives, networks, communities, processes and objectives of citizens themselves, at least initially independent of government policies and detached from participatory planning procedures.
> (Boostra and Boelens 2011, 109)

Therefore, in contrast to participation, self-organisation can also emerge without intervention of the local government and even despite of it – for example out of missing citizen participation – or it can deliberately be started by citizens as a protest movement against political or administrative action. Self-organisation does not necessarily have to

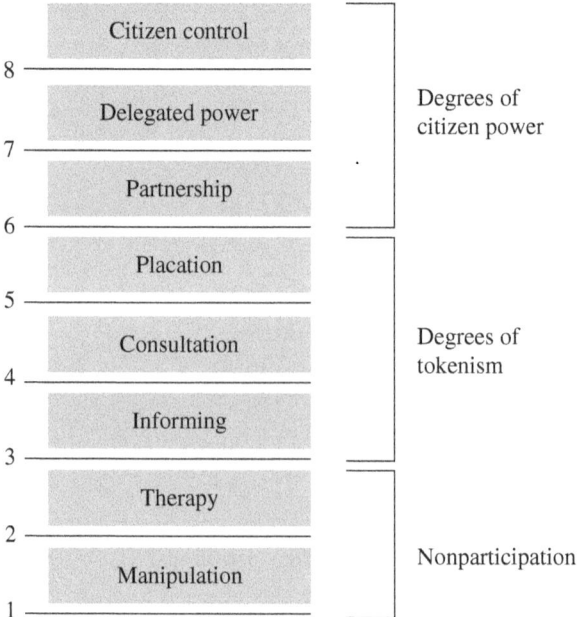

Figure 3-1 Eight rungs on a Ladder of Citizen Participation

follow the 'rules of the game', namely, be organised via established formal institutions; activities can instead happen in a more spontaneous, self-managed way.

Another perspective might be introduced by the seminal Ladder of Citizen Participation of Sherry Arnstein (1969), as presented in Figure 3-1. It is interesting how Arnstein divided the degrees of citizen participation into three major categories: *nonparticipation*, characterised by manipulation and therapy, where the citizens appear as objects of public administrations; *tokenism*, where the citizens are simply persuaded as if they would participate for real; and *citizen power*, where all citizens have a real voice in collective decision-making, independent of their socio-economic power resources. "At the topmost rungs, (7) *Delegated Power* and (8) *Citizen Control*, have-not citizens obtain the majority of decision-making seats, or full managerial power" (Sherry R. Arnstein 1969, 217). In 1969, as Sherry Arnstein published her article, the "have-not citizens" she had in mind were people without significant assets that should be empowered to get a voice in community governance which they did not have before. In current times, and in this research, it might be an issue whether delegated power and citizen control are really a sequence of increasing citizen power or equally valid alternatives of it. This assumption would transform the Arnstein ladder into a 'Y of citizen control'. The Arnstein ladder appears in the literature on public participation in many variations, extended or abridged, like the one by the International Association for Public Participation (IAP2) and the Theoretical, Empirical and Policy Foundations for Social Innovation in Europe (TEPSIE) project (Table 3-1). Maybe the newer spectra of public participation are not as judgemental as the seminal Arnstein ladder, but they miss her reasonable distinction between citizen control and delegated power.

Table 3-1 IAP2/TEPSIE spectrum of public participation

	Inform	Consult	Involve	Collaborate	Empower
Public participation goal	To provide the public with balanced and objective information to assist them in understanding the problem, alternatives, opportunities, and/or solutions	To obtain public feedback on analysis, alternatives, and/or decisions	To work directly with the public throughout the process to ensure that public concerns and aspirations are consistently understood and considered	To partner with the public in each aspect of the decision including the development of alternatives and the identification of the preferred solution	To place final decision-making in the hands of the public

Source: Anna Davies and Julie Simon (2013, 5), following International Association for Public Participation

3.1.2 Goods and commons – the difference

Commons are no ordinary goods, as in the imagination of neoclassical economists who

> [d]efine a good as an object or service of which the consumer would choose to have more. Then the collection of goods he chooses when he has more money to spend . . . must represent more goods than that he chooses when he has less money to spend. . . . Hence we derive both parts of the law of demand from the definition of goods. The hypothesis from which we have deduced it is that goods are goods.
> (Harry Johnson 1958, 149)

From this neoclassical perspective, the resilience of ecological systems, like global climate, groundwater basins, lakes, fisheries, forests, and so on, is no good in the sense that people would buy more if they could afford to do so. Resilience defines the common wealth in the sense that human life depends on the mere existence and functioning of these ecological systems, and not of its growth. Humans have to understand how they could maintain the resilience of crucial ecosystems and to avoid their collapse. Thus, there is no choice than to have simply more of the same.

Commons are neither public goods nor "collective consumption goods . . . which all enjoy in common . . . that each individual's consumption of such a good leads to no subtraction from any other individual's consumption of that good" (Paul A. Samuelson 1954, 387). In contrast to public goods, such common-pool resources are characterised by a high degree of subtractability, which may even lead towards a collapse of the overall ecological system. In contrast to private goods, it is highly difficult to exclude potential beneficiaries from using common-pool resources.

Unfolding the conventional binary terminology of goods ('private vs. public') towards a four-type scheme relies on the assumption that the institutional setting for the governance

Table 3-2 Four types of goods

Difficulty of Excluding Potential Beneficiaries	Subtractability of Use	
	High	Low
High	Common-pool resources: groundwater basins, lakes, irrigation systems, fisheries, forests, etc.	Public goods: peace and security of a community, national defense, knowledge, fire protection, weather forecasts, etc.
Low	Private goods: food, clothing, automobiles, etc.	Toll goods: theaters, private clubs, daycare centers

Source: Elinor Ostrom (2005, 24)

of commons is more diverse than the conventionally supposed delineation between the boundaries of market and government sectors. Put in another way, *is there a case for self-organised governance of common-pool resources beyond market and government structures?*

A first legal attempt to define urban commons is the Bologna Regulation (LABGOV 2014, 6) that defines it as

> the goods, tangible, intangible and digital, that citizens and the Administration, also through participative and deliberative procedures, recognize to be functional to the individual and collective wellbeing, activating consequently towards them ... to share the responsibility with the Administration of their care or regeneration in order to improve the collective enjoyment.

3.2 General model of socio-ecological transition

3.2.1 *An institutional perspective on socio-ecological transitions*

The term 'transition', the shift of socio-ecological systems from one state to another, expresses a certain degree of urgency (cf. section 1.1). Goal-directedness and urgency appear to predestine transitions as a subject of management, namely, transition management, solving technical problems of resource efficiency and so on. However, this could be a misleading idea if transitions entail the transformation of the overall system, including the emergence of new groups of actors. In his seminal book *The Great Transformation*, Karl Polanyi hints at "those critical phases of history, when a civilisation has broken down or is passing through a transformation, when as a rule new classes are formed, sometimes within the briefest space of time, out of the ruins of older classes, or even out of extraneous elements like foreign adventurers or outcasts" (Polanyi 1944, 155). Under such circumstances, it might be difficult to find transition managers accepted and trusted by these new actors. It appears to be more likely that such new social groups emerge as change agents of a Great Transformation (WBGU 2011).

Transition management is one of the most important concepts and frameworks for analysing and researching transitions towards sustainability. Its prominence in transitional research is undoubtable. The approach of transition *management* is the governance of transitions to provide guidance in a "radical transformation towards a sustainable society" (John Grin, Jan Rotmans, and Johan Schot 2010, 1). Since this 'radical' rupture can issue uncertainty and uncontrollable problems, the transformation is met with governance knowledge. "Transition management . . . is the attempt to influence the societal system into a more sustainable direction, ultimately resolving the persistent problem(s) involved" (Grin, Rotmans, and Schot 2010, 108). The goal is to provide an analytical framework, elaborated by "competent practitioners and researchers together" (Jan Rotmans, Derk Loorbach, and René Kemp 2007, 5) to initiate transitional changes in societal structures, cultures, and practices through means of technological and social innovations (Grin, Rotmans, and Schot 2010, 109–13).

Yet, there are certain critiques that transition management has to face and that we indirectly seek as a demarcation to our own demands for a theoretical framework. Criticising transition management needs to account for several levels that refer to its perspective, its approach, and its implications. To begin with the latter, the term '*management*' already implies a narrow and straight logic to grapple with transitions towards sustainability. *Management* suggests a view of transition as something that is *manage*-able, which means it is steerable. At the same moment, it finds itself in the common (modern) belief that management is a universal knowledge and logic of steering, organising, and controlling. Against management itself, a more and more noticeable opposition has been forming since the late 1980s and early 1990s, with *Critical Management Studies* being one of the more prominent representatives (cf. Yannick Kalff 2015). Not only sociologists feel a slight unease that a rather technocratic, instrumental form of knowledge dominates the control and organisation of nearly all societal domains (Mats Alvesson and Hugh Willmott 1992, 1996; Martin Parker 2002; Martin Parker, Valérie Fournier, and Patrick Reedy 2007). In short, the critique of management reflects the unilateral focus on instrumental knowledge and its applicability to any given situation. Thus, it is a neutral tool in a modern, fashioned way of means-to-ends relations. Ambiguity and ambivalence are neglected, and the ability to dominate nature and control human beings and their organisations is taken for granted (Parker 2002, 3–5; Elisabeth Shove and Gordon Walker 2007, 765). The critique in the cited work does not fundamentally oppose management except when it is too narrow, the most common interpretation (Alvesson and Willmott 1996, 29–36). Its roots in modern traditions of accountability, predictability, and controllability seem to be reminiscent of the dominance of humanity over nature that contradicts the 'postmodern' ambiguity and ambivalence of the world. At this point, transition management exceeds classic management definitions and is aware of its position in highly uncertain contexts with the need "for a new breed of managers schooled in the arts of transition" (Shove and Walker 2007, 766–67).

This directly leads to a critique of transition management's approach, which is, in the realm of trained and informed personnel, an exclusive and elitist undertaking by a 'classic' managerial caste of competent and capable experts (Rotmans, Loorbach, and Kemp 2007, 5). While this can be a politically motivated critique, it also points out that complex transitions over long time spans produce effects and outcomes that only different actors from different settings can assess or influence. This is also influenced by a general unease concerning the role of individual agency in transition processes (Felix Rauschmayer, Tom Bauler, and Niko Schäpke 2015, 214). The influence in processes is not clearly approached to integrate them into the picture, which at least suggests that they are underrepresented – or at worst are not capable of having agency at all. A rather scientific critique reflects the case study approach of unique technological innovations. Their trajectories usually represent 'success stories'. What becomes a case and what is left out of the picture is deeply entangled with its underlying story in socio-ecological transition (Shove and Walker 2007, 767).

The third critique reflects the inherent perspective and, with it, the heuristics that are applied to the research subject. Transition management takes a common interest in transitional motives for granted. In a sense, transitions are considered conflict-free without any contested or debated visions or ideas – especially contradicting movements are left out of the picture. Rauschmayer, Bauler, and Schäpke (2015, 214) reflect this aspect as a general "naivety to issues of power" that emerges from the three distinct levels and their institutional actors. For example, technological lock-ins or path dependencies are always tied to specific interests and power positions that are sincere in maintaining the status quo. Above that, a one-dimensional interpretation of innovation, which is a synonym to progress, blurs the perspective of transition management. A lot of discontent with this connotation of innovation refers to the underlying model of change in transition management, the multilevel perspective (MLP), which leaves other models of change out of the picture, especially those with a more conflict-driven approach. Although there is a distinct attempt to map self-organisation, it remains an evolutionary perspective that is partly blind for political and discursive means of change, for example by conflict. This contradicts the 'radical' of this transformation, since it is rather a mode of incremental change. Either way, the conceptualisation of system change by transitions is deeply connected to actors and specific forms of knowledge that are necessary to have insight into the system, the transition, and the targets. While transition management can lend decisive insights into transitional processes, the other two forms of knowledge are underrepresented (Rauschmayer, Bauler, and Schäpke 2015).

In short, several aspects make transition management a limited approach for urban socio-ecological transitions. Above all, transition management cannot inquire into the involvement of an active civil society or the engagement in productive conflict, in discourse, and participation, since it is not considered a constituting force. Especially in these fields, a simple instrumental means-to-ends rationality of management leaves out the dynamics of *movements*.

Thus, we develop here an extended socio-ecological system (SES) approach to the ongoing sustainability debate on sustainability transition theory, by focusing on the rules in use, which structure the interactions of the resource and the governance system. This appears to be the most appropriate way to capture the dynamic factors driving such transitions.

The SES framework as presented in Poteete, Janssen, and Ostrom (2010) can be seen as an advancement of the Institutional Analysis and Development (IAD) framework. According to Elinor Ostrom and Charlotte Hess (2007, 41), the IAD framework "is a diagnostic tool that can be used to investigate any broad subject where humans repeatedly interact within rules and norms that guide their choice of strategies and behaviors". It focuses on institutions that are guiding social interaction between actors that are negotiating either on markets or by state laws or are self-organising their interactions (Ostrom 1990). On a bottom level, our interest is focused on the functioning of institutional settings in certain governance paradigms. For the self-organising capabilities of local entities, the special functional settings of diverse institutional frames are assessed, since diversification of the institutional framework fosters a wider possibility to solve any shortcomings of the other two paradigms – markets and states – by addressing the diversity of the social structure and its scenarios.

A primary way analyses these "action arenas" (Ostrom 2005, 55–56), where the social exchange takes place and is guided by three major sets of variables: institutions and rules, characteristics of the community, and attributes of the physical environment (Ostrom 2005, 15). The benefit of using the IAD framework as a starting point lies in its strength as "a comparative method of institutional analysis" (Ostrom and Hess 2007, 42). Because this study aims at identifying the institutional relations that are crucial for a socio-ecological transition at the city level, the IAD framework seems to be appropriate to frame the research approach. Mainly in focusing and analysing an action arena, the sets of rules, community attributes, and the several distinct rule sets that determine positions and access to and restrictions from these arenas become assessable for a comparative analysis (Ostrom 2005). This could be used for comparisons of the governance of different resource systems in different institutional settings in Europe like in this study here.

To capture the institutional dynamics of socio-ecological transition, we assume that these kinds of transitions are driven by learning and norm-adopting individuals (Figure 3-2). These individuals are capable of (1) developing critical levels of trust that other individuals involved in the governance of the resource systems are reciprocators, (2) developing levels of cooperation which are necessary to solve social dilemmas like the 'tragedy of the commons', and (3) realising the net benefits of this cooperation. From this perspective, it is crucial for a general theory of socio-ecological transition to understand the variables inducing this kind of collective learning and norm adoption. It makes sense to distinguish between socio-ecological and micro-situational context variables and relate them to sets of rules governing the action situation under consideration.

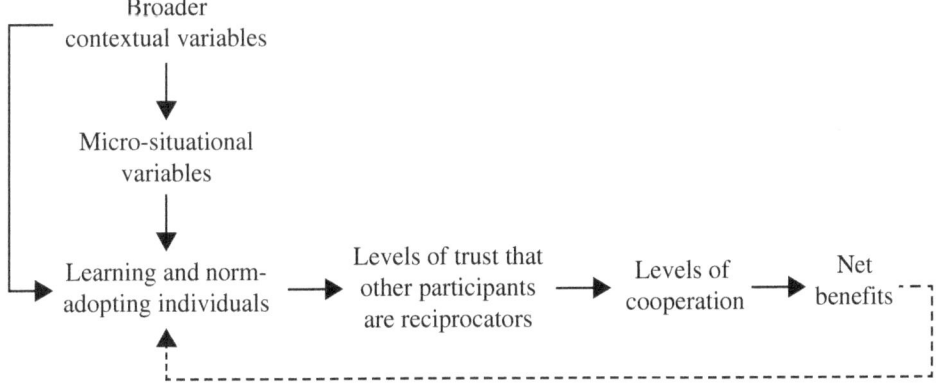

Figure 3-2 Micro-situational and broader context variables of social dilemmas affecting the levels of trust and cooperation

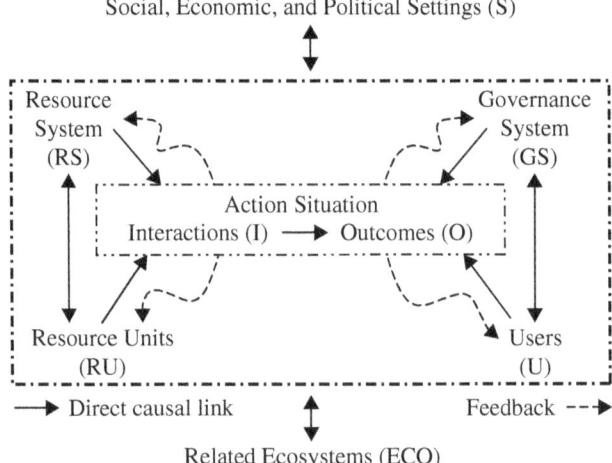

Figure 3-3 Action situations embedded in broader socio-ecological systems

3.2.2 The socio-ecological context variables

The broader context of an action situation (see Figure 3-3) could be conceptually modelled as a socio-ecological system (SES), consisting of the variables describing the resource system (RS), the resource units (RU), the governance system (GS), and the users (U), which influence the interactions (I) and outcomes (O) of the action situation. External to this system are variables of the social, economic, and political settings (S) as well as of the related ecosystems (ECO).

Poteete, Janssen, and Ostrom (2010, 237–38) identified a total of 53 variables describing the overall socio-ecological system. Furthermore, they considered 12 variables as particularly relevant for the capabilities of the users to self-organise the governance of the resource system under consideration. "Rather, it is the overall combination of these variables in particular settings that affects how participants judge the benefits and costs of new operational rules, and how trust and reciprocity have developed in a setting" (Poteete, Janssen, and Ostrom 2010, 238). The framework distinguishes two spheres: the social system and the resource system. The perspective focuses on reciprocal interactions between the two systems, where the ecological system is perceived as anthropocentric (Claudia R. Binder et al. 2013). What is important at this point is an explicit link between this systemic approach and a normative perspective. Although it is foremost an analysis-oriented concept, the description of rules, their emergence, and practical implications describes the role of norms in linking the two systems. These linkages especially occur in the topics of information, boundaries, and decisions, since a direct alignment takes place there between social and ecological system, and vice versa.

3.2.3 Micro-situational context variables solving social dilemmas

While the identification of broader context variables of socio-ecological research draws on a wealth of field research described in the works of Elinor Ostrom and her colleagues, micro-situational context variables are derived from repeated social dilemma experiments in the laboratory (Norman Frohlich and Joe A. Oppenheimer 2001; Eva Ebenhöh

Table 3-3 Variables that affect the likelihood of self-organisation

Resources	Governance
System RS3 – Size of the resource system RS5 – Productivity of the system RS5a – Indicators of the productivity of the system RS7 – Predictability of system dynamics	System GS6a – Local collective choice autonomy
Units RU1 – Resource unit mobility	Users U1 – Number of users U2 – Socio-economic attributes of users U5 – Leadership/entrepreneurship U6 – Norms/social capital U7 – Knowledge of SES/mental models U8 – Importance of resource

Source: Variables extracted from Amy R. Poteete, Marco A. Janssen, and Elinor Ostrom (2010, 237)

and Claudia Pahl-Wostl 2008). These experiments show on the one hand the very rigid assumptions leading to situations like the tragedy of the commons, where – at best – only a few users would cooperate.

> A social dilemma situation in which an individual has no information about who else is involved and makes an anonymous decision relieves many individual participants of the need to follow norms or value outcomes of others. . . . Overharvesting tends to occur when resource users do not know who is involved, do not have a foundation of trust and reciprocity, cannot communicate, have no established rules, and lack effective monitoring and sanctioning mechanisms.
> (Poteete, Janssen, and Ostrom 2010, 228)

However, trust and cooperation could also produce exclusive elitism and not necessarily advance socio-ecological transitions. Such elitist understanding of 'community' would construct a demarcation line and diminish the understanding sustainability transitions to the aspect of ecological transition alone. Including the societal aspect into the concept of transitions requires more inclusive forms of social integration than socially 'gated' communities would allow.

Elinor Ostrom's approach proves to be scalable in its reach, although empirically it has only been applied to local or regional resource systems. The process of negotiating rules of usage, scope, and boundaries can be extended to a broader level (Binder et al. 2013). In existing research, it was possible to identify a set of micro-situational variables in experiments by relaxing such restrictive conditions that led by definition towards noncooperative behaviour. These influence trust and positive outcomes in multiple social dilemmas (Table 3-4). These variables will be explained in the next section and extended by other variables we deem influential.

3.2.4 Institutional elements of action situations

The action situation is a key concept of the IAD and the SES framework as well. It can be used to describe a variety of diverse institutional settings such as markets, families,

Table 3-4 Variables influencing trust and the solution of social dilemmas

Positive	Positive, neutral, or negative impact	Negative
S1 – High marginal per capita return of cooperation	S7 – Size of group	S10 – Heterogeneity in benefits and costs
S2 – Security that contributions will be returned if not sufficient	S8 – Information about the average contribution is made available	
S3 – The reputations of participants are known	S9 – Sanctioning capabilities	
S4 – Longer time horizon		
S5 – Capability to choose to enter or exit from a group		
S6 – Communication is feasible with the full set of participants		

Source: Amy R. Poteete, Marco A. Janssen, and Elinor Ostrom (2010, 229–30)

hierarchies, legislatures, corporations, neighbourhood associations, common-property regimes and so on. Formal games could also be described, analysed, and compared as action situations regulated by seven normative elements concerning "participants, positions, actions, outcomes, information, control, and cost/benefit" (Ostrom 2005, 188). Each of these elements is governed by a special set of rules, which as an ensemble govern the overall action situation (Figure 3-4).

Assuming that these sets of rules define the governance regime of a socio-ecological system and defining transitions "as shifts from one regime to another regime" (Frank W. Geels 2011, 26) implies that any transition could involve a change of at least some of the rules governing the action situation of a socio-ecological system (SES). Rules – in contrast to norms – are sanctionable. This means that the breaking of rules results in a kind of regulating response of a specific body that is capable and eligible to sanction. However, the violation of a norm does not imply institutional corrections. The process of norm adoption precedes the changing of rules, as it is a broader foundation of any rule and sanctioning mechanism. This change of rules might be induced externally by superior governance levels, or internally by learning and norm-adopting individuals who are involved in the local action situation. The internal way of learning and norm adoption is crucial for a profound transition to strong sustainability, because it influences behavioural patterns in the action situation already before legal changes. Thus, this kind of learning is more informal and more directly involved in everyday activities than legislation by superior levels of governance alone.

The socio-ecological context variables are determining the capabilities of the users to self-organise the governance of the resource system, and the micro-situational context variables are influencing the feasible levels of trust and of cooperative solutions in multiple social dilemmas. They are probably responsible for the diversification and change of the norms ruling the action situation under consideration. Thus, they could be of crucial importance for the direction and success of socio-ecological transition.

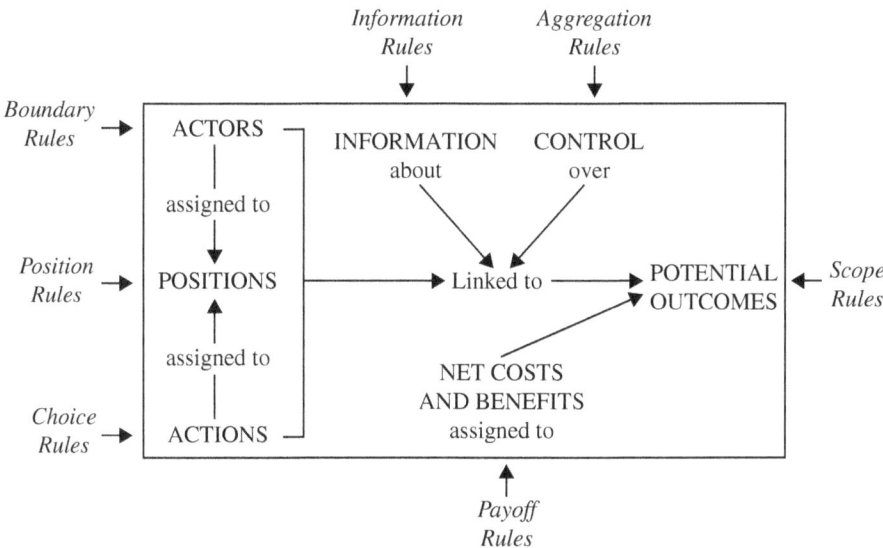

Figure 3-4 Rules as exogenous variables directly affecting the elements of an action situation

Summarising, we argue that the change of norms represented by this set of rules governing local action situations may be considered as the central characteristic of socio-ecological system transitions. Successful norm adoption could be decisive for approaching higher levels of trust and cooperation, and thus for the success of self-organised and more sustainable governance of common-pool resources in general.

3.2.5 Norms ruling socio-ecological systems

In our research, we focus on the interactions of the three different dimensions of resource system governance. Rules and socio-ecological and micro-situational context variables as an ensemble are assumed to determine the transition paths from one governance regime to another. For such an examination, the sets of rules regulating the action situation of an SES seem to be the appropriate starting point. They link the resource system and its units on the one hand and the governance system and its units, the users, on the other. Norms are considered here as the transition channels for negative or positive feedback loops between the SES and the action situation. This is why they could be stabilised or destabilised by these feedback loops, the latter case urging a transition from one governance regime to another. Table 3-5 presents the influence of the seven different sets of rules in interaction with (1) the socio-ecological context variables relevant for facilitating self-organisation of resource governance, (2) the micro-situational context variables enhancing trust and cooperation in local action arenas of SES governance, and (3) the potential signs of their impact on trust and cooperation. Hereafter, we discuss the connections of these sets of rules with both kinds of context variables.

(1) Scope rules could be considered as a set of rules interacting with both kinds of context variables concerning "a known outcome variable that must, must not, or may be affected as a result of actions taken within the situation" (Ostrom 2005, 209). Such scope

Table 3-5 Interactions between micro-situational and socio-ecological context variables with rules governing transitional action situations

Rules evolving	Socio-ecologic context variables (SECV)	Micro-situational context variables (MICV)	Trust impact
1 Scope	U7/RS7: Knowledge of SES, practical & shared/ Predictability of systems dynamics	S4: Longer time horizon	Positive
2 Information	U6/GS8: Norms, social capital & civil society/ Monitoring	S6: Communication is feasible with the full set of participants	Positive
3 Payoff (feasible)	U9/RS5: Technology used/Resource system productivity	S1: High returns of cooperation	Positive
3 Payoff (net)	RU1/RS3: Resource unit mobility/Size of resource system	S8: Information about the average contribution is made available	Unclear
4 Position	U5/U3/U4: Leadership, entrepreneurship/History of use/Location	S3: Known reputations of participants	Positive
4 Position	U6/GS8: Norms, social capital & civil society/ Sanctioning	S9: Sanctioning capabilities	Unclear
5 Boundary (entry rules)	GS6a/U1: Local collective choice autonomy/ Number of users	S7: Size of group	Unclear
5 Boundary (exit rules)	GS6a/U2: Local collective choice autonomy/ Bargaining & conflict resolution, Voice & exit	S5: Capability to enter or exit from a group	Positive
6 Participation (aggregation rules)	GS6a/RS3: Local collective choice autonomy/Size of resource system	S2: Security of returned contributions, if not sufficient	Positive
7 Choice (creation and distribution of power)	U2/U8: Socioeconomic attributes of users/ Importance of resource	S10: Heterogeneity of participants	Negative

Source: Original, based on Ostrom (2005) and Amy R. Poteete, Marco A. Janssen, and Elinor Ostrom (2010)

rules depend strongly on the practical and shared knowledge about the SES considered (U7), which is necessary to predict the dynamics of the resource system (RS7) and, thus, responsible for the time horizon of the decision-making about the SES (S4). A longer time horizon (S4) might be the result of trust-building and positive outcomes in many common-pool experiments. However, it might also improve the willingness to commit in long-term investment positively: "Participants can reason with themselves that showing a willingness to contribute early may lead others to contribute and the longer the time horizon involved, the better the return on individual investment" (Poteete, Janssen, and Ostrom 2010, 229).

(2) **Information rules** "affect the level of information available to participants" (Ostrom 2005, 206). Thus, an important assumption in our research is that the higher the information levels of all participants about the resource system, for example the local energy system, the higher the probability that trust and cooperation in the governance of the resource systems could emerge. As indicators for this hypothesis may serve the degrees to which civil society and private households are involved in the monitoring of the resource system (GS8) and the extent to which communication is feasible with the full set of participants of the resource system (S6).

(3) **Payoff rules** are a third set of rules relevant for the institutional setting of SES assigning "external rewards or sanctions to particular actions that have been taken or to particular readings on outcome state variables" (Ostrom 2005, 207). They determine whether a motivation for transitional activities regarding the governance of the common-pool resource under consideration may exist or not. The significance of the payoff rules depends on different kinds of variables:

1   The factor facilitating a positive experience with the self-organisation of SES governance is a high marginal per capita return of cooperation (S1): Participants learn that their contribution makes a difference. This is obviously the most important payoff rule: The net benefit should be high enough to convince the potential actors to act. The basic socio-ecological context variables for allowing such high returns are the technology used for harvesting the common-pool resource (U9) in interaction with the productivity of the resource system (RS5). For example, the energy transition towards the exclusive use of renewable energy will change the technologies used for energy harvesting and storage significantly. At the same time, productivity of energy use could be enhanced significantly – due to the decentralisation of the resource system governance allowing tighter feedbacks between users and providers. In contrast to that, grassroots activities on urban green spaces are inherently local with high returns on cooperation because the results are very soon visible. On the other hand, the water system in dense urban agglomerations does need large, long-term investments in fixed capital – probably hard to handle by self-organised interventions of civil society.

2   The information made available about the average contributions (S8) of all resource users appears to have an ambiguous impact on trust-building in common-pool resource governance: "[I]nformation about past overuse may lead some individuals to pull back and harvest less out of fear of losing all future opportunities, while others might increase harvesting" (Poteete, Janssen, and Ostrom 2010, 230). The information about resource contributions and use of others might be easier to receive in smaller resource systems (RS3), which are probably characterised by slower resource unit mobility (RU1), such as land use compared to water use in an urban area. The availability of reliable information on resource use by other participants would decrease information costs and risks of individuals calculating the probable net payoff of their own contribution to the resource maintenance. Thus, this kind of information is relevant for the payoff rules as well.

(4) **Position rules** are connecting participants and authorised actions in the action situation under consideration (Ostrom 2005, 193–94). It could be assumed that this authorisation to act will strongly depend on the known reputations of the participants

(S3) gained by them in the location under consideration (U3), by using the common-pool resource (U4) and resulting in a kind of leadership of some of them which is appreciated by all other participants (U5). Thus, the variables determining the known reputation of participants might be of special importance for trust-building: "[K]nowing enough about fellow participants' past history of being a contributor is likely to increase cooperation levels when the reputation is positive" (Poteete, Janssen, and Ostrom 2010, 229). Here is a special link to a second knowledge issue: "Prior experience with other forms of local organisation and development of local leadership (U5) greatly enhances the repertoire of rules and strategies known to local participants as potentially useful to achieve various forms of regulations" (Poteete, Janssen, and Ostrom 2010, 240). Thus, we can assume that leadership and entrepreneurship could build on prior experience with the management of socio-ecological systems and may motivate less experienced users to collaborate in long-term endeavours. Such linkages between participants and authorised actions could lead to the evolution of corresponding position rules.

(5) **Boundary rules** are relevant for a theory of socio-ecological transition with a focus on the aspect of institutional change. They "define (1) who is eligible to enter a position, (2) the process that determines which eligible participants may enter (or must enter) positions, and (3) how an individual may leave (or must leave) a position" (Ostrom 2005, 194). Core micro-situational context variables, like the capability to enter or exit from a group governing a resource system (S5), as well as the size of group allowed (S7) and the eligible heterogeneity of the participants (S10), are defined by these boundary rules. On the micro-situational level, the capability to access and leave the action situation will probably have a positive impact on trust-building, while the size of the group may have diverse impacts and a high degree of heterogeneity, a negative one.

(6) **Aggregation rules** determine "whether a decision of a single participant or multiple participants is needed prior to an action at a node in a decision process" (Ostrom 2005, 202). Thus, they define the degree of participation feasible in the user groups of the socio-ecological system considered. In this sense, they could also be termed as *participation rules*. It is plausible to expect a higher degree of participation in a more decentralised SES with significant *local collective-choice autonomy (GS6a)*. Here, the inclusion of all participants is an important precondition for successful decision-making processes. According to Poteete, Janssen, and Ostrom (2010, 241), this kind of autonomy

> tends to lower the costs of organizing. A group that has little autonomy may find that those who disagree with locally developed rules seek contacts with higher-level officials to undo the efforts of users to achieve their own new rules. With the legal autonomy to make their own rules, users face substantially lower costs in defending their own rules against other authorities."

This appears to be particularly true for defining the size of the resource (RS3) as well as for the security of returned contributions (S2), for setting the rules to enter or exit a group (S5), and the size of the group as such (S7).

(7) Finally, **choice rules** define "what a participant occupying a position must, must not, or may do at a particular point in a decision process in light of conditions that have, or have not, been met at that point in the process" (Ostrom 2005, 200). In some sense, choice rules and scope rules are the residuals of all other sets of rules and could substitute each other: "If a rule is not a position, boundary, information, pay-off, or aggregation rule,

then it is either a choice rule (if the AIM is an action) or a scope rule (if the AIM is an outcome)" (Ostrom 2005, 209). Choice rules indicate the creation and distribution of power in action situations:

> By widening or narrowing the range of actions assigned to participants, choice rules affect the basic rights, duties, liberties, and exposure of members and the relative distribution of these all. Choice rules may allocate to positions high levels of control over many different state variables; in other words, authorize powerful positions. Choice rules empower, but the power created can be distributed in relative equal manner or grossly unequal manner. Choice rules thus affect the total power created in action situations and the distribution of this power.
>
> (Ostrom 2005, 201)

Thus, choice rules are crucial indicators for the degree of citizen empowerment towards the self-organised use of resource systems. We can imagine urban farms on local green spaces organised as cooperatives where every associate has an equal voice on important decisions on what to plant, how to nurture, how to distribute the harvest. This could be an example of full citizen control in the sense of Arnstein's ladder. On the other end of the scale, we have the urban water systems, where one-time investments in the fixed infrastructure determine the form of water provision for perhaps the next 70 years. It is hard to imagine that such decisions could be an issue for direct citizen control. More likely, it could be an issue for a delegated power to the local government, if this is in the position to own the local water utilities or to hold the decisive share in it at least. Depending on the technologies available – and there are profound innovations under way now, and on the legal market design, for example by feed-in tariffs – there are now many options for how to organise the decision rules in the energy sector. Here we expect to observe the highest diversity in choice rules due to the diversity of national rules governing the energy sectors and the technological infrastructure already in use.

3.2.6 Sustainability transitions as a sequence of norm changes and interactions with the socio-ecological resource system

Concluding this section, we propose to analyse transitions of socio-ecological systems, as a sequence of rule sets with increasing complexity and dynamics (Figure 3-5). As developed in our socio-ecological systems transition model, we assume that, if self-organised and cooperative use of common-pool resources emerges, this is due to a complex set of variables and norms. They help us to formulate the following definitions and research assumptions as basis for the specific research questions following subsequently:

1 **Scope rules** affect the very basic issues and the time horizon of known outcome variables of the sustainability strategy under consideration.

    A commonly agreed understanding of the sustainability transition concept, including agreement on the priorities of such transitions on the local level and on strategies, enhances the possibility to grasp topics and fields the sustainability transition encloses. This tacit knowledge facilitates the initiation of transition processes of the socio-ecological systems towards stronger sustainability since strategies and approaches refer to the same scope and allow consensual solutions.

2 **Information rules** affect the level of information available to each participant of the considered SES. Thus, they provide the basic precondition for citizens' participation and the possible starting point for developing higher levels of trust and cooperation.

Considering the information rules applied in the local context, the degree of citizen participation in the governance of local resource systems like energy, water, and green spaces might be higher if better information is available to the citizens.

3 **Payoff rules** assign awards or sanctions to actions regarding the outcomes, thus defining possible returns and the motivation to implement specific sustainability measures for a multitude of actors.

Another crucial precondition for the initiation of socio-ecological transition processes is the emergence of attractive opportunities to invest in new institutional arrangements, promising a sufficient per capita return for the cooperation of local actors. Investments as well as returns need not necessarily be monetary, but could rather be of other qualities, like resources, social acknowledgement, or replenishment rates of resource units.

4 **Position rules** determine the actors who are authorised and capable to act, considering the reputation gained and the possibilities to sanction by potential actors.

We assume that the existence of a certain degree of leadership, that is the reputation gained by innovativeness, practical experience, and trustworthiness in the urban action arena, is supportive for the local self-organisation of common-pool resources. If these individuals gained a reputation as reciprocators, this is particularly helpful for a cooperative approach towards the governance of local socio-ecological systems.

5 **Boundary rules** define criteria and processes for including and excluding actors in socio-ecological systems, the degree of overlap between resource and governance systems, as well as the size and heterogeneity of the actor group.

If such eminent people – established as reciprocators and specialists for the local resource system – exist, this facilitates a kind of norm adoption in favour of new institutional arrangements, and their acceptance by the local citizenship. In the case that the concerned stakeholders accept such trusted evolution of norms and their sanctioning, this transforms these new norms into rules. The shift of boundary, position, or choice rules thus follows lessons learned in the local action arenas.

6 **Aggregation rules** determine the degree of communication and participation of actors involved in the decision-making on the SES at the considered location. They depend very much on the level of local decision-making autonomy.

If norm adoption shifted the boundary rules in favour of local action arenas, this could pave the way for a more autonomous decision-making on the local level, leading to a harmonisation of ecological and social boundaries. This implies an enhancement of the local decision-making autonomy.

7 **Choice rules** characterise the extent of power distribution and citizen empowerment in self-organising the governance of local resource systems.

Finally, unambiguous choice or decision-making rules are the most complex indicators of citizen involvement in the governance of local resource systems, either via

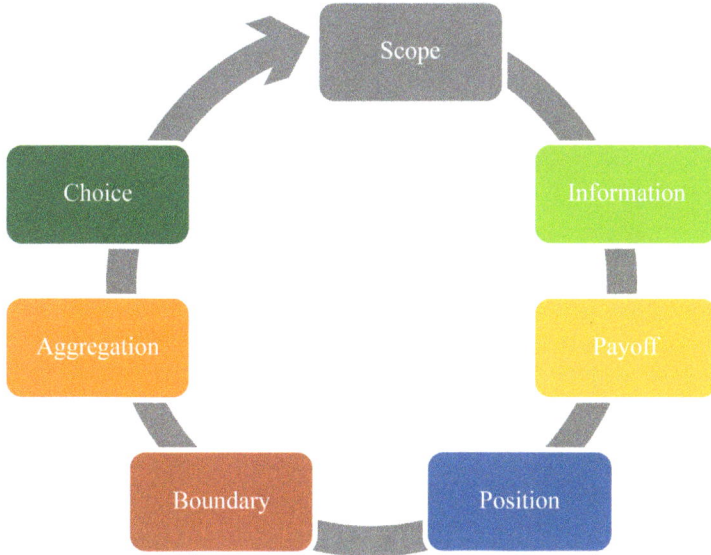

Figure 3-5 Socio-ecological systems transition model as a sequence of norm set adoption

delegation of power or full-fledged citizen control. We assume that a specific set of choice rules empowers local actors, and is most productive, if this power is distributed equally between the actors, to allow a thorough form of self-organisation.

Rather than reading the set of rules in Figure 3-5 as a cascade, it should be seen as a process of learning and norm changes in a helix structure. Rules are altered in a complex and interconnected way. The cycle will repeat itself limitlessly and regularly reinforce itself.

3.2.7 Research questions

To this point, we have derived seven related assumptions from Ostrom's rule set to guide our research interest that imply a certain mode of influence on critical aspects of the socio-ecological transition process towards sustainability. As a result, these assumptions are compared to a detailed description of the case studies of the resource field. Therefore, it is mandatory to understand the research assumptions as a preliminary interpretation of the field, not as testable hypotheses. These assumptions lead to research questions, indicating an exploratory approach to the field. The strength of the framework lies in its openness to produce explorative insights in the field, to be assessed by other scientific means later. In detail, the seven research questions, derived from the seven rules and assumptions, are as follows:

1. Is the urban governance of ecological resource systems observed in European cities framed by a common understanding of sustainability transition?
2. Which kinds of citizen participation and user self-organisation can be observed in local urban resource systems like energy, water, and green spaces?
3. Who are the actors, and what are the factors motivating them to pursue a socio-ecological transition in these urban resource systems?

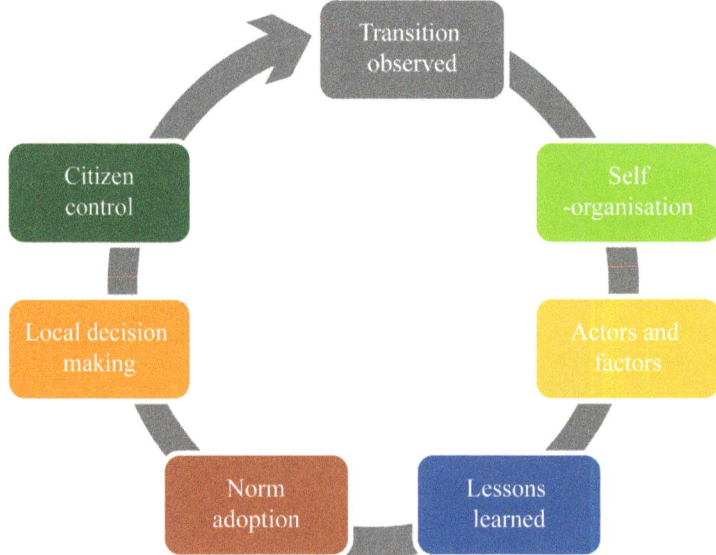

Figure 3-6 Research questions derived from the SES transition model

4   What are the lessons learned and the reputations gained from leadership in local resource management?
5   Could we observe transitional socio-ecological norm adoption towards trust and cooperation in the urban context?
6   Does local decision-making autonomy matter in socio-ecological transitions in relation to superior governance levels?
7   To what extent do citizens have an equal voice in the governance of urban resource systems in terms of delegated power and citizen control?

Based on the preceding theoretical concept, Figure 3-6 specifies the connection between the foundational assumptions on the effects of rules and the main direction of the respective research questions. Departing from this view on the socio-ecological structure of the field, its institutional settings, and the interactions between its elements, the research follows an abductive understanding rather than a deductive or inductive approach: This means that the research goal lies in confronting preset assumptions in the field with empirical evidence to create a picture of the empirical reality. These assumptions narrow down the research perspective and allow a focus on the elements that have the greatest influence.

Chapter 4

Socio-ecological transitions in the energy system

The local government view

Yannick Kalff

4.1 The role of the energy resource system in sustainability transition

The energy sector is the foremost leverage to bring forward transitions towards sustainability, since a central aspect of climate change relates to CO2 emissions, energy use, and global warming. This chapter describes, analyses, and discusses its role in the socio-ecological transition of European cities. As a main system in urban contexts, the energy system is highly significant for achieving sustainability goals (Jonathan Rutherford and Olivier Coutard 2014). On a technical level, this is achieved by actively changing the means of energy production to renewable ones and by passively increasing the efficiency of either the energy production or the energy consumption (e.g. substituting coal with gas, installing housing insulation, etc.). Henrik Lund points out that, in a more simplified grouping, "three major technological changes: energy savings on the demand side, . . . efficiency improvements in the energy production, . . . and replacement of fossil fuels by various sources of renewable energy" (Lund 2007, 912) are undertaken. Thus, this field gives way to several, heterogeneous movements towards a socio-ecological transition in urban fields. Yet, on several occasions, the research shows that especially greater energy efficiency can provoke rebound effects (Jeroen van den Bergh and Miklos Antal 2014). Increasing technological efficiency reduces the per unit price, and thus the gained advantage is wiped out due to increased (cheaper) consumption (Lorna A. Greening, David L. Greene, and Carmen Difiglio 2000). Others conclude (in this case, for Norway) "that efficiency gains have interesting, nonintuitive, and maybe provocative impacts on energy consumption and carbon emissions" (Sverre Grepperud and Ingeborg Rasmussen 2004, 279). On an individual consumption scale as well as on an economic and industry scale, this rebound effect is measurable (Horace Herring and Steve Sorrell 2009), but results on macro levels are also contested (cf. Lee Schipper and Michael Grubb 2000).

On a broader understanding, the issue of energy sustainability deeply connects with the topic of CO2 emissions. Therefore, energy topics touch topics of urban transportation, mobility, heating, and housing, which are all CO2-intensive. This makes the energy field a complex system, hard to separate from other systems in urban contexts. To be more concrete on the role of the energy system for either the city as a whole and for the socio-ecological transition towards sustainability, this introductory section tries to evaluate its relations to the city and the other resource systems. The conducted questionnaires showed that the experts assess the energy system as *one of the most important* resource systems in our research sample. The focus on energy topics relates to the perceived urgency of a transition: Due to their dense populations as well as the income produced by industry and businesses, cities consume more energy than rural areas. In addition, city lifestyles differ and are more energy-intensive (Jukka Heinonen et al. 2013a, 2013b). Considering urban areas for a socio-ecological transition towards sustainability is crucial. This is even more important since nearly half of the world's population lives in urban areas, thus showing the importance of assessing them thoroughly as social, economic, governmental, and ecological factors for a transition process.

Next to the structural needs of modern society and industry for electricity, a historical development is observable. Energy production had become highly centralised and decoupled from places of energy consumption. The shift from renewable to fossil resources during the carbon era implied higher energy density and lower energy transport costs, facilitating production of primary energy far from the location of energy users. "Counterfactual estimates of city population sizes indicate that our estimated coal effect explains at least 60% of the growth in European city populations from 1750 to 1900" (Alan Fernihough and Kevin H. O'Rourke 2014, 3). The current energy transition towards renewable resources, like wind, water, or solar power, partly reverses this development. Relying on new energy sources comes along with the necessity to link back together spatial production and consumption. Due to electric resistance in long-distance grids, energy loss is too high. Relying on CO_2-neutral energy production means that this energy has to be produced in a local and decentralised manner. Excluded from this is nuclear energy, which in parts of Europe is considered a low-emission technology, neglecting the difficulties of the final disposal of nuclear waste and the fundamental safety and risk estimation of nuclear power plants. This shows nuclear energy's flaws as a bridge technology and especially overshadows its low life-cycle greenhouse gas emissions, which are nearly as low as with hydro energy (cf. Ralph E.H. Sims, Hans-Holger Rogner, and Ken Gregory 2003; Manfred Lenzen 2008).[1] Nevertheless, the socio-ecological transition basically has to be described as a spatial 'recoupling' of energy production and consumption, like in the pre-coal era, when energy sources were windmills, watermills, or local forestry, located in the vicinity of the energy consumption. It is an interesting detail that the term 'sustainability' first appeared in the emergence of modern forestry in the eighteenth century. In his treatise on forestry, Hans Carl von Carlowitz (1713) discussed the problems of uncontrolled (unsustainable) woodcutting. He argued that one ought to cut down only as many trees as one could regrow in a certain period. This origin was reflected upon by several interviewed actors, although it is apparent that this is a trait for German-speaking regions only (e.g. Freiburg, a1, 11; Linz, a2, 11; Kiel, a1, 14; St. Gallen, a1, 10). The term gained broader popularity thanks to a publication in the 1980s, *Our Common Future* by The World Commission on Environment and Development (1987). The focused result, however, is not autarchy. It is an increased level of self-subsistence, however also generating trade-offs (Johannes Schmidt et al. 2012). They include volatility of local electricity grids with insufficient back-up potentials and the general problem of quickly adapting to changing consumption patterns and equally insecure energy provision.

Central developments that occur alongside spatially recoupled energy production are the construction of 'smart grids' that aim at a combination of production, consumption, and infrastructure for the distribution. This has to happen especially in respect to provision fluctuations due to the uncertain availability of renewable energy sources.

This first of four empirical chapters presents the relevant findings extracted from the material of quantitative and qualitative analysis. Section 2.3 describes the mixed methods approach deployed in this research. It combines qualitative interviews with quantitative statistics. Practically, this is realised by reciprocal reference of data from both domains. It presents an interpretation along the discussed research questions. The structure of the chapter is as follows: Section 4.2 discusses the self-organising capabilities in accordance to the presented theoretical extensions of Ostrom's IAD framework. It focuses on the central argument of the study that self-organisation can be considered as a transition driver and lays out the status of the sustainability transition. Section 4.3 depicts actors, actions, and transition factors that are involved in, undertaken in, and fostering socio-ecological transitions in the cities. The section concludes with an account of lessons learnt by local actors. Section 4.4 describes the processes of norm adoption and emergent changes in local frameworks to assist in transitions. Local decision autonomy as a foundation for self-organising capabilities is assessed in the light of local city transition processes. The last section discusses the findings and contextualises them.

The insights for this research come from a quantitative inquiry of 480 key actors in the field of urban socio-ecological transition for the basic survey and of 151 for the specialised part on energy: 57 government actors, 54 business actors, and 40 civil society actors. Further insights were gained from 69 qualitative expert interviews that covered 32 political, 34 administrative, and 3 business actors. It covers the cities Aalborg, Barcelona, Birmingham, Copenhagen, Dortmund, Freiburg, Giurgiu, Glasgow, Gothenburg, Innsbruck, Istanbul, Jihlava, Kiel, Larissa, Leeds, Linz, Lodz, Lublin, Lugano, Madrid, Milan, Naples, Nice, Paris, Potsdam, Prague, Rennes, Rome, Saarbrücken, Sibiu, St. Gallen, Strasbourg, Thessaloniki, Timisoara, Trieste, and Umea.

4.2 Self-organisation capabilities and sustainability transitions

The first subsection introduces two main parts of socio-ecological transitions. First, it provides insight into the current state of the transition and describes an understanding of sustainability, the state of the resource system, as well as perceived and experienced challenges. In a second subsection, the self-organising capabilities are assessed next to the state of participation in political processes, the transition, or other.

4.2.1 Socio-ecological transitions

At the beginning stands an outline of the transition processes towards sustainability. This includes statements about the understanding of sustainability as a concept and descriptions of the ongoing socio-ecological transition in the cities. Experienced and expected challenges as well as influencing factors are also subjects of our inquiry.

Initially, in both the questionnaire and the topic guide for the interviews, the experts were asked to give a brief definition of the term 'sustainability' to assess a common understanding. As a first insight, Table 4-1 shows a distinct estimate from the experts' questionnaire responses about the importance of several issues. These issues match the set-out sustainability goals, defined by the European Union (Council of the European Union 2006; Eurostat 2009, 2011, 2013a). The European sustainability goals partly overlap with the former Lisbon Strategy and now the Europe 2020 strategy. They can be divided into three aspects, social, environmental, and economic sets of goals, which conform the core definitions adopted by the United Nations in 1992 that became known as Agenda 21 or as

Table 4-1 Importance of sustainability issues (scaled from 0: none to 4: very high)

Variable	Obs.	Mean	Std. Dev.	Median
Public transport	441	3.41	0.746	4
Clean energy	447	3.36	0.786	4
Management of local water resources	442	3.29	0.847	3
Education	439	3.29	0.820	3
Management of local green spaces	441	3.21	0.866	3
Management of local land resources	439	3.18	0.860	3
Climate change	446	3.03	0.971	3
Poverty and social exclusion	436	2.98	0.910	3
Labour markets	437	2.98	0.871	3
Consumption behaviour of the citizens	440	2.92	0.947	3
Private transport	440	2.85	1.016	3
Production patterns of local enterprises	430	2.82	0.923	3
Demographic changes	439	2.69	0.931	3
Migration	421	2.47	1.006	3

Rio 1992, in reference to the hosting city Rio de Janeiro. From the experts' point of view, the topic of public transport is the most important field, followed by clean energy second and local water resource management and education together in third place. Generally, social aspects for sustainability like migration or demographic changes are considered less important than resource issues. The interviewees commonly name these 'three pillars' as a framing for sustainability definitions. These pillars are a standard approach, considered a "conservative perspective" on sustainability (Dortmund, a1, 12). "The three P's: profit, people, planet" (Aalborg, a3, 13) have become solid knowledge of a university's curricula (Prague, a1, 13). Interviewees occasionally referred to an additional fourth pillar. The questionnaires cannot give further insights, since they did not inquire after them. However, the interviews highlight significance of governance and institutional or governmental aspects for sustainability (e.g. Milan, a2, 11; Nice, a2, 16; Strasbourg, a3, 14). The broad reference to the three-pillar model indicates that, to a certain degree, the definitions of sustainability are common knowledge and suggest a convergence to the EU sustainability goals, although they are not considered equally relevant.

Regional comparisons of the importance of sustainability issues show significant differences for climate change as well as clean energy for North and South and education for East and South (cf. Figure 4-1). In the case of clean energy, the differences, also to the other two regions, are moderate although highly significant. Education is an important issue in countries that suffer from weak economies and from not-yet solidified social security regimes. Thus, for Southern and Eastern Europe, the importance of education is fundamental in order to gain on the already advanced educational standards of other European regions.

Interviews depict a holistic understanding of sustainability processes, bringing to attention that a socio-ecological transition cannot be achieved through one item alone. It is

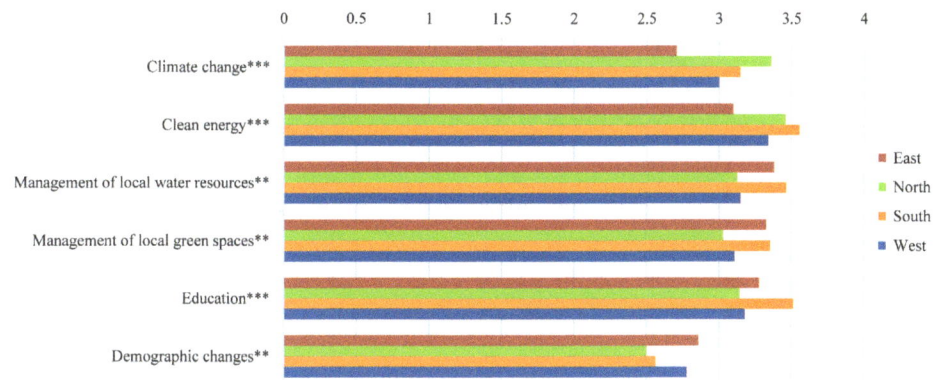

Figure 4-1 Differences in sustainability perception according to European region (scaled from 0: none to 4: very high)

of utmost importance to address all facets of sustainability in all sectors and systems (e.g. Birmingham, a2, 13; Paris, a2, 12–15; Strasbourg, a1, 17). This underlines the high complexity and heterogeneity of the sustainable transitions in cities that makes the process hard to define (e.g. Innsbruck, a2, 21; Linz, a1, 11; Timisoara, a1, 22). In a broader sense, sustainability is referred to as an attitude in thinking and a specific set of moralities and values that harmonise with ecology (e.g. Freiburg, a1, 19; Innsbruck, a2, 21; Larissa, a1, 25; Nice, a2, 14; Paris, a1, 12; Prague, a2, 11). In addition to this holistic approach, a temporal dimension becomes important, which aligns sustainability to the future for following generations. When it comes to the treatment of scarce resources and long-term preservation, a "compromise between history and future" is found (Prague, a2, 9). Bequeathing the planet to *future generations* is a specific motivation (e.g. Barcelona, a1, 20; Copenhagen, a1, 12; Madrid, a2, 18; Umea, a1, 19). This temporal dimension is by definition a crucial part of sustainability although not accordingly mentioned in every city.

In contrast to these quite homogeneous definitions of sustainability, the estimations of the local socio-ecological transitions are more heterogeneous. They include problematisations of the transitions, perceived challenges, as well as results. Intersecting is the relevance of action plans and strategies derived from European policies (e.g. Europe 2020, Agenda 21, etc.) as well as underlying programmes and networks like the Covenant of Mayors[2] (Adrien Labaeye and Thomas Sauer 2013). Timeframes for the transition processes begin around 1992, directly influenced by the first Rio conference. In relation to the Europe 2020 programme, they are estimated to end in the year 2020 – at least for achieving the set-out goals, not for a completely successful transition (e.g. Barcelona, a1, 22; Kiel, a2, 16; Timisoara, a1, 25). These strategies are directed towards reducing CO_2 emissions and pollution levels of the cities and relate to energy and public transport as well as traffic in general (Birmingham, a1, 14; Thessaloniki, a2, 13–17). Individual aspects of the cities can complement this.

Further, the state of the socio-ecological transition is connected with awareness and awareness-raising. Efforts to change citizens' consumption patterns go along with information campaigns and use individual behaviour as leverage in fostering transitions from the 'bottom up' (Bilbao, a1, 22; Lugano, a2, 11; St. Gallen, a1, 11). Although the term 'sustainability' frames these efforts, one actor consistently avoided the term. The interviewee argued that if a city pursues goals of economic and social cohesion, the overall result would be 'sustainable' (Leeds, a2, 12).

The state of the local resource systems is very heterogeneous. The divergences even within cities suggest difficulties in correctly assessing them. In terms of energy efficiency, the cities have unanimously taken steps to increase these levels. This is achieved by a variety of programmes or projects, for example SMART cities, the changing of street lighting with LEDs or implementing new directives and laws that request energy-efficient building. Also legally binding standards are introduced to make administration and municipal buildings energy efficient (e.g. Birmingham, a1, 40; Glasgow, a1, 17–19; Paris, a1, 33). The estimated proportion of locally produced energy is also very heterogeneous and substantially differs within cities. Two cities aim at implementing a "circular economy" (Freiburg, a1, 18; Rennes, a1, 74) and combine production and continuous use of residuals in other production steps. For example, water treatment facilities produce sewer sludge that biogas digesters use to generate energy (Nice, a1, 38). All in all, the proportion of locally produced renewable energy is low. In several locations, it is not distinguishable because local municipal utilities merged with (inter)national companies (Freiburg, a1, 41). Occasionally, a biodigester not working to capacity buys the needed biowaste from distant communities (Potsdam, a2, 93–98). This shows that the proportion of renewables in the local energy mix is hard to estimate and coherent information is urgently needed.

Local energy efficiency was also difficult to assess in the interviews. Nonetheless, distinct actions and decisions were being taken to increase efficiency according to Europe 2020 objectives.[3] Above that, cities provide help in increasing energy efficiency, for example by establishing a solar cadastre (Potsdam, a1, 94) or by helping to spot "energy thieves" (Umea, a2, 46). In addition to this, the productivity of the resource system for renewable energies faces the problem that urban areas – in contrast to rural areas – do not have the same preconditions (Potsdam, a1, 92) as well as spatial problems: "[P]utting photovoltaic panels on all roofs might not be the solution" (Nice, a1, 60). The prerequisites for different types of renewable energies are not given everywhere. This is also true for spatial use, where solar panels can be more easily downscaled for individual use than a wind power plant or a biodigester.

Cities set goals for their socio-ecological transitions, which they derive from distinctive programmes and strategies (like Europe 2020) and provide the cities with key figures and timeframes. Occasionally, they project to the year 2050, depending on the set of goals. They involve interconnected social, economic, and environmental issues and refer to the three-pillar model of sustainability. A special focus lies on the social dimension: Several statements pronounce the necessity for cohesion and adequate mechanisms to treat social problems (e.g. Aalborg, a2, 89; Nice, a1, 66). Another important aspect is education, as has been mentioned above (e.g. Linz, a2, 95; cf. Table 4-1). This has to be backed financially, and thus social cohesion goals include economic goals for an 'integrated economy' in relation to municipal agenda and urban development (Strasbourg, a1, 99; Lublin, a2, 50). Setting goals provides a reference point for planning and a 'translation' of socio-ecological transitions into a language accessible for administrative and political processes as well as for public understanding. Therefore, goals have to be clear to allow better performance and measurement (Copenhagen, a1, 79).

A last aspect for assessing the sustainability transition in the empirical data contains challenges perceived and expected, problems that the actors have dealt with or are assuming to encounter. Above that, their relevance for the future of the transition was part of the

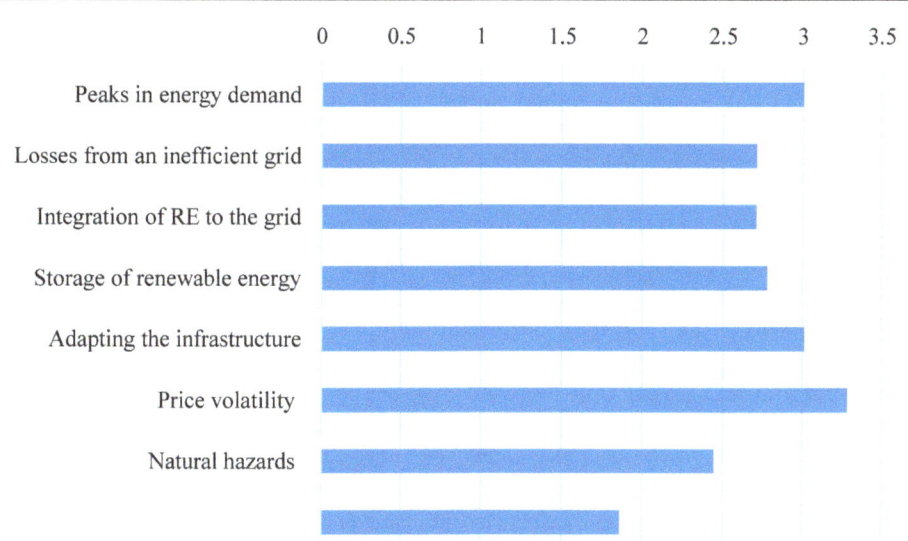

Figure 4-2 Anticipated challenges to the availability of affordable energy (scaled from 0: very low to 4: very high)

inquiry. The questionnaire asked for anticipated challenges to the availability of affordable energy in the future (cf. Figure 4-2). Especially, peaks in energy demands, an adequate infrastructure, and price volatility pose key threats to the local resource system. The several statements are, again, very heterogeneous and thus are more diverse in the interviews than in the questionnaire. In addition, they reflect individual features of the according cities. The assessments can be summarised into different categories. First, social problems like segregation, energy poverty, and gentrification are concerns that emerge from transition processes especially when cities improve their overall living quality. Cities are expected to realise a socio-ecological transition that is affordable for everyone (Aalborg, a3, 15; Madrid, a2, 28). Closely related to this is the problem of high costs for citizens to get entrance to these 'communities', for example for constructing houses or the mandatory consumption of (more expensive) renewable energies (Bilbao, a2, 81–82; Thessaloniki, a2, 77). Here lies a problem of so-called *boundary rules* (cf. subsection 3.2.5) that prohibit entry into local resource systems and make sustainability an exclusive, socially closed privilege (Max Weber 1978).

Problems erupting from structural aspects reinforce social problems. Individual histories of cities, their industrial layouts, and affiliations with the service sector, the dynamics, and structural changes resulting from it create challenges that influence the cities' social structure as well as political dynamics, financial means, and so forth. This refers especially to structural changes, mainly in urban districts that relied on heavy industries. With their decline, social and economic problems have gone hand in hand and are still felt today (e.g. Bilbao, a2, 28; Glasgow, a2, 19; Rome, a2, 26). A broader problem is posed by 'the crises' (financial crises, economic crises, crises of the EU and the euro) and the continuing austerity politics (Aalborg, a1, 35; Barcelona, a1, 30). The socio-economic backbone of cities interferes with transitions towards sustainability and is an important challenge, especially if transitions towards postindustrial cities are incomplete or were unsuccessful. However, successful industrial transitions provide a certain vantage point for socio-ecological transitions (e.g. Dortmund, a2, 26–28). The interconnectedness between social, economic, and ecological well-being is obvious to this point.

Other problems are legal and juridical challenges. Concerning the approaches to transitions, implementing edicts, legal standards, and laws are common to direct the possible actions of actors in a more sustainable direction. This happens on a variety of levels from the EU level to the local level. Nonetheless, juridical intervention is often felt as paternalism that cuts individual freedom. Second, a prohibitive culture is accentuated more than a culture of encouragement towards sustainability (Milan, a1, 19; Trieste, a1, 12). Third, the laws are, occasionally, contradictory, inconsistent, or ambiguous on the different levels from the EU ;eve; to the local level. They add further complexity that makes "the interpretation of the law ... quite complicated" (Prague, a2, 21).

Urban areas are vastly developing, especially in given conditions of socio-economic changes and ruptures of crises. Sustainable transitions and developments towards new resilient states are often ambiguous and accompanied by risks that a society has to cope with. Planning as an ultimately insecure and risky endeavour still reflects on a possible open-ended development – and suffers from lacking knowledge of resource systems (Barcelona, a2, 28). A transition always involves the risk that something will not develop according to plan and that a plan ultimately *can* fail. One of the challenges perceived is thus first to plan somehow (and reduce the risk of failure) and second to follow the plan until successful completion. As the definitions of sustainability have shown, they are considered heterogeneous and complex. Therefore, the planning processes are – and planning inherently is – uncertain and has to reflect social, ecological, and economic dimensions alike (Lugano, a2, 11). Istanbul has a slightly different problem: Its development follows no plans. Moreover, developments 'happen', and the administration 'plans' afterwards to 'cover' these uncontrollable developments (Istanbul, a2, 13).

Lastly, funding issues of sustainability programmes are another challenge that is related to juridical problems (Innsbruck, a2, 27). Financing programmes and campaigns are central in socio-ecological transitions, especially in terms of decision autonomy. Thus, the possibilities to acquire funding on the EU, national, or local level are important for an ongoing transition towards sustainability – especially in times of 'crisis' and EU austerity politics – and for structurally 'weak' cities per se (Leeds, a1, 23–25).

4.2.2 Self-organisation capabilities

Developing self-organising capabilities and citizens' participation are the foremost mechanisms to realise a bottom-up transition towards sustainability. As transition drivers, they press urgent matters in local communities that are negotiated in "action arenas" (Poteete, Janssen, and Ostrom 2010). The steps towards successful self-organisation necessarily include the ability for citizens to participate in local decision-making processes, in politics, and in public spheres and to engage in public discourse (Jürgen Habermas 1989). This possibility to 'get involved' in public affairs has to be granted and institutionalised. Thus, to assess the self-organising capabilities, first of all, the state of citizens' participation has to be evaluated.

Foundations for participation in a local energy transition lie in several local aspects. A central necessity for constructive participation is rooted in information. On the level of individual citizens, efforts to become informed on processes and developments that are fostered by municipalities exist, for example by holding public discussions or informing the citizens in advance (Prague, a1, 39; Kiel, a1, 82). However, occasionally information about decisions serves transparency purposes only. It does not intend to allow citizens to influence the decision process itself (Innsbruck, a2, 83). The other way around, municipalities seek insight into the needs of the local population and initiate surveys for the citizenry, although this is a rather rare phenomenon (Jihlava, a1, 15). In addition, a municipality provided equipment for citizens to measure their own energy efficiency (Rennes, a2, 45). A more substantial necessity is general awareness of ecological problems and a technical understanding of the underlying mechanisms (Nice, a2, 113; Paris, a2, 50). To allow and foster participation in political processes, citizens require a forum to seize voicing options. These can be discussion rounds, surveys, or public meetings of the city administration (Nice, a2, 67; Rome, a2, 30). One interviewee states that a specific "energy culture" is helpful as it provides awareness and motivates participation (Barcelona, a2, 58). In general, the interviewed actors from politics and administrations see distinct importance in participation. Although it is a challenge to involve and motivate the citizens, it is a basic requirement to achieve a socio-ecological transition (Larissa, a2, 20; Madrid, a2, 35; Paris, a1, 38). In addition, the pooling of creativity and innovativeness produces more and more elaborated ideas (Strasbourg, a3, 63). Participation cannot be enforced. The citizens have to be enabled and motivated to get involved – above that, nothing else can bring them to participate than awareness, idealism, and conviction (Linz, a2, 93).

The quantitative analysis shows that there are substantial differences between the actors taking responsibility and leadership as well as how those inquired perceive the leadership (cf. Figure 4-3). Especially the mayors' roles and those of the politicians of the majority are critically assessed by civil society, whilst governmental actors perceive their leadership as more valuable. The other way around, this can also be stated for the role of local

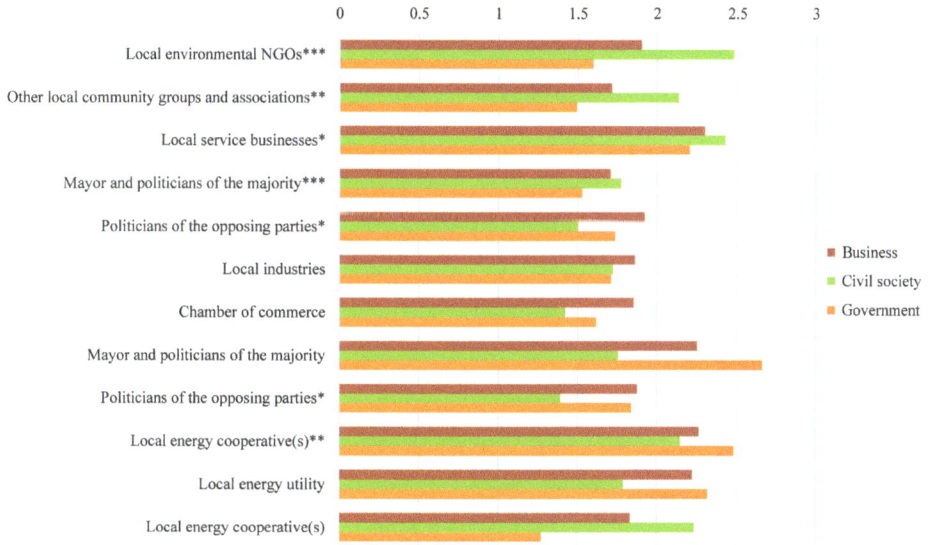

Figure 4-3 Leadership shown by local actors in developing local renewable energy (scaled from 0: none to 4: very high)

civil society groups or NGOs. Another important aspect is the overall assessment that leadership in the development of local energy efficiency is higher than the potentials for creating new energy sources. This indicates the perceived complexity in rendering new sources accessible in contrast to increasing the efficiency of existing ones. On this point, universities and research institutions are considered to take the leadership, along with the ruling parties and the governmental administrations (cf. Figure 4-4). The participation of citizenry is low.

One direct approach to participating on the local level is to get involved in political proceedings. As above, in some places, there are possibilities to get involved in public discussions on decisions, although sometimes they take place only once the decision has been taken. Nonetheless, there are positive examples where this possibility exists and can influence administrative procedures (Jihlava, a2, 39–41). Participation is even a juridical precondition for political processes on different levels. For example, consultative neighbourhoods with the capability to assign budgets on local projects for one year exist, or social media is used to integrate citizenry. In this case, the law obliges the provision of structural mechanisms to participate (Timisoara, a1, 85–86). Involving citizens in local campaigns also plays a role in Birmingham. Open planning processes and the delegation of emerging topics to open forums that handle them on the citizen level are described (Birmingham, a1, 48 and a2, 62). Although there is a certain understanding of the importance of citizens' participation, there are also cases where genuine participation efforts are obstructed. For example 'round tables' for energy planning are only open to technical experts or to actors from the economy – discussions on planning and strategies are generally kept on a professional level that excludes the citizenry (Aalborg, a2, 64; Lugano, a1, 87; Milan, a1, 33). Business representatives and politics further make the important decisions, "since at important decisions money talks" (Innsbruck, a2, 79). On top of this, socio-ecological movements can be 'institutionalised' and absorbed by political/administrative structures (Kiel, a2, 92). A unique case is Switzerland, which has a specific constitutional framework.

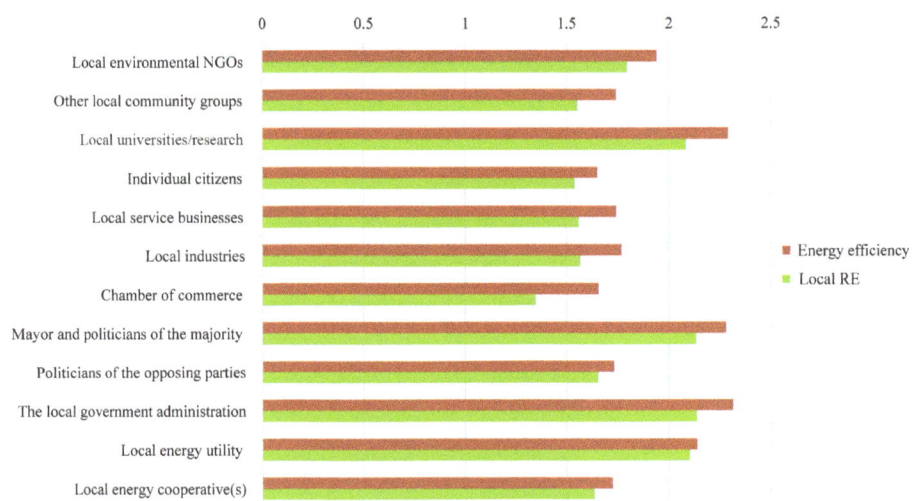

Figure 4-4 Leadership in improving energy efficiency and developing renewable energy locally (scaled from 0: none to 4: very high)

Direct democracy, the possibility to vote on every political decision, constitutes citizens' participation as rooted in the constitution of the country and is part of the political self-conception (St. Gallen, a1, 50 and a2, 29, 39).

Participating in energy-related topics in urban contexts faces several problems, challenges, and hindrances.[4] A first hindering factor is the complexity of energy issues on a technical and infrastructural basis. Further, political processes are bureaucratic; administrative procedures, time-consuming and opaque (Gothenburg, a2, 52; Strasbourg, a3, 91). An important question about responsibility arises as a diffuse participatory movement hardly allows for clear structures, hierarchy, and so forth; addressing and taking responsibility is nearly impossible but mandatory for the interviewed politician (Dortmund, a1, 51). In addition, the process is too complicated since it is not politics that has a direct influence on energy issues but the administration, and they do not easily "change a winning horse" – assuming that the current system works well (Rome, a2, 66). This leads to the problem of representation by citizens' participation. Since initiatives are usually a small(er) group of people, they are not adequately representing the citizenry (Larissa, a2, 60). The governance of energy policy of a country also determines successful or possible participation: In several cases, energy system policies are set on a national level without any local decision autonomy (Barcelona, a1, 55; Lugano, a2, 59).[5] Especially lack of motivation and awareness of relevant topics add to issues of disputed participation. The majority does not take interest in specific issues (Madrid, a2, 72, 72–74; Umea, a1, 73) or take interest in other matters like transportation (Trieste, a1, 49). The preference of citizens for convenient, traditional democratic representation undermines participation. Getting involved contradicts their urge to be 'caressed' by politics (Glasgow, a2, 66; Leeds, a1, 52–54). One politician puts it straight: "I think participation is overrated" (Kiel, a1, 68). He refers to a project where participation was offered but not seized, even not by environmental NGOs. However, these statements are not an adequate assessment of social reality but only one distinct view.

Out of or alongside citizens' participation, self-organisation can emerge. The relation between participation and self-organisation is not easy to depict; it can be argued that the correlation works both ways. Participation fosters and sustains self-organisational processes – or it hinders them, since citizens are included in decision-making processes and consider this situation as adequate and discard the possibilities to self-organise. Further details about forms of self-organisation are discussed in section 3.1.

The foundations for successful self-organisation lie in several aspects, according to the interviewed and inquired experts. A first cornerstone is coherent legal frameworks that structure self-organisation and allow for a degree of reliability and predictability. In a sense, bottom-up projects still need to be controllable for politics. While local or national laws back self-organised projects, constitutional rules determine their influence. Acting in a complex field, a framework provides a 'playground' for self-organised socio-ecological transition (Barcelona, a2, 75; Bilbao, a2, 123). A contrasting case is Istanbul, where openly no citizens' initiatives exist; the citizens' role only includes informing the city council or the administration about problems (Istanbul, a2, 50, 64). Further, political or governmental support sustains self-organised movements, for example by socialising local energy production and transforming it to "community-based energy association[s]" (Copenhagen, a1, 72; quote: Potsdam, a1, 106). Administration offers needed information about the resource system in the form of a solar cadastre (Dortmund, a1, 31 and a3, 58; Kiel, a2, 118; Paris, a1, 50; Potsdam, a1, 94). Providing adequate tools for citizens' initiatives is also important to cope with the demands of self-organisation. However, administrative and governmental institutions do not necessarily fulfil this task (Rome, a2, 80). It can be stated from the quantitative analysis that in no region are energy cooperatives common. On top of this, the overall assessments about cooperation and conflict remain neutral; in terms of conflict, Western Europe seems to be more harmonious (cf. Figures 4-5 and 4-6). This can be interpreted in different ways. Either there is no conflict, or there is no form of cooperation in the first place that could lead to conflict.

With the solar cadastre, a requirement for adequate local-level plans is articulated. It represents knowledge of the local resource system that is obligatory for successful self-organisation. These can be interpreted twofold: as knowledge of the local context and as having a plan – an idea of how to advance (Aalborg, a2, 81–84). The role of local or (inter)national NGOs is also important. Citizens' movements are guided by NGOs that have existed for some time and can draw on experience and knowledge; or they form NGOs to recur to a form of organising – although these are not always long lasting. An actor describes the frustrating short lifespan of NGOs as cooperation partners for

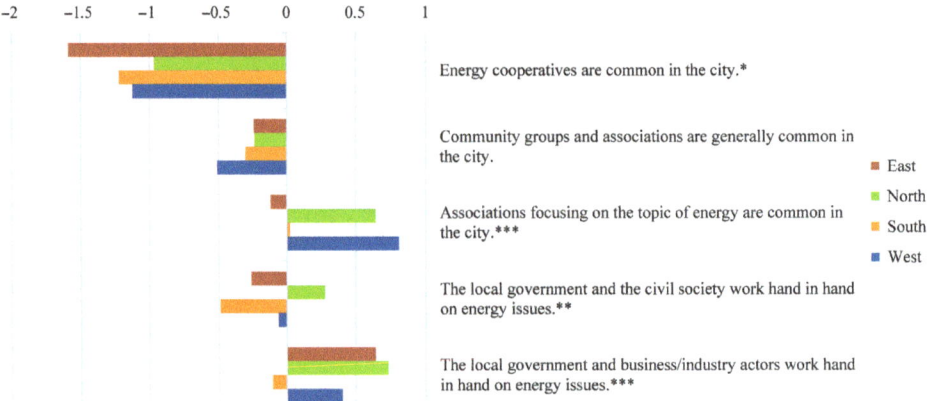

Figure 4-5 Cooperation and conflicts (scaled from −2: strongly disagree to +2: strongly agree)

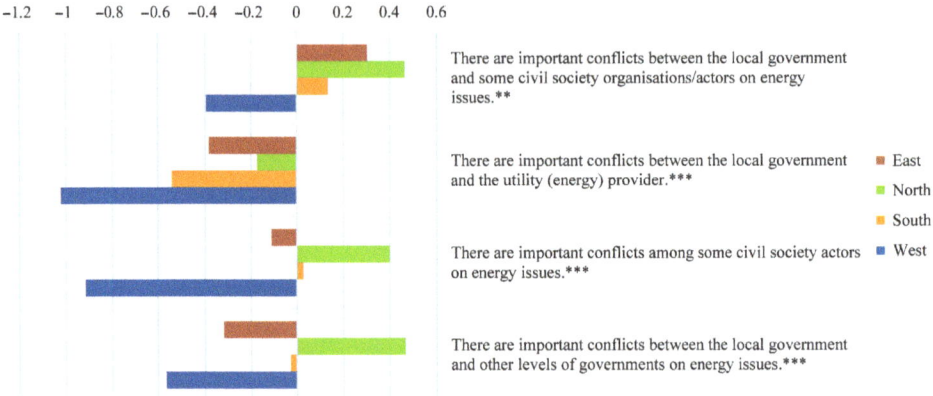

Figure 4-6 Cooperation and conflicts II

administrations, which rely on longer timeframes (Thessaloniki, a2, 69). A central precondition (and a challenge) is to guarantee and secure sufficient funding of self-organised endeavours (Madrid, a2, 90); without funding, ideas remain ideas – and there are many of them (Timisoara, a2, 128).

A last step extracts the state and shape of self-organisation from the interviews. A socio-ecological transition of the energy system has to be considered as "a decentralised revolution" (Freiburg, a1, 79). The state cannot govern an energy transition on its own but has to distribute the responsibility to local entities and movements. Partly, this includes experts' opinions on socio-ecological transitions that primarily have to change individual decisions, behaviour, and consumption (e.g. energy saving, energy efficiency). Influencing, changing, shaping, or incentivising behaviour is seen as a task of the state, government, or local administration, and politics (Barcelona, a1, 73; Freiburg, a1, 82; Milan, a2, 89; Potsdam, a2, 170; Trieste, a1, 53). This coincides with statements about citizens' participation considering it individualised behavioural changes. The question is whether this perception of participation and self-organisation is reductive and neglects and inhibits bottom-up organised initiatives. Participation is restricted to a passive role in socio-ecological transition that has no influence on the process, but only on its consumption. Focusing on individual behaviour change complies with activation policies that strengthen citizens' responsibilities. Participation then is a personal affair. If it were about influencing political decision processes, participation would be an intervention on governmental sovereignty.

The state of self-organised energy transitions in the city sample is hard to assess for the interviewed persons. This, on the one hand, has to do with the overall organisation of the resource system (e.g. on national or regional level – Rennes, a1, 139; Larissa, a2, 78); on the other hand, it is hard to distinguish organisational forms, especially since the sample did not include civil society actors. The latter point is a pitfall, since it is not possible to conclude from the interviews a distinct state of self-organisation in the perspective of civil society. Further, the state of self-organisation depends on the kind of renewable energy resources: While wind energy is a collective undertaking, biogas digesters might be too expensive, and solar panels on rooftops could be too individual for a citizens' initiative (Leeds, a2, 67). Diverging from this, self-organisation *takes oppositional influence* on planning processes introduced by municipalities. The citizens' initiatives do not start individual campaigns; they only involve themselves in governmental projects (Umea, a2, 64; Trieste, a1, 64–67). To foster grassroots or bottom-up self-organisation several key aspects can be found. First, the governance level for resource systems sustains civil society initiatives if self-organisation is positioned on the local level. Also the state (spatial, quality, etc.) of the resource system is of importance (Bilbao, a2, 123). Other important issues to enable self-organisation are awareness and a coherent mentality, which are motivational drivers for individuals to participate and self-organise (Lugano, a2, 87; Umea, a1, 115–120).

4.3 Actors, factors, and lessons learned

This section describes involved actors and influencing factors on socio-ecological transitions. A second part will focus on lessons learned in the process of transitions.

4.3.1 Actors, actions, and factors

Nearly everywhere, the involved actors were very heterogeneous. This means that transitions involved all aspects of urban characters from politics, economy, and the third sector or civil society. Every group has its own interests, involvement, and motivations, which differ in importance or influence on the matter. In any event, the realisation of socio-ecological transition as 'decentralised revolution' necessarily can only take place if central actors are involved and cooperate eye to eye. The main groups come from politics and administrations, economy, civil society, and from (higher) education and science. In Freiburg, one actor stated that the whole city is involved in a collective undertaking (Freiburg, a2, 84–85). Additionally, pronouncing individual responsibility is not the same as an active civil society that interacts, cooperates, and collaborates. The results of the quantitative inquiry suggest throughout all inquired actors, local as well as national or global business and industry actors have the highest influence on the local energy mix, with peaks in Northern and Eastern Europe (cf. Figure 4-7). In addition, national governments and the EU have high influences (especially in Northern and Southern Europe). For Western and Northern Europe, local governments have a solid influence, which stems from the specific autonomy of local governments, especially in Germany or Sweden. Very interesting is the importance of local private households: While assessing the impact and possibility of self-organisation as a transition driver, the roles of individual behaviour and consumption choices were emphasised. The inquiry shows that local households are least important for constituting a local energy mix although the argumentation for self-organisation tends to pronounce a market-driven 'supply and demand' mechanism as a driving force. This contradicts the described citizen-driven socio-ecological transition, which is facilitated by a sustainable consumption choice and individual behaviour. Households – individuals – are least capable of shaping such a transition, which suggests that aggregated individual choice is not sufficient. This supports the argument for a vivid civil society. In addition, the overall possibility of civil society to influence the local energy mix is low to medium.

Cooperation spans a diverse set of actors that includes politics and administration nearly everywhere as well as business associations and business companies. On several occasions,

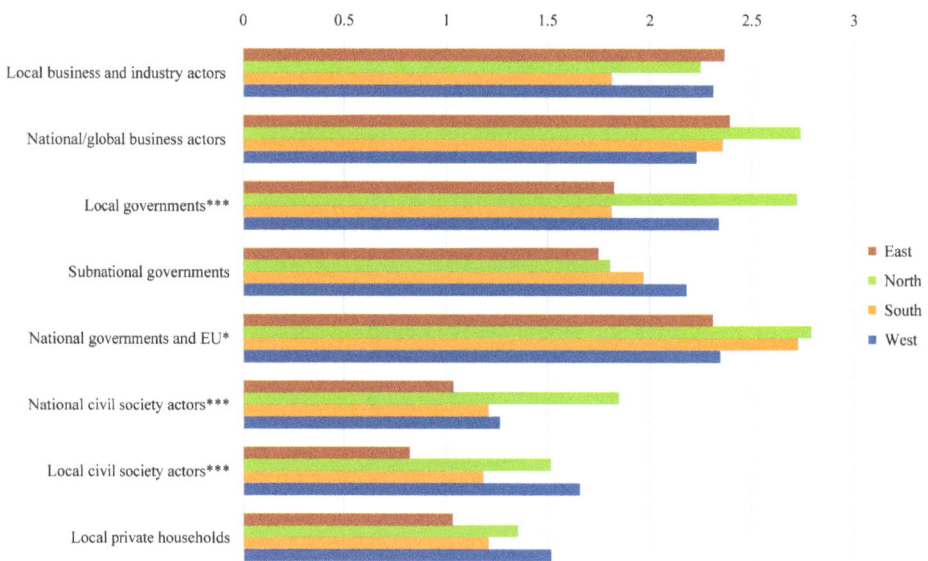

Figure 4-7 Influence on the local energy mix (scaled from 0: none to 4: very high)

NGOs or citizens' associations were additionally included (e.g. Madrid, a2, 46; Milan, a2, 50). A special cooperation partner is found in universities that are taking part in education and research (Copenhagen, a1, 41–44; Dortmund, a3, 74; Freiburg, a1, 120; St. Gallen, a1, 46).[6] Freiburg constitutes a vivid example where university and research institutes participate in a public discourse on sustainability, which commenced as generating counter-knowledge against experts from the nuclear industry in the 1980s (Freiburg, a1, 54). The field of education includes kindergarten, preschools, or primary schools where they teach children basic sustainable behaviour anticipating that they reintroduce this knowledge at home (Giurgiu, a2, 46). The influence of NGOs is sensible and reflected; their success in projects, frames, and so forth, though, is quite different. They participate either directly in projects, or foster social cohesion, but they do not initiate developments on their own (Kiel, a1, 40; Rennes, a1, 73; Saarbrücken, a1, 40; Thessaloniki, a1, 51). Besides, sometimes only political actors were mentioned to have a part in the dynamics, for example in parliamentary processes (Paris, a1, 20; St. Gallen, a1, 37).

Elaborated networks that institutionalise collaboration are particularly important. These emerge either as a response to urgent socio-ecological transitions (Birmingham, a2, 41; Glasgow, a1, 49; Rome, a2, 38), or because of longer ongoing fundamental changes in socio-structural dynamics of cities, such as transformations towards postindustrial cities (Dortmund, a3, 36). Within these collaboration networks, different heterogeneous actors are involved, like unions or churches, especially to address economic and social topics.

The interviewees discussed only a few conflicting constellations: The chamber of commerce worked against environmental goals (Kiel, a1, 40). The construction industry in Rome proved to be a specific conflicting sector, since energy efficiency in buildings contradicts the intentions of industry magnates (Rome, a2, 26). A complete deficit of cooperation between industry and the municipality occurred in Timisoara (a2, 59). All in all, this parallels the indicated low level of conflicts inquired into by the questionnaire.

The actors undertook different kinds of actions in socio-ecological transitions. These were collected and put together into a collage of local activities. Overall, many diverse activities and actions can be reconstructed, but in this context, they will be grouped according to underlying functions.

Incentives are used to trigger active sustainable behaviour. This is sought through different mechanisms like reducing prices for public transportation, or introducing eco-tickets (Linz, a1, 41). In addition, clean vehicles are subsidised while polluting ones are penalised, for example by raising taxes (Madrid, a2, 86). These measures aim at reducing CO_2 emissions. Moreover, actions directly related to energy incentives were undertaken, such as subsidies for switching to long-distance heating, changing to energy-efficient boilers, and so forth (Linz, a1, 113; Madrid, a2, 62). A more general approach was fostering local circular or 'close' economies that are energy efficient in the sense that spatial dimensions were reduced and product cycles were kept to a minimum (Leeds, a2, 78).

Planning procedures and strategies for local transition processes are additional activities related to transition processes. It has already been discussed that sustainability goals were derived from programme strategies negotiated internationally. Translating these global agreements into local strategies and action plans is a decisive step to reach the set-out targets. Setting up plans for local circumstances referred not only to energy issues but also to CO_2 emission reduction and traffic/public transportation topics. They included for example the planning of a public transportation system (Rennes, a1, 57); a "table of mobility" (Madrid, a2, 22); a "master plan energy transition" (Dortmund, a3, 34); or were derived from Agenda 21 goals (Rome, a2, 36). Planning makes local problems visible and lays out fields of action to a broader public (Trieste, a1, 41 and a2, 99). The planning and deriving of strategies bring local stakeholders together and fosters their cooperation, since their interests are included in the discussions (Aalborg, a1, 46). Especially joining networks like the Covenant of Mayors is a particular initiative of the cities' political actors to exchange on specific topics (Bilbao, a1, 38; Naples, a2, 12). This intersects with 'networking', which tries to bring together several different stakeholders. Especially for interviewed business actors, this produces local synergies (Aalborg, a3, 19–20; Dortmund, a3, 64). Networks also include universities and institutions of higher education (Aalborg, a3, 54; Nice, a1, 83). This fosters integrating social innovations (Leeds, a1, 40; Leeds, a2, 35; Rennes, a2, 15). The performed actions indicate that municipal institutions especially set their goals in catalysing the cooperation and information exchange in networks – but also in participating in such networking contexts.

To a smaller degree, actions undertaken consisted of actively funding projects. The cities' tasks are financing and maintaining cost-intensive projects or buildings (Jihlava, a1, 11). Backed by the EXPO Framework for the World Exposition 2015, financial assets were made available for example for a public transportation project (Milan, a1, 27). Funding is provided for building refurbishments to support individual contributions to better energy efficiency (Innsbruck, a2, 47).

The most substantial part of activities consisted of distributing information, raising awareness, and educating about sustainability in general or very detailed and specific aspects. The range went from information campaigns to the installation of fixed public relations departments to address citizens. Among these was the implementation of a festival with 70 events about sustainability as a joint undertaking of a broad coalition of the municipality, business, and civil society actors (Aalborg, a2, 48–49). Expert lectures were also considered as a way to provide the city with detailed information (Aalborg, a3, 39). Dortmund started an information campaign that addressed the population and tried to reach them with local football enthusiasm and identification ("Climate is a home match" and "We are climate fans"; Dortmund, a2, 80, 82). Further, an information centre was opened to inform citizens and to provide consultation services (Dortmund, a2, 72). A business actor acts as an "information broker" on new technologies and developments sensitising local business companies (Dortmund, a3, 34, 64). Information via leaflet drops (Prague, a1, 39) covered more basic information about sustainability issues, but more detailed and concrete information about the resource system were also made available by cartographies of energy consumption (Nice, a1, 28). The local work of NGOs is supported by providing an information space (Saarbrücken, a1, 41). More generally, a focus lay on distributing information and raising awareness among the citizens and sometimes also among industry and economy; these actions were in all regions sensible but dominant mainly in Eastern and Southern European countries (Birmingham, a1, 48; Giurgiu, a2, 46–49; Larissa, a2, 45; Strasbourg, a1, 55; Thessaloniki, a1, 51 and a2, 31).

The last point describes individual actions. This refers to residual activities and programmes that resulted in specific outcomes. For example, Trieste refurbished old buildings from the 1960s and 1970s (Trieste, a1, 12). Energy efficiency and awareness was increased in the past by increasing energy efficiency on several levels, from light bulbs at home to street lighting (Birmingham, a1, 36; Lodz, a1, 49; Saarbrücken, a1, 41; Trieste, a1, 33). Another, yet disciplinary, approach actively changed taxation and charged specific unsustainable behaviour. This correlates with goals in traffic and emission reductions to "challenge the citizens to make them understand" (Milan, a1, 21). In another sense, this creates incentives to act and behave in an environmentally friendly way and solves problems with dense traffic and pollution, such as the pollution badge for older cars that are forbidden to enter inner cities in Germany. Another variety of actions directly undertaken was the renovation of public and administrative buildings in the cities and municipalities. They are updated with new insulations and new heating systems and by installing solar panels and the like (Larissa, a1, 72; Nice, a1, 29; Paris, a1, 33). Usually these measures only apply to public buildings, since the local administrations do not have any direct influence on the private sector. A more specific insight delivered by the questionnaire described influences on energy consumption: An especially high effect is had by the retrofitting of buildings by governmental or private owners. Civil society actors additionally named the greening of businesses as a factor. The business actors claimed that behavioural changes in transport habits and in energy consumption are responsible for decreased energy use, thus each pointing to past activities and different leverages (cf. Figure 4-8).

The further topic of factors that foster or hinder – or more generally have an effect on – socio-ecological transitions is divided into three distinct groups. Interviews assessed local and nonlocal factors and, additionally, temporal aspects. These factors influence transitions in certain ways and are a key to understanding the action situations of local sustainability campaigns and decisions. They relate to manifold aspects of the urban system, stretching from material texture to dynamics of society and technology. A clear distinction between hindering factors and challenges was not always possible.

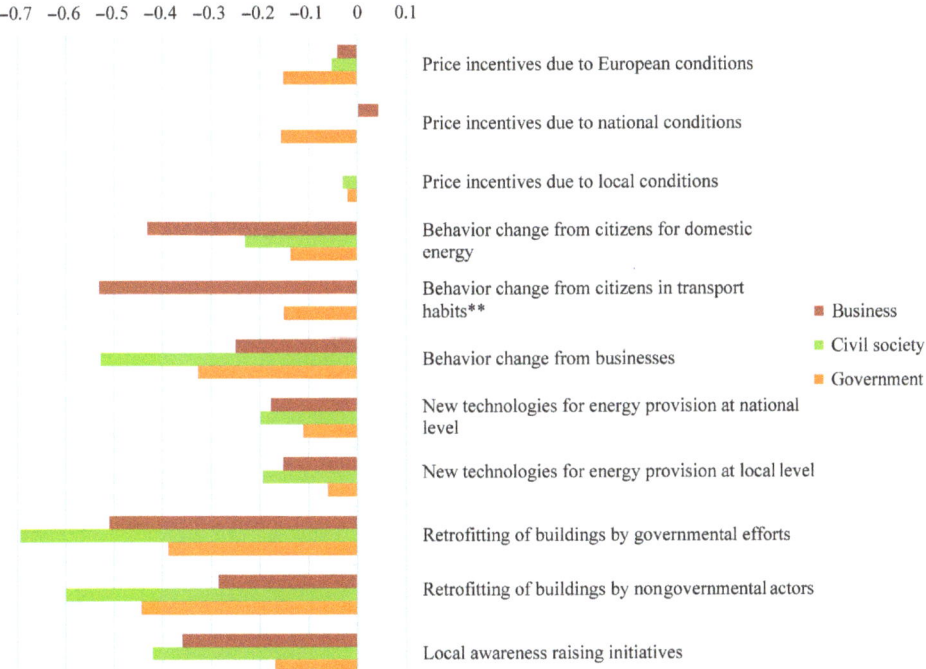

Figure 4-8 Influences on the energy consumption in the past ten years (scaled from −2: decreased a lot to +2: increased a lot)

As a first estimation, the goal to set examples can be considered: Taking a pioneering position in the transition process, two actors explained that providing good examples is a key factor for their cities (Copenhagen, a1, 46; Freiburg, a2, 198–200). Especially, Freiburg's self-conception as a beacon for other cities in transition displays itself as a 'best practice' example.[7] Another local factor that influences sustainability transitions is the importance of awareness. This also has been discussed above under the topic of challenges for participation and self-organisation as well as in the light of concrete actions undertaken in the transition. This clearly shows the acknowledged importance of awareness by the interviewed actors. Education is a primary aspect to raise awareness (e.g. Dortmund, a1, 32; Gothenburg, a2, 27–31; Linz, a1, 67 and a2, 31; Rennes, a1, 50). Timisoara relies on consumption self-monitoring, an individualisation of sustainability development to make citizens aware of their consumption (Timisoara, a2, 94). Likewise, the relevance of planning processes was stated, especially in combination with setting goals and 'translating' EU or national strategies into local action programmes. Planning and steering is realised by environmental management systems that imply to a certain degree that controlling the transition is possible (Aalborg, a3, 77; Freiburg, a2, 158). An actor compares reflections on planning to a "Stalinist view" indicating rigidly planned steps of a centrally planned economy (Rennes, a1, 32). Further, planning is a "tradition of prospective, of territorial planning" (Rennes, a2, 14) that structures and guides transition movements (also Kiel, a1, 112; Kiel, a2, 38; Strasbourg, a1, 43).

In addition to these factors, the structural changes of cities act as transition factors. In light of postindustrial cities, this has been discussed above and can be denoted as a factor. Structural ruptures can provide the drive for a socio-ecological transition and can also be an obstacle for the development. Successful developments from industrial to postindustrial cities ease sustainability transitions (Bilbao, a2, 38) and may lead to new fields for sustainable socio-cultural and economic developments (Linz, a1, 67). Several actors operate as transition factors. Especially universities and institutes for the environment play a major role, especially in knowledge exchange and technology (cf. Figure 4-4). Their tasks consist of research as well as education, for example "green university" and the Institute for Applied Ecology (Freiburg, a1, 40, 66, 120); PIK[8] (Potsdam, a1, 60); and EMPA[9] (St. Gallen, a1, 46). A more subtle factor can be described as a 'proactive' culture of problem-raising – a well-functioning public discourse about local problems and challenges among several stakeholders is considered helpful (Rennes, a1, 50). This can be extended by collaboration among a majority of involved actors (Dortmund, a2, 41; Timisoara, a1, 57–61).

The last point covers structural aspects, a variety of heterogeneous factors that influence socio-ecological transitions in many different ways. For example, spatial attributes of the urban region influence transitions (Barcelona, a2, 35; Lugano, a2, 31). Socio-structural aspects, like the population and its affinity to cars in a "class city" – a city that is characterised by class distinctions – are distinct traits that have effects on socio-ecological transition (Birmingham, a1, 32). Further, the local influence of specific political parties – especially ecological parties – or political guidelines for the administration (Freiburg, a1, 39; Saarbrücken, a1, 29–30) as well as legal frameworks that enforce sustainable behaviour (Rome, a2, 26) have their influence. Finally, the overall context of a city is unique, and thus there are no one-for-all solutions (Potsdam, a2, 54), and this uniqueness influences transition towards sustainability individually (Glasgow, a2, 37).

Nonlocal factors include regional, national, or European influences. First, the given legal frameworks have their own influences on socio-ecological transitions. Especially, the degree of local autonomy is directly connected to the impact of national administrative frames and European directives – thus, the state of decentralisation is an essential indicator for the overall independence of the local level and its possibility to enact a transition (cf. subsection 2.2.1). In a broader sense, local actors have to correspond to legal standards in a varying degree with the level of (de)centralisation (Saarbrücken, a1, 36–38). More generally, "regulation pressure always makes things move" (Strasbourg, a3, 50), although this is a one-dimensional argument that has a potential to neglect hindering aspects of legal frames. Their influence as transition factors is at least ambivalent, as their assessment for self-organisation capabilities has shown (see above). Funding issues can be included into legal frames since they relate to specific development programmes or directives that provide financial coverage (Dortmund, a1, 32). Legal frameworks as well as funding policies on national or European levels are the main foundations and are central for promoting and advancing socio-ecological transitions. These consist of several parts like goal setting and the controlling of goal attainment (Potsdam, a2, 74) or like the support of pilot projects on the local level for later use in a national application (Giurgiu, a2, 44; Lugano, a1, 61–64) – above all, controlling functions are fulfilled by national governmental levels. Contrasting this, governmental levels can also hinder transitions equally by legal means or by denying the importance of sustainability, by neglecting regions or specific urban areas (Barcelona, a1, 39), or by being "unbearably conservative" (St. Gallen, a1, 31).

The temporal dimension converges with time horizons in set-out goals, discussed in subsection 4.2.1. More specifically, time horizons can be interpreted as transition factors. Actors consider the temporal frame as an important and contested factor in socio-ecological transitions (cf. Figure 4-9). The road towards sustainability is a long one – in part, it is argued that its endpoint is never entirely reachable (Barcelona, a1, 36) – and changes will take a long time to have any visible and sensible effects (Umea, a2, 80). Therefore, socio-ecological transition has to aim at long-term investments, for example in education, which has an impact on the individual behaviour of future generations (Trieste, a1, 24). In addition, depending on the size of a local project, it takes respective time to realise an endeavour. This means to accept, plan, and implement or build the deliverable, since

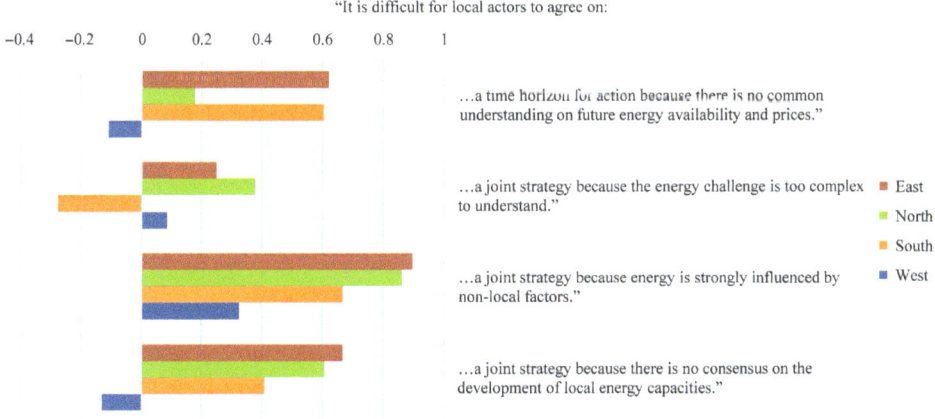

Figure 4-9 Difficulties to agree on local energy strategy (scaled from −2: strongly disagree to +2: strongly agree)

the complexity of a project increases in relation to its size (St. Gallen, a1, 52). Development plans have different time horizons in respect to the ownership (public, municipal, or private economy) and the desired development path (Aalborg, a3, 35). Condensed, short-term economic gains stand against long-term goals of sustainability – as reflected above in the common definitions of sustainability (Umea, a2, 30). The long timeframe perspective is not the only central temporal factor. Depending on different measures, different timeframes in realisation, efficiency, and impact exist (Timisoara, a1, 65–67). Radical shifts, though, are rather uncommon as "constant dripping wears away the stone" (Potsdam, a2, 52).

4.3.2 Lessons learnt

In the process of a socio-ecological transition, the involved actors gain experience in a wide variety of fields. 'Social learning' is an important asset in transition processes that are participatory or self-organised (Eneko Garmendia and Sigrid Stagl 2010). These experiences help in successfully achieving upcoming projects, tasks, and so on; they are lessons learnt about different facets of a complex, contingent, and unstable transitional process. These lessons learnt can be grouped into different categories. In this context, the experts' narrations reflected especially the roles of actors and actions undertaken, processes and details of the field, governance issues, contexts of the resource system, and individual experiences as a residual category. Figure 4-9 shows that there are difficulties in agreeing on common strategies on the local level. These extensive issues are difficulties arising from nonlocal factors. Here, Eastern and Northern Europe achieve the highest approval, although it is – in relation to the initial scale – low (around +0.8). The only significant group differences exist in a 'time horizon' and a 'joint strategy'. Especially Eastern and Southern Europe anticipate difficulties in finding a common time horizon. Joint strategies for developing local capacities are common in Eastern and Northern Europe and a bit in Southern Europe. The highest agreement (without significant group differences) was scored by the topic of joint strategies influenced by nonlocal factors.

A first point discusses experiences made in interaction with local stakeholders. The reference to these was rather general. Administrative processes have to involve stakeholders in socio-ecological transitions, and they should ask for their visions and scepticisms (Innsbruck, a2, 85). Any new undertaking can face resistance from the population, so integrating them into processes can ease common doubts (Linz, a2, 75). Mainly, the problem is to satisfy every single citizen, since the population does not always perceive local projects well (Bilbao, a2, 110). Cooperation and keen leadership are strong influences on a transition that tries to outmanoeuvre the problems of disinterested or opposing citizens (Gothenburg, a2, 53–55). Glasgow's actors argue for the involvement of as many people as possible and the importance of a socio-ecological transition on everybody's agenda (Glasgow, a1, 64; Glasgow, a2, 71). Therefore, a specific culture of discussion that consists of compromising, negotiating, and respecting others' ideas is imperative (Prague, a2, 55). Moving things together and having a common task and goal are essential points that have major impacts on local transitions (Aalborg, a2, 66). The linking of actions is important: In reflection of the denoted 'holism' in sustainability definitions, each action is meaningful, but only together do they "become a pertinent policy" (Nice, a1, 84).

A second field provides insights into learning processes, experiences, and especially issues about information and educational facets. More and especially more detailed and transparent information is important and sustaining in socio-ecological transition (Linz, a1, 97). Associations to help local businesses switch their sources could address questions and problems about renewable energy (Strasbourg, a3, 96). Cooperation helps a lot, especially when exchanging experiences with other cities in networks, like the Covenant of Mayors (Lublin, a2, 48). Cities are potent actors, so the wish to cooperate is there from other actors – at least in the self-description (Leeds, a2, 53). Interviewed actors pronounced the value of information and cooperation already with regard to participation and self-organisation. This indicates that there are learning processes and that the importance of these two aspects cannot be neglected. To be successful in bringing together several different actors and engaging in cooperation as well as motivating civil society and others, a strong narrative of sustainability that activates all parties is required (Birmingham, a1, 52). Lastly, there remains a more general question about how to handle these gained experiences and insights. A basic structure for assessing and saving lessons learnt is important to draw value from experiences (Kiel, a2, 110). Nevertheless, the urge for cooperation is not a distinct alternative to levelling out external market effects or as an opposition to governmental hierarchy.[10]

The third group of lessons learnt applies to governmental processes, issues, and topics related to financing and funding. The latter assesses that especially projects need secured funding possibilities, for which a reliable and straightforward government system is required (Nice, a2, 54). The urge for European funding is pointed out on several occasions and especially for pilot projects that introduce prototypical technology, processes and so on (Trieste, a2, 107). In addition, renewable energy projects should guarantee cost efficiency in economically reasonable dimensions. This emphasises that any socio-ecological transition also relates to market mechanisms (Strasbourg, a2, 105). Another aspect is the realisation that energy efficiency and energy savings come with the benefits of saving financial resources (Freiburg, a1, 87). However, this neglects *rebound effects* that slowly reduce these efficiency gains, for example through increased consumption or changed behaviour that stems from additional financial resources (cf. section 4.1). The other set of experiences concerns governmental processes and experiences made with governmental institutions, like interactions or their relevance to transitions towards sustainability. Regarding the installed and maintained frameworks, consideration might differ: In some actors' perception, frameworks on the European, national, or local level are helpful and productive to initiate campaigns (Rennes, a2, 54). However, governmental institutions can slow down and delay processes due to their bureaucratic nature (Potsdam, a1, 118). These problems exist from local levels to European institutions (Naples, a1, 45). Especially legal frameworks exist to accordingly guide and standardise efforts towards sustainability. However, this also includes a somewhat lax interpretation of 'binding' regulations: An actor states that (national) governmental instances do not necessarily follow them (here this refers to EU policies; Thessaloniki, a2, 57). To a certain degree, the implementation of new regulations is considered helpful in Istanbul (a2, 52). It has been realised that with changes to and extensions of the legal framework, the efficiency and understanding of renewable energies can be improved – directly easing financial needs.

In Germany, the focus on industry exempts businesses from higher reallocation charges for renewables. This especially affects private persons, who are burdened with higher charges (Dortmund, a2, 70). A severe imbalance in the cost distribution between actors is perceived. Lacking collaboration between local actors produced tensions. In one specific case, public authorities with insufficient competences and the administration of the city council faced situations where complicated actions and decisions had to be made (Barcelona, a1, 57). On top of that, one interviewee reflected on better monitoring capabilities that inquire more frequently and more intensively to ensure better and faster project realisation – overall a more comprehensive project management approach (Timisoara, a2, 107).

Structural aspects learnt from socio-ecological transition processes concerned the local resource systems. A first insight is the complex nature of the resource system that is influenceable by many diverse factors. Thus, a development plan and transition towards sustainability has to include many interacting factors (Strasbourg, a1, 75). The importance of these context factors expresses itself in city planning in relation to design, nature protection, public opinion, and physical aspects of the resource system (Saarbrücken, a2, 111). Above all, the energy sector has a diverse connection to economic and social topics (see above; Thessaloniki, a1, 71). One actor could not assess clearly what experiences he could draw from the ongoing processes, since the field was too fragmented (Milan, a2, 74). Overall, energy topics touch a wide variety of different actors, mechanisms, policies, and leverage points – it is a sensitive sector with many interests that requires well thought-out actions (Lugano, a2, 65). Individually experienced factors are for example economic aspects. Although Leeds is very "backward" and not energy efficient (Leeds, a1, 56), a complete economic sector has been developed that is concerned with sustainability and produces jobs and economic growth (Leeds, a2, 59). Technology has a significant influence on the energy resource system, coupled with social improvements for citizens (Lublin, a2, 46; Barcelona, a1, 67). Further, stricter behavioural constraints assist in sustainable action, for example recycling to make available the potential energy deposits in waste or maintaining strict levels of resource use to save scarce pools (Madrid, a1, 80; Umea, a2, 56).

Lastly, there were individual lessons learnt that derived from individual actions. Especially dealing with individual behaviour is a key for sustainability transition, since aggregated individual behaviour is a driver to a sustainable movement. This is also part of the experts' reflections: Individuals can achieve much, if they get involved (Saarbrücken, a1, 67). And even the worst city can reach a state of sustainability, if the citizens were to actively take part in a transition process (Larissa, a1, 63) and change behavioural patterns (Naples, a2, 42). However, citizens often lack motivation and – inherently – awareness, a fact that lets an actor demand imposition instruments (Trieste, a2, 69). However, sustainability is about energy efficiency in many different fields, and thus several distinct access points lead to increased sustainable developments – but only in a holistic relation (Madrid, a2, 78).

4.4 Norm adoption and local decision-making autonomy

Section 4.4 is concerned with norm adoption and local decision-making autonomy. Missing or to be adjusted governmental mechanisms are covered by the first subsection while the second describes the possibilities of local-level governments to decide autonomously.

4.4.1 Norm adoption

Stemming from lessons learnt in the transition process, actors were asked for their experiences and, beyond that, for policy instruments that could support their goals and if changes to them could increase their effectiveness. A basic indicator is the building of trust and the development of a common understanding of the transition process. This means increased insight into the individual features and requirements of the transition as well as a trusting group cohesion that fosters reciprocity.

A part of this initial question has been discussed as *difficulties to agree on local energy strategies* (cf. Figure 4-9). The nearly neutral assessment of shared understandings requires great explanation. In the sections above, actors have discussed facets of socio-ecological transitions and sustainability that referred to the time horizon of transition, to the influences of nonlocal strategies and programmes as well as to the development of local-level resource capacities by raising energy efficiency. These reoccur to some extent in this question. Also in light of governance principles, results are not distinct (cf. Figures 4-10 and 4-11). The most striking aspect here is the felt absence of local arenas for resolving conflicts in Eastern Europe; in other regions, this item is neutral. Other items with diverging opinions include a slight disagreement on the possibilities of authorised participation in rule changing for Northern Europe as well as an agreeable stance towards the monitoring of contribution and benefit levels. For a more specific agreement on governance principles, clear-cut boundaries are missing in Northern and Southern Europe, indicating that the range of the system is unclear.

The qualitative inquiry yields a variety of interesting assessments of local political processes and their limitations. A first point covers legal aspects of policies and refers to more direct obligations, such as taxation to increase the pressure on unsustainable behaviour (Innsbruck, a2, 117) or in building laws to force sustainable renovations (Paris, a1, 57). In a broader context, relying on a higher level, legal frameworks are concerned. Especially the European procurement law has flaws that lead to bad quality and price dumping (Prague, a2, 60–63). Existing laws and frames should also be 'greener' and support or enforce topics of sustainability (Aalborg, a1, 110; Dortmund, a2, 110; Lodz, a1, 60). Further, consistency of legal frameworks is contested. One actor directly states that he wants

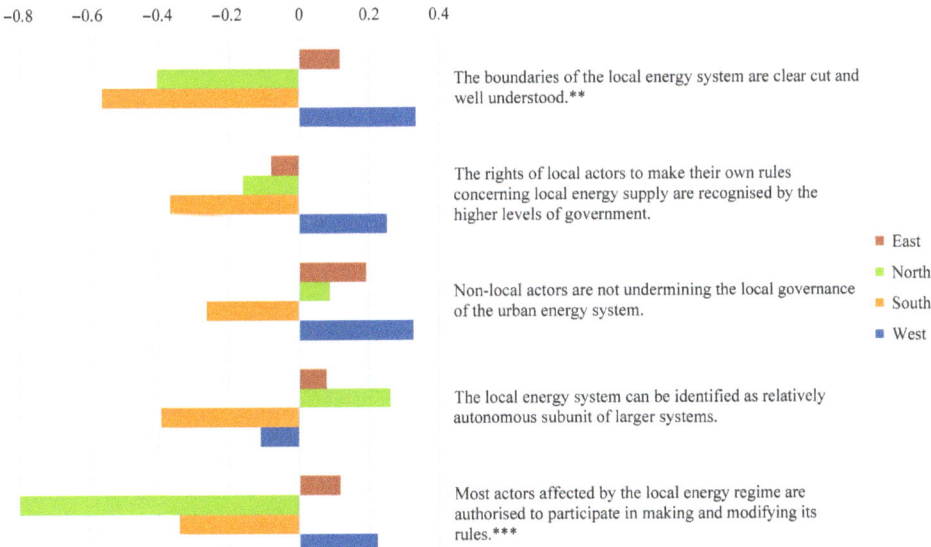

Figure 4-10 Agreement with governance principles for the local energy system (scaled from −2: strongly disagree to +2: strongly agree)

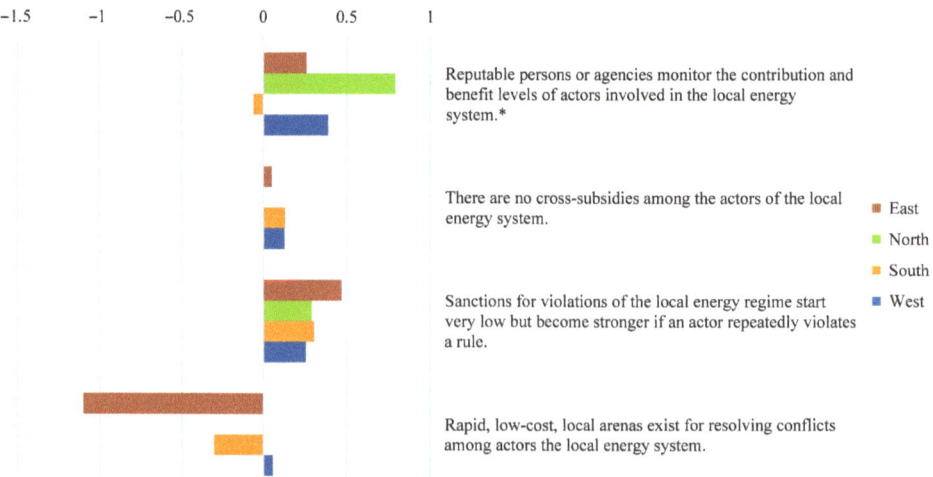

Figure 4–11 Agreement with governance principles for the local energy system

to "'clean up' the legislative environment" since incoherent laws persist especially on a national level (Prague, a2, 61). This is also a point of criticism in Barcelona, where clear rules are missing and lobbyists and the economy influence existing regulations (Barcelona, a2, 88). In another case, the authority of legislation should be increased to facilitate processes (Aalborg, a2, 97). Elsewhere, the focus is that EU policies should be reconsidered. For instance, the EU should change the emphasis of its policies from economic to social and environmental issues (Linz, a1, 141) and foster more supportive policies that do not only rely on changing people's behaviour (Dortmund, a3, 101–104). This intersects with statements that emphasise the necessity to raise awareness of topics instead of seeing EU standards as impositions (Milan, a1, 67). On climate issues, actors demand more authority from the European Union; the EU should be responsible for all topics related to climate and consider a "single European Climate Mitigation Bill" (Potsdam, a1, 180–182). This asks the EU to take a strong leadership position (Bilbao, a1, 90). Without the EU, an interviewee assesses, there would be fewer regimentations and standards for ecological sustainability. Thus, increased pressure from EU institutions fosters sustainable development (Saarbrücken, a1, 96).

Funding represents another field of EU policy; experts pronounce financial support of housing refurbishments and – generally – the increased incentivising of funding processes (Rennes, a2, 54; Milan, a2, 101). The funding process is difficult and bureaucratic; here the EU should lend assistance with the complex process (Glasgow, a2, 98). Funding covers issues related to the amount of financial resources that are made available. Funding is always too scarce; more financial means nearly everywhere are seen as increased potential and improvement (Dortmund, a1, 94; Nice, a1, 71; Rennes, a1, 133). "[M]oney is not everything but without money, it's not much either" (Potsdam, a2, 226). Another factor is the allocation of the financial resources at hand: Topics related to CO2 emissions, such as transportation and housing, are preferred over energy topics (Umea, a2, 80). The distribution process on the national level to local entities must be optimised (Prague, a1, 71). The EU has established a framework to initiate projects – the European Regional

Development Fund (ERDF) grants 5 per cent of its resources directly to cities, which is seen as insufficient (Linz, a2, 116). Cases with a general lack of financial support exist, too, and in providing the money, for example for pilot projects, a socio-ecological transition is more likely to succeed (Naples, a1, 80; Trieste, a2, 107). There is also a necessity for EU funding since the structurally weak regions lack investment activities from private or public hands (Lodz, a1, 60). A last point concerns autonomy: Regions should distribute the financial resources and entrust cities to act on their own (Leeds, a1, 95). Combined with requirements in sustainability goals, the granting of funding could be tied to specific criteria that foster a local transition and rely more on mechanisms of incentivising (Leeds, a2, 80; Milan, a2, 101).

In terms of available instruments to foster socio-ecological transitions in cities, the promotion of Agenda 21 and the consolidation of the CO2 exchange have to achieve better performance. Agenda 21 has proved to be a powerful tool in supporting cities in sustainability transitions and therefore needs to be disseminated. It proposes a variety of tools, plans, and strategies that already describe a detailed sustainable development for a socio-ecological transition (Bilbao, a1, 80; Nice, a2, 67). In addition, the EU has to implement the CO2 trading exchange "the way it was intended", and it should handle it entirely (Potsdam, a1, 178; St. Gallen, a2, 83). Instruments that are more diverse cover the increase of local autonomy to support cities in decision-making (Copenhagen, a1, 84–87). In addition, an alignment of politics and decisions to global scales is necessary (Istanbul, a2, 74). The most basic tool for approaching local problems is a vivid discussion and a public discourse (Prague, a2, 59). This last statement shifts the 'instruments' to a broader perspective and emphasises the necessity of an active civil society. As a sum of political factors, interviewees referred to the necessity of strong EU leadership in renewable energy topics. For one actor, even dictatorships promise adequate results, since they can be "damn effective" in prescribing laws (Aalborg, a3, 107). In terms of local levels, regional and national governments dominate and have to take the policies for renewable energies and energy transitions more seriously (Freiburg, a1, 134–135; Kiel, a2, 132). This requires a supportive stance from national governance. In this light, the European Union is a potent actor that could shape and influence local markets accordingly (Saarbrücken, a1, 96). This aspect further neglects an increased claim for more independence and autonomy of local levels. However, the barriers to communicate with the EU due to bureaucratic hindrances are high (Trieste, a1, 89), and the request that the European Union should directly address cities, without having to include national or regional governments and institutions, is stated (Rome, a2, 75). For Turkey, Istanbul's actor responded that the EU should take in Turkey to accelerate the sustainability process and foster innovations (Istanbul, a2, 80).

The last point reflects the city as a social institution. This means that cities are conglomerates that emerge from socio-historic, cultural, and economic contingencies. Their uniqueness lies in this specific historical development, which shows itself in political, economic, and social thriving. Cities' social structures have a particular role in socio-ecological transition. Their specific role and their influences on socio-ecological transitions should be reflected by installing a ministry of cities, since cities are considered the most severe contributors to CO2 emissions and climate change (Birmingham, a2, 105). However, the actor does not go into any further detail. The city as a social institution is seen as a relic from the nineteenth century that evolved alongside an industrialising society on the threshold of modernity. On the one hand, the question the actor implicitly raises is about the *sustainability* of the city as a concept. The "problems are cities, and the problems of cities are created by the fact that they were nineteenth century institutions in the main, and they've been run at best with twentieth century governance" (Birmingham, a2, 105). The solution would be an 'up-to-date' governance of the twenty-first century (Birmingham, a2, 107). On the other hand, this position is contrasted, however, by a return to a "European city" (Kiel, a1, 124), which represents traditional urban planning and development that centres around a market place with short distances between private and public spheres. No matter how the role and form of cities are considered, their importance and their structural problems cannot be neglected.

4.4.2 Local decision-making autonomy

The final research question reflects local decision-making autonomy and the financial autonomy of the cities. These two greatly influence the possibility and the efficiency of self-organising capabilities. The state of the socio-ecological transition, self-organisation, the involved actors, and influencing factors as well as actions undertaken are entangled and produce experiences that drive the process to norm adoption according to the lessons learnt. These then influence institutions that constitute potentials and constraints on the local level.

The individual estimates of autonomy in the city sample are quite heterogeneous and show a diverging meaning of 'autonomy'. The degree of administrative decentralisation directly influences the degree of independent decision-making. EU policies and programmes also influence the level of autonomy, especially in countries that are under fiscal control and subject to austerity politics. Depending on the national constitution of legal frames, certain policies are not decided at the local level but at other levels. Exemplary, this can be seen for energy policies that are the subject of national politics in Germany or France; local autonomy refers to city planning and urban development but always reacts to standards 'from above' (Dortmund, a1, 86; Rennes, a1, 111). Especially Germany has a very high degree of local autonomy, rooted in the lowest administrative level, the communal level (Freiburg, a1, 98; Potsdam, a1, 174). In terms of infrastructure, for example, municipalities can decide for themselves, but projects with a higher investment volume have to be realised in business partnerships (Potsdam, a2, 160). Locally made decisions always influence or are influenced by actors from other sectors. One of the most common assessments points out the nexus of different reciprocal positions. The possibility to make decisions is embedded in a social field of conflicts and interests. Therefore, they have to reflect either their influences on the economy (employment rate, location factors, etc.) or on the opinion and behaviour of individuals (consumption choice, energy saving, etc.). The latter point refers to sustainability frames that are set by municipalities and address the behavioural aspects of socio-ecological transition (e.g. Giurgiu, a2, 86; Gothenburg, a2, 61; Umea, a1, 101 and a2, 60).

Two interesting cases are Switzerland and Greece. The first has a specific constitutional framework of direct democracy that suits bottom-up initiatives and decisions. Also, on the cantonal level, governance structures are very independent (Lugano, a2, 75). However, these possibilities could be used more efficiently (Lugano, a1, 109). Cantonal independence in St. Gallen is visible where the local directive consists of "as little government as possible and as many private initiatives as possible" (St. Gallen, a1, 56). Greece, on the other hand, had to undergo administrative reform to comply with the imposed objectives of austerity politics. This 'Kallikratis' reform included an enforced decentralisation of administration and shifted decision-making capabilities to the lower levels. A more implicit goal was to impede the possibilities for corruption and the downsizing of bureaucracy. In the interviews, this transfer of competences is assessed quite differently: It is (still) seen as a bad situation where local administrations are helpless against central government's decisions and especially concerning smaller problems on local levels (Larissa, a1, 75 and a2, 87). Contrary to these opinions, the Kallikratis transition is considered a smooth process that has already transferred many competences to the local level (Thessaloniki, a2, 65). Other interesting examples are Germany and France, which are quite opposite cases. While Germany has a high degree of decentralisation, France is a centralised state in energy politics and in the local decision-making autonomy, where "[l]ocal authorities don't have anything to say" (Nice, a2, 101). The effectiveness of local decision autonomy in France is differently assessed, though (cf. the statements from Rennes). In contrast, the independence of Istanbul from national governmental levels does not exist; all authority is centralised although the local level has the best insight into local problems and the interconnectedness of actors and factors. Altogether, local administration is powerless (Istanbul, a2, 25).

Municipalities or administrations have different possibilities to decide relevant local strategies and policies, depending on their decision-making autonomy. The sphere of influence of local decisions touches strategies and planning processes. First, according to the quantitative analysis, governmental institutions have the most important role in energy issues. There are almost no legal constraints to the mandates of each group of actors, according to the inquiry (cf. Figure 4-12). City or urban planning as well as the implementation of sustainability strategies and the like are rooted in local-level activities and decisions (Gothenburg, a2, 63; Lugano, a2, 77; Prague, a2, 57; Rennes, a1, 111; Timisoara, a2, 118). This is reasonable since the handling of local environment falls to local-level actors with in-depth knowledge. This marks the complaint of the Turkish actor in Istanbul, stated above. The capability to set or alter laws is usually not given to local actors since

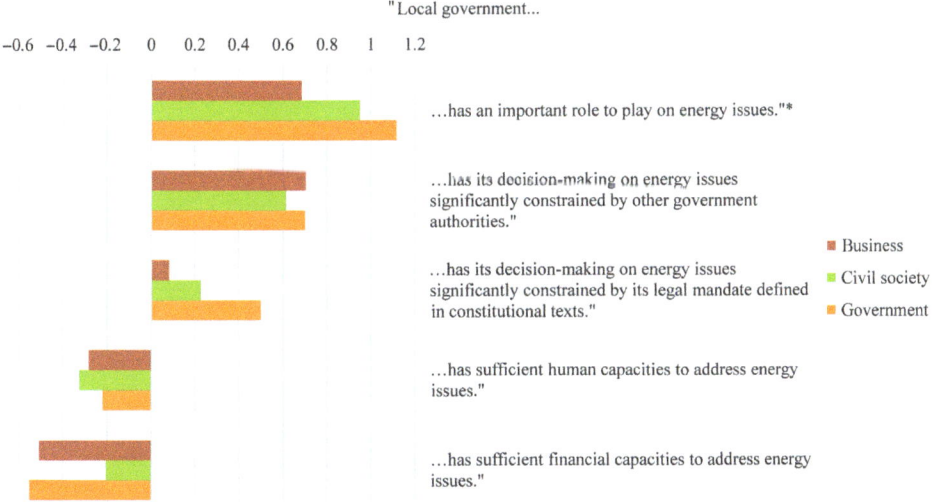

Figure 4-12 Local decision-making autonomy for different sectors (scaled from −2: strongly disagree to +2: strongly agree)

the legal frameworks are handled on the national level. Urban areas thus cannot decide upon constitutional and legal frameworks, and so on. One possible intervention is achievable by introducing rules like a land use plan that can be outfitted with binding guidelines on energy efficiency for newly built houses. In some cases, this potential only reaches as far as municipal buildings and leaves out individuals (Innsbruck, a2, 93; Linz, a1, 105). A key factor can be the power to direct the municipal energy utility – at least if it is in public hands and city owned. This opens up potential for direct influence on the use and production of renewable energy (Timisoara, a1, 102–105).

More interesting – and in a way structurally more important – are the obstacles in local decision-making. Their evaluation allows for a thorough interpretation of institutional and structural preconditions for and effects on local-level decision autonomy. A first important factor is (in)dependence from higher governance structures. Especially centralised states undermine local-level autonomy (Larissa, a1, 75; Rennes, a1, 103; Strasbourg, a2, 40). It is striking that centralisation is a problem in France, since the energy provider, EDF, has a powerful position in the energy market and additionally cannot even be influenced by the national government. Further, Greece still suffers from a high level of centralisation although the Kallikratis reform aimed at shifting responsibilities and influences to lower levels. One reason might be the short timespan this constitutional and political reform has been in place, which can result in a lack of consolidated procedures. Additionally, the political responsibilities for the local level were not extended far enough. On central topics, the local administration has little to no influence at all (Thessaloniki, a1, 92). In general, if regulations of the energy system are in national or European hands, the decision-making capabilities of the local level are restrained (Strasbourg, a2, 115), and – also relating to this issue – if higher levels have not yet made certain decisions, local hands are tied (Aalborg, a2, 72–75). Next to governmental obstacles, the role and influence of economy and business actors on local decision-making autonomy is important. Particularly the interests of business actors with an economic logic – realising profits and prevailing on the market – fosters antagonistic behaviour. This relation shows itself in decisions that interfere with economic interests, for example by introducing higher environmental taxes or enforcing the use of clean energy. The influence of individual business actors can be felt in local decisions (Rome, a2, 57). An interviewee dramatically asserts that this problem is "blackmail" (Kiel, a1, 88). The leverages are jobs and economic growth, directly related to the financial and social well-being of a city. Tax revenue and jobs (which lead to a socially secured population) are driving forces that secure the financial autonomy of the cities at the cost of cuts in decision autonomy, since adversely affecting the economy is not considered an option (Saarbrücken, a2, 134). Thus, cities are both dependent and independent at the same time, since their decisions have to evaluate and account for different interests (Kiel, a1, 88). Being dependent on national funding can also be a pitfall for local autonomy if the local plans and programmes are not backed by politics on higher levels, for instance if different parties are governing the local and the national level (Naples, a1, 52). The relation to financial autonomy will be discussed in detail at the end of this section.

Other obstructions to local decision autonomy can be found in strategy and planning issues as well as in the resource system itself. The planning process is usually embedded in a legal framework that can restrict autonomous decision-making. Especially Greece and Italy refer to preservation laws to safeguard historical buildings. This prohibits the altering of existing buildings and hinders the construction of new buildings (Thessaloniki, a1, 79–80). Also, a lack of decisive national planning for sustainability and clear-cut programmes and strategies have a negative impact on local-level autonomy since no clearly derived goals are available and local action appears contextless or is not initiated at all (Milan, a1, 43). The planning policies and strategies for a socio-ecological transition need to remain on the local level though, since the administration and municipality in cooperation with local actors are best aware where problems occur and what actions are best suited to solve them (Leeds, a1, 89). With regard to influences and special features of the resource system, decision-making autonomy is limited, too. This results from the spatial dimension of certain resource systems. Energy can easily surpass urban areas of influence (Rome, a2, 61). Another effect on autonomy is the spatial constitution of the urban area. It has already been stated above that spatial attributes delimit local possibilities (for example it is not possible to cover an entire city with solar collectors). This leads to the problem that local decision autonomy might not have enough space to decide upon (Bilbao, a2, 116). Too large an area in a municipality is not productive, either. The far-reaching territory suffers from a dispersion of responsibility, since the municipality cannot cover the whole territory (Thessaloniki, a1, 79–80). Additionally, the energy resource system is a field that focuses on interventions on the individual level, like consumption behaviour, and awareness (Strasbourg, a2, 99–102). However, possible actions only involve incentivising individual sustainable behaviour or the banning of unsustainable products like light bulbs. A direct influence on energy-efficient behaviour or consumption exceeds the possibilities of local or national governments – happily.

Nonetheless, an actor states that more and more cities are successfully engaging themselves in sustainability issues on their own, decoupled from national politics (Birmingham, a2, 93). However, this cannot mean that urban areas need to be left alone to tend to themselves. On the one hand, it is crucial for local governments to influence respective frameworks; on the other, national governments depend on the information and inputs coming from the local level to design their funding and support programmes. Structural and supportive embeddedness are important key factors to guarantee cities become "masters of their own destiny" (Birmingham, a1, 72). This last point stresses financial autonomy for the cities. In particular, tax revenues and the like should remain in the cities and be reinvested locally (Birmingham, a1, 72; Timisoara, a1, 51).

Overall, the topics of local decision autonomy and financial autonomy are closely connected. Decisions need to be backed financially in order to translate them into concrete action or to support further engagement (Timisoara, a1, 101). A broad selection of interviewees assesses the state of financial autonomy negatively. This also matches the quantitative analysis (cf. Figure 4-13). Especially Eastern and Southern Europe suffer from insufficient financial means to address energy issues. Budget assurance concepts restrict autonomous decisions on finances when municipalities are in debt (Dortmund, a2, 87). This is comparable to the field of austerity politics on a national scale, which has an impact on the local level as well. Broadly, the absence of financial autonomy directly influences the potential to act and decide independently (Milan, a2, 81; Potsdam, a2, 162). Further, the dependence on other private actors as partners for financing undertakings bears too much complexity (Barcelona, a2, 73). Financial autonomy has to be secured by funding programmes from the national level (Naples, a1, 50). This underlines an aspect of autonomy that concerns financial sustainability and self-sufficiency in relation to financial autonomy: The interviewee does not necessarily connect one with another – more particularly, a general availability of financial resources is sought whereas the sources are not important. In terms of energy and financial autonomy, city-owned energy utility providers

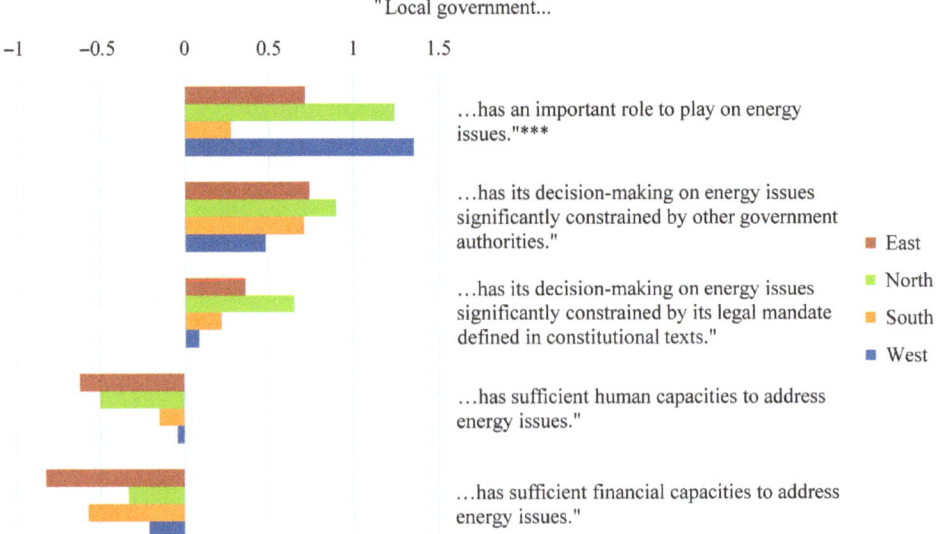

Figure 4-13 Local decision-making autonomy for different regions (scaled from −2: strongly disagree to +2: strongly agree)

are helpful. Energy markets play a particular role in generating revenue. Thus, subsidies and other distorting actions lead to decreased market prices and are potentially threatening much more expensive renewable energies (Umea, a1, 110). Strasbourg, for example, sold its energy supplier and traded parts of its financial independence to a national corporation (Strasbourg, a1, 80). To allow the municipality in Leeds to initiate plans, solid business cases are mandatory. Self-sustaining economic activity that relieves the city administration from overhead financial resource use is mandatory (Leeds, a2, 65).

The necessity for financial resources is clearly visible. Funding is required, not only for financial autonomy and thus for extending possibilities to realise local decision autonomy, but also for general investments and procurement activities. This is also shown in the interviews above: Financial resources could always be increased. In relation to self-determined decision-making, financial backing is a central requirement. The interviewed actors state that several policies enforce national and/or local-level government institutions to rigid saving and budget discipline and endanger this special relation. The impact of these measures on socio-ecological transition has to be seen in the future. Until now, only a few direct effects are noticeable and visible, but the full scale might only be recognisable after a specific timespan.

4.5 Discussion of the findings

The empirical inquiry shows interesting details of socio-ecological transitions in the 40 selected cities. The research questions that guided the field research produced a kaleidoscopic picture of distinct sets of institutions.

Starting with the state of transition, this chapter shows the different local features of the cities but also the underlying frames of thought visible in definitions of sustainability.

Within the European Union, a cohesive image of sustainability transitions exists, referring to a three-pillar model and to common strategies like Agenda 21. Some actors extend this model by a fourth pillar, which indicates the necessity to transform governance structures as well. Sustainability in governmental administration and governance structures displays itself in its reoccurring challenges. The transition processes face several distinct problems that show that a socio-ecological transition must be seen and treated holistically. Moreover, it has to take into account social, economic, legal, governmental, and societal problems and societal needs (Fjalar J. de Haan et al. 2014).

Concerning the main research question about self-organising capabilities, the inquiry covers the dynamics of civil society and the role of self-responsibility. This is best shown by the increasing demand to individually participate in the transition process and adopt sustainable behaviours and awareness. A complex and multifaceted process like a socio-ecological transition can be realised neither solely by individual citizens nor by a national or local government alone. The interviews indicate that increased individual awareness is essential to change consumption patterns and usage behaviour of energy – and that this is the foremost leverage for political and administrative action. Central is the relevance of the individual, although the questionnaires indicated that especially on local energy mixes, citizens only have little influence. Expanding education is a goal set to raise awareness among the citizens and change their behaviour accordingly. Political and administrative actors judged this form as *self-organisation*. The misunderstanding is clear, since this does not refer to a bottom-up organisation of civil society. The nucleus of transition remains aggregated individual actions. Moreover, the interviewees refer primarily to participation, which is a misinterpretation of self-organisation. Self-organisation would require the establishment of alternative political processes *next to existing ones* that are formed by citizens to foster an individualised but still collective form of energy transition. Such parallel structures do not exist in any surveyed city.

Especially actors from the United Kingdom state that, in terms of decision autonomy, some cities are initiating their own sustainability transitions. It is striking that the individualised responsibility – for individuals and cities – is clearly observable in nations where liberal welfare state regimes are in place. Individuals are addressed as subjects, responsible for their own well-being and for the well-being of the socio-ecological 'space' they live in. This approach shows itself in the emphasis of education, private energy efficiency and so on (Birmingham, a1, 40). The key factors are frameworks that facilitate liberty to act and decide in a wide variety of topics and give responsibility to the individual. Against rigid sets of rules, diffuse activation of sustainable behaviour and action is imposed. The concept relies on aspects of economic self-sustainability, which in turn means that a central aspect to organise action relates to market logic with supply-and-demand mechanisms, like an invisible hand that guides the individual and benefits all. However, this approach can hinder the idea of bottom-up processes that rely on the ideas of the community. There is an inherent opposition of two different political philosophies.

Local actors advance holistic socio-ecological transitions, which must involve a variety of resource systems, strategies for sustainability, and finally different and heterogeneous actors in the transformation process. It is important for the research to assess the involved actors and to ask for the representation of local stakeholders. This also involves the cooperation of local actors and special challenges that emerge in interactions. Almost every city had a variety of its actors taking part in the energy transition but not always with equal rights and will to participate. Very interesting is the role of local universities and scientific institutes – and the sciences in general – that provide knowledge and technical assistance or uphold a counter-discourse for sustainability issues (Harald Rohracher 2008; Marko Joas et al. 2013). The discourses that are brought forward in the process of any transition need to be analysed to understand the mechanisms of knowledge production and distribution in the field (Philipp Späth and Harald Rohracher 2010). Especially, the creations of networks were efficient actions to generate a drive for sustainable movements – and more broadly to exchange experiences with other cities. Conflicts in cooperation are common, and the interviews showed that especially conflicting aims are an issue. Local transitions faced manifold factors that influence socio-ecological transitions. They can be differentiated into political, administrative, structural, and legal factors. The influences of politics and administrations are quite clear and include different levels of governance, from the local to the European level. Particularly interesting are structural effects on the transition. Socio-structural features and traits of the cities influence their performances as well as global aspects like economic crises.

Regarding perceived problems on an institutional level, the inquiry indicates that funding is a fundamental issue. This is not surprising, since financial means are the first bottleneck when initiating transition projects. The topic appears together with a general urge to simplify bureaucratic procedures and make administrative processes more accessible on the European level. The relevance of local autonomy is visible, especially from national governments, while on behalf of legal frameworks European directives indicate increased leadership. The influence of national legislation should be more coherent and/or reduced, and at the same time, the leadership of EU directives should be increased. This includes more local autonomy, and the European Union should draw the constituting rule framework for it. This would strengthen local decision autonomy to an extent. Nonetheless, differing interests of other local actors affect this autonomy and limit it. Autonomy is always constrained to certain degrees, since local interests are diverse and contradicting. A more direct influence on decision-making autonomy is the possibility to enact financial resources. Cities that are suffering from debts are less able to make decisions accordingly. This points back to funding issues and involves the European Union to assist with funding programmes and national states with a more generous distribution of financial resources. Especially in the United Kingdom, actors request greater shares of revenue generated by the city to reward economic success.

However, there exists a severe imbalance between successful and challenged cities – and on a greater scale also countries. The problems can be seen in structurally weak countries like Greece, which suffers from a variety of problems. Especially rigid austerity politics, the restructuring of administration, and the vast pauperisation of the population led to distinct phenomena. CO_2 emissions from cars were reduced due to a decrease in usage that mainly resulted from high fuel prices – but these CO_2 reductions were entirely eradicated by the development of alternative heating. By burning crude oil in old stoves, residuals and emissions were set free – and illegal clearing of woodlands around several cities produced CO_2 emissions and destroyed green spaces that compensated for pollution (Thessaloniki, a2, 52; Daniel M. Knight 2014). The relations are very complex, and this example indicates that a healthy ecosystem also needs a healthy socio-economy. This aspect is not always given in cities transforming from industrial to postindustrial structures.

Further, the forms of cities need to be scrutinised. The city as a social institution from the nineteenth century developed itself into its recent form from the beginning of industrialisation, the beginning of modernity. Cities – as institutions – never rest, are changing, and transform more or less rapidly, according to many different aspects. The process of urbanisation is continuing with no foreseeable end, thus cities and urban areas have to be shaped accordingly to allow and foster a socio-ecological transition. This is especially urgent for the energy system since cities have the highest energy density, correlating with population, jobs, industry, and other aspects of societal life. These cannot be prescribed developments, derived by social engineering. They instead need to be rooted in a broader basis. The possibilities of self-organisation in socio-ecological transition and in sustainable reforming cities cannot be underestimated. However, the central conflict lies between an ingrained system of political representation and a bottom-up system of public initiative and active civil society. Solving this contradiction is a priority to enable a democratic and holistic transition.

To draw the conclusion for self-organising capabilities, a central problem revolves around the misunderstanding of participation and self-organisation – at least in the interpretation of central political and administrative actors. The role of the European Union could be to strengthen the possibilities for citizens to participate in (transparent) institutional processes and beyond that to initiate their own independent programmes or cooperations on the local level. These need structural coupling to funding channels and programmes. This also implies that the two modes of democratic interventions of the citizens need to be thoroughly defined and distinguished: participation and self-organisation. Nonetheless, the central problem of an active, informed, and political public sphere remains. The lack of such a public sphere leads to an absence of critical opposition against institutional structures. In conflicts between a healthy public sphere on the one hand and governmental representation on the other lies the key to productive public discourse – and to changes necessary for a successful socio-ecological transition. This refers to conflicts as driving forces behind models of social innovations. The interviews and the questionnaires have shown that self-organising capabilities need to meet essential aspects. First, awareness about the resource system, the need for a transition, the process, and so on are crucial. Second, the possibility to meet and engage in discussion and to mobilise others is needed. Third, institutional channels to communicate opinions and local decisions to politics and administration are required. These points all need the specific constitution of a public sphere. The shifting and transformation of this public sphere has been extensively discussed in sociology and political sciences (cf. Richard Sennett 1976; Habermas 1989; Richard Sennett 1992). The depoliticisation of the public sphere and the expansion of the private sphere into public life is a broad diagnosis that takes into account many different aspects from the individualisation of responsibilities to the emerging faces of consumerism and the new roles of media. The arguments consolidate movements of individualisation, a profanation of public discourse, a rapidly developing political focus that addresses individual self-responsibility, and a depoliticisation of the masses by political beliefs that are 'without any alternatives' in an era of "post-democracy" (Colin Crouch 2004).

An alternative development can be seen in the topic of green spaces (cf. section 5.5) and more generally in the emerging discussion about participation in and self-organisation of urban spaces (Harvey 2008, 2012). The targeted democratisation process as a 'Right to the City', of living in and shaping cities, might yield a potential for a 'holistic' approach to sustainable cities that covers political, social, economic, and ecological topics. In the words of Jürgen Habermas, the shift from 'culture-debating' to 'culture-consuming' (Habermas 1989, 159–67) has to be reversed again to enable a public decision process, a discourse about living together – and about alternatives. For energy, this can mean completely different approaches to urban energy production and consumption. Therefore, different modes of organising energy as a common good need to be assessed, for example in the sense of an 'energy democracy': "de-centralisation and independence from corporations, distribution grid use rights and control over municipal energy suppliers, moderated forms of reconciliation of interests, and union co-participation" (Conrad Kunze and Sören Becker 2014, 8). Moreover, 'governing the commons' (Ostrom 1990) implicitly refers to alternative modes of organising: 'organising in common', 'organising for the common', and 'organising of the common', which refer to the act of 'commoning', what actually "is done in common" (Valérie Fournier 2013, 448). Self-organisation of a resource system exceeds the political dimension, it inherently includes a broader approach to production, consumption, as well as social organisation – all of which has to be reflected.

Notes

1 Low-emission affinity of nuclear energy is – along with nuclear energy in general – an issue of dispute. It is imperative that arguments are also considered in the context that generated them, since a certain proportion of studies is conducted on behalf of nuclear energy corporations and interest groups; for a summary of several studies, cf. Nuclear Energy Institute (n. a.).
2 The covenant is a voluntary programme that aims at increasing energy efficiency and the use of renewable energies in the participating cities. Also by commission, it has sought to exceed the CO2 reduction goals set by the European Union. Cf. The Covenant of Mayors (2015).
3 These goals are derived from a 'strategy for smart, sustainable and inclusive growth' of the European Commission (2010): reducing greenhouse gas emissions (like CO2) by 20 per cent in relation to the levels of 1990, increasing the proportion of renewable energies to 20 per cent, and increasing energy efficiency by 20 per cent.
4 It is important to keep in mind that nearly all the following statements on citizens' participation were gained from political or administrative actors. Thus, they show *their* opinion that follows the *logic of their field*. Therefore, statements have to be assessed carefully: Representatives of energy cooperation and the like might have different stories to tell.
5 Generally, France could be added to this group, since energy policies are in the hands of a single national corporation, Électricité de France (EDF). However, EDF does not have a monopoly on electricity production. It is interesting that, in these statements, Lugano and St. Gallen differ. At least on a general position on citizens' participation, the statements do not diverge, except on energy policies, which is a cantonal responsibility.
6 Especially in France, the Grandes Écoles, elite universities, which train the "Grand Corps" (Paris, a3, 59), are a central part of creating influential expertise. Graduates like engineers fill important positions and are thus able to make important decisions on the resource system and energy topics (e.g. Rennes, a1, 103; Strasbourg, a1, 94).
7 The term 'best practice' is problematic. Since it implies a normative approach to sustainable transitions that is believed to be generalisable for other cities, it neglects the uniqueness of a city. It implies that 'one size fits all' is a valid approach to individual and unique urban systems.
8 Potsdam-Institut für Klimaforschung – Potsdam Institute for Climate Impact Research.
9 Eidgenössische Materialprüfungs- und Forschungsanstalt – Swiss Federal Institute for Material Testing and Research.
10 Organisation theory has made several approaches to this issue. Following Walter W. Powell (1990), networks are a growing alternative to 'classical' forms of organisation – in the sense of business units. This is extendable to some degree to other forms of social cooperation as well.

Chapter 5

Socio-ecological transitions in the green spaces resource system

Judith Schicklinski

5.1 The role of the green spaces resource system in sustainability transition

This chapter describes, analyses, and discusses the role of green spaces in the socio-ecological transition of European cities. In the European Union, land use changes are mostly and increasingly marked by land consumption, due to ongoing urbanisation with concomitant urban sprawl leading to a decreasing density of cities (Stefan Bringezu et al. 2014, 50). Biodiversity, threatened by the introduction of invasive species and the "replacement of natural areas by artificial green areas" (European Environment Agency 2012, 32), is additionally endangered by this development (Bringezu et al. 2014, 50). Another problem linked to the process of structural change is soil degradation and contamination on abandoned brownfield sites (European Commission 2011c, 15).

It is the European Commission's aim, as expressed in its "Roadmap to a Resource Efficient Europe" section of the Europe 2020 Strategy, that its policies consider their consequences on land use in order to prevent net land take by 2050 (European Commission 2011c, 15). To reach the goal of no additional land consumption by 2050, land take has to be reduced "to an average of 800 km² per year in the period 2000–2020" (European Commission 2011c, 15). Measures to reach this goal include favouring concentrated development and redevelopment of urban areas, minimising soil sealing, ensuring sufficient and connected green spaces, and avoiding invasive alien species spread (European Commission 2011c, 24). However, achieving the aforementioned goals is complicated by the fact that the finite and shrinking resource of land is subject to competing pressures. Specifically across European cities, the use of green space is highly controversial and is torn between diverging interests, yielding high conflict potential.

Nevertheless, achieving sustainable land use management is crucial for a socio-ecological transition in Europe. The role and governance of the resource system of green spaces in European cities play an important part in this process due to increasing urbanisation and the multiple functions urban green spaces provide. They offer various social, economic, and ecological benefits that are not distinct but mutually influence each other.

By their mitigation and adaptation capacities, urban green spaces play an important role in building climate-resilient cities (e.g. in "post-disaster" cities; Yuki Kato, Catarina Passidomo, and Daina Harvey 2014). In cities, climate change impacts are exacerbated by the urban heat island effect,[1] making them especially vulnerable. As a counterweight, green spaces limit the accumulation of heat in concrete surfaces (European Environment Agency 2012, 6, 10, 31). The high proportion of imperviously sealed ground increases the risk of urban drainage flooding because extreme amounts of rainwater cannot drain into the ground (European Environment Agency 2012, 6, 41; also cf. chapter 6). Here, green spaces' mitigating capacity for absorbing rainwater, attenuating surface water run-off, and fostering groundwater infiltration is greatly needed. In times of water scarcity and droughts, green spaces' "capacity of storing water" (European Environment Agency 2012, 60) is essential. They prevent soil erosion and significantly ameliorate the urban climate by improving air quality by their capacity to filter the air. They are capable of sequestrating carbon, absorbing air pollutants, releasing oxygen, and regulating air humidity. This is especially important in times of rising average temperatures, which increase the probability of air quality problems (European Environment Agency 2012, 29–31). Green spaces also contribute to biodiversity conservation by providing habitats for plant and animal species (Tüzin Baycan-Levent, Ron Vreeker, and Peter Nijkamp 2009, 195), even more so if urban green spaces are interconnected, providing the "possibility of species migration" (European Commission 2011c, 7).

Numerous values can be subsumed under social benefits. Green spaces improve the quality of life of city dwellers inter alia by their high recreational value (Baycan-Levent, Vreeker, and Nijkamp 2009, 195). By providing space for social interaction taking place outside in nature, they foster social and environmental practical learning across generations and cultures. They provide opportunities for informal hands-on learning, for experimenting with rule making, and coping with conflicts and group dynamics. Thus, they also constitute a counterweight to the trend of virtual communication.

Urban green spaces can be productive also in economic terms. By producing urban timber, fruits, compost but also increasingly vegetables originating from urban agriculture, they can enhance the attractiveness of city districts by creating new employment opportunities (Baycan-Levent, Vreeker, and Nijkamp 2009, 196).

The analysed qualitative data, 1 to 4 interviews per city, stems from 29 cities covering all regions and participating countries (Aalborg, Bilbao, Copenhagen, Cracow, Dortmund, Gothenburg, Glasgow, Innsbruck, Istanbul, Jihlava, Larissa, Leeds, Linz, Lodz, Lublin, Lugano, Madrid, Milan, Naples, Paris, Potsdam, Rome, Saarbrücken, Sibiu, St. Gallen, Strasbourg, Thessaloniki, Timisoara, and Umea). Six interviews from political, 1 from administrative, 21 from business, and 27 from civil society actor(s) were obtained. This data is supplemented by 40 case study reports, 1 per city, written by the respective field researcher with a section on the characteristics of the resource system of green spaces. The analysed quantitative data stems from 167 questionnaires (41 administration, 63 business, and 63 civil society) including the interviewed actors (cf. chapter 2).

5.2 Self-organisation capabilities and sustainability transitions

This section provides insight into two major components of socio-ecological transitions. The first subsection describes the observed sustainability transition, while the second one examines existing self-organisation capabilities.

5.2.1 Socio-ecological transitions

The collected quantitative and qualitative data yields insights into the actors' understanding of the sustainability concept into their estimation of the state of the socio-ecological transition in general as well as into the status of the green spaces resource system in particular. Additionally, their perceived transition urgency, experienced and expected challenges as well as existing conflicts are inquired into.

As with the resource systems energy and water, when asked to define sustainability, most frequently and independently of the sector, interviewees explicitly or implicitly refer to the "three pillars" (Istanbul, a1, 9–11; Linz, a3, 11; Sibiu, a4, 19–20; Umea, a3, 11) (cf. chapters 3 and 6). Some actors, however, also explicitly refer to green spaces. They define sustainability as the necessity to preserve them, to consider the sustainability aspect in investments made in public green spaces (Timisoara, a3, 19 and a4, 49–61). It is the necessity to find innovative ways of "sustainable maintenance . . . to maintain them without using many resources" (Madrid, a3, 16) in times of very restricted local budgets for green spaces, for example by choosing plants needing less care and water.

The concept is considered to be a very ambitious one (Bilbao, a4, 19), especially due to its abstractness and wide scope (Glasgow, a3, 14; Gothenburg, a3, 11; Timisoara, a4, 21), which make it extremely difficult to define (Leeds, a3, 30–31, 120; Timisoara, a4, 21). Actors also note an increased misuse of the term, having become a catchphrase (Cracow, a3, 14; Glasgow a3, 13–14; Sibiu, a4, 21; Strasbourg, a4, 16). Some actors stress that there cannot be one overall definition but that locally varying ones are needed according to each region's specific challenges (Cracow, a3, 14, 26; Larissa, a3, 17).

Regarding the status of the local resource system, in the majority of cities of all regions, a good to very good *availability* of green spaces is reported. However, the quantity of most types of green spaces is higher in the North and West than in the South and East of Europe. In some cities in the East, West, and South, availability is rated as not good to very bad. Patterns are very diverse. Whereas availability in the city centre can be good – there are for example well-maintained parks – the outer districts might be overlooked (Naples, a4, 46–47), up to the situation that almost no green spaces exist at all. The inner city can also be very dense with large sealed surfaces (Lugano, a3, 107–109 and a4, 49–56; Paris, a3, 29; Strasbourg, a4, 76–87), not providing any ecological corridors (Timisoara, a4, 30, 98–100). The reason for the bad availability is without exception building and infrastructure development.

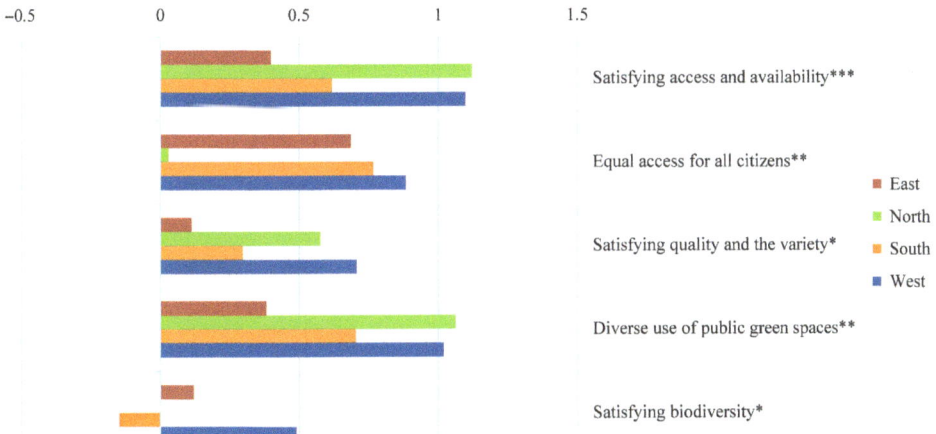

Figure 5-1 Regional differences in assessing the status of green spaces (scaled from −2: strong disagreement to +2: strong agreement)

In several cities in the East, West, and South, there is very good to good *accessibility* (Larissa, a4, 59; Madrid, a4, 43–50; St. Gallen, a4, 9; Timisoara, a4,108, supporting Figure 5-1), showing the low rate of equal access for all citizens in the North. Concerning the *diversity* of green spaces, public parks and lawns are most common, followed by sport facilities and forests. Green roofs hardly exist. Whereas green spaces are very often used for recreational activities and as a community gathering place, they are still far less often deployed for growing food, illustrating that this is still a relatively recent phenomenon in European cities (cf. Barthel, Parker, and Ernstson 2013).

A good *quality* linked to a high maintenance level is reported from several cities in all regions (Larissa, a4, 54–55, 58–59; Leeds, a4, 79–88; Lodz, a3, 62–72; Saarbrücken, a3, 31–36). The same holds true for *(bio)diversity* (Lublin, a1, 17; Madrid, a4, 54–55; Potsdam, a3, 135–140; Umea, a3, 59). Respondents from the majority of cities report that biodiversity is threatened by the continuing decrease of green spaces due to construction development, with Figure 5-1 revealing the lowest level of biodiversity in the South. A varying quality is reported from a smaller number of cities in all regions. It varies according to the district (Naples, a3, 33; Strasbourg, a4, 76); the type of green space (Aalborg, a4, 60; Lodz, a4, 37–38); or their size – for example it is good in bigger parks but moderate in smaller ones (Cracow, a4, 40). Cities also report insufficient quality of green spaces, mostly due to insufficient maintenance. This mainly stems from lacking financial resources, which sometimes limit even basic maintenance. With the privatisation of maintenance services and due to the critical financial situation, most often the lowest bidder is selected, leading to a significant decrease in quality (Thessaloniki, a3, 49–53). Soil pollution due to former industrial activities or (illegal) dumping activities without immediate subsequent soil reclamation is named in a handful of cities (Milan, a3, 27, 55; Naples, a4, 25–26; Sibiu, a2, 122).

Altogether, Figure 5-1 shows that three out of five subcategories on the status of green spaces are rated lowest in the East while the same proportion is rated highest in the North. However, a generally better situation in the North cannot be derived from the qualitative data.

Looking into the future, the actors' statements are sometimes contradicting, depending on which sector they belong to. For example, the political actor claims that the percentage of green spaces is slowly increasing (Cracow, a1, 38), while the business actor admits that urban sprawl will create immense costs since infrastructure will have to be built and maintained (Cracow, a3, 23–25). Civil society fears the diminishing of green spaces due to densification and urban sprawl, calling it "developers' aggressiveness" (Cracow, a4, 40). Green spaces are threatened if they have a low status in municipal planning, which can result in their constant reduction for construction development, leading to an acute overuse of the remaining ones (Istanbul, a4, 43–46). Dependencies across resource systems become apparent for example where forests near the city were damaged for the construction of water lines. This was done because the city cannot provide drinking water from its own area for its growing population any more (Istanbul, a4, 81–84).

Apart from being specifically questioned on the state of the local resource system, actors were interviewed on their general estimation of the local state of the socio-ecological transition. Positive and negative estimations are given in all regions. Positively, *structural change* can be used to increase the level of sustainability, thus increasing the amount of green spaces. This visibly improves quality of life and the cityscape (Bilbao, a3, 20, 38 and a4, 21; Linz, a3, 103, 109). A *common understanding* of sustainability transition for green spaces is evolving across sectors in several cities. This "new way of thinking city" (Copenhagen, a4, 15) includes developing *joint, transdisciplinary strategies* as well as *institutional changes*, such as setting up a sustainability department. Roots for this are a *change of awareness and attitude*. In a Swedish city, the community commenced with this in the 1990s already. This evolved into a large movement leading to the ongoing vivid implementation phase involving political and technical solutions as well as *constructive conflicts* (Gothenburg, a4, 21–23).

However, other actors admit that the socio-ecological transition is still in its infancy. Several reasons are invoked for this. Actors state a lack of a clear joint vision and of a long-term strategy combined with long-expired urban plans (Timisoara, a4, 23), a persisting conservative attitude in the administration (Lublin, a4, 16), the complexity of city governance as such (Leeds, a3, 20–23) as well as insufficient local autonomy (Lugano, a3, 14).

Further actors give an even more negative estimation up to denying the existence of any transition. Reasons range from not providing common public space for discussions (Strasbourg, a4, 126) and the *lack of financial resources* (Milan, a4, 15–18) to continuously sticking to the logic of ever-increasing population. In addition, *economic growth* manifesting itself in ongoing construction and consumption leads to soil sealing (Istanbul, a4, 12), by paving instead of extending green spaces (Strasbourg, a4, 20–25).

The perceived transition urgency can be derived from named *goals* as well as from the time horizon indicated. Concerning goals specifically related to green spaces, the quantitative data reveals that actors across cities and sectors consider 'avoiding land use change – turning green spaces into constructed land', 'improving the ecological quality and biodiversity of available public green spaces', 'enlarging their size and number', 'increasing the demand for them', 'adapting to climate change', 'avoiding their misuse by human activities', and 'improving the legal framework for green spaces' as important. The significance of almost all named objectives is rated higher in the South and East than in the North and West, which could point to backlogged demand in the first two regions.

In the interviews, few goals directly relating to green spaces were named but rather general environmental, social, and economic ones. The majority of actors from all sectors and regions believe that environmental, social, and economic goals must be balanced against each other with none being more important than the other (Glasgow, a3, 12–14; Paris, a3, 14; Sibiu, a2, 144 and a4, 200). "[W]ithout money nothing can be done, without the environment no money can be generated, without people it is not working" (Gothenburg, a4, 12–13).

Yet, for some – mostly civil society – actors, the economic aspects should not be on the same level as the environmental and the social ones (Istanbul, a4, 92–95; Strasbourg, a4, 17–18; Umea, a3, 109–112). These respondents stress that the environmental aspect, "a functioning ecosystem" (Umea, a3, 31), is crucial, since it is the *basis* of everything, including of the economy. In this regard, the "no net loss" (Umea, a3, 72, 131–132) policy is recommended. This means not to lose even more nature, species, and ecosystem services, trying to keep what is left. Otherwise, compensation areas need to be created. Just as the whole of human society has to be managed within the global biosphere, the same is true for the local level. Each municipality, each community "has to manage its impact within its own co-system" (Leeds, a4, 127).

The economy "only makes sense in a constituted society with its rules. The economy is part of society's creation but is not a tangible, vital element like social and environmental issues" (Strasbourg, a4, 18). Solving social problems is considered of utmost importance for the socio-ecological transition: "Only if the basic, short-term needs are met can one start thinking about sustainability, long-term environmental issues, and the common good" (Gothenburg, a3, 106–109, 132–133). Well-being is defined as increasing the citizens' quality of life by combining "economic prosperity with the creation of a sustainable environment offering quality of life and social cohesion" (Larissa, a3, 22), while respecting the environment in the short and long run (Glasgow a3, 14 and a4, 116; Larissa, a4, 25; Madrid, a4, 102; Thessaloniki, a4, 14, 79–80). Bringing nature back into the city by preserving and expanding green spaces is a well-being element, especially important for city dwellers who cannot afford to leave the city for holidays (Paris, a3, 56–57).

The named economic sustainability goals disclose contradicting opinions, which can be clustered into two strands. The first group of actors, mainly from the business sector, rely on *economic growth* as the overarching goal that is the basis for and facilitates the implementation of social and ecological sustainability goals by providing jobs and wealth (Cracow, a3, 34; Innsbruck, a3, 142–43; Potsdam, a3, 173–174). Following this logic, sustainability must be financially affordable for producers and consumers. Making profit remains the core goal. A variation in this logic is also brought up, that "sustainability has almost become a commodity" (Copenhagen, a2, 21). Sustainable commodities have already become cheaper, creating financial, economic, and political interests. It is suggested to end the prevailing of economic over social and environmental aspects "by introducing a governance mechanism taking into account and making visible social and environmental externalities" (Copenhagen, a2, 107–109).

In contrast, the second group of actors, coming mainly from civil society, argues for a *post-growth logic*, claiming that "[t]he economic system based on growth has to be drastically rethought to become sustainable" (Linz, a4, 113–114). This can be done by relying on and promoting local human, economic, and cultural assets (Naples, a3, 77–80, 85–86). Concrete actions include suggesting the use of local resource cycles (Potsdam, a4, 17) and preferring the use of local knowledge instead of foreign experts. This means promoting local businesses instead of attracting big foreign investors at all costs with public grants but minimal obligations (Sibiu, a3, 130–133), since these investors often generate social and ecological externalities locally, such as pollution, only skimming off profits before moving to an even cheaper location after a few years (Sibiu, a3, 131–132).

Having only been "a topic of environmentalists" (Bilbao, a3, 21–25) some decades ago, the mainstreaming of sustainability has partly been achieved. Sustainability has become an integral section of business plans, showing that this even saves costs in the long run (Innsbruck, a3, 42–43; Linz, a3, 17–19), or where it has been mainstreamed into all city policy fields (Copenhagen, a2, 18–21). Goals must be seen in small actions, reached step by step, starting from the bottom (Milan, a3, 71) since the 'crisis' does not allow for "big steps" (Thessaloniki, a4, 77–78).

The majority of actors expect a long time horizon to realise the goals. This is due to the difficulty of changing mentality and habits (Aalborg, a4, 14–16; Umea, a3, 101–108) and of reaching financial feasibility (Aalborg, a4, 14–16). Further reasons are "the slowness of the political decision processes" (Saarbrücken, a4, 77–80) and the dependency of political decisions bound to elections and thus to short-term goals. Stated time spans range from up to 5 (Linz, a4, 99–100; Madrid, a3, 78–79; Potsdam, a4, 196–199; Rome, a1, 69–70) to 20 years (Lugano, a3, 146–149), depending on the type of goal to be reached, with awareness-raising considered one of the most quickly attainable. Patience is needed altogether though, making it a "generational question" (Istanbul, a1, 78–79; Saarbrücken, a4, 77) and emphasising the transition's process character. It is perceived as a slow but steady, constant ongoing process, happening in small steps with a long-term perspective, without ever reaching a stationary system (Gothenburg, a3, 9–11 and a4, 11–13; Istanbul, a1, 9; Madrid, a4, 21; Sibiu, a2, 144 and a3, 23). With regard to the urgency of the transition, this could be a disappointing finding. Yet a longer time horizon might in the end lead to a higher degree of sustainability than fast-track actions, due to the fact that longer timeframes seem to have a positive impact on developing trust between actors and related positive socio-ecological transition outcomes (Poteete, Janssen, and Ostrom 2010, 229).

In trying to reach socio-ecological transition goals, challenges appear of which conflicts are part. In order to overcome them, they need to be clearly identified and grouped as a first step. Most experienced and expected challenges brought up can be classified as economic, political, or mental ones. A minor group belongs to social and environmental ones.

Amongst economic challenges, a *tight local budget* for green spaces is most often named in all regions (Glasgow, a4, 49–51; Madrid, a3, 77; Sibiu, a3, 35–37). This forces actors to find ways of decreasing costs and of finding new funding sources to keep up maintenance. In all regions but the North, *construction development pressure* is seen as a danger to existing green spaces. Partly resulting from a tight local budget, this pressure sometimes takes the form of excessive building speculation, which reduces housing space for real needs and provokes urban sprawl (Naples, a4, 26; Lodz, a4, 23; Lugano, a4, 27; Timisoara, a4, 52–53).

Political challenges include legal and institutional ones and are equally brought up in all regions. They are quite diverse and sometimes opposed. Whereas a low *turnover rate*, meaning politicians staying in power very long, can hinder the transition (Paris, a4, 52), a high turnover rate, with politicians changing "too fast to establish a constructive relationship between civil society and politics" (Glasgow, a4, 44–45), can be equally problematic. Bad *city management* can lead to de facto inability in coping with numerous challenges in urban planning, not following any sustainability vision (Istanbul, a4, 12; Milan, a4, 25).

Actors pointed out the lack of goals, strategies, and effective legal frameworks. The latter either means that regional and state laws do not prevent the consumption of the territory (Milan, a3, 27, 39) or that state and local laws do not leave manoeuvring room for local actors due to the local level having the least power (Istanbul, a1, 61). Furthermore, *lobbying against sustainability* is mentioned, keeping it "socially accepted to be unsustainable" (Aalborg, a4, 114). This makes it difficult to change public opinion, also because the "deniers" (Aalborg, a4, 114) misuse science to draw a less alarming picture. Still, public opinion should still be changed by introducing "small doable things" (Aalborg, a4, 114). *Institutional* challenges emerge in all regions. An overly large administration makes cross-sector communication between departments difficult (Strasbourg, a4, 52). Complicated budgetary procedures increase bureaucracy, since it is often unclear to civil society actors which department deals with what issue (Glasgow, a4, 44–48). Administration is often perceived as not proactive but as hindering (Madrid, a4, 70).

Mental models are considered a challenge in all sectors and regions. It is deplored that urban dwellers "have lost their relationship with nature" (Paris, a3, 44–49) and that many politicians are not aware of the necessity of education to understand the need for the socio-ecological transition (Paris, a3, 51–53). Apart from that, some cities report a conservative mentality in the administration: "[I]t can't be done. . . . The developer knows better what's good for people" (Lublin, a4, 24).

Interestingly, only a few environmental and social challenges are named, even fewer directly relating to green spaces. Most environmental challenges raised refer to air pollution

(Cracow, a2, 15 and a4, 19–21; Timisoara, a3, 23–25 and a4, 74). The problem of invasive species is only mentioned once (Bilbao, a4, 59). Although the quantitative research reveals that the majority of respondents assess climate change as an important aspect for defining a future local sustainability strategy, climate change does not seem to be perceived as a big threat. Only a few actors explicitly raise it as a challenge. They warn for example that heat stress will become a major social challenge, also due to the fact of an ever-ageing population in Europe for which cities will have to find strategies to cope with (Saarbrücken, a3, 20–23).

The reduction of green spaces due to infrastructure and building development, often linked to privatisation, has generated conflicts between urban stakeholders with highly diverging interests and a different understanding of the value of green space (e.g. Cracow, a1, 70–75; Istanbul, a4, 47–48; Lublin, a1, 22–23; Milan, a3, 54–55). This often leads to diametrical visions for city development. Conflicts are a challenge on the one hand and part of the problem-solving process on the other, if stakeholders have institutionalised conflict management tools. Such tools seem to be widely missing, since only a minority of actors consider conflicts as a constructive component of the sustainability discourse driving forward the socio-ecological transition.

Named conflicts can be clustered into four different types:

First, they emerge due to different ideas on the *use of existing green spaces*. These can be intergenerational conflicts (Strasbourg, a4, 88); conflicts about different forms of usage (Aalborg, a4, 73–75), for example between dog owners and non-dog owners (Milan, a3, 54–55; Saarbrücken, a4, 52–53); or between cyclists and pedestrians (Glasgow, a4, 23–28; Madrid, a3, 48–49). Conflict can also emerge on the conversion of use, for example when urban gardening activities are started on public green spaces (Innsbruck, a3, 77; Strasbourg, a4, 92), or around the usage for recreational activities and nature protection (Copenhagen, a3, 81–82; Innsbruck, a3, 80–85; Rome, a1, 42–43; Saarbrücken, a3, 37–38).

Second, conflicts emerge around the *accessibility of green spaces*. Parks can be closed (Strasbourg, a4, 88–92), or access can be restricted by entrance fees (Potsdam, a3, 141–145). The city can partly assign the management of public green spaces to associations, which can also lead to restricted access (cf. section 5.3.1).

Third, in all regions, there are conflicts *between preserving green spaces and building and infrastructure development*, which in some cities heavily reduce green spaces (Cracow, a4, 48–49; Leeds, a3, 60–63; Milan, a4, 72–75; Saarbrücken, a3, 26), often entailing persisting citizens' protests (cf. section 5.2.2).

Fourth, conflicts can emerge *between sectors* – mostly between civil society and local authorities (Cracow, a4, 50–51; Milan, a3, 54–55) – but also within a sector. For example, conflicts between civil society actors (Cracow, a1, 50–52; Gothenburg, a4, 35) or within the city administration between departments (Copenhagen, a2, 103–106) have been reported.

5.2.2 Self-organisation capabilities

To understand a possible impact of self-organisation on the transition in green spaces management, it has to be examined to what extent citizens are involved in local decision-making regarding green spaces and if opportunities for citizens to self-organise exist (for an overview cf. Johan Colding et al. 2013).

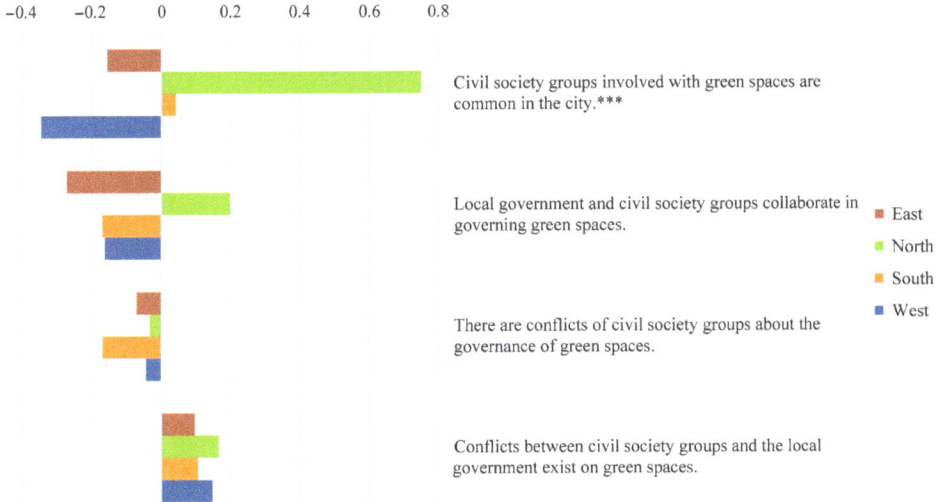

Figure 5-2 Regional differences for civil society involvement in green spaces governance (scaled from −2: strong disagreement to +2: strong agreement)

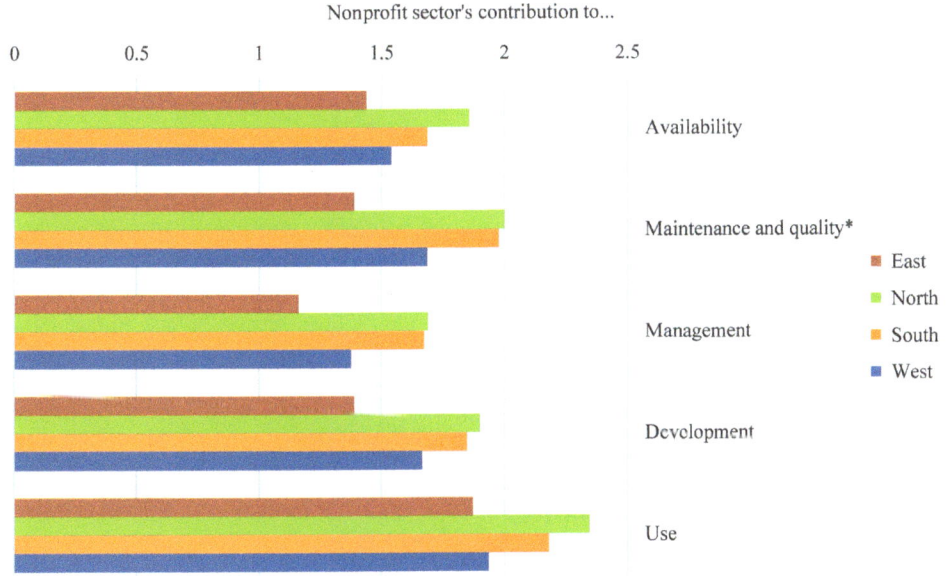

Figure 5-3 Regional differences in the contribution of the nonprofit sector to green spaces (scaled from 0: none to 4: very high)

The regional differences (cf. Figures 5-2 and 5-3) point to a higher degree of civil society action and of interaction between civil society and government in the North compared to the three other regions. It supports the thesis that the least civil society influence in the governance of green spaces is in the East. According to the quantitative data, only in the North are civil society groups involved with green spaces common, and local government and civil society closely collaborate. Concerning conflicts between civil society and the local government, the sector analysis reveals that administration clearly rejects the existence of conflicts between itself and civil society, whereas civil society and business confirm the existence of such conflicts.

The case study report (Garzillo and Ulrich 2015) analysis points in the same direction. Out of 40 cities, 21 cities could be classified as having a very active civil society in the field of green spaces, 9 as having an active one, and only 10 as having a less active one, of which 6 belong to the East (Cracow, Giurgiu, Jihlava, Lodz, Prague, and Sibiu). Thus, the majority of cities with least civil society action in the field of green spaces as well as with the lowest degree of cooperation between civil society and local government are to be found there. However, these indications should not be overestimated since the qualitative data shows that forms of participation and self-organisation are to be found in every region.

Participation procedures are enshrined in the legal framework of most countries in the European Union. Yet the level of participation actually applied on the local level greatly differs across the cities. Observed forms of participation are clustered as best as possible referring to the participation models explained in section 3.1:

- The lowest stage of *information* exists for example when providing a citizen phone hotline and a website (Madrid, a3, 52–53) or when letting citizens attend municipality council sessions (Istanbul, a1, 48).
- The second stage of *consultation* can be seen across all regions. This can happen on the district or the municipality level. Local authorities listen to citizens, citizens associations, and neighbourhood commissions in information sessions or get their opinion via questionnaires (Gothenburg, a4, 63–66; Istanbul, a1, 70–71; Lugano, a3, 77; Sibiu, a2, 166–175). Citizens give input to the elaboration of the zoning plan in a workshop and afterwards via the Internet (Jihlava, a3, 40), or the mayor broadly invites a public reflection on green areas (Copenhagen, a4, 52–53). District councils with a right to be heard by the municipal council exist for local decisions, constituting the intermediary link between the municipality council and the citizens (Copenhagen, a2, 55; Larissa, a4, 62–63; Lublin, a1, 24–25 and 39–41; Milan, a4, 76). They organise for example citizen meetings whose results are communicated to the municipality. Nongovernmental organisations participate in round tables, or a committee for public dialogue was created (Cracow, a1, 53 and a3, 16).
- The third stage of *stakeholder engagement* is also mentioned (Naples, a4, 18–19, 80–85). Here, city consultative committees on the municipality level exist, for example the Environmental Committee, for which each citizen can enrol to participate. Citizens take part in decision-making by elaborating a joint group proposal on a round table, which is then presented to the Chancellor. He/she has to consider it yet is not obliged to present it to the Council.
- The fourth stage of *delegated decision-making* can be found in the form of the participatory budget through which citizens have a say in allocating the city's resources, as mentioned in several cities (Lodz, a3, 58–61; Lublin, a4, 34–36; Potsdam, a3, 113).
- The fifth stage of *co-decision-making* exists where there is collaboration in different councils – for example in a green council in which associations are involved (Aalborg, a4, 82–87). With Switzerland, generally known for its system of direct democracy, another example is a referendum on a regeneration project of a park (Lugano, a3, 46–47). Citizens' committees approving of local decisions on green spaces also fall

into this category yet can only wield influence if decisions on green spaces are taken by the council (Naples, a3, 29–30, 51–56).

Amongst the different reasons for allowing citizen participation, as traced for example by Liisa Häikiö (2012, 421–23) and earlier by Jürgen Habermas (1976, 136–37), the one of *increasing legitimacy* is mentioned by several actors, stating that participation is necessary since "citizens do not accept projects being imposed from above" (Rome, a1, 34–35). To avoid legal problems at a later stage of the planning process, citizens should be involved early (Lugano, a3, 110–120). Even social peace can be endangered if no options for citizen participation exist (Bilbao, a3, 103). Participation is further considered necessary for *improving the quality of decision-making*, stressing that participation is "necessary to find the best policy solution due to the inclusion of local knowledge of citizens" (Sibiu, a2, 166). This means that all stakeholders are taken seriously and are considered as experts. Participation is also a means of *creating social support amongst stakeholders*. An active civil society can support the work of politicians working for the transition. This is for example the case if individuals or associations' representatives become involved in different councils (Aalborg, a4, 82–87). Monitoring and evaluating local politics and policies is a form of citizen participation that can contribute to *rising levels of transparency and trust*. The right to do so needs to be in citizens' hands, for example by monitoring the local budget (Thessaloniki, a4, 86, 89–90; Naples, a3, 45–46). Here, self-organisation and participation is seen as a basic control element of local authorities in a democracy, especially in the case of a weak opposition.

Self-organisation capabilities regarding the green spaces resource system are reported from all regions. They range from small citizens' initiatives on the neighbourhood level, often emerging in opposition to planned construction on public green spaces, to the formation of bottom-up social movements, for example in the field of urban food production. They also arise in bigger associations and nongovernmental organisations with a higher organisational degree and financial structure (Innsbruck, a3, 114–115; Larissa, a4, 80–83; Leeds, a3, 87 and a4, 15–19, 113–116; Naples, a3, 71–74 and a4, 56–57). Forms of self-organisation can be clustered according to often-intertwined goals. The main ones are to *protest against building or infrastructure development on public green spaces* (cf. next paragraph) and to *use common green spaces for urban food production* (cf. section 5.3.1), sometimes after citizens have appropriated these spaces. These initiatives show that city dwellers become more and more aware of the need to protect urban green spaces in the face of ongoing urbanisation producing urban sprawl and the decimation of green spaces. They have understood that these spaces are not only essential in ecological but also in social terms, and they are willing to fight for their preservation. Their joint actions, such as the (re) appropriation of urban green spaces, make clear that they do not inactively tolerate an urban development strategy mainly based on economic growth and profit interests, but that they claim their right to the city by turning with their diverse actions these spaces into commons.

From all regions, *citizens' protests* due to conflicts between preserving public green spaces and building and infrastructure development are reported. Urbanisation increases building density and sealing and is exacerbated by real estate and infrastructure speculation. This creates conflicts, out of which self-organisation can emerge, often starting with protests of informal citizens' movements (Cracow, a2, 36–39, 81 and a3, 73–76, 125–134). Measures to achieve the *(re)appropriation of public green spaces* take various forms, ranging from protest movements (Lodz, a4, 35–36) and going to court – often with organised nongovernmental organisations filing a suit against the government – (Istanbul, a1, 39 and a4, 47–48) to fruitful collaboration amongst various civil society actors (Saarbrücken, a4, 67–73). Initiatives sometimes succeed, sometimes not or only partially, due to existing power structures or due to the fact that they come late in the planning phase. Some examples are given below:

- Citizens self-organise for protests against tree felling or planned traffic infrastructure projects (Linz, a3, 62–67 and a4, 65–68).
- A social movement has taken possession of abandoned areas (such as old military fields) to prevent construction on them and to develop green corridors by urban gardening activities (cf. section 5.3.1; Madrid, a4, 61–64).
- Conflicts on the accessibility of green spaces end in protests, with the most famous one being the Gezi Park protests (Istanbul, a4, 47–48). Local nongovernmental organisations and district politicians jointly fight against construction plans on public green spaces that provide for mosques with underground shopping malls in public parks. Actions range from demonstrations to court hearings (Istanbul, a1, 23–29, 42–47 and a4, 47–48).
- City residents self-organised with the support of a nongovernmental organisation against the city's plan to sell pieces of land of a public park to the highest bidder for construction purposes. A consensus was reached in several meetings. Some green spaces were preserved, resulting in a significant monetary loss for the city's budget, whereas the rest was put up for sale (Cracow, a2, 36–39 and a3, 76, 125–134).
- Civil society actors founded an association to counter real estate development in the outer city district. They achieved an institutionalised hearing process for a participated planning procedure consisting of informative meetings with all stakeholders involved, which was led by an external facilitator (Lugano, a4, 19–20, 61–68, 83–86).

In a rising number of cities, self-organisation helps to *mitigate public poverty*. Especially in cities in which local governments have severe difficulties in affording the provision of green space, new self-organised initiatives have emerged on the grassroots level for maintaining and even developing those, thus tackling local challenges and becoming active players in local governance processes (cf. section 5.3.1). Tasks previously accomplished by public authorities are taken over by civil society, citizens, or associations, and in some cases by business actors, alleviating the public budget. This tendency has been intensified because of the multiple financial crises in 2008–2009 and subsequent austerity policies hitting hard on local public budgets (Rome, a1, 35). In some places, self-organisation also *mitigates rising private poverty*. Using urban green spaces for growing food for self-consumption is a poverty-combatting strategy that has its roots in Europe's nineteenth-century industrial cities (Cordula Kropp 2011, 78). This function was driven back by economic growth in the second half of the last century and is now reappearing, especially in Southern European cities. Individuals take the crisis as a starting point to join others in becoming active. Public authorities can equally launch innovative processes.

According to the quantitative data, the strongest motive for citizens to self-organise in the management of green spaces is to beautify their neighbourhood. Other popular reasons are to contribute to societal life and to create things. To act independently from local government and to be self-sufficient in food production are not focal motives. This picture slightly changes when looking at the regional distribution, which shows that there are no significant differences for the strongest motive. However, the aims to contribute to societal life and to create things are weaker motives in the East than in the other regions (cf. Figure 5-4).

This is supported by the qualitative data, which shows that actions around urban food production have emerged in all regions but the East. However, the motive of self-sufficiency in fresh, healthy food at low costs, especially for citizens with a low economic status, is only raised in the South. When analysing the factors for successful self-organisation and participation, two aspects are striking. First, all factors are raised in the North, West, or South. Second, most given factors are identical with the ones referred to as factors for a successful socio-ecological transition, suggesting that a successful socio-ecological transition is strongly linked to self-organisation and participation.

Political will and courage in the administration is seen as a precondition to allow for self-organised initiatives. The municipality must have the sincere intention of involving citizens and believe in the value of citizens' input in the long term. This means to acknowledge and to acquire citizens' local expert knowledge (Copenhagen, a3, 61–64 and a4, 52–53; Saarbrücken, a4, 67–73). Depending on the level of participation, participation can be influenced by aggregation rules, which are one of the seven rule types defining the institutional setting of an action situation (cf. section 3.2). Aggregation rules determine "whether a decision of a single participant or multiple participants is needed prior to an action at a node in a decision process" (Ostrom 2005, 202). The more actors are involved in the decision-making process, the more the mastery of increased complexity in decision-making is needed. Participation procedures cannot be improvised but follow certain criteria. Clear rules as well as training for political and administrative staff on these are necessary (Naples, a4, 44–48).

Figure 5-4 Regional differences in citizens' motivations for self-organisation in green spaces management (scaled from −2: strong disagreement to +2: strong agreement)

The administration must transparently transfer information towards the citizens (Lugano, a3, 124–125; Naples, a4, 90–93). This confirms the need for information rules that "affect the level of information available to participants ... [and which must] relate to the set of all possible channels connecting all participants in a situation" (Ostrom 2005, 206). Clear communication also means that when participatory tools are employed, administration has to break the technical administrative language down into a language easily understandable by citizens.

Due to the complexity and the higher costs of citizen participation in the short term, some actors suggest exclusively applying it in decision-making situations in which a conflict is emerging, in other words where there is a need for people to get information and where a debate can be created (Copenhagen, a2, 82–85). The importance of *being involved from the beginning* of the planning process is stressed by actors from all sectors (Aalborg, a4, 82–87; Copenhagen, a2, 61; Lugano, a3, 121–128; Saarbrücken, a4, 54–59). Furthermore, the importance of *involving a wide range of actors* in the participatory procedure to make sure to not only take into account the best-organised groups with the best lobbying capabilities, such as associations, is acknowledged (Copenhagen, a2, 93–94). Experience has shown that successful involvement is done by activities appealing to different groups of people; otherwise, only the already committed come (Copenhagen, a3, 65–66; Leeds, a4, 15–19).

Apart from that, *education* and *awareness-raising* are seen as crucial, since they enable people to participate and to self-organise (Naples, a4, 31–32; Strasbourg, a4, 93). It is necessary to inform citizens and public authorities about the benefits of participation. It is about to activate bottom-up action and to reach those that are not sensitised yet in a process of communication. Perhaps these sensitisation processes can more easily be obtained in cities that follow rigorous growth logic despite already existing immense socio-ecological problems, since the environmental and social externalities of growth are most evident there. If citizens want to participate, and thus are politically very aware, this makes it easy for nongovernmental organisations to gather support (Istanbul, a1, 42–47 and a4, 61). Raising citizens' interest for participation is also easier with *concrete issues* directly related to their neighbourhood than with more abstract planning procedures (Lublin, a4, 34–36).

The existence of *funding* schemes, for example from foundations, is a decisive factor (Copenhagen, a3, 36–37). Furthermore, *expanding participatory policy tools* such as consultative committees to district level as well as holding city referenda and civil audits[2] in order to give citizens a veto power on decisions is deemed necessary (Naples, a4, 86–93). This is because these tools serve to control politics. Thus, they surpass the state of mere consultation, for example on how resources are consumed, to increase the transparency of the political process. Regarding projects of the European Union, it is suggested to set stricter participation requirements instead of just having participation indicators (Naples, a4, 78–79).

Barriers to self-organisation and participation are reported from all regions and partly mirror the named success factors. It is mentioned by actors from all sectors that organising participatory procedures is difficult and *complicated*, needs a lot of time and resources, and thus is *expensive* and can *prolong decision-making* (Copenhagen, a2, 79–81 and a3, 65–66; Linz, a4, 81–84; Lugano, a3, 152–153; Strasbourg, a4, 93). This increases the risk that in times of tight local budgets, funds to support self-organisation are cut (Thessaloniki, a4, 71–76). *Policymakers want to be in control* since politicians are responsible for the political decisions taken (Copenhagen, a2, 79–81). Whether participation tools are applied and room for self-organisation is given depends on the *political will* of local authorities. Some are very proactive (Aalborg, a4, 42–45; Gothenburg, a4, 45–46), yet political will can also be missing (Lublin, a4, 24; Madrid, a4, 70; Thessaloniki, a3, 32–33 and a4, 32–35). Citizens with the will to self-organise and participate might even be considered a "disturbing factor" (Naples, a3, 76), believing that citizens are not able to decide for the common good but just vote according to their own interests (Lugano, a4, 61–68). Local authorities might also be afraid of being criticised by citizens when allowing participation (Lugano, a3, 110). In numerous cities the will to let citizens participate exists and is required by law, yet concrete policy tools are lacking (Madrid, a4, 84–91; Rome, a1, 77–78). For example, there is *no institutionalised regular mechanism of participation*, for example via regular council meetings (Bilbao, a4, 40–47; Milan, a4, 76). Instead, citizens are involved case by case.

Institutional barriers include *complicated* and *inefficient administrative procedures* and a high degree of bureaucracy, as well as *nontransparency* (Milan, a3, 44–45, 67; Naples, a3, 90–91 and a4, 50–51). Even if participation tools exist, citizens might not be well informed about the possibilities to use them (Bilbao, a3, 103; Cracow, a4, 74–77; Milan, a4, 76–83; Sibiu, a3, 85 and a4, 114–115).

Missing trust in public institutions is reported from every region but the West (e.g. Cracow, a4, 22–27; Glasgow, a3, 49–58 and a4, 77–80; Lodz, a3, 119–126). It can be due to experiences of secret – sometimes illegal – entanglement between the public and the private sectors with concomitant exercise of influence (Milan, a3, 83–84). As a result, people even refrain from joining associations and stop caring about the common good (Milan a3, 56–59 and a4, 26). Citizens might not trust association leaders any more if they were led by personal interests in the past (Larissa, a3, 72–75) or if they are scandalised by politics on higher levels or by the inefficiency of the legal system (Jihlava, a4, 80–83). It can also be that existing participatory tools have been badly managed by the administration so that citizens are tired of them (Bilbao, a4, 40). The *local mentality* and *culture* on the citizens' side and on the public authority's side is quoted in several cities in all regions but the South as a reason for a low participation and self-organisation rate. It includes not being used to the idea of citizens becoming active in common good matters beyond their voting right (Glasgow, a3, 49 and a4, 77; Sibiu, a3, 104–110 and a4, 189–190; St. Gallen, a4, 9–10; Strasbourg, a4, 93). Historic reasons for citizens rejecting participation are invoked in the East, saying that they associate it with "old-time communist social activism" (Lublin, a4, 49–50).

The *lack of education* (Thessaloniki, a3, 60) and a *lack of time* for voluntary activities are also mentioned, with the latter raised in the East and the West as a reason for citizens' nonparticipation, due to their "fight for survival" (Sibiu, a3, 85) or employment (Bilbao, a3, 103; Strasbourg, a4, 93). Furthermore, *political oppression* – from hindering nongovernmental organisations' operation to physical violence during demonstrations – intimidates citizens and can demotivate them from becoming active (Istanbul, a4, 73). In addition, *legal barriers* are put up by the centralised political system giving little power to the municipal council (Larissa, a3, 78–79).

The regression analysis (cf. Table 5-1) shows that, on the one hand, high local government autonomy in improving and expanding as well as in investing in green spaces is beneficial to the *commonness of civil society groups* (cf. section 5.4.2). The same holds true for a high degree of leadership of the local authorities in ensuring the availability and quality of green spaces.[3] On the other hand, if the capacity of the local government in providing financial and human resources is high, this makes the commonness of civil society groups less probable. The same holds true for a satisfactory level of monitoring of local land quality, pollution, and biodiversity. From this, it can be concluded that a high degree of local autonomy, combined with a high degree of leadership of local authorities, provides the right framework conditions for civil society groups to enter the stage. If the local administration is then capable of providing a satisfactory level of monitoring, closely linked to its capacity of financial and human resources, civil society groups become less involved than in cities in which public authorities have problems in ensuring a satisfactory level of green spaces management.

Actors also raise positive and negative outcomes of self-organisation and participation. Positive outcomes are named in all regions except the East. Participation leads to *shared experiences of a community*, thus building a more attentive community, which is the basis for sustainability (Rome, a1, 33). It is seen that the results of participatory processes are better than those achieved in top-down procedures without participation (Linz, a4, 81–84). *The more people are involved, the more satisfied they are* with the result and the more they use the city, identifying with it and its public space (Copenhagen, a2, 79–81). Even if citizens did not succeed with their opinion, participatory processes increase the acceptance of political decisions, since citizens have the feeling of having been listened to, thus of having been taken seriously (Copenhagen, a4, 52–53). Participation creates a feeling of *ownership* and *responsibility* with the citizens, raising their interest in the common good (Copenhagen, a3, 36–37; Potsdam, a4, 194–195; Rome, a1, 34–35). Local participatory processes can be seen as joint experiments that are evaluated after implementation. If they work, they can be scaled up "think big – start small – scale fast" (Copenhagen, a3, 36–37). In Spain, citizens' movements mushroomed after the end of the dictatorship. They have achieved an increase in green spaces in the neighbourhoods and have gained influence in the management of parks (Madrid, a4, 56). The adoption of public green spaces by civil society and business

Table 5-1 Influences on civil society groups' existence in green spaces

Civil society groups in the field of green spaces are common in the city	Coef.	Std. Err.
Satisfactory access and availability to public green spaces in general	0.417	0.270
Involvement of local civil society actors in governance of green spaces***	1.221	0.324
Local government's autonomy in improving / expanding green spaces***	0.741	0.272
Capacity of the local government (financial capacity and human resources)*	−0.620	0.335
Leadership of local government administration in ensuring availability and quality of green spaces**	0.641	0.248
Monitoring of local land quality, pollution and biodiversity is satisfactory*	−0.433	0.238
Autonomy of the local government in investing in green spaces***	0.724	0.274
Local government and civil society groups closely collaborate in governing green spaces***	1.336	0.299

Notes: Ordered logistic regression, 128 observations, p-value = 0.000; Pseudo R^2 = 0.3815, Log likelihood = −117.92 (control variables: city and sector)

actors (cf. section 5.3.1) can be a counterweight to private actors' building and dumping activities on empty spaces (Naples, a4, 48–49). This can even weaken organised crime as in the case of associations managing land withdrawn from the mafia (Naples, a4, 65–75). This exemplifies civil society's correcting role towards the state and the market from below.

Negative outcomes and shortcomings of participatory procedures are also named. The "*participation paradox*" (John E. Seley 1983, 20), meaning that groups with higher capacities to express their opinions are primarily listened to by policymakers, disadvantaging less powerful civil society groups, is existent. This implies that there is the risk of only the strongest and best lobbyist influencing political decisions with the rest remaining unheard (Gothenburg, a4, 67). The *misuse of participation*, either for political reasons or for particular interests of citizens, is mentioned in every region (Cracow, a3, 27–28). Individuals and associations try to get through particular interests, sometimes related to a NIMBY[4] attitude, hindering the socio-ecological transition (Cracow, a1, 50–53; Gothenburg, a4, 67). In several places, participatory tools are only applied because they are required by law ("tick a box" – Copenhagen, a3, 36) without having an influence on further policy outcomes (Copenhagen, a3, 36–37, 61–64; Istanbul, a4, 33, 61; Lodz, a4, 13; Paris, a4, 65–66). They are often only applied if they fit the political planning process and are only suggested at a late stage (Cracow, a4, 74; Saarbrücken, a4, 54).

5.3 Actors, factors, and lessons learnt

This section gives an overview of actors, actions, and factors driving the green spaces transition across the cities and summarises the lessons that actors have learnt from local resource management. Insight is gained by studying examples of (un-/less) successful actions and actors' (non-)involvement in them. In all cities of the green spaces sample there are political, business, and civil society actors involved, yet the degree and quality of their collaboration differs greatly from city to city. Defining factors are subdivided into local and nonlocal factors and analysed along success and failure factors.

5.3.1 Actors, actions, and factors

Across cities, actors from politics, administration, and civil society have shown *leadership* in the governance of green spaces (the local government administration, the mayor, politicians of the ruling parties, local environmental NGOs, other local community groups). In contrast to the other resource systems (cf. chapters 4 and 6), local community groups play a major role in green spaces. Reflecting less civil society influence in the East (cf. section 5.2.2), local environmental NGOs and other local community groups are less important there compared with the other regions (cf. Figure 5-5).

The qualitative data shows that, in all regions, individual persons coming from all sectors are highly influential and can become key change agents. They often have a known reputation, such as a dedicated mayor driving forward sustainability issues (Sibiu, a2, 68–71). Highly driven individuals working as civil servants in the Environment Department can be decisive (Gothenburg, a4, 45–46). The same applies for well-informed leading figures from civil society that are good networkers implementing innovative ideas, for example in the field of urban food production (Leeds, a4, 69–72). In addition, the position of the city's semi-public companies[5] on sustainability issues influences the city's orientation towards sustainability (Copenhagen, a2, 57–58; Saarbrücken, a4, 32–34).

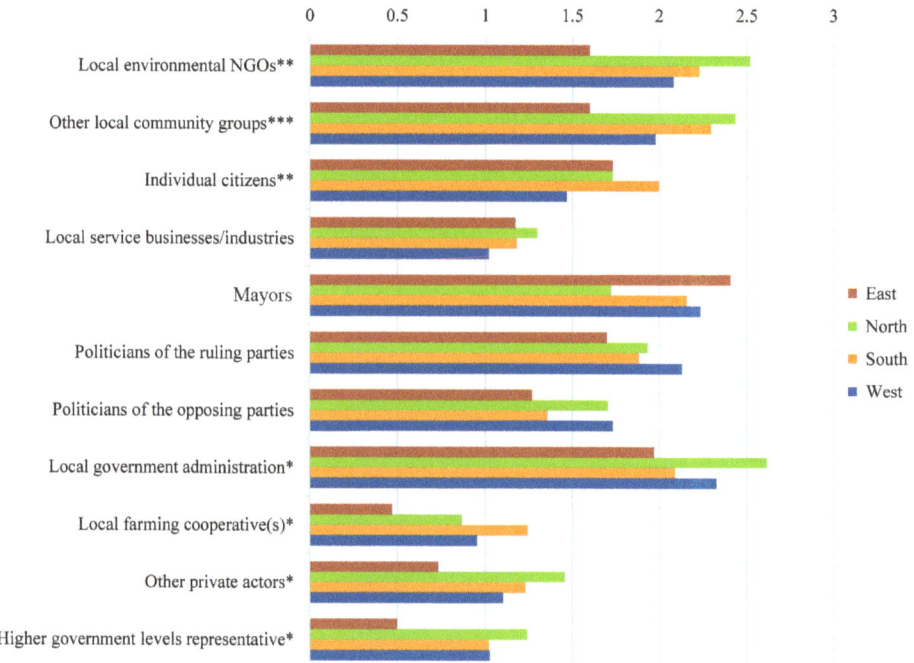

Figure 5-5 Regional differences in actors showing concrete leadership (reputation and capability) in green spaces management (scaled from 0: none to 4: very high)

The role of science is seen as bringing in a neutral perspective, highlighting problems, and pointing to the future (Linz, a3, 46–47). Universities should be rooted locally, work in an innovative, project-oriented way, and collaborate with local authorities and the business sector (Aalborg, a4, 46–51; Lodz, a3, 99–108; Lublin, a1, 42–51; Rome, a1, 73–78; St. Gallen, a4, 10). Innovation means strengthening these university–community linkages (e.g. Leeds, a4, 30–36). Science plays an important role in underlining the urgency of sustainability issues in the public opinion and therefore can deliberately be misrepresented (Aalborg, a4, 114 (cf. also section 5.2.1). Civil society can be influential (Copenhagen, a4, 38–39; Lodz, a4, 31–36; Lugano, a4, 41–47; Thessaloniki, a3, 41–44 and a4, 13): In some cities the sustainability topic was brought up by citizens' movements, then taken up by politicians. High pressure from nongovernmental organisations on local authorities can lead to the official involvement of civil society actors in local politics, for example in committees. This can have a spillover effect to also involving individual citizens, for example via local councils (Copenhagen, a2, 53–54).

A high level of cooperation is expressed in *regular institutionalised collaboration* between civil society representatives and the local council. Collaboration can be direct or indirect. For example, regarding the involvement of citizens in decisions about public green spaces, citizens can participate directly in town councils, which are open to everyone. Indirectly, they can be represented in a city's green council by a member of a citizens' association. Often different civil society actors collaborate, for example a nongovernmental organisation supporting citizens' initiatives joining forces and increasing chances of success (Copenhagen, a4, 62–64; Lugano, a4, 41–47; Saarbrücken, a4, 71–72). A high degree of cross-sector cooperation can manifest itself for example in numerous activities in the field of urban food production in cooperation with local authorities, schools, and universities (Leeds, a4, 30–36).

A minority of actors claim that cooperation between civil society actors and the local government does not exist at all. They deplore that there are no common projects between administration and civil society and that there is no response from the government to civil society actors' propositions or that it only happens by chance, for example via a personal relationship with government employees (Sibiu, a2, 123–128). This is often the case if a general lack of organisation and knowledge is noted with local authorities, stemming from understaffing due to financial hardships or position assignment along clientelistic 'criteria'.

The various conflicts around urban land use raise the question of what kind of local control system is adequate to deal with this *new complexity and multiplication of actors* entering the governance of green spaces. This increases the conflict potential since rule definition, for example around fallow land, permanent permits, and so on, is further complicated by a rising number of involved actors. In some cities, boundary rules have partly been shifted: New actors from civil society and business are now eligible to enter positions that before were reserved for state actors only. The process determining which eligible participants may enter – or must enter – positions and, at a later stage, how participants may or must leave a position (Ostrom 2005, 193) has only just started. This leads to conflict and sometimes disappointment and to the retreat of new actors that had invested time and commitment. Due to not yet clearly defined boundary rules, they become tired of participating or self-organising.

There is a wide range of successful actions referred to in all regions: Numerous *information* and *awareness-raising* events have been held all over Europe. These include lectures (Jihlava, a4, 24–25); research studies conducted by nongovernmental organisations (Larissa, a4, 14–17, 47–49); tree-planting actions (Jihlava, a4, 24–25); park-cleaning events (Larissa, a4, 67); or picnics (Thessaloniki, a3, 41–44). They are organised, depending on the city, mainly by civil society or by local authorities, often in collaboration with each other, sometimes also involving the business or science sector. Tendering *sustainability prizes* within the city or taking part in (inter)national tenders as a whole city is becoming more common and seems to be a functioning incentive (Copenhagen, a4, 14–15; Innsbruck, a3, 146–149). In several places, the *adoption of public green spaces* by associations as well as private companies to take care of them has become common (cf. section 5.3.1), and in several cities, citizens' movements get together to protect endangered green areas (cf. section 5.2.2). Local authorities can encourage and facilitate participation and self-organisation, for example by coordinating volunteers' involvement and by supporting emerging initiatives financially or by providing space, material, and soil. Actions across sectors help to mitigate *public poverty*. Civil society and sometimes business actors contribute voluntarily to public green spaces management (Milan, a3, 36–37 and a4, 101–102; Naples, a3, 71–76 and a4, 31–32, 46–47, 56–57; Thessaloniki, a3, 20–21, 41–44, 85 and a4, 13). Cooperation takes different forms, for example *spontaneous self-organised initiatives* from the bottom or actions proposed by the city, such as the *adoption of public green spaces* by associations and private companies to take care of them. This new collaboration is in most places not yet anchored institutionally. It often still lacks clear rules, so that responsibilities are not clearly assigned to stakeholders, as the following examples show:

- Accessibility of green spaces was reduced by assigning their management to a golf association that restricted access to its members (Milan, a3, 54–55).

- Two civil society groups together with a business actor, providing material, volunteers, as well as financial means, started park renovation initiative. The only thing they requested from the local administration was to provide them with soil, which would have cost around 500 EUR, which did not happen (Thessaloniki, a3, 73–76).
- Across European cities, urban commons are increasingly used for *food production*. In some cases, these movements start as small spontaneous bottom-up initiatives, evolving into growing social movements in which sometimes associations join or out of which in some cases new associations or cooperatives are formed. For example, an *urban garden network* was created by individuals/neighbourhood associations without any support from the city council, operating on public abandoned space (Madrid, a3, 58–59).

Urban food production can be a means of *combatting private poverty* by providing fresh local food to contribute to food security: Examples come from Greece, where the ongoing transformation of a former military camp into a composting site done by city employees was suddenly stopped by the 'crisis' and concomitant budget problems. The staff was dismissed, and the place turned into an illegal dumping ground (Thessaloniki, a3, 84–85). Citizens reacted to the city's difficulty in providing sufficient management of public green spaces by self-organising in a large *urban agriculture initiative*. They have created gardens for vegetables and fruits in several sections of the city on abandoned military camps, cleaning, embellishing, and making the spaces available for food production designated for self-consumption (Thessaloniki, a3, 78, 85). In Larissa, the administration initiated a *municipal vegetable garden*, which gives citizens with low or no income the possibility to grow their own food. The garden is a successful project and has already been expanded (Larissa, a3, 49–50 and a4, 41–42).

The quantitative data illustrates three points. First, the availability of green spaces is influenced by several factors, of which the national regulatory framework is not important while *local regulations* tend to be important. Second, the most often named factors improving green spaces are the *availability of unbuilt land, local building codes and sectoral plans, local political commitment*, the *capacity of the local government*, and *citizen empowerment*. Third, most actors see more *support for sustainable management of green spaces* coming from European and national policies than from local ones. This tendency is most distinct amongst civil society actors. Only in the North does local policy play a bigger role than the national one, which could be ascribed to municipalities' high levels of autonomy there. This third statement seems at first sight to contradict the preceding two from which it can be discerned that the green spaces resource system is mostly influenced by local factors. Possibly, actors associate political support more with funding options than with legal frameworks. Apart from that, looking at the various benefits of local green spaces (cf. also section 5.1), their positive influence on the microclimate is rated highest. Probably, the importance of ecological effects depends on the specific conditions of each city since there are little regional differences but many between the countries within a region. Apart from ecological benefits, the social ones, for example the possibility for citizens to relax, are also of a high value for actors.

The qualitative data provides a detailed insight into transition success factors across the cities. In cities most advanced in the transition, a process of *collaboration* and *compromise-finding* can be detected (Bilbao, a3, 39–44; Innsbruck, a3, 44–45; Linz, a3, 36–37; Rome, a1, 30–31). It is coordinated by proactive local authorities that jointly elaborate a *long-term strategy* for sustainability with all stakeholders, comprising a high degree of *citizen participation* from the beginning of the process. Concrete options for citizen participation exist and are pointed out (Cracow, a3, 50). The basis for this is *political will* (Bilbao, a3, 37–38; Leeds, a4, 58; Linz, a4, 36; Saarbrücken, a4, 28–29; Sibiu, a2, 52–55). Political actors can even be transition drivers, then interacting with other actors from a proactive administration, business, and civil society to "carry it through" (Aalborg, a4, 42–45). Not surprisingly, the lack of political willingness "to make sustainable development principle number one" (Lodz, a4, 28–30) is mentioned as a *failure factor* (Leeds, a3, 38–41; Potsdam, a3, 101; Thessaloniki, a3, 32–33). *Networking* between stakeholders is facilitated by an *innovative committed administration* that then carries the political decisions out (Larissa, a3, 39–41; Potsdam, a4, 116; Rome, a1, 30–31; Timisoara, a3, 59).

Local authorities along with business should invest in the potential, the activities, and ideas coming from civil society actors by creating a social dialogue. It should take place regularly in institutionalised form, creating *communication channels* between citizens and local authorities. Media has to communicate ongoing activities and sensitise citizens to the necessity of the socio-ecological transition. Now it does not sufficiently support the sustainability topic. Awareness must be raised via *information* and *education* campaigns (Larissa, a4, 41–42).

This comes along with existing *funding options*, of which European Union funds are a major part (Milan, a4, 97–98; Sibiu, a4, 88; Timisoara, a3, 69). Individuals and institutions with the *knowledge* of how to successfully apply for funding (for example from the European Union) are of key importance here.

Generally, a high degree of local autonomy is seen as a transition factor everywhere apart from Switzerland, where some actors regard the high local autonomy as hindering (cf. section 5.4.2). Though non-Swiss actors do not explicitly describe local autonomy as hindering, actors from all regions stress the importance of a *strong national and European Union legal framework*, for example in the field of nature protection or building development, which forces the local level to abide by it (Copenhagen, a3, 80; St. Gallen, a4, 77). For example, if the city has to comply with federal law in the field of nature protection and building development (Saarbrücken, a4, 30–31), if the national environmental law prescribes the amount of surface of green spaces according to the number of inhabitants (Sibiu, a2, 56), or if a clear regional environmental framework exists (Bilbao, a3, 39–44), this can foster the transition. Primarily, in the East, an overly permissive European Union legal framework, not sufficiently forcing the national and local level to reach sustainability goals in the field of green spaces, is deplored (Lodz, a4, 57; Lugano, a4, 100; Timisoara, a4, 73–76).

5.3.2 Lessons learnt

The socio-ecological transition is "driven by learning and norm-adoption individuals, who are capable . . . to develop critical levels of trust, . . . to develop levels of cooperation . . . [and] to realize the net benefits of this cooperation" (Poteete, Janssen, and Ostrom 2010, 240). In the interviews, the majority of actors are quite specific about what they have learnt and what should be improved regarding sustainability issues in the city in general and the green spaces resource system in particular. The quantitative results particularly gain insights into lessons learnt on green spaces governance.

While the *amount of green spaces and greenery*, their *quality*, and the *access* to them has increased on average moderately over the last ten years, *biodiversity* has stayed more or less the same. This should not lead to the assumption that the level of biodiversity is satisfactory everywhere. The qualitative and quantitative findings displayed in section 5.2.1 draw a differentiated picture, showing that especially in the South biodiversity is threatened. In the last ten years, the availability and quality of green spaces has been improved mainly by reclaiming land or by opening new spaces either by the local government or by residents or community groups, by investments or new regulations by the local government and by community actions with or without changing the function of existing open green spaces. The impact of new spaces by residents or community groups is stronger in the South and North than in the East and West. Community actions that do not change green spaces' function are relevant especially in the North and South, and community actions that change the function of the green spaces are not common in the East.

Altogether, no privatisation trend can be seen. The majority of respondents from all regions believe that public green spaces better guarantee equal access than private ones. Also, there is strong opposition from citizens in the city to privatising green spaces, and in recent years, there have been land transformations in favour of constructed areas, with civil society being most critical and government most supportive (cf. Figure 5-6).

If a future joint strategy exists, there is also a *culture of sustainability*, meaning that the need for it is clear to everyone and that everyone identifies with it as a goal. The transition is seen as a mutual *continuous learning process* in the day-to-day work of all participating stakeholders, often leading to new innovative solutions (Madrid, a3, 62–63). These emerging solutions have then to be tested if they work locally with all stakeholders participating before being scaled up. Local good practice examples should be made visible and then be spread (Paris, a3, 60–62; Timisoara, a4, 156–157). This is helped by *networking* via participation in European Union projects, which promotes the learning process across cities, groups, and individuals (Potsdam, a4, 116).

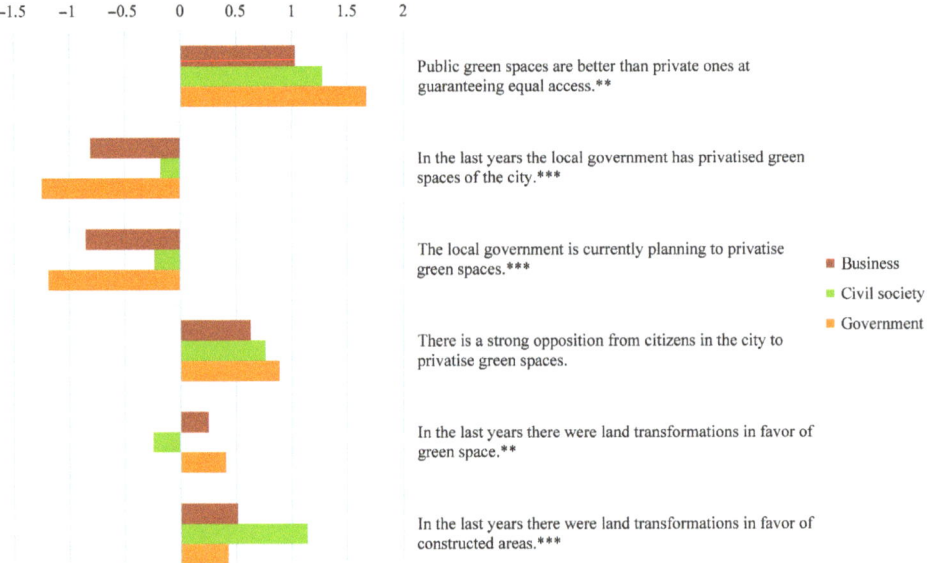

Figure 5-6 Sector differences on statements on privatisation (scaled from −2: strong disagreement to +2: strong agreement)

Knowing that the path to sustainability is arduous, it requires a lot of *stamina* (Copenhagen, a3, 65–66 and a4, 54–55). Predominantly civil society actors, when asked for their motivation, name strong will, self-confidence, positive thinking, patience, and dedication instead of being in a hurry or despair (Leeds, a4, 107–108; Thessaloniki, a4, 61–62). The work is done, though knowing that in the end perhaps only a small step is achieved and no quick results are produced (Bilbao, a4, 76–79; Istanbul, a4, 51).

Concerning *participation* and *self-organisation*, citizens are motivated to participate if they can engage in a concrete aspect, a practical issue. In order to involve different groups of citizens, they must be addressed with activities that appeal to them. Citizen participation helps to achieve sustainability aims, since "an informed and aware citizen is always the best ally for an administration that wants to pursue certain objectives such as sustainability" (Rome, a1, 54–55). If citizens are faced with a fait accompli, they react with resistance. What is known is more easily accepted and appreciated. The comanagement of common goods fosters civic environmental education, underlines their value and benefits as well as their costs and the need to protect them (Rome, a1, 54–55). Civil society actors suggest the monitoring and the evaluation of policymaking by citizens, asking for a combination of a top-down organisation plan for sustainability with an interactive, bottom-up, citizen-led control system, so that local authorities take the citizens' needs into account (Thessaloniki, a4, 86). This must be embedded in a *multidisciplinary approach* to avoid important aspects being missed.

To achieve fruitful collaboration between civil society, business, and local authorities, the rights and duties of each party, for example of public authorities, citizens, or associations, need to be clearly defined. This means that *rules* have to be established (cf. section 5.3.1). Otherwise, civil society actors do not understand which tasks are delegated to them. These defined rules need to be controlled because there is always the risk of someone taking advantage of his power (Rome, a1, 48–49). *Conflicts* emerge because of the stakes of actors whose power position might be threatened by newly incoming actors. Thus, in a first step, existing local power structures need to be analysed and understood. In a second step, ways of involving potential stakeholders in rule finding without bypassing present stakeholders must be found. In this process, the local government's task is to offer an institutionalised transparent meeting and discussion platform and to coordinate this process.

Concerning European transition factors, the European Union's *funding schemes* seem to be, in spite of their complexity, a functioning instrument to drive the transition on the local level. In order to receive European Union funds, sustainability criteria must be met. This can be the trigger to elaborate a local sustainability strategy. European funds, accessible also for local civil society actors, for example small associations, help to raise people's sustainability awareness, since they enable networking, learning from others, and the sharing and spreading of good practices. European directives, which have to be implemented down to the local level, are equally helpful, for example in forcing the local level to introduce a register for green spaces. Therefore, according to many actors, stronger environmental *legislation* on the national or European Union level with more solid and clearer rules is needed, where noncompliance on the local level is also consistently sanctioned (e.g. Lugano, a4, 98–99; Madrid, a3, 91–92, 95–96; Timisoara, a3, 167–171 and a4, 183–185). Furthermore, the national and European Union level can set financial and fiscal incentives to force local authorities to act more sustainably, for example by predetermining the goals concerning land consumption, land taxes, and so on (Madrid, a4, 39–40; Paris, a4, 18–19; Saarbrücken, a4, 90–91; Timisoara, a4, 72). In this regard, civil society regrets the halt in Turkey's EU accession process, since working towards European Union accession would have meant working towards compliance with the European Union's legal framework, which would have advanced sustainability (Istanbul, a4, 100–103).

5.4 Norm adoption and local decision-making autonomy

According to Poteete, Janssen, and Ostrom (2010, 226–227), successful norm adoption by participants in an action situation leading to shared norms raises the level of trust between participants and is thus decisive for a higher degree of cooperation (cf. also chapter 3). The underlying question is whether and how values change, which could be observed in a transitional socio-ecological norm adoption towards trust and cooperation. Thus, this section investigates the evolution of norms in the governance of local resources and tries to answer the question whether local decision-making autonomy matters in the socio-ecological transition.

5.4.1 Norm adoption

Respondents agree that the following statements on norms govern the local green space policy: 'The conservation and development of green areas is of strong importance for the local government.' 'It should be avoided that the current levels of real estate and land prices have a negative impact on the current and future availability of green spaces.' 'It should be avoided that the current levels of real estate and land prices have a negative impact on local food production.' Sector differences can be detected for the importance of the conservation and the development of green areas, the monitoring of local land quality, and access to information. Government representatives' opinions are most positive, civil society representatives' are most negative, and the business respondents' statements lie between these (cf. Figure 5-7).

Three governance principles that can be derived from these norms are also agreed on across cities: 'The amount and location of green spaces are known.' 'External actors do not undermine the local governance of green spaces.' 'The local green space system can be identified as relatively autonomous.' The last statement means that the boundaries of the resource system are clear-cut in green spaces and that green spaces are a relatively autonomous subunit of a larger system.

When asked specifically about rules and policy instruments that are supporting or missing or that need to be changed in order to achieve a socio-ecological transition, interviewees named the existing *legal framework* as obstructing. This can be due to its *complexity* and *complicatedness*. It can be bureaucratic and even chaotic. With the recently decentralised administration or the national ministry, it is often not clear which government level is responsible for a specific action (cf. chapter 3). It hinders for example the transformation of former military camps into green spaces (Thessaloniki, a3, 32–33, 36–38), or European Union regulations are interpreted differently on the national level than intended in Brussels and thus the final national law is complicated (Jihlava, a3, 66).

A *too flexible or even missing – or not enforced* – legal framework can equally be hindering. For example, the local legal framework for tree-cutting and replacement might not be strict enough without a local law protecting trees, meaning that tree-cutting – also in private areas – is possible without replacing them elsewhere (Linz, a4, 76). The national legal framework concerning construction can be too permissive, making it difficult to

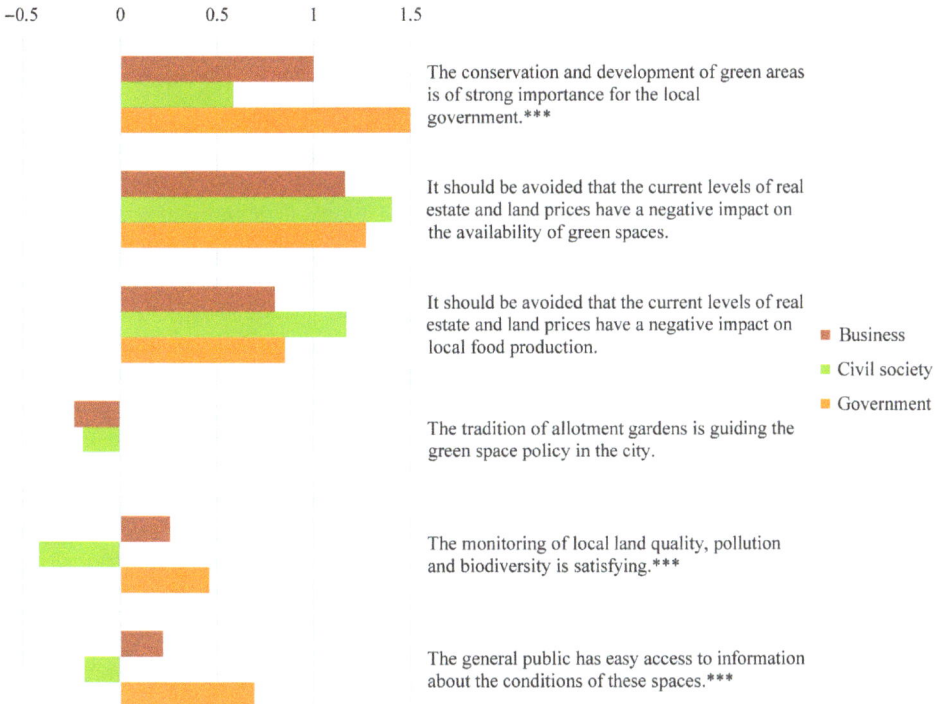

Figure 5-7 Sector differences in agreeing with statements on norms governing the local green space policy (scaled from −2: strong disagreement to +2: strong agreement)

protect green spaces (Cracow, a2, 32–33). If the value of nature is further disregarded in legal texts, green spaces will continuously be considered as relatively insignificant. This is for example the case where penalties for the removal of trees were removed in an amendment to the national Environmental Act and where the green spaces category has not been incorporated as public purpose into the law on spatial planning (Lodz, a4, 55–59). An example from the past comes from Romania, where in the 1990s, there was no legislation on construction, leading to uncontrolled building activity (Sibiu, a2, 57–63).

A *too inflexible* framework can be hindering as well. It can be too general and abstract (Timisoara, a4, 123–124). An inflexible public procurement law setting price as the primary criterion can hinder project implementation (Lublin, a1, 54). Innovative bottom-up solutions might meet legal obstacles, for example by the interdiction to sell food produced in urban gardens in schools (Gothenburg, a4, 87–92). The European Union's legal framework might not be flexible enough to be adapted to local conditions. For example, the European Union's rules on organic farming need to be adjusted or local exceptions have to be made, since in some Northern European countries organic farming is not possible without additional lighting (Gothenburg, a4, 103–107).

Missing or obstructing policy instruments are named. Ongoing land consumption is not sufficiently countered because of the lack of applying appropriate policy instruments. Bringing local authorities and universities closer together is missing in most cities but would be very important also for green spaces planning (Rome, a1, 73–78). Insufficient steering tools are often the reason for only single strategies followed by piecemeal actions without a sustainability drive and an overarching sustainability vision for the city behind it (Leeds, a3, 38–41; Lodz, a3, 47; Potsdam, a3, 87–88; Thessaloniki, a4, 21, 35). Yet an overall concept can only emerge with a clear political will behind it. A lack of urban planning can also stem from a desolate financial situation, as is the case in cities having suffered from severe mismanagement, sometimes linked to the misappropriation of public funds in the past (Larissa, a3, 32, 45, 78–79). Creating a local development strategy is even more important in times of crisis when overarching national strategies on sustainability development are often missing and financial resources are very much limited. The 'crisis' has aggravated the tendency of always awarding public project tenders to the lowest bidder, combined with decreased quality and sustainability criteria (Thessaloniki, a3, 49–53). Investing in oversized, expensive prestige projects, mostly in the field of building and traffic infrastructure construction, is seen as counterproductive to sustainability, also in an intergenerational sense, leaving future generations with high debts (Saarbrücken, a4, 76).

Supporting policy instruments are equally stated: Strategies at the local and the regional level are a good starting point (Aalborg, a4, 107–112), such as a master plan on biodiversity (Paris, a3, 58–59). Citizens need to be involved in the planning process from the beginning – in consultations, dialogue meetings, coordination groups (Umea, a3, 125). Making plans is relatively easy though, compared to implementing them afterwards, due to diverging interests and arising conflicts (Aalborg, a4, 28–32). An existing *implementation gap* is reported from every region (Lodz, a4, 25–27; Bilbao, a4, 79; Istanbul, a4, 96; Timisoara, a4, 32,169) yet can be tackled by policy tools adapted to the respective local context. Different examples of such successful tools are given: Political decisions can be liable to a 'sustainability check', which asks politicians to publish sustainability impacts of the planned measures (Saarbrücken, a4, 83). The 'Environmental Diploma', an environmental management system for small and medium enterprises and municipalities, was invented on the local level and was so successful that it is now enshrined in the national law (Gothenburg, a4, 43–44). Furthermore, the 'no net loss' tool can be applied in land use planning, demanding ecological compensation measures when building on green areas. However, the principle has not become obligatory by entering the national Environmental Code (Umea, a3, 69–72). The last three examples show how "rules [can be] used as tools to change the structure of action situations" (Ostrom 2005, 68) by actors on the local level to drive the socio-ecological transition. If all these tools became part of legislation, entering the legal system of the respective country, compliance with them could be claimed by actors and could be enforced via sanctions.

Moreover, interviewees suggest *additional policy instruments that could be developed*. They stress the necessity of policy instruments underlying the link between today's investments and their positive effects in the future (St. Gallen, a4, 10) to reveal the superiority of sustainable alternatives to cheaper versions in the long run by also uncovering the social and ecological externalities of these cheaper versions. Instead of going into oversized prestige projects, funding should be invested in key lighthouse projects that upgrade the city as a whole, promoting ecological, economic, and social aspects (Saarbrücken, a3, 65).

To achieve real participative urban planning, powerful citizen participation tools should be applied (Bilbao, a4, 97; Istanbul, a1, 80; Lugano, a3, Madrid, a4, 95–103). This means for example shifting from consultation to citizens' budgets, referenda, and civic audits to reach all citizens – apart from those organised in associations (Naples, a3, 87–91 and a4, 86–93). Advanced technology development facilitates these steps (Lodz, a3, 58–59). This is necessary, since progress in the socio-ecological transition can only be made with a citizen perspective, certainly not with a sector perspective. Local authorities need to know what is important to citizens and need to have them as well as the business sector on their side (Copenhagen, a2, 100).

City administrations are often large institutions with *insufficient interdisciplinary cross-sector* communication and cooperation (Strasbourg, a4, 51–52, 74–75), sometimes due to being headed by different political parties, weakening the whole city (Copenhagen, a2, 103–106). This can produce contradictory sector policies (Glasgow, a4, 45–48). For example, environmental protection and municipal policies can be consistent with the general strategy in terms of environmental protection, yet the urban development policy by the City Planning Office might not contain a reference to green spaces. Equally, the responsibility for trees might be split between three different departments, yet there is no collaboration between them, even if officials are fully aware of this (Lodz, a4, 25, 30, 59). According to the cited actors, a uniform structure of administration with one resource being handled by one department could be a concrete solution here. However, additional cross-sector strategies need to be developed. This is the case where policy strategy on sustainability is coordinated and promoted by the specially created sustainability departments. They give input into the sector plans to keep them as cross-sectoral as possible (Aalborg, a4, 15). Innovative integral thinking is needed instead of keeping within the boundaries of one's own profession (Copenhagen, a4, 22).

Observed norm adoption by increased self-organisation and participation has in some places shifted boundary rules of local action arenas (cf. section 3.2), for example where citizens have founded an association to fight against construction development in the outer city districts (Lugano, a4, 17–20, 23–24, 57–60), having achieved an institutionalised hearing process (cf. section 5.3.1).

5.4.2 Local decision-making autonomy

According to both qualitative and quantitative data, across cities, the local level is perceived as best suited for governing the resource system of green spaces. Furthermore, it has a high level of autonomy compared to the resource systems water and especially energy (cf. chapters 3 and 6). The level of local decision-making autonomy in investing, planning, and regulating green spaces is high, but not very high, on average according to respondents from all sectors. There are no differences between the regions as a whole but between the countries of the regions, showing that the degree of autonomy granted to the local level differs across countries (cf. chapter 3).

According to all sectors, the local government is the most important actor in *defining rules on use and access to public green spaces* in green spaces governance. Local associations and civil society groups as well as local users have medium influence, whereas the existing local cooperative initiatives are of low importance. For *ensuring the availability of high-quality green spaces*, according to all sectors, the local level of the city is most relevant, followed by the district level, while the subnational, national, and European Union level are of medium to low importance.

In addition, the interviews support the conclusion that local decision-making autonomy matters for the socio-ecological transition in the green spaces resource system. Most actors estimate local autonomy as *conducive* to the transition, considering it to be necessary to *formulate local policies according to local goals, needs, and interests* for reaching sustainability

(Copenhagen, a2, 89–92; Istanbul, a1, 81 and a4, 67–72; Sibiu, a2, 185–188; Thessaloniki, a4, 86). This is because local authorities are *most aware of the city's existing problems*. In lots of places, it is stressed that local autonomy is essential since local authorities know best the citizens' needs in order to develop a corresponding policy (Bilbao, a3, 122–125; Larissa, a3, 78–79; Thessaloniki, a4, 86). This underlines the importance of the local level in a system of polycentric governance for the socio-ecological transition.

In Istanbul, missing local autonomy[6] is seen as a major obstacle to achieving sustainability. Due to a highly centralised system, the central government has to approve of all projects on the city level. This responsibility is not shared with the regional or the local level, leading to *minimal local autonomy* (Istanbul, a1, 40–41, 76–77). Thus, sustainability plans conceived on the local level can easily be thwarted by the national level (Istanbul, a1, 12–13, 16–17). The district level is the politically and financially weakest unit of all government levels; also, for decisions directly concerning green spaces governance in the respective city district, "They tie your hands with laws and regulations" (Istanbul, a1, 60–61). Yet, due to the small size of many green spaces in cities, this resource system especially lends itself to being governed also on the lowest level. For example, the district level could organise maintenance in collaboration with civil society actors, for example volunteers, associations, and schools, while responsibility for bigger green spaces as well as for street greening and other general issues would remain with the city level. Indeed, the option of involving civil society actors in the maintenance of green spaces to save costs is already practised in several cities (cf. section 5.3.1).

According to the cited interviewees in this section, Danish local authorities were granted extensive responsibility in relation to management and economics from higher government levels. Therefore, the commitment local authorities have towards the national government and the European Union are also bigger than elsewhere. They are subject to strict rules, which leave however a wide scope for *autonomous management*. Municipalities showed little interest in experiments of running an even more autonomous local management, proving their satisfaction with the current quite flexible framework which allows them to "produce a form of self-government within the framework" (Copenhagen, a2, 86–88). Municipalities are the counterpart of the national parliament, forming a good division of power and a control mechanism (Copenhagen, a3, 69–70). The municipality manages green areas and can take important decisions independently, setting priorities in agenda and budget (Copenhagen, a4, 58–61). In Copenhagen, the administration is, with 45,000 employees, the city's largest employer, with as many as 180 people working exclusively on the environment, bundling expert knowledge from many different disciplines. Thus, having the authority and the human and financial resources to be innovative, the economy follows up (Copenhagen, a2, 89–92).

Local autonomy is also understood in the sense of having a *direct communication channel from the city to the European Union's institutions* for not wasting time and opportunities due to an intermediary body for European project planning (Rome, a1, 80).

The 'crisis' and subsequent austerity politics have aggravated cities' *financial situation* and intensified their dependency on European Union funds (Naples, a4, 18–20, 58–64). There is a great need for building up knowledge of writing European Union project proposals to attract funds (Naples, a4, 78–79). Local green spaces investments often depend greatly on external funds (Lublin, a1, 34–37; Sibiu, a2, 129 and a3, 98–103). There is an attempt to match each green spaces project with national or EU funding programmes (Larissa, a4, 74–75). The findings about the greater dependence on European Union financial resources in the East and South are supported by the quantitative data, which show only one regional difference in the relevance of different government levels in ensuring the availability of green spaces. The East and the South attribute a medium relevance to the European Union's level, whereas the West and the North only see a low relevance (cf. Figure 5-8).

A minority of actors depict local autonomy as hindering the socio-ecological transition. They deplore the overly large autonomy of the local government in green spaces governance that can also be *misused* by local actors or lead to overly piecemeal planning when regional coordination might be required. For example, if the national and regional urban planning laws leave much room for manoeuvre for local governments, this can be misused to the detriment of sustainability, opting for profit, thus turning green spaces into construction sites (Milan, a3, 63–64). In Switzerland, federalism with a high degree of local autonomy concedes much power to the local government with each municipality levying its own taxes and making its own rules. Planning and collaboration on the regional (canton) level is deemed necessary by some actors to avoid *fragmentation* of the territory (Lugano, a3, 20, 26–27, 135 and a4, 77–82).

Apart from the legal framework limiting local autonomy by prescribing a more centralised system, local autonomy is influenced and can be limited by specific interest groups and private investors. Due to a desolate budget situation, cities often depend on such investments (Linz, a3, 72–73; Potsdam, a3, 181). This displays the situation reported from cities in all regions, claiming that political local autonomy, in the sense of being legally authorised to decide independently in the field of green spaces, is given in theory. However, in practice it is highly limited by the *lack of financial means* needed to implement policies (e.g. Leeds, a3, 79–86; Naples, a4, 58–64; Saarbrücken, a3, 51–54; Sibiu, a2, 129, a3, 55–57, 98 and a4, 175).

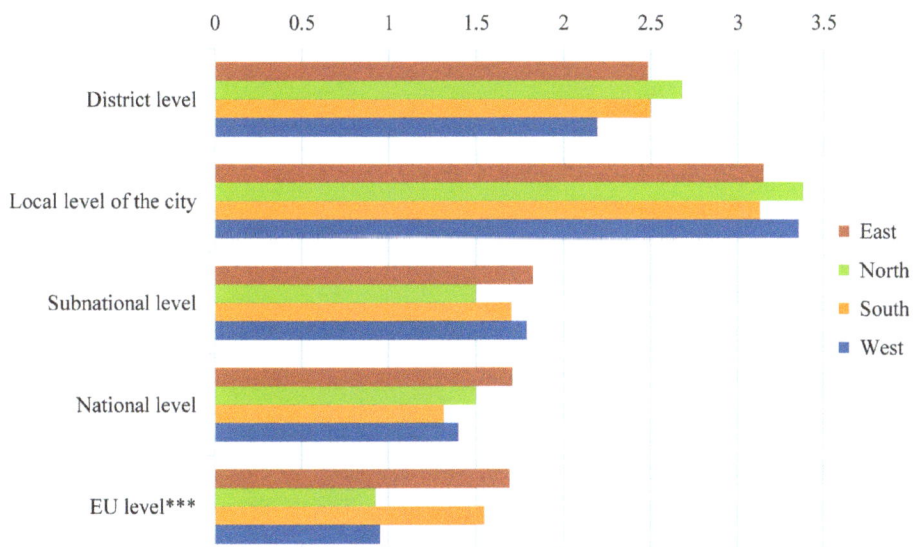

Figure 5-8 Regional differences in the relevance of different government levels in ensuring the availability of green spaces (scaled from 0: none to 4: very high)

According to Greek interviewees, the crisis has reduced local governments' room for manoeuvre (Thessaloniki, a3, 84 and a4 67–72). This virtual decrease in local autonomy stems from extremely tight local budgets and post-'crisis' European Union austerity policies pushing the central government to financially control municipalities even more. Cities face problems of covering even the operating expenses for maintenance and often are not even able to support civil society and business initiatives (cf. section 5.3.1). A comparative situation is reported from Italy and Romania, where the legal framework allows for local autonomy; yet in Italy the threat "to be thrown out of the stability pact" (Naples, a4, 18) reduces public spending to a minimum, not leaving room for action on the local level. In Sibiu, despite being chronically understaffed in the administration, the city cannot hire due to its current budgetary position (Sibiu, a2, 129). Cash-strapped cities have to find ways of economical maintenance and new funding sources or have to create income at all costs (Leeds, a3, 79). Thus, cities opt for building on the last inner-city green zones, being offered to wealthy private persons (Saarbrücken, a4, 62) or for selling big sections of their agricultural land to foreign investors, often without the public even noticing (Potsdam, a3, 191).

In Madrid, within the last five years the budget for green spaces maintenance has been cut by almost 40 per cent, and quality could only have been upheld because of the knowledge and creativity of the city's employees caring for green spaces. If the budget further decreases, quality will suffer (Madrid, a3, 26–29, 44–45, 61, 68–69). In Poland, less than 20 per cent of the cities' budgets stems from direct local taxes. The rest comes from national taxes redistributed to the regions and cities. Already stretched city budgets have additionally been burdened by tasks shifted from the national to the local level – for example in education – without providing the equivalent funding (Cracow, a1, 86–87). This disregards the *principle of connexity* according to which "legally described functions (duties) should correlate with the resources allocated" (World Bank, United Cities and Local Governments 2009, 145). The situation is not only severe in Eastern Europe. Insufficient implementation of the connexity principle is also criticised by Katja Rietzler (2014, 1–2). She states that municipalities report a clear depletion stemming from a sinking public investment ratio that leads to an investment bottleneck.[7] In order to avoid future follow-up costs, higher tax revenues are suggested. They could be generated on the one hand by the taxation of high incomes and assets, with municipalities receiving an adequate share of them, and on the other hand by better financial support for municipalities, especially for financially weak ones.

5.5 Discussion of the findings

Findings from the empirical data were displayed around the six guiding research questions (cf. subsection 3.2.7) to understand the role of self-organisation in the governance of green spaces. The conditions conducive to the emergence and the unfolding of bottom-up initiatives in the design and the preservation of common green spaces were depicted. Reasons for failure or success of local transition processes were identified and analysed by looking both at the green spaces ecological system and connected social structures to better understand how they interact.

The green spaces resource system is, more than the energy and water system, determined by local factors, yet not exclusively, as the influence of European Union and national environmental regulations on local green spaces governance shows. Self-organisation and participation emerges more easily and occurs more often in the field of green spaces than in other resource systems. This is due to the comparatively high degree of local autonomy in this field and to the tangibility of green spaces. They are visibly situated in the citizens' living environment, and attempts to reduce them immediately affect their daily quality of life. It is also easier for citizens' associations to gather support for concrete issues, such as the protection of a green space, than for lobbying the more complicated logic of self-sufficiency in the energy system or the introduction of an integrated water cycle. Thus, *self-organised and cooperative forms of management of green spaces emerge*, greatly differing in terms of numbers, shares, duration, and growth rates according to different urban contexts.

They are accelerated by *advantageous framework conditions*, for example highly motivated innovative experts working as civil servants in the local government who are little bound by bureaucracy and have a sufficient budget. Cities advanced in the transition run innovative projects with citizens' involvement that are then carried on, on a voluntary basis, or they take up and support ideas emerging from self-organised citizens' groups. These successful examples have emerged out of *collective learning processes* in which changing and new rules have been internalised. These processes are very often driven by committed key persons from all sectors that have first adopted changing and newly evolving norms and significantly pushed for their manifestation in rules. Here, successful norm adoption has led to higher levels of trust and cooperation between stakeholders and to vivid institutionalised interaction processes with the joint goal of a socio-ecological transition.

The examples of participation and self-organisation from cities across Europe show that people are able to cooperate, to organise themselves, and to take over responsibility for green spaces, while also introducing new practices that support sustainability transitions. They contribute to the maintenance of existing green spaces, which are available and accessible for all and possibly being expanded whilst ensuring biodiversity and allowing diverse use for local needs at the same time. In some cities, civil society actors have fought for their influence, whereas in others it has been granted to them by local authorities. Whereas in the majority of cities these are still *niche projects*, in a minority they have become important players in green space governance, meeting public authorities *at eye level* and cooperating with a wide range of actors. However, in all cities, responsibility for local green space governance remains with local authorities on whose cooperation self-organised actors are highly dependent to scale up successful bottom-up actions.

It cannot be judged yet whether local self-organised and cooperative management of green spaces yields better results in terms of a better internalisation of related social and ecological externalities, meaning higher levels of equity, sustainability, and efficiency, than market- or government-based provisions. This is because, on the one hand, many bottom-up activities have only started recently, and some more time is needed to evaluate their impact. On the other hand, it is sometimes difficult to attribute successful outcomes to a specific sector. *Social innovation* is not bound to the civil society sector but can equally emerge in the state and market sectors. Very often, it is collaboration across sectors that lets initiatives succeed. In addition, numerous actors on the local level take double or even triple roles, being present and active in more than one sector,[8] thus complying with Ostrom's thoughts on the benefits of *institutional diversity*.

The data demonstrates that the *logic of economic growth*, accepting its social and ecological externalities, still determines the legal framework as well as most local actors' decisions. Rules – expressed in the legal framework from local to European Union levels – are still not sufficiently modelled around sustainability outcomes, meaning taking into consideration long-term social and ecological externalities with a concomitant shift in incentives.

The persistence of the economic growth logic manifests itself in *increasing numbers of sealed surfaces* and continuing *urban sprawl* due to infrastructure and building development pressure. Swimming against this tide is possible, as numerous examples from across Europe show, yet requires not only awareness and stamina on the individual level but also a joint vision, political will, a supporting legal framework setting the right financial and fiscal incentives, as well as a certain degree of local autonomy. Otherwise, short-term profit interests will continuously determine actors' choices, be it for the mere need of closing holes in strapped public budgets or for securing jobs.

This situation shows that mere state and market solutions for the problems of ecological resilience and further ecological and social outcomes of the green spaces resource system are not sufficient and meet high obstacles in times of scarce public resources. Here, diverse forms of local, self-organised, and cooperative management of green spaces, which voluntarily take over important functions, become important. *Solutions counting on the innovation force of bottom-up actors* in interaction with open-minded representatives of the state and market sector are spreading across Europe. In this sense, a counter-power from below emerges with the potential to surpass its current niche status. Most often it originates in civil society but is then also carried into the business and government sectors, thus being institutionalised, depending on whether political, social, and economic framework conditions are conducive or hindering.

Especially in the field of green spaces, a resource system in which high profit rates are expected from the privatisation of public land, a strong legal framework is necessary to prevent these tendencies, allowing municipalities to exit the growth logic and to provide for *growth-neutral land use* within European cities. It seems that this ultimate goal can only be reached with the strengthening of participation and self-organisation capabilities in order to create a counterweight from below to a binary state and market logic of commodification.

Notes

1 The urban heat island effect refers to "the increased temperature of the urban air compared to its rural surroundings" (European Environment Agency 2012, 21). This is due to "a high amount of artificial surfaces [which store] heat and cause raised temperatures in cities compared to the surrounding region" (6). Therefore, the difference is particularly big at night.
2 Meaning groups of actors from different background organise an investigation on a field of city management. The city has to deliver the requested information and the audit identifies problems. At the end, the city is accountable to the group.
3 The correlation between the variables "Involvement of local civil society actors in governance of green spaces" and "Civil society groups in the field of green spaces are common in the city" proved to be insignificant. Both variables indicate different situations. Whereas the dependent variable refers to self-organisation, which can emerge with or without cooperation with local authorities, the other variable relates to citizen participation, thus implying as a precondition an interaction between civil society and local authorities.
4 "Not In My Backyard".
5 Semi-public companies are more than 50 per cent owned by the city yet function like private enterprises.
6 Some respondents from big cities refer the term 'local autonomy' to the city level but also use it for the lower district level, wishing this level to receive more power from the city level (respondents from Istanbul, Rome, and Naples).
7 Rietzler's analysis focuses on Germany, yet other countries of the European Union face equal problems.
8 For example, the head of the green spaces department of a German city, who also writes scientific articles, holds lectures and is an active member of the NGO Friends of the Earth Germany.

Chapter 6

Socio-ecological transitions in the water system

Stephanie Barnebeck

6.1 The role of the water resource system in sustainability transition

Water covers more than 70 per cent of the Earth's surface. However, only 2.5 per cent of the total volume is freshwater. The water system is in many regards special, as the natural and cultural functions of the resource are diverse and strongly influence each other. Human activity can affect water quantity and quality. Natural functions of water are life sustainment, habitat, and regulation like the energy balance, the hydrological cycle, and the matter balance (the self-purification of nature, solvent and transport medium, hydromorphology). The cultural functions of water are consumption and withdrawal for food and drinking, cleansing and agricultural as well as industrial production. Withdrawal of water reduces the quantity of the water resource and may also change water quality, as some original characteristics of the water can get lost. Likewise, water is used, but not withdrawn, for transportation, energy production, fisheries, aesthetics, and recreational or spiritual purposes. These types of use can also lead to pollution, and the habitat functions of the water can be impaired (cf. WBGU 1997, 45–48). Moreover, climatic changes can affect the hydrologic cycle (Richard G. Taylor et al. 2013), since the main water inflow happens by atmospheric deposition. Regional surface and groundwater resources are often interconnected.

In contrast to the energy system, the geographical boundaries of the urban water system are well defined. However, it is strongly linked to the environmental compartments of air and soil and, due to its mobility and solvent properties, functions as a transport system for all types of pollutants (Malin Falkenmark and Johan Rockström 2004, 22–24). As a result of pollution and withdrawal, the natural functions of streams, lakes, and groundwater are impaired, which has negative impacts on the environment. Sustainable and environmentally healthy water resource management is necessary to ensure drinking water quality and quantity in the future (cf. David R. Marlow et al. 2013). 'Integrated urban water cycle management' is one connected catchphrase. The elements of the urban water cycle – water supply, sewage, and storm water – are managed as interlinked components of an institutionally and organisationally integrated water basin system. Water resource sustainability should be improved by the connection of human and ecosystem requirements. Nevertheless, practical evidence of the benefits is ambivalent (Wietske Medema, Brian S. McIntosh, and Paul J. Jeffrey 2008). The institutional context to enable a shift from a traditional, centralised water infrastructure towards a more decentralised one was, for instance, analysed in Briony C. Ferguson et al. (2013).

The management of the resource water is influenced by the values found in the particular sociocultural context of the society using the water (cf. WBGU 1997, 47). Protection and sustainable use of freshwater can often be attained efficiently on the local level, namely, in the corresponding water catchment areas (cf. WBGU 2011, 42). The research on the transition towards sustainable water management on the city level in 14 European countries ties up to these declarations.

The loss of drinking water always refers to insufficient infrastructure, either through leaking water pipes or through malfunctions in facilities of the waterworks, which lead to water pollution. Missing resources through losses, pollution, or high consumption levels can cause scarcity of drinking water. Climatic phenomena like droughts and floods may also cause scarcity, the latter because of its polluting impact. In addition, sealed surfaces in urban areas can lead to water scarcity, since they prevent the refilling of groundwater reservoirs by natural infiltration. Any kind of pollution negatively affects the quality of the drinking water. It can thus be improved by establishing water protection areas. Drinking water is usually extracted from surface water (lakes, springs, and rivers) – replenishing rather fast – or groundwater reservoirs that take about eight years to replenish. For instance, nitrates and pesticides through intensive agricultural land usage, contamination due to industrial production practices, pollution based on dense settlement in urban areas, and new types of contamination by antibiotics and hormones as well as hydraulic fracturing[1] directly threaten these water sources (John-Karl Böhlke 2002; Thomas Heberer 2002; Marta Carballa et al. 2004; Prem. K. Goel 2006, 1–3). Overconsumption of drinking water (for example by irrigation of green spaces) puts additional pressure on the availability of water. Thus, the endeavour to prevent pollution and the loss of drinkable water is crucial for a sustainable management of water reserves and for ensuring the good quality and broad availability of drinking water in the future.

Wastewater needs to be cleaned before it can be re-fed into the hydrological cycle. Wastewater treatment plants consume a high amount of energy for operation if they are run by an aerobic process. Modern technologies furthermore allow the production of electric energy out of effluent sludge as well as the provision of heating for nearby residential areas (Perry L. McCarty, Jaeho Bae, and Jeonghwan Kim 2011). After using the effluent sludge, there are still substances like phosphorus and nitrogen in the digestate that could be reused (Harry van Veldhuizen, Mark C.M. van Loosdrecht, and Sef J.J. Heijnen 1999; Xinchao Wei, Roger C. Viadero, Jr., and Shilpa Bhojappa 2008). Infrastructural modernisation is therefore an opportunity for local water suppliers to take a step towards more sustainable water management. The tight interconnection between the water resource system and the energy system is visible here as well.

Summing up the findings from the case study reports on the topic of water shows that the status of the water and sewage system is very different throughout the four researched European regions; so the perceived challenges and urgencies are quite heterogeneous, too. In general, there is a trend towards overall decreasing water consumption; only some growing cities face an increase. Particularly in Eastern Europe, the awareness of (potential) problems by public authorities is low. There are some water quality problems, and the still high per capita water consumption should be restricted more efficiently. Development plans most often affect modernisation of the water infrastructure. In the South, problems are already present and the most serious in Europe. There are high water losses due to bad infrastructure and also high water consumption. Water scarcity and poor quality can be observed at times. Approaches for solutions refer to infrastructural measures, awareness-raising campaigns addressing users, and pricing policy. In North Europe, problems refer to the pollution of water reserves and negative climatic influences. Proceeded solutions are environmental protection, education, and innovative wastewater treatment technologies. Problems addressed in Western European cities are rising water prices, required conformations to EU regulations, water pollution, and decreasing consumption levels.[2] Approaches to the problems are monitoring, increasing the efficiency of sanctions, or campaigns promoting the drinking of tap water. Citizens' initiatives contradicting the privatisation of water utilities came up especially in Italy. Groups dealing with seawater protection formed in some Western coastal cities. Civil society action can be observed where apparent problems occur (Garzillo and Ulrich 2015).

The potential of civil society involvement in sustainable water management exists, but local citizens' initiatives dealing with drinking water quality and availability are confronted with a very different scope of action compared to the green spaces or energy systems. Characteristics of the water network (including its indivisibility and invisibility of large parts of it), legal framework, and time horizon of investment allow, for instance, new institutional arrangements with the aim of influencing decision-making processes, to inform and raise awareness, or to set up frames for cooperation of all stakeholders. It is usually neither reasonable nor possible to act separately from governmental bodies and/or the water utility providers, as these decision-makers have to implement or at least support sustainable solutions. In addition to local civil society action, there is a European movement against the privatisation of the water resource. The first successful European Citizen's Initiative Right2Water collected more than 1.8 million signatures and called on the European Commission "to implement the human right to water and sanitation in European law" (Human Right to Water 2014).

The analysed qualitative data (1 to 3 interviews per city) originate from 18 cities covering all regions and 12 of the participating countries except Denmark and Greece, where no interviews on the water topic were conducted. Interviews from Barcelona, Birmingham, Freiburg, Giurgiu, Innsbruck, Istanbul, Kiel, Lodz, London, Lublin, Nice, Prague, Rennes, Rome, St. Gallen, Trieste, Umea, and Valencia will be analysed. Two interviews stem from political actors (a1), one from an administrative actor (a2), 14 from business actors (a3), and 14 from civil society actors (a4). Findings about the characteristics, challenges, and solutions concerning the water resource system from 40 case study reports – one per city in the whole sample – supplement the data (Garzillo and Ulrich 2015). The analysed quantitative data stems from 135 questionnaires on 'sustainable water use with regards to quality and availability'; 37 questionnaires were filled by government actors (from administration, cf. chapter 2), 49 from business actors, and 49 from civil society actors. Most actors from qualitative research are included in the quantitative sample, as actors a2, a3, and a4 gave interviews and afterwards filled in questionnaires.

6.2 Self-organisation capabilities and sustainability transitions

Following the logic of the socio-ecological system (SES) approach's transition model (cf. chapter 3), the focus of the following sections is set on the water resource system and the underlying governance system, as well as interactions within and outcomes from the system. First, two research questions, whether a common understanding of sustainability transition can be observed and if self-organisation is a transition driver, will be answered.

Alongside the understanding of transition, the cities' initial positions in the process as well as present and future challenges will be observed.

6.2.1 Socio-ecological transitions

Definitions of sustainability have already been discussed in earlier chapters. There is a consensus that human activities should not harm the natural environment (Prague, a4, 11), or expressed differently "Don't steal from your grandkids" (Birmingham, a3, 10–13). Also the three pillars economy, society, and ecology are brought up, with different foci on the one or the other element (e.g. Rennes, a4, 9; Rome a4, 9; Giurgiu, a4, 14–15; Lublin, a3, 19). It is agreed that sustainability is a complex matter and that it must be seen in a greater context than in just one resource system, that is sustainability is important in all fields of action (Giurgiu, a3, 16). That might be the reason why most respondents would not give an isolated view on sustainability in the water system but gave rather generalised definitions. More precise definitions of sustainability in the water system are that the water chain must be kept in balance, including fish, insects, quality, and so on (Birmingham, a4, 14) and also that the networks must be modernised and rivers renaturalised (Lodz, a2, 12).

The actors involved with the water system assessed the socio-ecological transition differently depending on the regarded cities. An approach to sustainability needs to be tailor-made, as every city has different characteristics (London, a3, 15–16). Some actors see the expansion of new energies as the main system to be developed and regard water, mobility, and other fields as additional (e.g. Nice, a4, 25–32; Innsbruck, a1, 15; St. Gallen, a3, 10). In some cities, political will and interests lead the way to transition, which goes from the local level to the EU (e.g. Rennes, a4, 139–142). In others, civil society enables transition paths by opposing profit-driven private organisations (e.g. Prague, a4, 29, 41). It is a widespread belief that a successful transition is driven by awareness, personal experience, and individual behaviour. Awareness allows for behaviour change and willingness to invest in sustainable solutions. Additionally, if sustainable solutions also maximise economic profit, the general support of these solutions will intensify (e.g. Istanbul, a3, 60; Valencia, a3, 22). Sustainability can also be limited and used as an alibi for profit and economic development, especially when water supply is fully or partly privatised. Privatisation is assessed as contradictory to the understanding of sustainability that profit is not the first priority (Freiburg, a3, 19–20).

The status of the resource water can be assessed by regarding the quality and availability of drinking water and the frequency of complaints about several aspects regarding the drinking water system. Water quality is on average very good in North and West Europe and good in the East and South. Water availability is worse in the South compared with the rest of Europe. However, currently no bigger problems are recorded through the questionnaires. In general, complaints are rarely made, especially in North and West Europe. If so, most often citizens complain about the pricing of tap water and about surface water quality. Bad taste or smell of tap water, for example through high chlorine content, are brought up occasionally in the South and East, but close to never in the other regions. Users complaining about being forced to buy bottled water due to bad tap water quality can be seen occasionally in Southern Europe, but never in Western countries. The proportions of bottled water and tap water used for nutrition differ in the four regions. In the North, East, and West people use 80 to 90 per cent tap water and equally less bottled water. In some countries like Austria, Denmark, and Sweden, it is very unusual to drink bottled water, and the proportion of tap water is even higher. In the South, the proportion of tap water is only about 70 per cent on average, and people use more bottled water than in any other region, reaching up to over 80 per cent bottled water in some cities with rather bad tap water quality.

Most cities withdraw drinking water from surface water and replenishable groundwater reservoirs. Fossil groundwater reservoirs and long-distance water sources (over 100 kilometres) are only of low or medium importance. Desalinated seawater and rainwater play a minor role. Most commonly, cities do not rely on only one source but combine different water sources (e.g. Freiburg, a4, 46–47; Nice, a4, 73; Prague, a3, 101–103). Long-distance water sources are nevertheless relevant for cities with insufficient reserves of their own (e.g. Istanbul, a3, 49; Rennes, a3, 40). Depending on the size of the water system, consumption levels, and climatic conditions, the present and future availability of drinking water according to EU quality standards is very different in the cities. Some actors assume that water availability will "always be sufficient" for their cities (e.g. Innsbruck, a1, 63; Birmingham, a3, 45; Kiel, a4, 41–43; Valencia, a3, 60), whilst others think they will face serious problems in the future or already experience occasional water scarcity (e.g. Barcelona, a4, 57; London, a3, 36; Lublin, a3, 35; Rennes, a3, 31–32). Many actors state that water availability is not currently an issue but that this could change if the use of water resources does not become more sustainable (e.g. Prague, a4, 15; Umea, a4, 57; Valencia, a4, 42). There is general sensitivity for the need of sustainability concerning water.

The productivity of the drinking water system can be assessed by relating the produced output (drinking water) to the input into the system. The cleaner and easier to access water resources are, the higher the productivity, as only little further processing is necessary to meet quality standards for drinking water. As illustrated in section 6.1, the quality and quantity of ground and surface water also depend on the condition of the wastewater released back into the natural water system and on the quantity of rainwater that can be absorbed by the soil. Especially in the South and parts of the East of Europe, high loss rates of up to 50 per cent due to outdated infrastructure are reported (e.g. Giurgiu, a1, 28–34; Prague, a4, 15–17; Rome, a4, 47; Trieste, a3, 46–48). In combination with high consumption patterns, losses can cause the overexploitation of natural resources (Rome, a4, 47). If the quantity of rainwater replenishing the water reservoirs is much greater than the quantity of water lost through leaking pipes, these losses cause no severe problems (Trieste, a3, 48). Water that cannot get back into the water cycle, not only endangers the replenishment of groundwater reservoirs, but also affects the ground, where soil and debris are carried away (Innsbruck, a4, 31).

The reuse of wastewater with appropriate methods helps to safeguard water quantity and quality and to reduce the pressure on the ecosystem, but it is not yet implemented in all cities. In many cities, most of the water requires purification (Barcelona, a4, 59; Kiel, a3, 149–152; Lublin, a3, 31; Valencia, a4, 40). Sometimes the capacity of the system is too low or too big (Prague, a3, 113; Giurgiu, a1, 28–34). Investments in infrastructure and especially in modern technologies are instruments to increase productivity. Technology is getting cheaper and more efficient (e.g. Kiel, a3, 24–26; Valencia, a3, 62), so "you can make drinking water out of every puddle of water. . . . You have to be willing to invest in this know-how in case of need" (Freiburg, a3, 42). Technology offers opportunities but can also increase the cost of water (Valencia, a3, 62). For example, desalination plants require a huge amount of energy, but the gained amount of water is quite low (London, a4, 76). The transport of water over long distances is energy intensive, too (Istanbul, a3, 80). Wastewater treatment also consumes a lot of energy, but energy can also be produced by using sewer sludge in biogas digesters, reducing the overall energy consumption of the treatment plants or even providing surplus energy to be sold (Freiburg, a4, 72; Nice, a3, 25–35; Rennes, a3, 69). The questionnaires showed that the impact of investments in water infrastructure has been high for the cities and the impact of the adoption of new technologies has been medium on average. These aspects of productivity ensure the availability of drinking water according to EU quality standards. Especially in the East, investment in infrastructure has had a very big influence. In the West, the impact has been below average. This reflects the different states of the water systems in these regions described in section 6.1 and the case study reports (cf. chapter 2; Garzillo and Ulrich 2015).

The cities experience or expect a variety of challenges concerning their drinking water systems. Challenges faced are the increase or decrease of water consumption; an insufficient state of infrastructure; the degradation of ground, spring, or surface water resources; a decrease in drinking water quality; and a decrease in water availability due to droughts and climate changes (cf. Figure 6-1). These challenges are rated as of between low and medium relevance in West Europe, which faces relatively small challenges overall, especially in Austria. The Eastern and Southern countries rated these challenges as of medium to high relevance. The state of infrastructure and a decrease in drinking water quality are, however, less challenging in Polish cities than in the Czech and Romanian cities. The pressure on the water resource system seems to be strongest in the South. The Northern countries mainly face challenges of degradation of water resources, though the UK also reports an insufficient state of infrastructure, an increase in water consumption, and a decrease in water availability.

An increasing number of built-up areas and a decreasing number of green areas hinder storm water from being soaked in and accessing groundwater, so systems for discharging these waters must be built and "sewer systems must be sufficiently expanded",

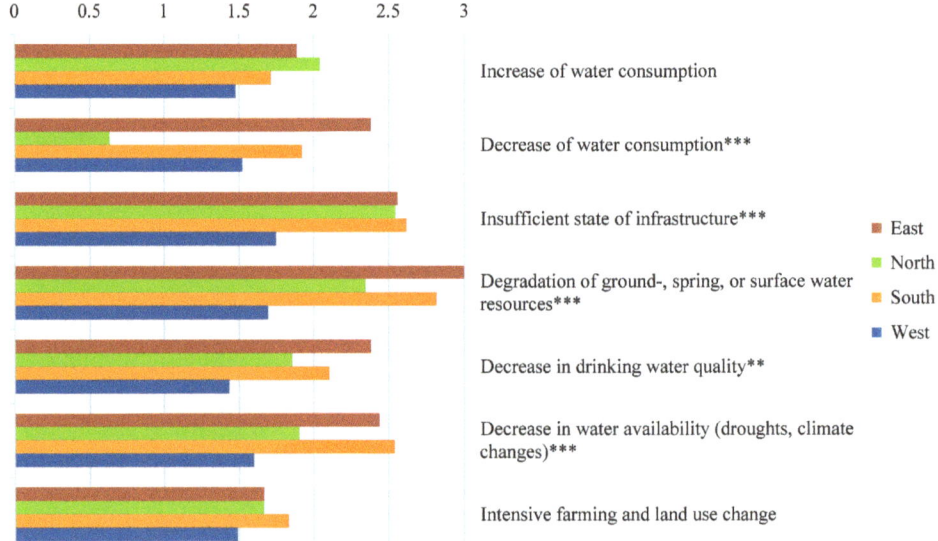

Figure 6-1 Challenges for the water provision until 2030 (scaled from 0: no relevance to 4: very high relevance)

being expensive and sometimes technically challenging (Lublin, a3, 37; Prague, a4, 45). For instance, in pedestrian redevelopment, the drainage of paved areas can be constructed in a way that "water would not run on the streets but would soak into the grass next to it" (Prague, a4, 29). Many cities still use drinking water for irrigation. In several places, drinking water is also used for the cleaning of urban spaces. In some cities, systems were developed to use water from other sources, for example reused sanitation water or reclaimed rainwater to irrigate green spaces or to clean the streets (Barcelona, a4, 99). Especially big and growing cities already tend to overuse their groundwater resources, which cannot be renewed to the extent necessary (Prague, a4, 45).

The lack of awareness of water-related issues concerning consumption patterns and sustainable water and sewage treatment amongst citizens and politicians is reported from various cities throughout Europe (e.g. Barcelona, a4, 33; Freiburg, a4, 73; Giurgiu, a4, 45–46; Rennes, a3, 25 and a4, 103–109). Information about the exploitation of resources and on sustainable feed-in is rarely available (Kiel, a3, 68; Trieste, a3, 25). The fact that environmental education has to start in kindergarten and that cultural imprints can only be changed slowly is mentioned as well (Barcelona, a4, 33; Giurgiu, a3, 31; Nice, a4, 113 and a4, 34–49; Rennes, a4, 113). Communication patterns to educate and inform people must be considered. People who are bored about environmental action plans will not listen and change their behaviour, but if the potential benefits for them are pointed out in a clear language, they will be interested (London, a4, 38).

The size of the city is a factor concerning water issues. Especially integrated, holistic solutions must take into account the uniqueness of cities and even neighbourhoods, which is quite challenging. The developments in different areas like green spaces, tourism, buildings, or commuting should be harmonised through smart solutions (Kiel, a4, 21; London, a3, 26). Big cities with a high population density and many governance levels controlling the planning processes of their borough face special problems. These structures antagonise superior sustainability plans. Furthermore, environmental aspects are sometimes poorly integrated into the rest of urban policy (e.g. Barcelona, a4, 34; London, a4, 16; Valencia, a4, 19). In contrast, some actors stated that their cities developed plans, taking into account environmental and social parameters (Rome, a4, 27; St. Gallen, a3, 10). Long-term sustainability of water supply can only be achieved by finding a balance between supply and demand. A lack of long-term thinking in planning in general has sometimes been stated (e.g. Giurgiu, a1, 47 and a3, 39; Kiel, a3, 42; London, a4, 70; Rennes, a4, 13).

Pollution as a result of human activities is an issue in some cities (e.g. Nice, a3, 29; Trieste, a4, 41; Valencia, a3, 54). Regulations force cities to reduce pollutants in order to catch up with EU quality standards, or old infrastructure has to be modernised for technical reasons. Investments must be made regularly, since infrastructure needs to be maintained as well (Barcelona, a4, 59; Giurgiu, a3, 40). However, many cities face problems in funding necessary water infrastructure projects (e.g. Giurgiu, a3, 29; Kiel, a4, 113; Prague, a4, 59; Trieste, a3, 9). In some regions, the European Regional Development Fund supports these investments, but not all kinds of projects can be financed that way. In addition, bureaucratic hurdles or failures in acquiring funding can play a role (Lodz, a2, 18–22; Nice, a3, 38–39; Trieste, a4, 47). Some municipalities feel the pressure by citizens' referenda to keep the water supply public but lack the necessary financial means to invest in the maintenance of the water system (Trieste, a3, 58; cf. section 6.3.2). The liberalisation of the water market creates additional fear and uncertainty for the future (Freiburg, a3, 26; Innsbruck, a1, 9). The background is the increasing private sector involvement in the water system over the past decades. The main drivers in the liberalisation process are financial and ideological factors. Forms span from private sector participation to full privatisation, which is rather exceptional. Alongside liberalisation in the network industries, significant changes exist in the mode of market regulation. However, properties of the water systems impede the liberalisation of the water market – which is a kind of 'natural monopoly' and essential to human existence – by requiring institutions to guarantee the coherence of organisational and technical as well as human needs. Thus, the water market stayed rather strongly regulated, regardless of implemented reforms (Claude Ménard and Aleksandra Peeroo 2011, 310–316).

Ecological and social objectives sometimes collide. When industries disappear from the cities, pollution vanishes too, being positive from an environmental point of view but disastrous from a social position, thus likewise not being sustainable. It is also argued that, if social problems and poverty are central, there is no room and no interest to think about sustainability for the people (Birmingham, a3, 28; Giurgiu, a4, 38). Also social incentives like free water provision for schools and public organisations instead of – for instance – water-recycling incentives contradict environmental sustainability objectives (Istanbul, a3, 78).

Goals and their time horizons depend on the transition urgency perceived by the cities. Meteorological conditions play the main role here. Rain is crucial to refill water sources; if rain stays away, problems occur. Additionally, new water sources need to be found (Nice, a3, 89; Rennes, a3, 34 and a4, 57). "Either we continue until there is a catastrophic drought, . . . or we do large-scale water efficiency programmes, or we . . . build desalination plants" (London, a4, 74). In addition, different climatic changes worry many cities. In the Alps, glacial retreat, defrosting of the permafrost, and resulting mudslides as well as heavy rainfalls already show impacts (Innsbruck, a1, 65).

Goals exist on different dimensions and across resource systems and topics. Some cities are looking for a collaborative way to manage resources and social targets, so coordination and communication between different levels of government (local, regional, and national) is necessary. Trans-regional sustainability should focus more on the local than on the national level, whilst local development must be harmonised with EU policies (Freiburg, a3, 69; Kiel, a4, 39; Rennes, a3, 76 and a4, 143; Trieste, a4, 71, 81). It was also claimed that information on the planning of projects reaches the citizens and a focus on participation by empowering citizens and by promoting collective decision-making (Kiel, a3, 188 and a4, 73; Prague, a4, 70). The appropriate value of common goods should be added and taken into account when implementing actions and allocating funds (Trieste, a4, 69). Investment in human capital together with a modernisation of company structures and adequate salaries for families to afford a good life are further important economic and social goals (Innsbruck, a4, 104; Kiel, a3, 122, 132; Rennes, a4, 135). The ecological goals are interwoven and affect all resource systems, such as renewable energy development, energy efficiency, district heating, sewage plant modernisation, or mobility management (Freiburg, a4, 21; Innsbruck, a1, 15 and a4, 102; Kiel, a3, 155–156, 264 and a4, 71; Prague, a4, 62; Trieste, a4, 59). Especially relevant for the water system are

- the focus on ecological farming and sustainable agricultural development,
- the protection and conservation of flora and fauna,
- an appropriate water resource management,
- the regulation of consumption patterns,

- recycling of the substances contained in sewage water,
- water network renovation, and
- eco-friendly practices instead of hazardous substance used in industry and households.

The time horizon to achieve sustainability goals varies between 10 and 35 years (Innsbruck, a1, 9 and a4, 102; Prague, a3, 104–105; Kiel, a3, 187–190; Trieste, a3, 86). Some see a pessimistic scenario, where sustainability will never be achieved (Prague, a2, 15). Some assess that sustainability will be difficult to achieve, especially in the short or medium term (Barcelona, a4, 111; Istanbul, a3, 100). Furthermore, "[i]nfrastructure in the form of canalisation and sewage plants is very, very enduring. To transmogrify this, you inherently need two generations" (Freiburg, a4, 69).

Many cities experience that a transition in the field of water has already begun. "During the last 15 years very significant efforts have been made" (Rennes, a3, 38). Contamination has been reduced in many water bodies by better sanitation technology, better monitoring, rehabilitation, ecological landfills, or regulation of farming activities (e.g. Barcelona, a4, 54, 59, 64, 75; Birmingham, a4, 16; Giurgiu, a3, 74, 95; Rennes, a3, 36–38 and a4, 54–55). Freiburg began as early as in the 1980s to cooperate with farmers at eye level. Pollution with pesticides and nitrates could be reduced significantly, and the "trend could be reversed" (Freiburg, a4, 42; 56). Some cities already use modern integrated methods on mixing water, rainwater treatment, and desalination (Barcelona, a4, 86). Initiatives exist to drink tap water instead of buying bottled water in cooperation with local councils, citizens, and community organisations (e.g. London, a4, 45–50, 60). There are also examples where action has been taken but are seen as insufficient or ambivalent or where projects were never implemented (Innsbruck, a4, 25; Istanbul, a3, 49–51; London, a4, 14).

6.2.2 Self-organisation capabilities

Whether citizens (can) participate and self-organised initiatives (can) emerge depends on a variety of factors. There is a difference between mere participation and self-organisation, as described in chapter 3. In many cities, some form of participation exists, but the citizens' influence on the decision-making process is very different. The impetus to participate can derive from the citizens themselves (Innsbruck, a4, 45). There are a few cities with a strong history of participation dating back to the 1970s or 1980s but not necessarily on water issues (Freiburg, a4, 40, 48). In other cities, associations, cooperatives, and initiatives are recently flourishing. Their fields of action are the cleaning of water streams and seawater protection or the monitoring of water projects including consulting and the provision of operational support (e.g. Barcelona, a4, 51; Innsbruck, a4, 51; Nice, a3, 62; Prague, a4, 47; Valencia, a3, 46).

Criticism focuses on the lack of interest by citizens to get involved in water issues regardless of participation possibilities. The reasons are a lack of awareness of problems and motivation and the general opinion that water will always come out of the tap (e.g. Kiel, a4, 53–57; London, a3, 42–46 and a4, 57–58, 77–86; Rome, a4, 45; Trieste, a3, 69–74; Umea, a4, 62–67; Valencia, a3, 97–99). Sometimes it was stated that citizens only got involved in water issues in the case of privatisation plans or pricing issues and on the question of whether water was a common good (London, a4, 77–86; Rennes, a3, 48; Rome, a4, 45; Trieste, a3, 69–74). It is also quite difficult for a public without subject-specific background to engage in technically complex topics like drinking water, thus limiting participation capabilities. "Basically, this is a problem of time.... As a private person, I would not have the time for it.... To my mind, this is the main reason why it does not work.... The subject matter is way too complex for everyone to be able to give a qualified opinion on it" (Freiburg, a3, 48).

Local NGOs and other civil society organisations show on average only little leadership on water issues. Government and business actors consider their reputation and capability as especially low. This assessment could point to ignorance about existing civil society initiatives by official bodies and business actors involved in water management (cf. Figure 6-2). Interviewees also stated that some voluntary initiatives and civil society groups lack in scientific or specialist human capital or are considered as naïve or unimportant by decision-makers (Istanbul, a3, 31–34; Trieste, a3, 42).

Participation can be misunderstood as monitoring on the household level or changing personal habits. Real participation does not only mean sending letters of complaint or commenting on urban challenges but finding ways of interaction between administration and civil society in terms of problem-solving and decision-making (Birmingham, a3, 71–72; Trieste, a4, 35–37 and a3, 42; cf. subsection 4.2.2). Providing information and consultation is an important part of civil society participation in water management, but it should not be limited to this (Trieste, a3, 40–42). Individual behavioural changes in water use, the sharing of information on water quality and availability, and reporting and monitoring are commonly possible (e.g. Barcelona, a4, 93–95; Rome, a4, 71).

Political support is crucial for successful participation of civil society initiatives. There are possibilities for administration to be close to the citizens and provide open communication and cooperation channels (St. Gallen, a3, 10). In some cities, committees or councils exist through which civil society members can participate in deciding on local projects and plans. Sometimes limited financial resources are allocated through these councils. Usually, these are not constrained to water issues but deal with different local matters (e.g. Barcelona, a4, 76–77; Birmingham, a4, 73–81; Giurgiu, a1, 82–89; Lublin, a3, 40–44; Rome, a4, 39). The possibility of being heard by decision-makers through petitions, proposals, consulting, and consumers' consultation bodies, and through participating in debates and discussions, is given in some cities (Rennes, a3, 52; St. Gallen, a3, 10; Valencia, a4, 34). In a few cities, civil society organisations have the opportunity to participate via formalised 'round tables' or in advisory boards, where their opinion on drinking water topics is heard

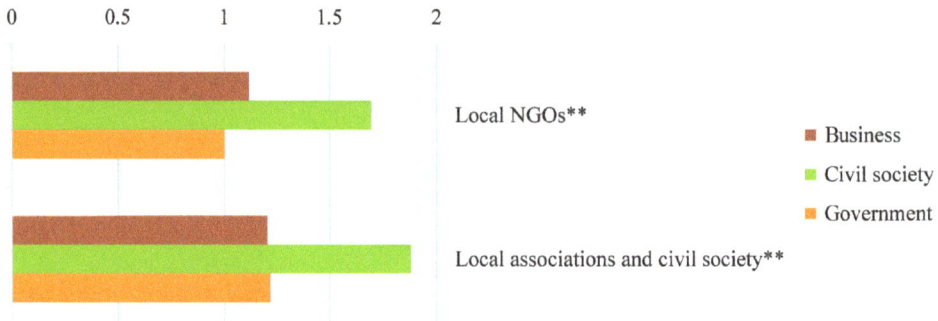

Figure 6-2 Leadership of civil society organisations (in terms of reputation and capability) in ensuring the quality and availability of drinking water (scaled from 0: none to 4: very high)

and discussed. The quality or efficiency of cooperation depends on its actual conditions and contents, though (Rennes, a3, 46; Rome, a4, 53). Transparency initiatives by public administrations exist (e.g. Lodz, a2, 47). Nevertheless, performance indicators on water services are still not efficiently compiled and published everywhere (Rennes, a3, 76–77).

Yet, the cases in which no or only very little participation regarding water is possible outweigh these examples. Low citizens' empowerment and weak NGOs in combination with a local government not paying attention to citizens' opinions cause situations in which political proceedings leave no room for participation (e.g. Birmingham, a3, 48–49; Istanbul, a3, 52–56; Rome, a3, 73). Even when the formal frame for participation is provided, there can be hindrances, aiming to avoid the influence of civil society actors in decision-making processes. Once-open participation channels can be cut off by not calling meetings anymore, for instance. Some local and central governments consider participation to cause a variety of 'troubles', amongst them the need for increased transparency and the necessity of considering citizens' proposals. In these cases, only the most motivated citizens find ways to participate (Giurgiu, a4, 68–74; Valencia, a4, 34, 44–50). Local governments need to reach out and be reachable at the same time. Participation and involvement do not occur by themselves; the authorities should approach the citizens. "The feeling of the population is: no matter what we say, they will do what they want anyway. . . . Overexposure of negative cases and bad models of practice made people have this type of feeling" (Giurgiu, a4, 106).

The formation of self-organisation might gather momentum in the case of very restrictive participation possibilities as well as in the case of open participation channels. On the one hand, civil society movements could emerge when local decision-makers are considered not to act in accordance with the wishes of the citizens. On the other hand, a fertile ground in terms of administrations inviting citizens to participate can support new institutional arrangements. Various cities' interviewees state an active civil society and self-organised citizens. Their tasks are diverse, from protesting against particular projects to broader activities like the promotion of sustainable living or the empowerment of citizens (e.g. Barcelona, a4, 52; Prague, a4, 29, 57; Rome, a4, 17, 39; Trieste, a4, 77). Self-organisation concerning water resource management is nevertheless rare and still in the early stages (e.g. Freiburg, a4, 68). Existing organisations mainly inform and educate citizens and officials about sustainable water use. There would be room for many more issues of water availability and quality like the mixing of grey water or wastewater treatment (Istanbul, a3, 71–78; Kiel, a4, 25; Nice, a4, 84; Rome, a4, 17). Funding is sometimes a problem, as initiatives have expenses, but are not financed by the municipality. Instead of direct funding of initiatives, also the infrastructure needed for their activities could be provided (Trieste, a3, 58, 92).

Networking becomes important in many cases for cities (e.g. Barcelona, a4, 57; Giurgiu, a4, 57–58; Valencia, a3, 46–50). However, cooperation with citizens' initiatives for water issues is still quite uncommon. Partnerships between civil society and local government on projects for water protection and on water resource management exist in only a few cities (Rennes, a4, 33, 46–48). Sometimes utility providers cooperate with universities (Rennes, a3, 17). As there is hardly any cooperation, few conflicts emerge. There seems to be more cooperation and even fewer conflicts between the three sectors in Western Europe (cf. Figure 6-3). Interviewees from different sectors stated several times the affected groups' willingness to cooperate. Even small projects can enhance networking and create good relationships between initiatives, NGOs, water utility, and politics. Sometimes problems

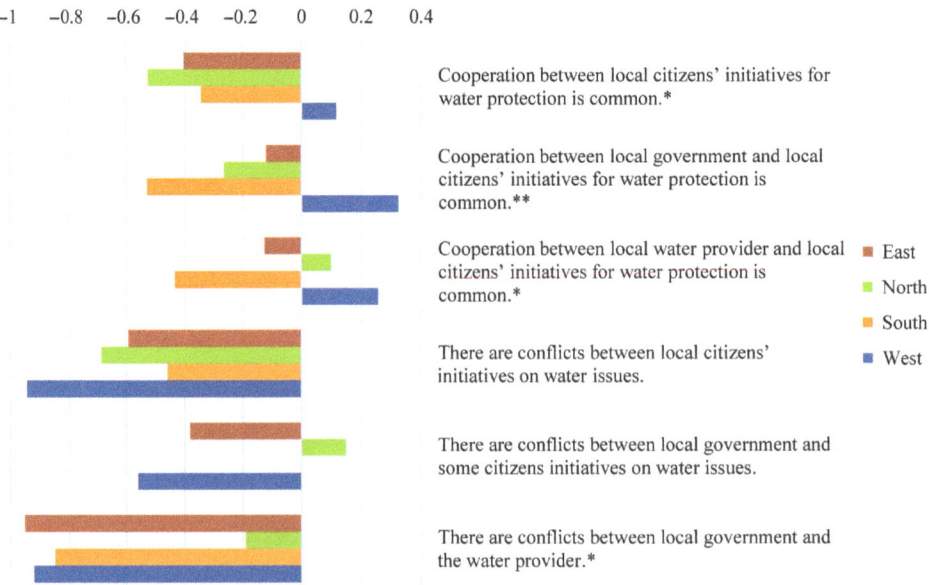

Figure 6-3 Statements on norms of trust (scaled from −2: strongly disagree to +2: strongly agree)

arise when funding from higher levels of government ends (Barcelona, a4, 78–80, 93–95; Birmingham, a4, 51–53, 89; London, a4, 53–56).

Conflicts can emerge between all kinds of interest groups, such as industries and civil society (e.g. Barcelona, a4, 59; Umea, a4, 61), utility provider and municipality and/or civil society (e.g. Giurgiu, a1, 80; Prague, a3, 107), or business/civil society and government (e.g. Istanbul, a3, 53). Subjects of these conflicts are varying: price developments of a cubic metre of water, pollution of resources by industries or agriculture, building projects endangering resources, legal obstacles for interest groups to participate in decision processes, or territory conflicts. Civil society respondents see more conflicts and less cooperation between citizens' initiatives on the one hand and the water provider or government on the other, compared to government or business respondents. A lack of consensus within civil society is obstructive (Giurgiu, a1, 82–89; Rome, a4, 13). Remarkably, conflicts between the local government and the water provider were only stated in Greece.

Some factors influencing the emergence of a civil society movement can be identified from the data. The positive impact of technology adoption on water availability in the past, the challenge of overall decreasing water consumption, a strong local government concerning water issues, and sufficient action from public authorities to prevent overabstraction of water resources tend to negatively influence leadership in terms of reputation and capability in ensuring water quality and availability of civil society organisations. These factors represent capability and action of local authorities. A decently performing authority makes self-organisation less likely. Factors that tend to have a positive influence on the evolvement of civil society organisations' leadership are the observed positive impact of technology adaption on water availability, the existing local challenge of degraded water resources, and the price elasticity of demand for drinking water as an aspect of social conflict. These factors stand for the environmental and social challenges and the local technological standards. Good cooperation between utility providers and civil society initiatives, sufficient support by authorities to install sustainable water technologies, and sufficient action from authorities to prevent infiltration also affect self-organisation positively. The first two variables work as indicators for the relationship between public authorities and civil society. Good contact and communication between these encourage self-organisation. Preventing the infiltration of pollutants is, in contrast to the prevention of overabstraction, a complementary task of civil society, public authorities, and utility providers and can be a vantage point for cooperation with civil society (for example farmers), explaining the different signs of the coefficients (cf. Table 6-1). Bias must be taken into consideration, as civil society respondents assessed the leadership of civil society organisations on average as stronger than business respondents and government respondents did. This shows throughout the complete quantitative research and reflects different interests, information, and objectives of the three sectors.

It is not possible to talk about a water transition process through active participation or even strong self-organisation, as participation options, civil society's motivation, and the current state of self-organisation are still relatively modest in this resource system's management. The possibility of self-organised monitoring of the water quality and availability and sanctioning is nevertheless used in some cities (Birmingham, a3, 73–76; Giurgiu, a3, 97–98; Rome, a3, 89). Some respondents, however, stated that their cities have highly motivated, very proactive citizens despite the unfavourable regulatory frameworks (e.g. London, a4, 117–128). Several influences on the development of self-organisation could

Table 6-1 Influences on the leadership of civil society organisations in the water system

Leadership of NGOs, civil society, associations	Coef.	Std. Err.
Drinking water quality***	3.473	0.841
Impact of technology adoption on water availability**	1.146	0.499
Impact of infrastructure investment on water availability***	−2.785	0.867
Intensity of water consumption dependence on price per cubic metre of water***	1.456	0.561
Challenge of decreasing water consumption***	−1.560	0.566
Insufficient infrastructure as challenge	0.952	0.629
Degradation of water resources as challenge††	1.156	0.469
Cooperation between the local water provider and local citizens' initiatives**	1.260	0.503
The local government plays an important role on local water issues*	−0.934	0.494
Support from public authorities to store and use rainwater is satisfactory***	1.654	0.574
Action from public authorities to prevent overabstraction of water resource**	−1.577	0.747
Action from public authorities to prevent infiltration of pollutants	0.624	0.510

Notes: Ordered logistic regression, 74 observations, p-value = 0.000, Pseudo R^2 = 0.5294, Log likelihood = -50.42752 (control variables: city and sector).

be identified in qualitative and quantitative research. Potentials are far from being fully exploited, and self-organisation is not a strong transition driver in drinking water management. Action can be observed especially in 'visible' parts of the system, like the opposition to privatisation – connected with pricing issues – and surface water protection.

6.3 Actors, factors, and lessons learned

In section 6.3, the following questions will be answered: What are the actors and factors driving the local water transition? What lessons could be learned and reputation be gained from leadership in local water management?

6.3.1 Actors, actions, and factors

Concerning actors driving the local water transition, in the majority of cases, the local water provider plays the key role. In addition, the local administration is quite important. The political majority, higher government representatives as well as local universities and research institutions show medium leadership. Political minorities, local NGOs, local associations, civil society, and private companies show only little leadership (cf. Figure 6-4). Interviewees most frequently named the local water provider and local administration or government as actors involved in sustainability transition of water management (e.g. Freiburg, a4, 56; Giurgiu, a3, 60–63; Prague, a3, 37; Umea, a4, 36–37; Valencia, a3, 79–86). NGOs and civil society initiatives were frequently named by representatives of the civil society sector but only once by a business actor (e.g. Freiburg, a4, 36; Kiel, a4, 43; Nice, a4, 92; Rome, a4, 39; Trieste, a3, 40 and a4, 49).

The regional comparison reveals that the local water provider shows the greatest leadership and the ranks of actors are almost alike for all regions. The ratings of the Southern countries are quite low in comparison with the other regions, perhaps representing a lack of capability concerning the solution of pressing problems in some countries mentioned

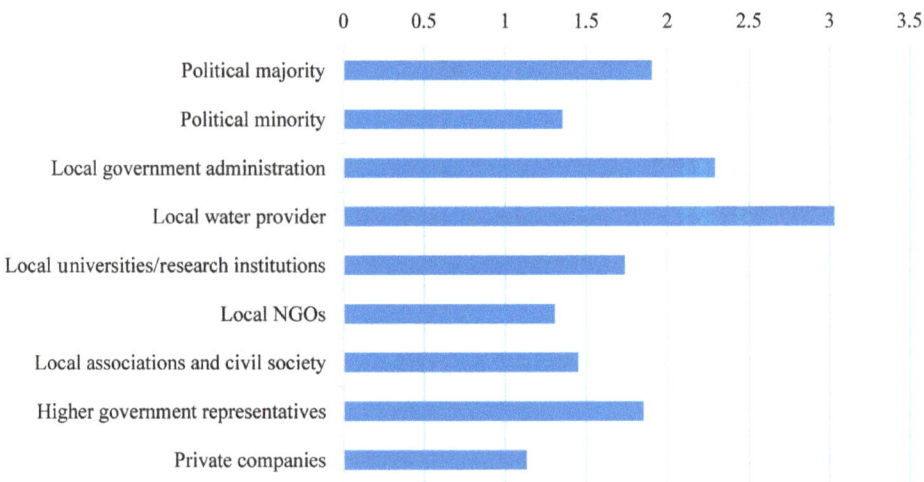

Figure 6-4 Leadership (in terms of reputation and capability) in ensuring the quality and availability of drinking water (scaled from 0: none to 4: very high)

earlier. In the West, the distance between the leadership of the political majority, the local government administration, and the local water provider on the one hand and the rest of the actors on the other is larger than in the other regions. The local universities as well as research and educational institutions, standing for the latest developments in research, have high influence in the North but show only medium leadership in ensuring the quality and availability of drinking water in the other regions.

Factors encouraging the local water transition are interwoven with the particular challenges the cities experience. From the challenges described in section 6.2, objectives and concepts for the future can be developed. Droughts and floods were rated as more risky for the drinking water system until 2030 than changes in population. Droughts are more relevant for Eastern and Southern European countries; floods are equally relevant in the four regions. The particular risk depends on the geographical characteristics of the city. Interestingly, cities with different population growth rates, except very fast growing megacities, did not rate the risk of an increasing population to the city's water supply significantly differently. Interviewees at times mentioned problems arising from densification and population accumulation in growing cities (e.g. Istanbul, a3, 30; Rennes, a4, 57; Umea, a4, 30–31). A shrinking population is significantly more challenging for shrinking cities. Nevertheless, these population risks are assessed as low on average.

Frequently mentioned was the factor of awareness creation for the sustainable deployment of resources. Amongst others, civil society, nonprofit organisations, and private businesses promote sustainability. Results are the creation of environmental consciousness and an increased awareness of the pollution of water resources as well as social responsibility. Consumers are thereby enabled to protest against high water prices and bad water quality. A city can only be sustainable when its citizens support sustainability issues and get involved. Thus, administration alone cannot actually impose sustainability but needs to address the people (Barcelona, a4, 106–107; London, a4, 129–130; Prague, a4, 36–41; Rennes, a4, 42). The EU is influential in creating environmental sensibility. In addition, some policymakers recognise that projects and issues related to water and sustainability can win votes (Umea, a4, 62–67; Valencia, a3, 41–44). Conversely, it was argued that city people are alienated from agriculture and show less awareness on issues like water pollution than people from the countryside. Their habits and established thinking patterns prevent sustainable action, and economic arguments dominate environmental ones. If consumers do not care about sustainable or 'green' markets, transition is slowed down significantly (Innsbruck, a1, 15; Istanbul, a3, 26, 41; Trieste, a4, 24–29; Umea, a4, 29). The level of citizens' awareness and willingness to act sustainably is very different in the observed cities. The impression of a North–South disparity arises.

Policy factors were frequently reported. There is a need for increased transparency, integration, and cooperation between all stakeholders, including the monitoring of water quality and technology management (Barcelona, a4, 45–47; Innsbruck, a1, 15; Rennes, a3, 56). Citizen participation depends on the information citizens receive from local government and media (Rome, a3, 75). Politicians set different foci; a 'green mayor' will focus more on sustainability issues (Freiburg, a3, 36). Political problems and corruption among public administration and politicians are likely to lead to citizens' mistrust and the inefficient allocation of funds (Barcelona, a4, 42–44; Kiel, a4, 35–37; Rome, a3, 75; Valencia, a4, 24). The situation is usually complicated when stakeholders and decision-makers with different backgrounds work together. Collaboration and trust are especially challenging for parties viewing each other with scepticism (Giurgiu, a1, 74, and a3, 82–83; Istanbul, a3, 36; Rennes, a4, 65–72). Apart from these local policy factors, nonlocal factors also play a role. Some regions participate in numerous EU-funded projects to improve living conditions for example through urban microclimate projects, sewage system modernisation, flood protection, or riverbed cleaning (Lodz, a2, 12, 28). The control and monitoring of water quality is frequently exercised by higher levels of government as well, for instance by the national and the EU level. These also determine the success of projects and the allocation of funds. Thus, projects are typically implemented according to national criteria and not according to local ones (Innsbruck, a4, 60–63; Rennes, a3, 35; Rome, a4, 93–94).

Cities have diverse objectives for ensuring or improving the quality of drinking water by 2030. The protection of groundwater, for example through ecological farming, is of high priority for many cities. The protection of surface water due to decreased limit values for sewage of households and industry, ecological farming and due to additional levels of sewage treatment also have high priority. The protection of surface water due to recultivation and the exploitation of new water sources (for example through long-distance water systems) are of medium priority. Added were objectives important to some cities concerning technological improvements, recycling of water, collaboration with users, and the protection of surface water from hydraulic fracturing.

In the North, most of the objectives are less prioritised than in the rest of Europe, but the exploitation of new water sources is of a higher priority than in the other regions. The protection of surface water due to additional levels of sewage treatment is of especially high priority in the East and the South (cf. Figure 6-5).

Water availability is an important challenge and transition factor. The priorities for ensuring the availability of drinking water by 2030 were requested. Some objectives ensure both quality and availability, as these aspects cannot be separated. The objective of reducing water loss (for example through investments in drinking water infrastructure) is of high priority on average. The priority of reducing water use (for example through intelligent water irrigation systems) is medium to high. The exploitation of new water

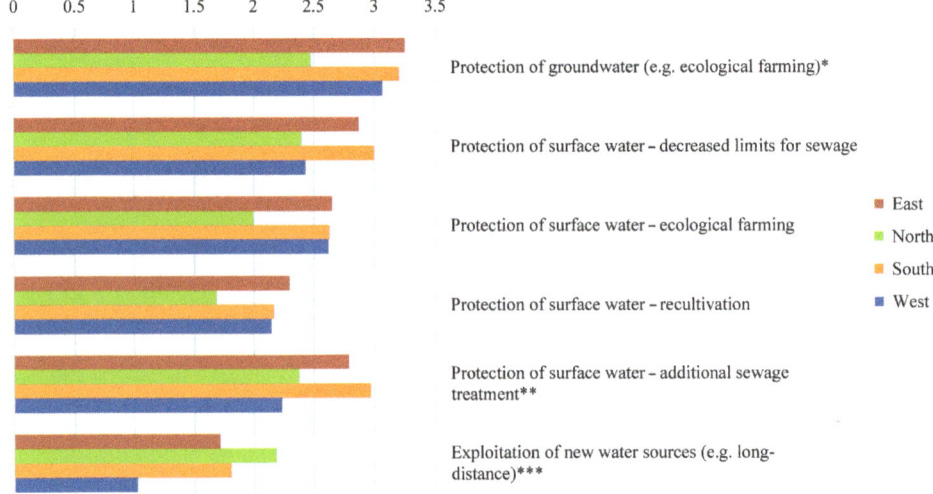

Figure 6-5 Priorities for ensuring or improving the quality of drinking water by 2030 (scaled from 0: none to 4: very high)

sources, the refilling of renewable water resources, and the reduction of the urban sealed soil are prioritised as medium on average by the cities. Additionally mentioned were the installation of rainwater management systems and the use of reclaimed water for industries, the renewal of infrastructure including effective well management, and the collaboration with and education in communes (Birmingham, a3, 34; Umea, a4, 62–63). Civil society respondents assess the objectives of reducing water use and the amount of urban sealed soil as of higher priority for drinking water availability in contrast to business and government respondents.

The objectives for water availability are seen differently in the four regions. The Western countries rated all objectives as less prioritised compared to the other regions, reflecting the image of fewer challenges and an already higher technological standard stated in section 6.2. The reduction of water use and water loss, the refilling of renewable water resources, and the reduction of the urban sealed soil are especially relevant for the South and East of Europe (cf. Figure 6-6). The exploitation of new water sources is, similar to the same objective for water quality, more important for the Northern countries than for the other three regions. There is a high correlation between the priorities of the exploitation of new water sources concerning quality (cf. Figure 6-5) and availability (cf. Figure 6-6) of drinking water.

In the questionnaire, most cities state that it will be rather easy, though not very easy, to deliver good water quality and enough water. It seems difficult to guarantee stable prices at the same time. The regional differences show that there are again more problems to be expected in East and South Europe. Sometimes, the countries of one region assess these difficulties very differently. Stable prices are supposed to be difficult to guarantee in all Southern countries except Italy and much easier in Austria than in the other Western countries.

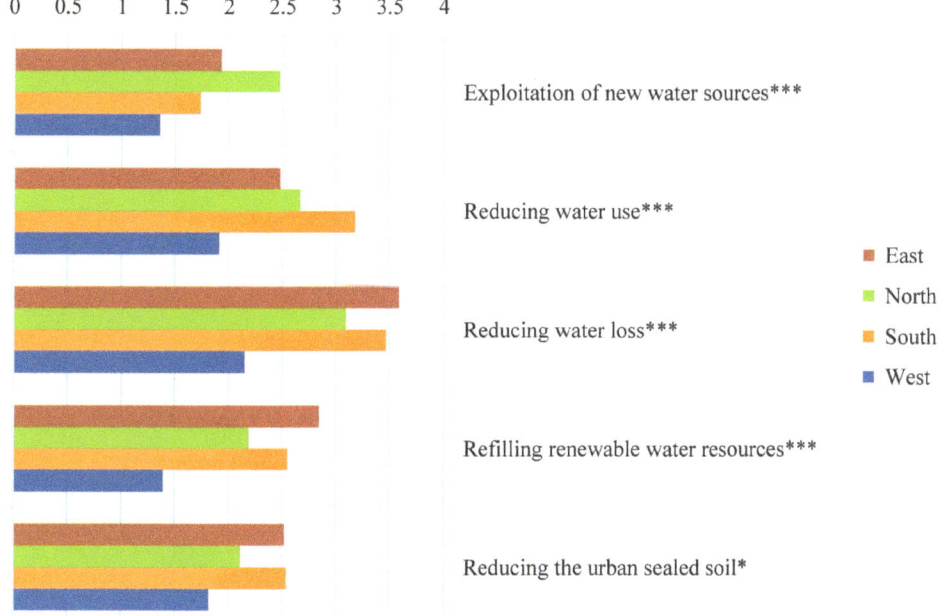

Figure 6-6 Priorities for ensuring the availability of drinking water by 2030 (scaled from 0: none to 4: very high)

142 Stephanie Barnebeck

Water quality and availability are regarded as easy to guarantee in Romania but as neutral in the Czech Republic and Poland. There is also a visible mechanism of large water savings leading to increasing prices, as fixed costs are apportioned to the cubic metre price of drinking water (Prague, a4, 41). In a few regions, poorer people dig wells in their yards, because groundwater is easily accessible. High water prices support these actions, while not every house is connected to the local drinking water system (Giurgiu, a4, 85–87).

The maintenance and renewal of existing infrastructure is the strongest cost driver of drinking water services. The investment in additional infrastructure to cope with degraded water resources, for instance through nitrate pollution, and other operational expenses are of medium importance. The least important factor is the investment in additional infrastructure to cope with scarce water resources, such as long-distance provision. This priority is the same for all regions. The degree of importance differs between the regions. It is lowest in the West for all items. For maintenance and renewal of existing infrastructure, for investment in additional infrastructure to cope with degraded water resources, and for other operational expenses, the importance is highest in the East and parts of the North; for investment in additional infrastructure to cope with scarce water resources, it is highest in the South and North. As local government budgets and EU funding tend to shrink, investments are difficult for some cities (e.g. Lodz, a2, 27–28; Rome, a4, 36–37; Trieste, a3, 58).

It is generally agreed that cultural habits[3] and pricing determine the level of water consumption in the cities. There is weak agreement on the influence of the production level of the industries within municipal boundaries. Concerning the income of the overall population, the production level of the service businesses within municipal boundaries, and the level of agricultural production within municipal boundaries, the respondents are neutral on average.

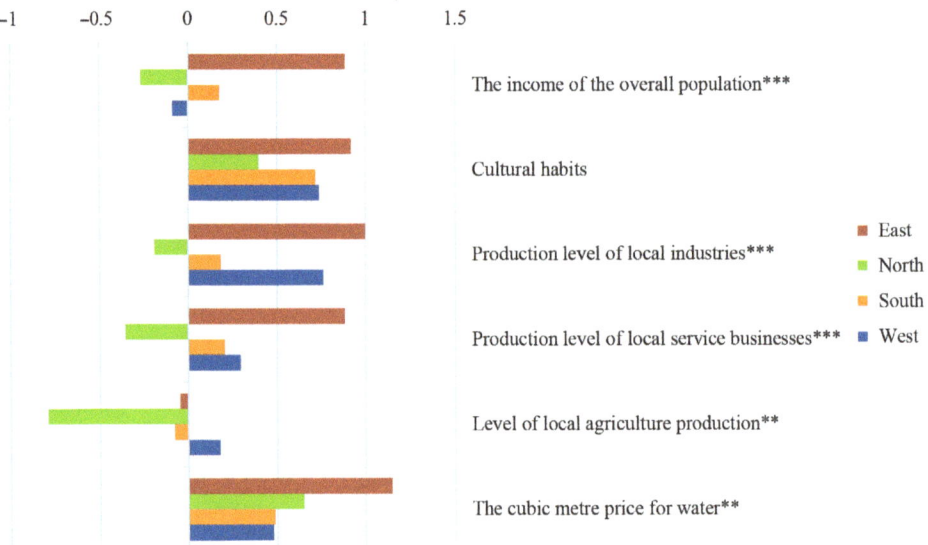

Figure 6-7 Aspects that determine the level of water consumption (scaled from −2: strong disagreement to +2: strong agreement)

The regional differences are huge on this question. In North and South Europe, only the cubic metre price for water and cultural habits determine water consumption. In the West, the production level of the industries within the municipal boundaries is a further determination factor for water consumption. In the East, all aspects except the level of agriculture production within the municipal boundaries play a role (cf. Figure 6-7).

6.3.2 Lessons learnt

During the more or less intense transition process of the last 10 or more years, important lessons could be learnt, and the actors involved could gain reputations. Energy efficiency programmes already showed that the same results could be achieved with less consumption. This knowledge can be transferred to the water system. For the water resource system, consumption patterns can change through innovative political frameworks, structural change, and efficient monitoring and sanctioning (Giurgiu, a1, 90–93; Istanbul, a3, 59–60). Water availability and quality depend on the way the resource system is treated. Water management, reuse, storage, and ecological agriculture are thus important. Investments in clean technology can facilitate sustainability transition but need to be supported by different levels of government. Local characteristics have to be respected in innovation (Barcelona, a4, 85–86, 114–116; Giurgiu, a4, 75–78; Istanbul, a3, 99–102; Valencia, a4, 68–69). Many things have to be revised to provide attractive, economic solutions for sustainability. If resources are limited, the rules of growth need to be defined differently. Taxation, incentives, and regulatory frameworks need to reflect that context (Istanbul, a3, 57–58; Umea, a4, 108–111).

Lessons learnt on actors and their actions concern for example conflicts and divergent opinions between the water industry, suppliers, and bottled water companies (Freiburg, a3, 50). Asked for difficulties in developing a common understanding regarding a joint strategy for drinking water provision, respondents were rather neutral on average. In general, a common understanding seems to be present, but awareness of the issues still seems low. Civil society obviously sees possible conflicts that government does not see, but the means are all very small and close to neutral. Nonetheless, the sectors' tendencies are clearly diverging (cf. Figure 6-8). There are no significant regional differences on this question and few between the countries of one region. The common understanding of how the quality of local water resources could be maintained locally causes conflicts only in the Czech Republic, Greece, and the UK. The questions of what an ecological level for local water abstraction is and how far users involved locally influence the provision of water are not issues of conflict at all in Austria and assessed as neutral in all other countries except Greece, where they are issues of conflict. Conflicts about scarce resources used up by neighbouring municipalities can emerge between local communities (London, a3, 60; Rennes, a3, 49; Valencia, a4, 41–42).

Other lessons learnt concern the relationship of top-down to bottom-up approaches. Transparency and citizens' commitment can improve current problematical situations, and public discussion can make project definitions more successful (Prague, a4, 55; London, a4, 101–106; Rome, a4, 59–61, 85–87). Monitoring and control of the allocation of funds and the implementation of projects are crucial. For projects, political and financial support is needed, as scientific relevance and sustainability reasons are not sufficient for their success (London, a4, 89–92; Rome, a4, 96–100). The success of projects cannot always be expressed adequately 'on a piece of paper'; the emotive component can be rather shown

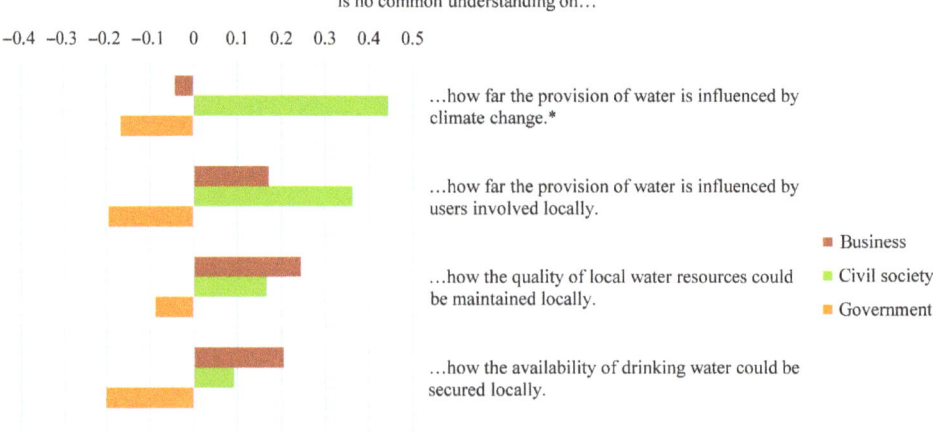

Figure 6-8 Common understanding regarding a joint strategy for drinking water provision (scaled from −2: strong disagreement to +2: strong agreement)

onsite, where the projects were realised. Unfortunately, politicians rarely show up there (Birmingham, a4, 111). Taking over 'best practice' solutions is not necessarily successful when institutional arrangements are unfavourable (Giurgiu, a3, 144–146). Some actors request changes in decision-making processes and water policy. Change has to come from all sides and all levels; consumption patterns need to be changed and companies should take over responsibility (Istanbul, a3, 63–64; Valencia, a4, 51–54).

Experiences on information and awareness or the lack of it are important in the transition process. Consumers and citizens often do not understand the subjects of discussion about sustainable development; the terminology used in water directives repels people. A more comprehensible language would help to create awareness and stimulate commitment (London, a4, 38, 94–96; Rennes, a4, 25; Trieste, a3, 53). Governments often only care about issues the public is actually interested in. Furthermore, personal interests sometimes interfere with sustainable development. The promotion of water issues by the media is biased towards pricing and consumption patterns (Giurgiu, a3, 107–108; London, a4, 148; Rennes, a4, 121–122). These aspects are connected with the need for a good educational system, including collaborations between schools and actors involved in sustainability issues (Birmingham, a3, 86–90; Giurgiu, a4, 35; Nice, a4, 74). "If you give people a choice between a sustainable and a nonsustainable option, they will go for the sustainable option" (London, a4, 38).

As already mentioned, many cities face funding problems. Indebted municipalities have a serious problem on the local level, since sustainability objectives are postponed due to lacking resources. Hence, their needs for external or EU funding increase. Especially infrastructure deterioration causes difficulties. Low water prices, used as a political instrument in some cities, intensify this effect (Giurgiu, a3, 99–102, 111–112; Kiel, a4, 117–121; Trieste, a3, 76). Private companies benefit from political decisions on the privatisation of water supply (Barcelona, a4, 85–86). Short-term profit and quick success are often put before sustainability, but sustainability can provide long-term financial stability. Long-term plans should be shielded from the influences of changes in the political scene, and short-term problems should be less focused on in favour of the common good water and long-term plans (Birmingham, a4, 150–157; London, a4, 34; Prague, a3, 125; Valencia, a3, 79–86).

The privatisation of the water supply is an aspect frequently brought up in the interviews. The initial situation is different, as in some countries private water supply has a comparably long tradition, for example in France[4] and the UK.[5] In some of these cities, the private water utility has recently been or will be recommunalised in the coming years. These developments are widely approved, because citizens expect considerably reduced water bills and improved water quality from municipal water providers (Nice, a3, 97–101; Rennes, a3, 23, 59). In most countries water supply has traditionally been a municipal task. Yet there is a current trend towards the privatisation of public services and the deregulation of markets. "[P]rivate profit and externalising costs towards society are the rules of operation" (Valencia, a4, 27). Many local politicians follow this mainstream. When profit comes into play, sustainability can become difficult (Freiburg, a3, 79). In some countries, citizens' referenda or protests prevented the cities from privatising water supply (Rome, a4, 59; Trieste, a3, 92). A nationwide referendum with more than 55 per cent of citizens voting was held in Italy in June 2011 regarding the privatisation of water services. Over 95 per cent of voters rejected private water suppliers (EPSU 2011). Other cities have recently privatised water supply (Barcelona, a4, 92). Less than one-fifth of the respondents stated that water provision has been privatised or will be privatised between 2003 and 2030. Privatisation is an issue especially in the Southern European states (cf. Figure 6-9). In most cities, no changes are expected within the next 15 years, but the topic nonetheless is present in many interviews and in various contexts.

Overall, the economic crisis has facilitated awareness and helped people to understand that community spirit and participation are very important. This shows in different fields of action, which are interconnected. The different needs of actors and resource systems need to be taken into account in progress (Birmingham, a3, 64; Prague, a4, 59). Nevertheless, there are drawbacks. Citizens fight over specific issues and thus create more tension rather than solving problems (Nice, a4, 43–48). A lack of self-criticism and courage in

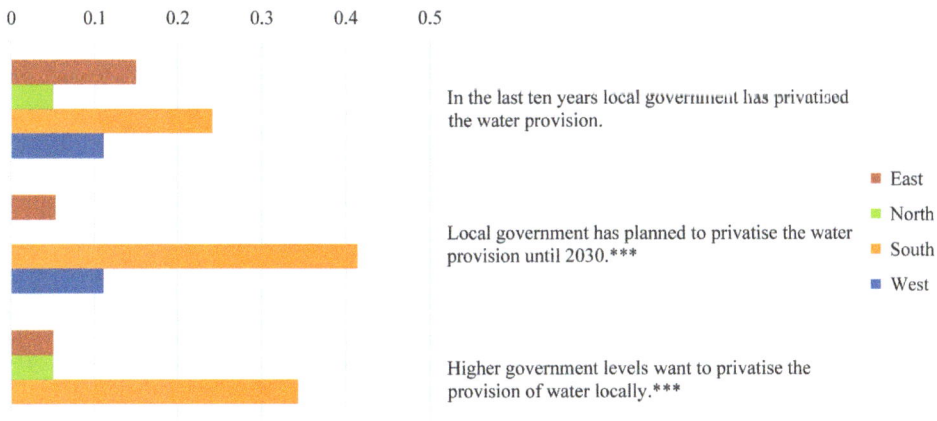

Figure 6-9 Status of privatisation (statements' applicability coded as 0: no or 1: yes)

politicians on all levels and the manipulation of citizens by politicians are also criticised. There is always opposition to sustainability projects, even if they are favourable for the region (Barcelona, a4, 51; Innsbruck, a1, 15; Lodz, a2, 38; Rennes, a4, 90–93; Rome, a3, 27). Changes take time in local and national administration, but a change of the system in favour of participation and self-organisation can be found. Young people as major motivators of society need to be involved (Barcelona, a4, 51–54; Giurgiu, a3, 147–152; Trieste, a4, 46–59). Political decisions and bureaucracy as well as the interference of higher government levels like the EU often slow down processes. The European Commission sometimes fails to ensure compliance with community law due to a lack of work force (Prague, a3, 129; Valencia, a3, 79–86 and a4, 68–75).

Individual learnings of the respondents concern an increased collective responsibility to maintain public common goods and the consideration of health aspects in water management as well as the fight against a still predominant perception of looking at growth only through economic benefit and the maximisation of profit (Istanbul, a3, 57–58; Lublin, a3, 45–46; Rome, a4, 53). Networking and collaboration of public and private actors is supposed to make the water resource system function better (Birmingham, a3, 68–70; Giurgiu, a3, 99–102; Lodz, a2, 41–44; Rome, a4, 59–61). In the opinion of some interviewees, the European Union provides the framework in which all stakeholders should join hands and create a network based on ethics and environmental values, involving different areas of economy and society. Citizens can benefit from legislation and 'best practices' applied in other cities and implement previously tested solutions (Giurgiu, a1, 106; St. Gallen, a3, 10; Trieste, a4, 77–81).

6.4 Norm adoption and local decision-making autonomy

The questions whether we could observe transitional socio-ecological norm adoption towards trust and cooperation and if local decision-making autonomy matters in socio-ecological transition processes are answered next.

6.4.1 Norm adoption

Most respondents clearly agreed that access to drinking water is a human right that should be guaranteed by public authorities. Only two business representatives and one government respondent answered neutrally. No respondents disagreed with this statement.

Inquiring into the value of clean drinking water, and whether subsidies have a positive or negative effect on sustainability, can be achieved by asking whether water should be free. The unanimous opinion of interviewees is that "water has to have its real price" (Giurgiu, a3, 105). Otherwise, the users would not value the resource. "People complain a lot about [costs for] water.... No one complains about paying for their mobile phone" (Barcelona, a4, 71). People should understand that the water prices relate, not only to the water currently taken from streams and other sources, but also to the provision of clean water for many people over a long period. The purification of water and the construction and maintenance of canals create high costs. These are included in the tariffs. The water providers then reinvest the money to ensure the operation of the cycle. Water for free would mislead the behaviour of people (Birmingham, a3, 112; Giurgiu, a3, 61–63, 104; Lodz, a2, 48–49). If water is too cheap, it leads to a serious depletion of the resource. Respondents expressed several ideas for efficient water pricing. Rising block tariffs could be incentives to reduce water use. Less than 100 litres per inhabitant per day could be free or in a low price category; beyond that, the tariffs would rise by volume. Instead of providing cheap drinking water, there could be encouragement to use recycled water or rainwater. If a low water price – followed by intense consumption stressing the resource system – is a political instrument, even privatisation of water supply could help to reflect the costs of water in its price (Barcelona, a4, 71–73; Birmingham, a3, 45; Istanbul, a3, 78, 90).

The clarity of system boundaries is one aspect defining the local scope of action and the need of cooperation. In all cities, the sources of the local water supply are well known. The availability of adequate local resources and the overall consumption level, depending for instance on population size, local industry, and agricultural use, determine whether cities are able to cover the needed quantity of drinking water. The availability of water resources and associated challenges were discussed in section 6.2. Most cities use more than one source for freshwater abstraction and discharge their wastewater after treatment into their local streams. The treated wastewater, especially of coastal cities, eventually ends up in the sea, so the preservation of the coastline and marine ecosystems are also relevant. In many interviews, awareness of the finiteness of water resources becomes apparent. There are only a few cities with households not connected to the sewage system in the sample (e.g. Giurgiu, a4, 85–89; Nice, a3, 28–29; Prague, a3, 101–103 and a4, 86). Many cities are using the water of neighbouring municipalities. Sometimes conflicts emerge from that, as external resources are used up by these cities. There can also be cooperation between

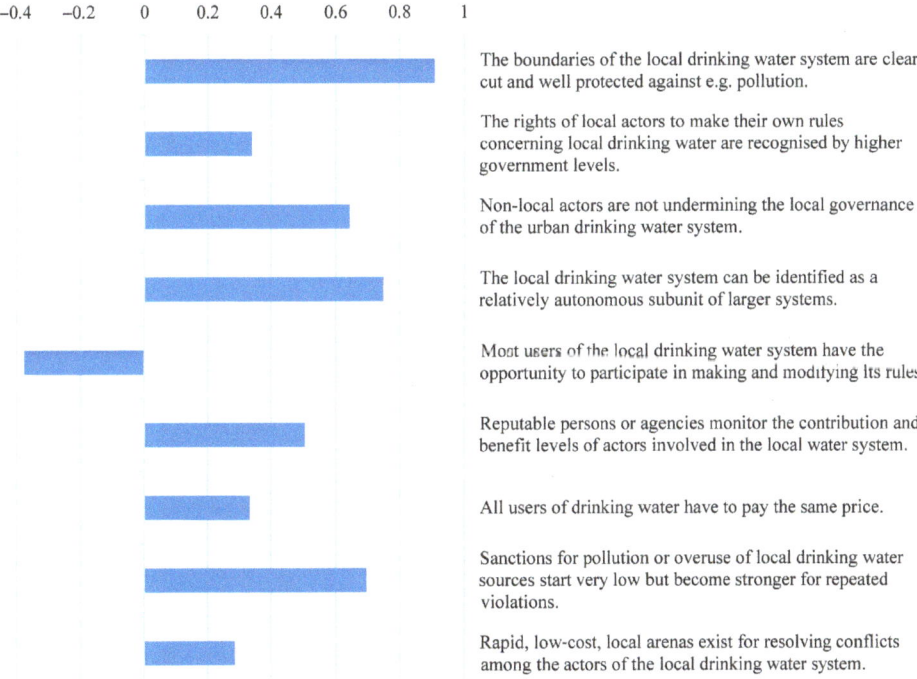

Figure 6-10 Agreement on governance principles regarding the local water provision system (scaled from −2: strong disagreement to +2: strong agreement)

neighbouring municipalities in wastewater management, in the coordination of actions, the protection of groundwater, and the mitigation of threats. The statement 'The boundaries of the local drinking water system are clear cut and well protected against for example pollution' is agreed on by most respondents of the questionnaire (cf. Figure 6-10).

An effective water basin management takes into account the regional needs. Depending on organisational structures and legal frameworks, various actors can be involved in the operation and control of water supply, for instance the public or (partially) private utility provider, the local or national administration, or various other businesses, boards, and committees (e.g. Kiel, a4, 51, 77; Rennes, a3, 49; Valencia, a4, 43). The statements 'The local drinking water system can be identified as a relatively autonomous subunit of larger systems' and 'Non-local actors are not undermining the local governance of the urban drinking water system' are commonly agreed to. The statement 'The rights of local actors to make their own rules concerning the local drinking water system are recognised by higher levels of government' is rated neutrally on average, but with a positive tendency. Only with the statement 'Most users of the local drinking water system have the opportunity to participate in making and modifying its rules' do respondents tend to disagree (cf. Figure 6-10).

In the majority of cities 'Sanctions for pollution or overuse of local drinking water sources start very low but become stronger if an actor repeatedly violates a rule' and 'Reputable persons or agencies monitor the contribution and benefit levels of actors involved in the local water system'. The statements 'All users of drinking water have to pay the same price' and 'Rapid, low-cost, local arenas exist for resolving conflicts among the actors of the local drinking water system' are rated as neutral with a positive tendency (cf. Figure 6-10).

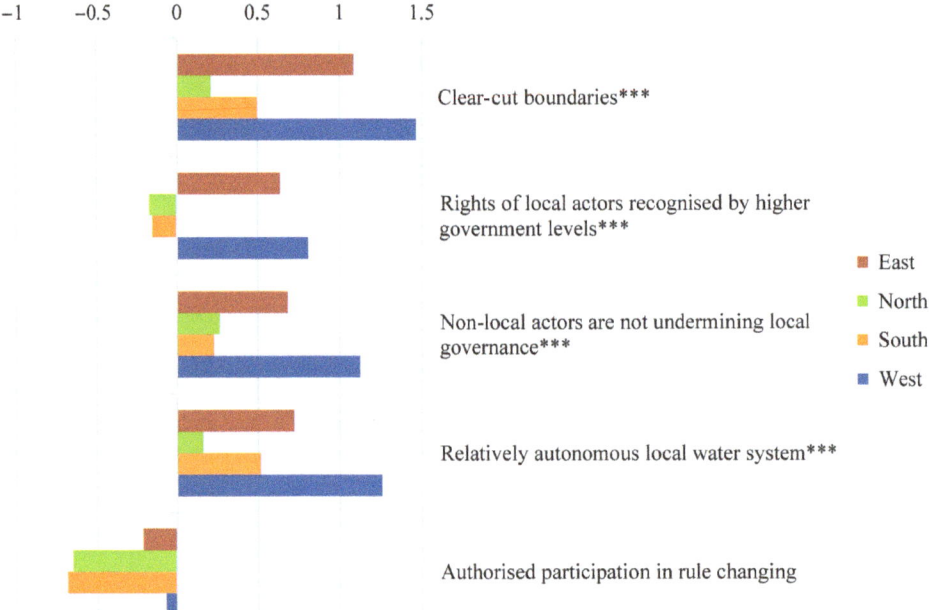

Figure 6-11 Agreement on governance principles regarding the local water provision system (regional differences I)

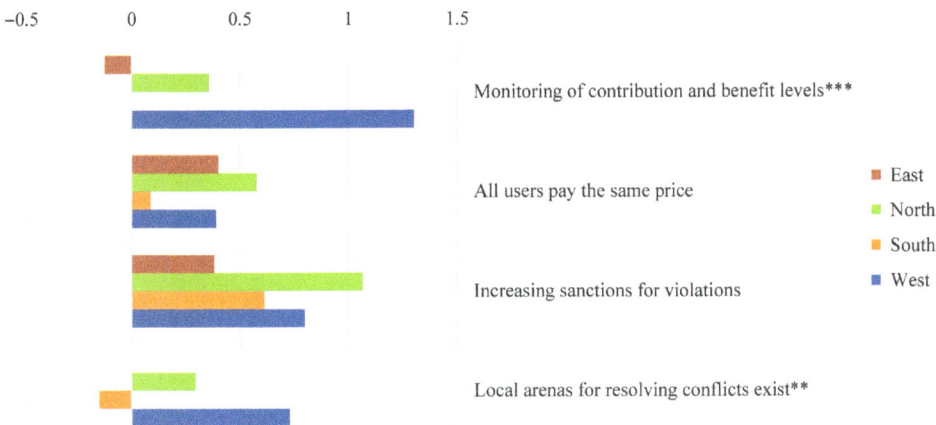

Figure 6-12 Agreement on governance principles regarding the local water provision system (regional differences II)

For some of the requested governance principles, the regional differences are huge. The Western respondents agree on all principles except that 'Most users of the local drinking water system have the opportunity to participate in making and modifying its rules'. The Northern and Southern respondents disagree on the statement and the Western and Eastern respondents are neutral. In no region can users participate in changing the rules of the local drinking water system, which corresponds with the findings about participation and self-organisation from section 6.2.2. Referring to the water system's boundaries, the recognition of local actors' rights, the absence of nonlocal actors undermining the local governance, and the autonomy of the local water system, these principles are agreed with in Eastern and Western Europe and are rated as neutral in the North and South (cf. Figure 6-11).

Concerning the principles of monitoring the contribution and benefit levels of involved actors, equity of water prices for all users, increasing sanctions for repeated pollution or overuse of water sources, and the existence of local arenas for resolving conflicts among the actors, the agreement from the Western and Northern countries is stronger than from the Southern and Eastern countries (cf. Figure 6-12). This confirms again the impression formulated earlier in this chapter and derived from the case studies that Western and Northern cities are further advanced in regards to water management and protection.

A public authority that ensures strong monitoring achieves good quality of water and services (Rennes, a3, 50). The monitoring of water use can be implemented by individual metering on household level. In some cities water metering is not mandatory, so the volume of water used has no impact on the individual water bill. As the installations of water meters create high costs, administration and water providers are ambivalent on the issue. It would create extra costs, but in the medium term households would save money, as they have an incentive to save water. Saving hot water also reduces fuel or energy costs (Birmingham, a3, 72, 112–115). The questionnaire revealed that the quality of the drinking water is monitored very effectively. The effectiveness of the monitoring of groundwater protection, surface water protection, water use, and water loss (for example through leaks) is high on average. There are differences between the answers of the actors from the three sectors. Government actors perceive the effectiveness of monitoring for quality, use, and loss of water as higher than actors from business and civil society. Regional differences exist as well. In the Southern countries, some shortcomings exist for all objectives compared with the other regions.

The effectiveness of sanctions is an important objective, as the compliance with rules must not only be monitored, but violations of these rules must be sanctioned. If these rules exist only on paper, their virtue is low. If there is no shift in environmental awareness, only sanctions can make companies involved in the production process and consumers change their habits and consumption patterns. The construction of the sanctioning system is crucial for its effectiveness. Penalties dependent on the volume of water polluted instead of the intensity of pollution can impair the success of sanctions (Barcelona, a4, 84; Istanbul, a3, 41, 60–64). The pollution of water sources is sanctioned at a medium level of effectiveness on average. The overuse or overconsumption of water is sanctioned at a low level of effectiveness. Other interventions sanctioned are the illegal use and theft of water. The sanctioning of the pollution of water sources is effective in the North and West but of medium effectiveness in East and South Europe (cf. Figure 6-13). Civil society respondents assess the sanctions on the pollution of water resources as less effective than government respondents do.

The contributions of actors to sanctioning the misuse and/or the pollution of water are unequal. The local water provider, local government administration, and higher government representatives contribute most. The local environmental NGOs play the next most important role. The contributions of the political majority, political minority, local associations, and users themselves are low. There are some regional differences to be found. The superior government levels' representatives' contribution to sanctioning the misuse and/or pollution of water is above average in the West, where it is as intense as the contributions of the local governments, the local administrations, and the local water providers, indicating shared control in these issues. In general, the contribution levels are assessed as higher in the West and North compared with the East and South.

Formal norms in the form of legal frameworks as well as informal norms are important bases for sustainability transition. Water companies primarily need to meet directives and distribute returns to their owners, yet an overreaching sustainability directive is missing in many cities. There are calls for changes in the regulation of these companies. Also the need for a more general change in legal frameworks to enable participation and sustainable

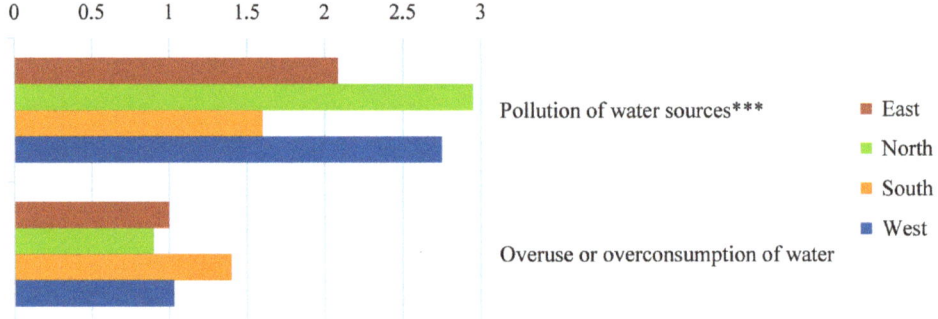

Figure 6-13 Effectiveness of sanctions (scaled from 0: not effective to 4: very effective)

actions in general was stated (Istanbul, a3, 60; London, a4, 18; Valencia, a4, 67). Water supply is almost a protected market, making it difficult and time-consuming to open (St. Gallen, a3, 10). Clear rules help the economy, the enterprises, the cities, and municipalities to take action (Innsbruck, a1, 111). Discrepancies between laws, concepts, and strategies and their implementation practice can be observed. In several cities, sustainability concepts exist only on paper and are poorly executed or not at all. Thus, no difference can be made. Also the control mechanisms do not always take effect, for instance due to money-saving measures (Giurgiu, a3, 146; Innsbruck, a1, 109; Kiel, a3, 41–42; London, a4, 146; Prague, a4, 64; Valencia, a4, 18, 71).

Regional, national, and supranational policies interdigitate and are linked hierarchically. These different level policies are supposed to be coherent, but problems and inconsistencies occur frequently (Barcelona, a4, 41; Giurgiu, a3, 137; Nice, a3, 43). As transition is difficult to manage, experience is needed, and environmental matters cannot be limited to the regional scope. Various respondents demand a less complex institutional landscape and more national or European responsibility for these tasks. Examples are regulations for the usage of wastewater sludge or water treatment technologies that should be made by higher government levels. Rule changes from 'above' can initiate change on the regional level (e.g. Barcelona, a4, 86; Istanbul, a3, 84; Lublin, a3, 23; Nice, a3, 43, 80; Prague, a3, 124–125; Rennes, a3, 61, 70; St. Gallen, a3, 10). Other respondents said that the EU can merely create framing conditions or that they are not sure whether the EU policy can have a real impact on local policies. There is also doubt on the intensity of interference of European legislation on local policies (Kiel, a3, 278; Prague, a3, 123; Rennes, a4, 138). Another aspect is that politicians believe that elections are not won on sustainability or wastewater issues. Investments thus lose political priority, creating an obstacle for long-lasting solutions. In times of crisis, politicians feel they have to leave behind these aspects, as social stability is more important (Barcelona, a4, 111; Nice, a4, 46–47; Rennes, a4, 97; Umea, a4, 79).

Cooperation between institutions is not always satisfactory. It might sometimes be difficult for financial reasons, as people, even from the nongovernmental sector, compete over grants and are not willing to involve others, as they would lose part of their endowments (Prague, a4, 37). For instance, important advances in sustainable agriculture would imply cooperation between national and federal governments. In addition, farmers and the food industry have to be involved. Another example is the comprehensive control and modernisation of the sewer system on private ground, where the municipality needs to consider funding and organisation together with other stakeholders like the association of homeowners and skilled crafts and trades (Innsbruck, a1, 103; Kiel, a4, 59). Engines for success are

> a transparent policy where citizens know what the state of the affairs is – that we know all the governmental actions in a transparent manner. A second step would be the participation where citizens and collectives can enhance their voice effectively. The third one would be accountability, where decisions are justified and at the same time are personalised. Thus, we can know who is taking the decisions and why these are being taken.
>
> (Valencia, a4, 64)

Funding – again – is an issue in norm adoption and decision-making autonomy. NGOs and other citizens' organisations cannot compete against large investment companies with vast funding options. Lobbying is also a problem, as many exceptions from the rules are made that are beneficial for economic interests. Many municipalities exceed their debt limits and cancel projects that would help to meet environmental goals. The austerity policy associated with the current economic crisis is further slowing down the implementation of sustainability objectives (Barcelona, a4, 111; Innsbruck, a1, 111; Kiel, a4, 113; London, a4, 144). There are possibilities of funding from higher government levels. Municipalities have to meet special requirements and handle the related bureaucracy. Apart from economic resources, also political ideas and good political practice are needed to drive these projects successfully and benefit from the advice of experts of European legislation (Barcelona, a4, 109; Lodz, a2, 51–52). There are also voices saying the goal in many projects is to spend available EU funds without giving enough thought to the aptitude of the projects (Lublin, a3, 57–58).

On average, respondents agree that public water providers are better than private ones at guaranteeing access to affordable water and that there is strong opposition from citizens in the city to privatising water provision. These findings correspond with the argumentations of sections 6.2.1 and 6.3.2. Respondents are on average neutral concerning the questions of whether the support from public authorities to store and use rainwater is satisfactory as well as if action from public authorities to prevent overabstraction of water resources and infiltration of water-polluting substances is sufficient. This support could indicate the authority's attitude towards sustainable water management. There are various sectorial differences in the answers. Civil society and, by tendency, government agree that public water providers are better than private ones. Business respondents are on average neutral on this question. Civil society is also more critical about the support from public authorities to store and use rainwater. Government finds action from public authorities to prevent infiltration

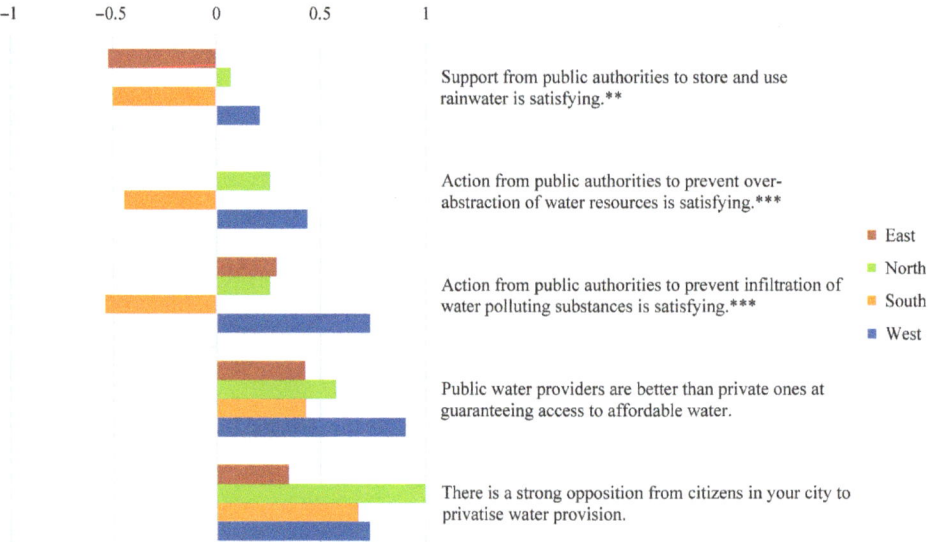

Figure 6-14 Statements on public support and the issue of privatisation (scaled from 0: none to 4: very high)

of water-polluting substances satisfactory, while business and civil society are neutral. Again, every sector plays its part in assessing the relationship between public authorities and civil society. Once more, especially the Western but also the Northern countries are more advanced in the implementation of sustainability principles (cf. Figure 6-14). There are, however, huge intra-regional differences in the West and North. Scandinavian respondents find these actions unsatisfactory in contrast to British respondents. Likewise, Austrian and Swiss respondents are more satisfied than German and French respondents.

6.4.2 Local decision-making autonomy

It is challenging to answer the question about the state of local decision-making autonomy regarding water issues. The interviews show many inconsistencies in the statements of different actors from one city. Hence, it could be concluded that there is a lack of transparency in decision processes. Some cities report a high independence of decision within the legal framework (Innsbruck, a1, 81; Prague, a4, 57; St. Gallen, a3, 10). Many city councils share decision-making autonomy with other governmental agencies on the regional or national level or with private companies operating the water supply. The influence of the local government can vary – from simple approval of the water supplier's plans up to deciding about defined tasks within a multilevel system of governance (Freiburg, a4, 58; Giurgiu, a3, 116 and a4, 82; Kiel, a4, 67; Rennes, a3, 56–57; Trieste, a3, 59–64; Valencia, a3, 92 and a4, 56). Some cities stated that the municipalities have very little to do with water issues. Reasons for municipalities' limited power often concern budgeting. Financial dependency on private business or other government levels implies also a certain amount of political dependency (Giurgiu, a1, 104; Barcelona, a4, 92; Birmingham, a4, 85–86; London, a3, 54–56; Rome, a3, 85). Especially cities with private water supply companies are constrained regarding decisions on water issues. "It's not their mandate. Water is private in England, . . . it's not up to them" (London, a3, 56).

Financial autonomy is sometimes described as "real autonomy" (Nice, a3, 101). As presented above, many cities lack financial resources. Formal competences without financial means are regarded as pointless. Especially in big projects, decision-making autonomy is thus constrained by other partners cofinancing them (e.g. Giurgiu, a3, 118; Kiel, a4, 67; Rome, a3, 85; Valencia, a4, 58). Typically, most of the money available for reinvestment in water infrastructure has to be earned by selling water. Therefore, no scope for financial gains exists for the cities (Trieste, a3, 66 and a4, 65; Valencia, a3, 94). The lack of financial autonomy can lead to further privatisations (Rome, a4, 69). Only financially autonomous cities are assessed as autonomous in decisions as well (Nice, a3, 101 and a4, 82; St. Gallen, a3, 10).

In general, the local government plays an important role in local water issues. It does not have its decision-making on local water issues significantly constrained by other government authorities or by its legal mandate defined in constitutional texts. The local government has its own capacities on infrastructures and has the financial and human resources to ensure the availability and quality of drinking water independently from other government authorities. Yet the statements on decision-making constraints and capacities are rated as neutral on average. There is no clear picture of autonomous local governments, as also visible from the interviews. In the East and West, local governments tend to have less autonomy than in North and South Europe (cf. Figure 6-15).

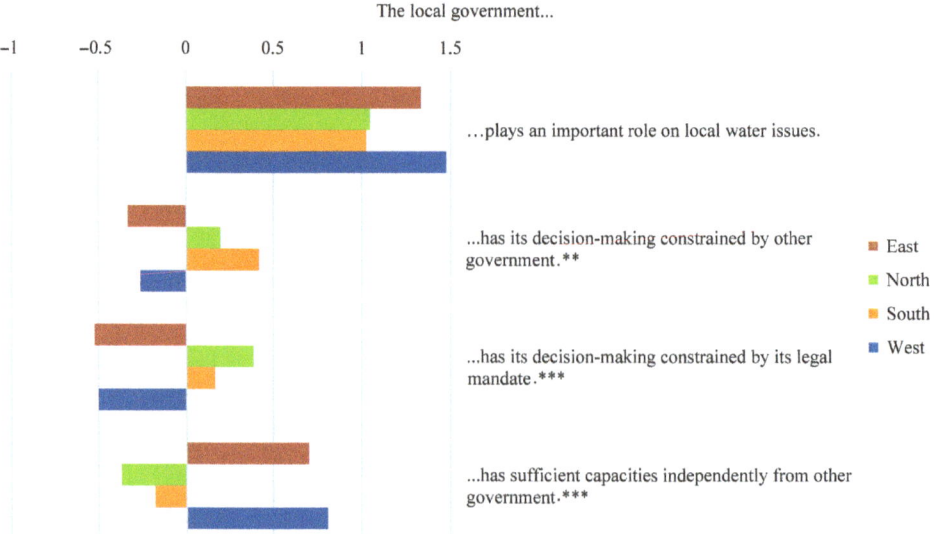

Figure 6-15 Statements on local decision-making autonomy (Scaled from −2: strong disagreement to +2: strong agreement)

The appropriateness of government levels to secure a stable supply of drinking water according to high quality standards is assessed differently. The local (i.e. municipal) level and the subnational level are assessed as most appropriate. The national level is also rated to be appropriate, but ranges behind these two. The EU level is seen as neutral and the neighbourhood or district level is considered as inappropriate to secure a stable supply of drinking water. Except from the neighbourhood or district level, which is found to be inappropriate in all regions, the respondents from the East find the government levels much more appropriate as they get lower. This effect is not that obvious in the other regions. Concerning the neighbourhood or district level, the opinions of government and civil society diverge. Government respondents find the district level clearly inappropriate, and civil society is neutral.

Many respondents view decision-making autonomy critically. Total autonomy seems not to be desirable for several reasons. Elected representatives are not capable of becoming water experts during their term of possibly only four years. Also for the reason that the water system is geographically dependent on neighbouring municipalities and regions, full independence is assessed as inappropriate. A joint treatment by national and local powers is more suitable for the water and sewage system. Furthermore, not all cities are supplied by waterworks in their own municipal area, so these are also outside of the area of responsibility of the city administration (Freiburg, a4, 62; Giurgiu, a3, 114, 120). Not every city's local authorities engage in the issue of water management, regardless of duties and responsibilities (London, a4, 108). More generally, the management of small projects should and can be local, but for larger plans such as the transition to renewable energies or sustainable urban water systems, a central coordination is preferable (St. Gallen, a3, 10).

6.5 Discussion of the findings

In section 6.1, the general potential of civil society involvement in sustainable water management was considered, and the possible scope of action by new institutional arrangements was assumed different from civil society's scope of action in green spaces and the energy system. The interviews as well as the questionnaires showed that this assessment was right, as local civil society action can hardly be observed on drinking water issues. More generally, NGOs and citizens' initiatives exist on the protection of lakes, streams, or seawater and the opposition to the privatisation of the water supply. The local activities of these organisations depend on apparent local challenges.

For the public, technical aspects are quite difficult to understand, and thus participation is difficult due to the complex character of many decisions connected with the drinking water system. Nonetheless, social aspects like the pricing of drinking water and privatisation frequently bring people to action. The 'Right to Water' European Citizen's Initiative as well as the Italian referendum against the privatisation of water services were rather successful. The citizens predominantly view privatisation plans of local governments as disadvantageous. There is the impression that good quality, socially acceptable tariffs for water and the maintenance of infrastructure will be sacrificed for the companies' benefits. In contrast, some financially weak municipalities see privatisation as a (good) option to catch up to technological standards and exonerate the city treasury. Private as well as public water suppliers are subject to the same rules and standards, so the scope for profit is limited. Expected private profits endanger the sustainability aspects in water management, as these might obstruct investments.

Many cities' financial problems are reasons for sustainability drawbacks in the water system. Their scope of action is very narrow without considerable financial means during times of economic crisis and austerity policy. Sustainable solutions frequently create higher costs at present and help reduce future costs. A need for current investments combined with tight budgets can hinder sustainable developments, as higher costs are avoided and thus transferred to the future.

Numerous actors are to be involved in sustainable water management. Water conservation cannot be contemplated without sustainable agriculture and industry. The system is very complex. Cooperation between these stakeholders on the content and funding of water transition are thus favourable, if not necessary. The main actors influencing the system and the ones concerned by these actions need to be brought *around one table* to seek solutions. The roles of the market and the state are in any event quite strong here, and apart from the creation of transition pressure, the role of civil society is limited. The economic crisis and discussions on climate change might have increased the general awareness of the need for new institutional arrangements apart from the state and the growth dynamic of the market, but the impact on the management of water is small. It is difficult to get people involved with water issues, as the system is in a way 'invisible' and the long time horizon connected as well as the slow results demotivate self-organisation. People more likely understand and are interested in tangible topics like urban food production, green spaces maintenance, or solar energy installations that can work as an 'entrance door' into the topic of sustainability and self-organisation.

One key issue in water transition identified by Yvette Bettini et al. (2014, 8) is access to information, knowledge, and expertise. From this perspective and the research presented here, it can be concluded that local governments, administrations, and water businesses hold the strings to invite citizens and other stakeholders to participate. Information can likewise be used to mislead decision-makers and the public, giving experts a powerful position. Transparency, proper information, and favourable institutional frames are necessary to bring people together and make people interested in water issues. Self-organisation and participation is, due to the complexity of the drinking water system, not likely to emerge from the bottom but can be encouraged from the top. In a supportive political environment, new institutional arrangements could add value.

As discussed in chapter 3, civil society participation and self-organisation must be appraised separately. Participation is often misunderstood by local authorities. The option of consumers to monitor their own water use and get information about water quality should not be called participation. Nevertheless, civil society can put pressure on decision-makers through actions emerging from collective awareness. A general citizens' awareness of environmental issues, not necessarily focused on water, is still expedient for the water system. Consumption patterns and habits concerning water and energy use, food production, waste disposal, or transportation preferences can be influenced by this general awareness. Citizens with a higher environmental consciousness expect their local government to act more sustainably. This influences elections and investment priorities. As discussed before, the water system is interwoven with many resource systems and thus gains from generally sustainable resource management. Corruption and/or ignorance among politicians as well as among citizens act in the opposite way.

One aspect frequently underlined in the research was the diversity of cities and the need for individualised solutions. A holistic or integrated approach is important for the water system, as water resource problems implicate the involvement of ecological, economic, technical, social, and legal sides. Urban water systems are, moreover, connected with riverbed management and rural ecosystems for example. These factors can be established quite differently in the cities. Water utility providers have to guarantee quality standards. Often, different actors (for example other departments in the city administration or of other locations) monitor for instance groundwater renewal rates or are responsible for water protection areas. Integrated water management has been intensely researched and evaluated. Numerous approaches exist and applicability appears to be difficult, at least for some standard approaches (Asit K. Biswas 2004; Medema, McIntosh, and Jeffrey 2008). An individualised approach, integrating the different aspects and spatial dimensions, and the specifics of the region, seems necessary for sustainable water management. Oliver M. Brandes (2005) postulates the need for an "institutional shift towards ecosystem-based water allocation and management that promotes innovative urban water management and fundamentally embraces conservation and demand management". His research shows that new, adaptable institutional arrangements that can handle these new requirements need to be formed.

Water is already assessed as a commodity,[6] referring to water resources being subject to market prices. There is a consensus amongst the interviewees that drinking water should have an appropriate price. Otherwise, users will not value it, and water use will not be sustainable. In addition, the treatment of water resources to meet drinking water quality standards, the distribution via aqueducts, and the treatment of sewage water create costs. In an extreme scenario, where water is viewed as an economic good only, the lower classes might not be able to pay water bills and are cut off from the drinking water supply. Among other things, no access to clean water is a serious health risk. At the same time, the agreement that water should be a human right is very high. Something being a human right would exclude the option of it being an economic good. Theoretically, commodification can be explained by the 'tragedy of the commons' (cf. chapter 3). It puts an economic value on an ecological resource, thus internalising the costs of using it. In this logic, a resource being valued correctly can be protected. Hubert H. Savenije (2002) argues that water is not a normal economic good due to its special characteristics. Water is essential for life, economy, and environment; it is scarce, it cannot be transported well in larger quantities, and it is nonsubstitutable. Thus, water is not freely tradable. Moreover water is complex, meaning it is a public good, bound to one location or system with high production and transaction costs for reallocation. The water market is not homogeneous (the willingness to pay of different user groups like industry, agriculture, or domestic users is very different), water markets tend to fail, leading to natural monopolies, and water has a high merit value. He concludes that only within the urban water supply subsector is pricing useful, but not on a larger scale. Adrian Walsh (2011, 90) discusses the "moral permissibility of commodifying water" and considers objections against it. We cannot lead a detailed discussion on the topic of the human right of water contra the commodification of water here, but we wish to point out the paradox described, one that is probably impossible to resolve as water is a unique resource.

Notes

1 Hydraulic fracturing (also fracking) is a technique where fluid (containing chemicals and sand) is injected with high pressure into a borehole. It can be applied for shale gas extraction. This economically attractive technique is highly controversial, as contamination and pollution of ground/surface water, air, and ground up to the triggering of earthquakes with the associated negative impacts for health and environment cannot be excluded. Detailed information can be found in Mark Broomfield (2012, 4) and in Thomas Spencer, Oliver Sartor, and Mathilde Mathieu (2014).
2 Decreasing drinking water consumption can be a problem if infrastructure has been designed for larger amounts of wastewater and is thus not used to capacity anymore.
3 The term 'cultural habit' was not defined or explained in the questionnaire. It refers to the common perception of habits of use, depending on factors like customs, education, climatic conditions, and society's social structure. Cultural diversity within EU countries probably contributes to a diversity of habits too, but as we only broadly talk about patterns of use, these aspects are not considered further here.
4 The private company Veolia Eau is managing drinking water in Nice since 1864 through a public service delegation contract. Water service will become entirely public in 2015. The case of Rennes is very similar. In Paris, water distribution was privatised in 1985. Veolia and Suez shared the market, with delegation contracts for 25 years. Eau de Paris (an autonomous branch of Paris' administration) took over the management of water in 2010. Detailed information can be found in Cristina Garzillo and Peter Ulrich (2015) for Nice, Paris, Rennes, and Strasbourg under the heading 'Water'.
5 There are ten regional water providers in England. These were privatised in 1989 along with other former public assets during the era of Margaret Thatcher. Scottish Water, unlike the rest of UK's water companies, is a public company that serves all of Scotland and is responsible for delivering water and wastewater services. Detailed information can be found in Garzillo and Ulrich (2015) for Birmingham, Glasgow, Leeds, and London under the heading 'Water'.
6 Privatisation commonly relates to water infrastructure; commodification, to water resources.

Chapter 7

The governance of regional labour market policies

Peter Huber

Social and labour market policy was chosen because it has been argued that existing national institutions may either hamper or improve both regional labour market development and adjustments. In this context, the interaction of national institutions with regional preconditions and developments is of particular importance. This chapter will first give an overview of recent trends in labour market governance, and then the conceptual framework used for analysis will be introduced. Finally, results from the 40 cities will be presented and discussed.

7.1 Trends in regional labour market governance: an overview

In regional labour market policy debates, decentralisation of tasks and/or devolution of decision powers to regional actor networks is often seen as a possibility to guarantee tailor-made labour market policies. These would take due account of the specifics of a region, promote innovation in and efficiency of labour market policy, improve accountability, and raise awareness of 'missing' policy elements in regional labour markets. Increasingly, it is also recognised that decentralisation alone is not a sufficient condition to guarantee efficient policymaking on a regional level. Decentralisation has to be accompanied by sufficient horizontal coordination between different policy actors and capacity building at the regional level to achieve its full potential (Randal W. Eberts 2009). The result of this recognition has been a parallel move towards increased networking among regional policy actors in recent years.

As a consequence, regional labour market governance has been one of the policy fields most strongly affected by the two main trends in policymaking in the EU in the last decades. The first of these was an increased dispersion of formal competencies from central states to regional and local authorities (Liesbet Hooghe and Gary Marks 2001; Regalia 2008; Andrés Rodríguez-Pose and Sylvia Tijmstra 2009; Arjan H. Schakel, Liesbet Hooghe, and Gary Marks 2015). As pointed out by Liesbet Hooghe and Gary Marks (2010), this trend has involved both general-purpose jurisdictions with systemwide and durable architecture that are nonintersecting in membership and organised in a limited number of levels (type I multilevel governance) as well as task-specific jurisdictions that have a rather flexible design and in principle can have intersecting memberships and no limits to the number of jurisdictional levels (type II multilevel governance). The second trend has been the increasing importance of policy networks in particular at the regional and local level (OECD 2004). In these networks, actors in various policy fields interact in a partnership-based approach in the provision of public services and coordination of policies (Eberts 2009). Again this trend has taken different forms and has in part also been driven by the European Union's strong emphasis on the partnership principle in designing regional policy (Christian Roth and Josef Schmid 2000; Michael W. Bauer 2002; OECD 2004; Xavier Prats-Monne 2004; Anastassios Chardas 2012).

European labour market policy, on account of lacking formal competencies of the European Commission, is mainly based on a soft (open) method of coordination, with EU authorities having only little coercive powers to influence labour market policy directly. It has been argued that this soft coordination, combined with the European Commission's repeated attempts to encourage more region-based approaches to employment and labour market policy, has empowered subnational government levels in this policy field (Mariely López-Santana 2006). At the same time, this empowerment has also resulted in the creation of large and diverse networks conducting labour market policy that include national and regional social partner organisations, NGOs, educational institutions, individual companies as well as potential further actors as members or stakeholders in their respective networks (OECD 2009a).

Furthermore, in this policy field the interaction of type I and type II organisations is particularly intensive (Liesbet Hooghe and Gary Marks 2010). In most European countries, labour market policy is conducted by various ministries and supported by Public Employment Services (PES). These according to the EU's definition "are the authorities that connect jobseekers with employers . . . through information, placement and active support services at local, national and European level" (European Commission n. a.). They are thus typical multi-tier type I institutions. At the same time, in many countries, a set of less formal organisations, often referred to as Local Employment Initiatives (LEIs) or Territorial Employment Pacts (Pacts), coexist with regional PES organisations. These have been defined in different ways by different authors. The OECD (2009b, 15) defines Local Employment Initiatives (LEIs) as: "Local in origin [they] respond to local needs and are created and controlled by individuals and groups in the community", while the European Commission (1999, 20) defines Territorial Employment Pacts as a "result of a debate leading to an agreement between local partners, published in a strategic document and accompanied by operational or financial commitments made by each partner [with] a bottom-up approach [and] a broad, active partnership". Irrespective of the concrete definition, Territorial Employment Pacts and Local Employment Initiatives (Pact/LEIs) are type II organisations according to the typology of Liesbet Hooghe and Gary Marks (2010), as they combine the characteristics of being task-specific, having a flexible design, and in principle allowing for intersecting memberships.

These organisations have received substantial attention in the literature. In particular, it has been argued that more decentralised PES organisations would allow tailor-made policies due to better knowledge of local circumstances. Thus, they would promote innovation as well as improve the accountability of local policymakers (Hugh G. Mosley 2011) and be associated with higher countrywide employment rates (Sylvain Giguère and Randal W. Eberts 2009). By contrast, critiques have stated that decentralisation bears the risk of leading to unequal standards in PES performance and duplication as well as 'reinventing the wheel'. This could even undermine accountability if regional systems of policy deliverance are inferior to national ones in terms of democratic control (Hugh G. Mosley 2009).

Similarly, the literature on Pact/LEIs (ECOTEC 2002; Buchegger-Traxler, Roggenkamp, and Scheffelt 2003; Huber 2005; OECD 2013b) argues that such initiatives have been successful in achieving goals of labour market policy, in raising awareness of 'missing' elements in regional labour market policy, in providing innovative new approaches to regional labour market policy, in improving the planning as well as in securing additional funds for regional labour market policy, and, finally, in helping communities to adapt policies to local needs and concerns. This literature, however, also stresses that the successes of these organisations have often been dependent on a number of context factors such as their interactions with other institutions, the policy space in which they operate, and the support they obtain from national policymakers. Furthermore, a number of case studies (Geddes 1998; Francesco Mantino 2011) have noted that the complexity of the partnership approach has a high potential for creating substantial transaction costs and may lead to the entrenchment of elite interests rather than to true bottom-up development initiatives. This literature also emphasises the substantial heterogeneity of these organisations. Thus for instance, in constructing a typology of Territorial Employment Pacts, which will also be used in the analysis below, ECOTEC (2002) suggests that these institutions may serve quite different purposes. According to these results, the most often found functions fulfilled by Pacts are those of a) a forum for the coordination of policy measures of the involved partners, b) an institution for designing and implementing policies, and c) an exchange platform for strategies and plans of regional actors, with some pacts serving only one of these functions and others more than one.

In this chapter, we use the questionnaires conducted among PES organisations as well as Pacts and LEIs (Pact/LEIs) in 40 cities (see chapter 2) to describe how these organisations evolved over the period 2008 to 2013 in terms of autonomy, partnership, objectives, and target groups. Furthermore, we use the results of the questionnaire to explore the potential validity of a number of hypotheses relating to the impact of PES organisations' autonomy on its stakeholders and target groups as well as to the interaction of PES and Pact/LEI organisations in a particular region. Thus, in contrast to the large number of studies focusing on the interaction of local initiatives with higher tier levels of governance such as the EU or national level (John Bachtler and Irene McMaster 2008; Ida Regalia 2008; Chardas 2012), this contribution focuses on how PES organisations (as type I organisations) interact with Pact/LEIs (as type II organisations) in a particular region. We explore how the parallel trends towards a devolution of decision powers to regional organisations and increasing importance of policy networks interact and shape the objectives of both PES and Pact/LEI organisations in a region. In particular, this chapter presents descriptive evidence on whether a PES or Pact/LEI organisation's capability to attract local stakeholders depends on its autonomy and whether its stakeholder structure and its autonomy have a discernible impact on the policies it follows. Furthermore, it also assesses how the organisation of the regional PES in terms of its autonomy, stakeholder structure, and objectives affects the chances for the formation and organisation of Pact/LEIs.

7.2 Stylised facts of local labour market governance in the EU

As described in detail in chapter 2, the data for this analysis was collected through questionnaires among two types of actors (regional PES organisations and Pact/LEIs) in the cities studied. The resulting sample of PES organisations and Pact/LEIs reflects the heterogeneity of the sample design. It, however, also reflects results in the literature with respect to the age and function of Pact/LEIs.

7.2.1 Heterogeneity of European labour markets

Fifteen of the PES organisations surveyed were located in smaller cities with less than 250,000 inhabitants and another 16 in medium-sized cities with between 250,000 and

1 million inhabitants, while only 9 PES organisations were located in large cities with more than 1 million inhabitants. Twelve of the studied cities were located in Western Europe, 9 in Eastern Europe, 8 in Northern Europe, and 11 in Southern Europe. Furthermore, the sample also includes countries which the economic crisis since 2009 has impacted rather differently (e.g. Poland and Greece). This also leads to rather different unemployment levels and labour market problems in the sampled cities.[1] Finally, while a PES organisation was sampled in each of the 40 cities, Pact/LEIs were only identified in 26 of the 40 cities, with the number of such institutions in large cities in particular being very low.

Table 7-1 Sample structure by city size, European region, territory serviced, and age and function of Pact/LEIs

Region	City size			
	Small	Medium	Large	Total
Western Europe	8 (7)	3 (2)	1 (1)	12 (10)
Eastern Europe	3 (2)	5 (3)	1 (0)	9 (5)
Northern Europe	2 (2)	4 (3)	2 (0)	8 (5)
Southern Europe	2 (1)	4 (2)	5 (2)	11 (5)
Territory serviced				
Corresponds to administrative city limits	3 (1)	7 (4)	3 (0)	13 (5)
Is larger than administrative city limits	11 (10)	8 (6)	4 (2)	23 (18)
Is smaller than administrative city limits	1 (0)	1 (0)	2 (1)	4 (1)
Covers part of city and part of other territories	0 (1)	0 (1)	0 (0)	0 (2)
Total	15 (12)	16 (11)	9 (3)	40 (26)
Characteristics of Pact/LEI				
Year of founding				
Before 1985	2	2	0	4
1985–1999	4	3	0	7
2000–2005	3	1	2	6
After 2005	3	5	1	9
Type of organisation[a]				
Coordination of policy measures of partners	1.9	1.7	1.3	1.8
Designing and implementing policies	1.8	2.0	1.7	1.9
Exchange platform for strategies and plans of regional actors	1.9	2.5	2.0	2.2

Note: City Size: Small = less than 250.000 inhabitants, Medium = 250.000 to less than one million inhabitants, Large = 1 million or more inhabitants; Region: Western Europe = AT, DE, FR, CH; Eastern Europe = CZ, PL, RO; Southern Europe = ES, GR, IT, TK, Northern Europe = DE, SE, UK. Values in brackets refer to the number of Pact/Lei institutions sampled. a) Average score on a scale from 3 = very applicable to 1 = not applicable.

Source: WWWforEurope questionnaire

This heterogeneity of the sample also leads to some differences of the territory serviced by the respective organisations relative to the administrative city limits (cf. Table 7-1). Among the interviewed regional PES organisations, 23 were responsible for a territory that is larger than the administrative city limits, while 13 serviced a territory according to administrative city limits, and for 4, this was smaller than the administrative city limits. As was to be expected, the proportion of PES administrations servicing territories larger than the administrative city limits is higher among small cities and lower among the medium-sized and large cities. The same applies to the interviewed Pact/LEIs. Among them, too, the proportion of organisations servicing territories larger than the administrative city limits is particularly large among small cities and smaller among medium-sized and large cities. Furthermore, the large majority (18 out of 26) of Pact/LEIs serviced a territory that is larger than the administrative city limits, while the territory serviced by these organisations accorded with the administrative city limits in 4 cities, and in 2, the territory serviced was smaller than the administrative city limits. In contrast to the PES questionnaire, however, two organisations partly serviced the city limits and partly other territories.

In accordance with the results of Ida Regalia (2008), who finds that while most Pact/LEIs are rather young, there are also quite a few examples of such institutions that have already existed for a rather long time. The oldest Pact/LEI in our sample was founded in 1970 (in Copenhagen), and among the 26 Pact/LEIs identified, 4 were already founded before 1985. Most of the Pact/LEIs (15) are, however, rather young and were founded after 2000. For historical reasons, the youngest Pact/LEIs are found in the Eastern European countries. The oldest are found in Northern and Western European countries (Denmark and Germany), while the development of such institutions – at least judging from our sample – set in after 1985 in Southern Europe. Large cities also seem to be latecomers to this development, since all of the Pact/LEIs sampled in large cities were founded after 2000.

Also in accordance with results by ECOTEC (2002), most of the Pact/LEIs surveyed at least partly serve as a forum of exchange on the plans and strategies of regional actors, which is followed (at some distance) by the function of designing and implementing and adapting policy measures. This is, however, primarily due to the importance of this function in Pact/LEIs in Southern and Eastern Europe and in large and medium-sized cities. While in small cities, all three functions are of about equal importance, in large cities and even more so in medium-sized cities the function of Pact/LEIs as a forum of exchange on the plans and strategies of regional actors is the most important one.

7.2.2 Autonomy, stakeholders, and objectives of PES organisations

Autonomy

The described heterogeneity is also reflected in other dimensions of the questionnaire. Thus, in the questionnaire, three indicators on the autonomy of PES organisations were collected. These relate to the share of autonomously decided budgets and organisational independence (i.e. whether a PES is part of a ministry or not) and a set of indicators measuring the degree of autonomy of the regional PES in the fields of designing programmes, allocating budgets, defining target groups, monitoring and evaluating, administration, and outsourcing. In addition, these indicators show substantial heterogeneity. This is mainly driven by differences in city size and national regulations but also varies substantially between the different aspects of autonomy considered: Of the 40 PES organisations interviewed, 28 are part of a (national or regional) ministry while 12 are part of an independent organisation.[2] The proportion of PES organisations that are part of an independent organisation is largest in small cities and smallest in large cities. This is, however, due to the strong impact of national regulations on the organisation of the PES and the sample of small cities that is strongly focused on Western Europe, as all of the interviewed Western European PES organisations are also part of an independent organisation, while the Eastern and Northern European PES organisations are all part of a ministry. By contrast, budgetary autonomy – in accordance with prior expectations – suggests greater autonomy of PES organisations in larger cities. While on average the proportion of total budget decided on autonomously by PES organisations is 46 per cent, this percentage reaches almost 49.8 per cent in large cities but only 43.3 per cent in the small cities.

The differences in autonomy between cities of different sizes with respect to different fields are somewhat less pronounced. Regional PES organisations in large cities tend to have more autonomy in allocating budgets, defining targets, and monitoring and evaluating. Regional PES organisations in small cities, by contrast, have more autonomy in designing programmes and performing administrative tasks. Furthermore, correlating the share of the autonomously decided budget of a PES organisation with the areas in which it has at least some responsibility suggest that many of the fields of responsibility are only weakly correlated to higher budgetary autonomy. Only the responsibility for deciding on active labour market policy budgets, designing passive labour market policies, and monitoring the success of active labour market policy are significantly (at the 10 per cent level) positively correlated with the share of the autonomously decided budget. Being at least partially responsible for placement services (i.e. services provided to jobseekers to match them to open positions), by contrast, is significantly negatively correlated with the budget autonomy. Differences in these indicators of autonomy also seem to be strongly driven by national differences.[3] The differences between PES organisations located in different European regions are particularly pronounced. Western European PES organisations have on average substantially more autonomy in allocating budgets and defining target groups, while Eastern European ones have more autonomy in monitoring and evaluating, administrative tasks, and outsourcing.[4] PES organisations in both Southern and Northern Europe as a rule have less autonomy in all fields.

The changes of the different indicators of autonomy (right-hand side of Table 7-2), however, suggest that the trend towards an increasing devolution of decision powers to the regional level – characterising the pre-2008 development of regional labour market policy – has continued since. The extent to which this is the case, however, depends strongly on the indicator or task considered. It was least pronounced in the share of the budget decided autonomously and also differs substantially between cities of different sizes. Four of the five interviewed PES organisations that responded to this question in large cities stated that they experienced an increase in the share of an autonomously decided budget since 2008, while the number of PES organisations in small cities experiencing a reduction in budgetary autonomy outnumbered the number of small cities experiencing an increase.

Similarly, the devolution of powers to regional authorities in other fields of activity has also continued more strongly since 2008. In all of the areas listed in Table 7-2, the number of PES organisations stating that they have experienced an increase in autonomy since 2008 exceeds the number stating that they experienced a decrease. This devolution of power to regional PES organisations has been highest in allocating budgets followed by

Table 7-2 Indicators for autonomy of regional PES organisations

City size	Small	Medium	Large	Total	Small	Medium	Large	Total
	Levels[a]				Change[b]			
	Independence							
Part of independent organisation	60.0	26.7	11.1	35.9				
	Budgetary autonomy							
Share of budget decided autonomously	43.3	47.4	49.8	46.0	-0.21	0.14	0.60	0.07
	At least partially responsible for							
Designing programs	28.6	25.6	22.2	25.9	0.15	0.22	0.17	0.18
Allocating budget	25.0	37.5	48.1	39.1	0.09	0.22	0.34	0.24
Defining target groups	46.2	42.3	37.5	42.6	0.15	0.27	0.00	0.18
Monitoring and evaluating	45.8	50.0	57.1	52.0	0.29	0.07	0.07	0.14
Administration	51.4	42.6	50.0	48.1	0.07	0.25	0.00	0.13
Outsourcing	32.1	32.1	26.2	30.8	0.13	0.06	0.00	0.08

Note: City Size: Small = less than 250.000 inhabitants, Medium = 250.000 to less than one million inhabitants, Large = 1 million or more inhabitants; a) Percentage of pacts responding positively (budgetary share = average percentage), b) Average score on a scale from 1 = increased to -1 = reduced.
Source: WWWforEurope questionnaire

competencies related to designing programmes and defining target groups, while in terms of outsourcing these changes have been lowest.[5] These increases in competences have also been correlated to city size. Large cities experienced a particularly strong increase in competences related to allocating budgets, while for small cities this increase was disproportionately high for tasks related to monitoring and evaluation as well as outsourcing. In defining target groups, designing programmes, and administration, medium-sized cities experienced the largest increase in autonomy.

Stakeholder involvement

Similar observations apply to the types of stakeholders involved in the decision-making of the regional PES. According to the results of the questionnaire, the average PES has 3.7 national and 4.3 regional stakeholders. Other stakeholders,[6] by contrast, are rarely included as the average PES has only 0.1 such stakeholders. As could be expected, the national PES, followed by national social policy and national employment policy actors, has an important role in almost all PES organisations. The national PES is named as a stakeholder by 70 per cent of the interviewed PES organisations and national social and employment policy actors by 68 per cent and 63 per cent, respectively (Figure 7-1). Furthermore, national policy actors in regional policy and national social partner organisations are named as stakeholders by over half of the PES organisations, while EU structural assistance committees (38 per cent) and NGOs (28 per cent) are only named by a minority of the PES organisations. Regional social partners, municipalities,

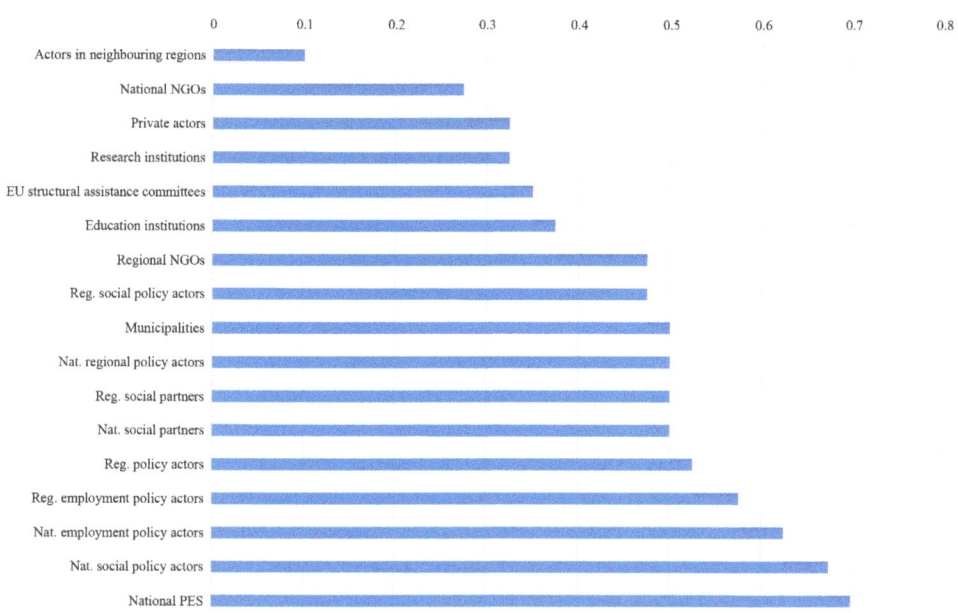

Figure 7-1 Stakeholders involved in PES decision-making by city size and region (share of positive answers)

and regional actors in employment and regional policy are stakeholders in more than half of the PES organisations. Regional NGOs are named by a little less than half of the PES organisations. Other stakeholders, such as research institutes and education institutions, are stakeholders even more rarely. Private actors, finally, are considered stakeholders only in about one-third of the PES organisations and actors in neighbouring regions are stakeholders in only a very small number (10 per cent) of the regional PES organisations.

Evidence on the change of influence of stakeholders in the PES organisations interviewed suggests that also the pre-crisis tendency in regional labour market policies towards the increasing importance of more varied stakeholder networks has continued since 2008.[7] The interviewed PES organisations stated that the importance of all stakeholders (except for actors in regional policy, where there has been no change) has increased since 2008 (Figure 7-2). These results, however, also indicate that this tendency has been far from uniform since 2008. In accordance with the finding of increased regional autonomy of PES organisations, regional social partners and regional NGOs as well as education and research institutions have experienced a particularly large increase in importance. In contrast, national social partner organisations, national employment policy actors, and national NGOs experienced a smaller increase in importance. Correlating aggregate indicators of the change in importance since 2008 with the level of importance reported in 2013, however, provides only very little evidence of a convergence across actors. Both less influential stakeholders as well as very influential groups gained more influence in quite a number of organisations. If anything, the data indicates an increased importance of regional stakeholders relative to national ones since 2008.

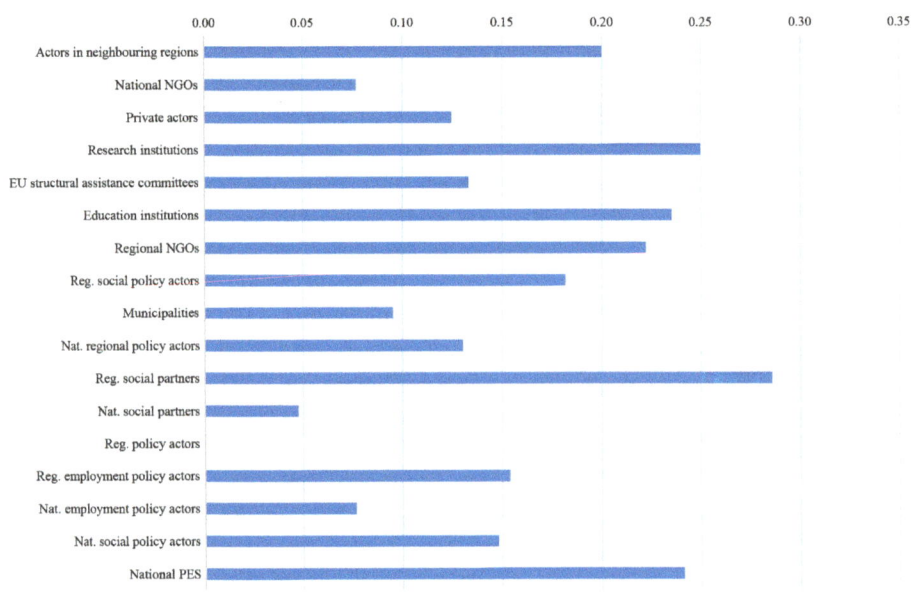

Figure 7-2 Change in the importance of stakeholders since 2007 (1: increased, 0: constant, −1: decreased; mean value; sorted by importance of stakeholder)

Objectives of PES organisations and Pact/LEIs

The results of the block of questions on the objectives of the interviewed organisations characterise the regional PES as primarily concerned with the unemployed. In aggregate, 98 per cent of the interviewed PES organisations stated that the long-term unemployed are a target group, and over 80 per cent stated that also young persons, older persons, and people with disabilities belong to their target groups. By contrast, persons who are employed, or belong to the core working groups (such as men in the main working ages), or are out of the labour force (such as the old or young employed as well as the employed in general and women on child leave) are target groups at less than 40 per cent of the interviewed organisations. Enterprises are a target group for only 38 per cent of these organisations, and 55 per cent of the organisations consider SMEs to be a target group, while 48 per cent also focus on newly founded enterprises (Figure 7-3). Sector-specific strategies, by contrast, are much less regularly followed in PES organisations than the core target groups. Even the most popular sector-specific strategies (related to the health sector and social services) exist in only slightly more than 50 per cent of the PES organisations. Strategies relating to tourism, domestic services, public sector employment, construction, and child care, all of which could be expected to be particularly important sectors in urban contexts, exist at between 30 per cent to 40 per cent of the PES organisations and less than a quarter of the PES organisations follow a strategy in leisure and cultural activities or in public utilities (Figure 7-4).

Comparing this objective structure to that of Pact/LEIs suggests that, for both these institutions, standard labour market objectives such as combating youth and long-term unemployment are in the top positions but that, for Pact/LEIs, there are also further important objectives that are not incorporated in the target groups of PES organisations, such as identifying job vacancies, creating intermediate and sheltered employment, providing training to meet employers' skill needs, identifying employers' skill needs, and securing national and regional funds (Figure 7-5). In accordance with results in the literature, Pact/LEIs are thus characterised by a wider set of policy objectives, which also include more policies designed to improve employment creation and the adaptability of the workforce in the region. Nonetheless, also in these organisations, standard regional policy objectives (e.g. implementing EU programmes, promoting the region, or increasing R&D employment) rank under the least important objectives.

In addition, sector strategies are less often followed in Pact/LEIs than in PES organisations. This applies in particular to the most important sector strategies for PES organisations. While 63 per cent of the PES organisations have a sector strategy applying to social services, as the most popular among both PES organisations and Pact/LEIs (Figure 7-6), the same applies to only 43 per cent of the Pact/LEIs. At the lower end of the pyramid, this difference is not so pronounced. While 15 per cent of regional PES organisations have sector strategies addressing leisure and cultural activities (the lowest ranking sector strategy for regional PES organisations), the same proportion of Pact/LEIs has sector-specific strategies for public utilities (which is the lowest ranking sector strategy for Pact/LEIs) (Figure 7-6). Finally, also the probability of the two institutions following a particular sector strategy in a particular city is positively correlated.[8] Thus in the vast majority of cases, if one of the institutions considered follows a sector strategy in a city, this increases the probability

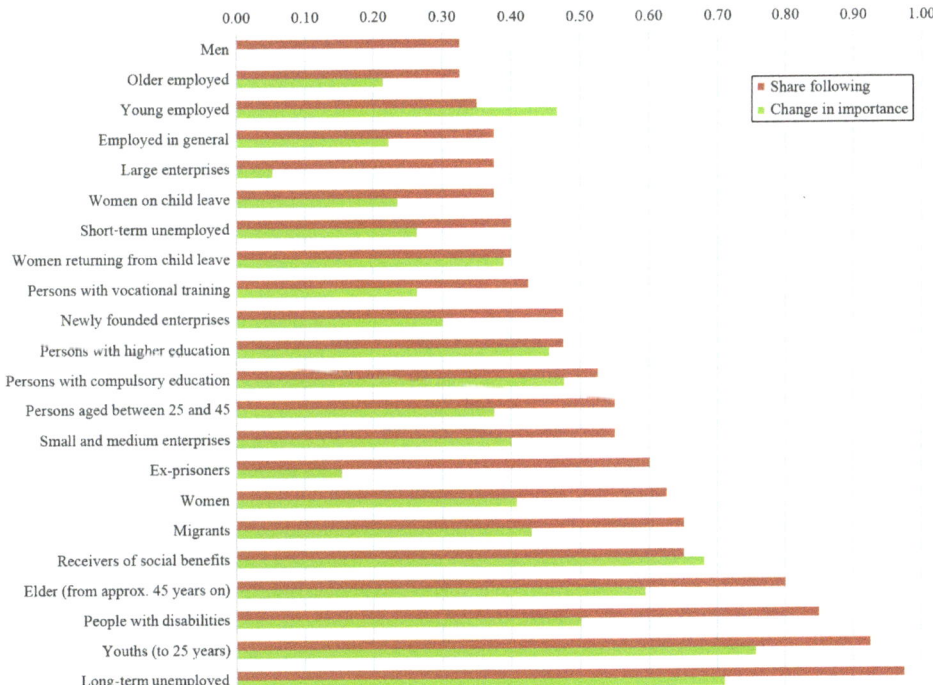

Figure 7-3 Share of PES organisations with target groups and change of importance in these target groups (Share following: share of PES organisations following target group strategy; change in importance: average score on a scale from 1: increased in importance to −1: reduced in importance)

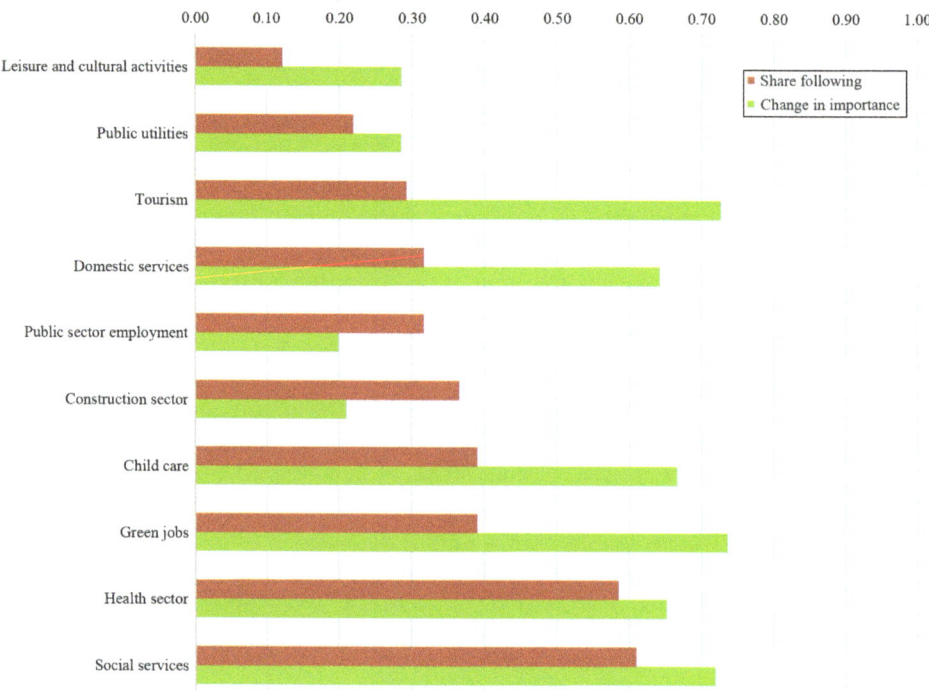

Figure 7-4 Share of PES organisations with sector strategies and change of importance in these sector strategies (Share following: share of PES organisations following sector strategy; change in importance: average score on a scale from 1: increased in importance to −1: reduced in importance)

of the other institutions in the same city following this strategy as well. This at least casts doubt on the claim in part of the literature (ECOTEC 2002; Buchegger-Traxler, Roggenkamp, and Scheffelt 2003; OECD 2004) that Pact/LEIs are mostly "filling policy gaps" left by the PES and suggests rather similar objectives of the two institutions, at least with respect to sector strategies.

The importance of target groups and sector strategies for PES organisations have also changed substantially since 2008. In this time period, increased unemployment and greater labour market difficulties have led to an increased importance of all target groups of labour market policy. As a consequence, a larger number of PES organisations indicates a higher importance, rather than a lower importance, for all target groups as well as for all sector strategies. The only exception is men in the main working ages, where an increased number equals a decreased importance, according to the PES interviewed (Figures 7-3 and 7-4). The strongest increases in importance, however, are reported for youths, the long-term unemployed, receivers of social benefits, and older persons. This accords with the increase in youth and long-term unemployment in the EU in this time period and the simultaneously increasing problems of older workers. It suggests as well that target groups outside the 'core' clientele of PES organisations seem to have relatively lost in importance, since the importance of groups such as large enterprises, ex-prisoners, and various groups

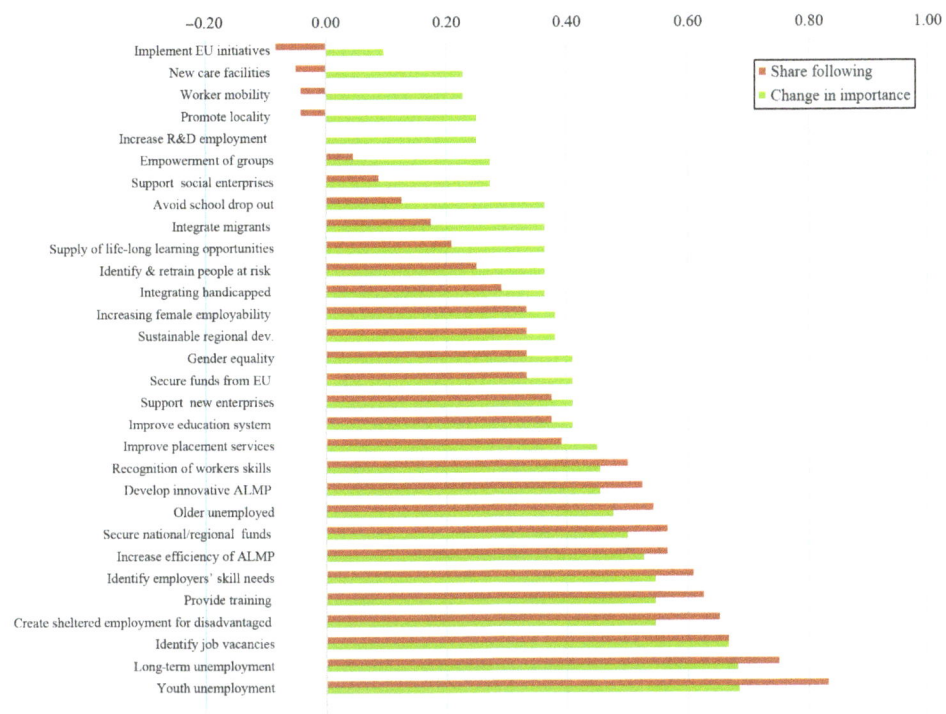

Figure 7-5 Importance and change of importance in objectives of Pact/LEIs (Importance: average score on a scale from −1: unimportant, 0: important, 1: very important; change in importance: average score on a scale from 1 increased in importance to − reduced in importance)

of employed persons as well as women on maternity leave has increased in much fewer PES organisations than in the case of youths, the long-term unemployed, older workers, and social benefit receivers.[9]

The importance of all objectives has also increased for Pact/LEIs in the last half decade. They are, however, also increasingly concentrated on their 'core' objectives, although this tendency was potentially slightly less pronounced for Pact/LEIs than for PES organisations. The largest increases in importance of Pact/LEI objectives were reported for reducing school drop-out rates, which belonged to the less important objectives in 2013. This reflects an increasing concern in many European countries with respect to the quality of education systems in the last five years. Outside this, however, the gains in importance in the last five years have been larger for the more important objectives in 2013 than for the less important ones. The second and third largest increases in importance were reported for identifying employers' skill needs and job vacancies, which belonged to the most important objectives in 2013, and the smallest increases in importance occurred for the implementation of European initiatives and the mobility of the workforce, which belonged to the least important objectives in 2013 (cf. Figures 7-5 and 7-6).

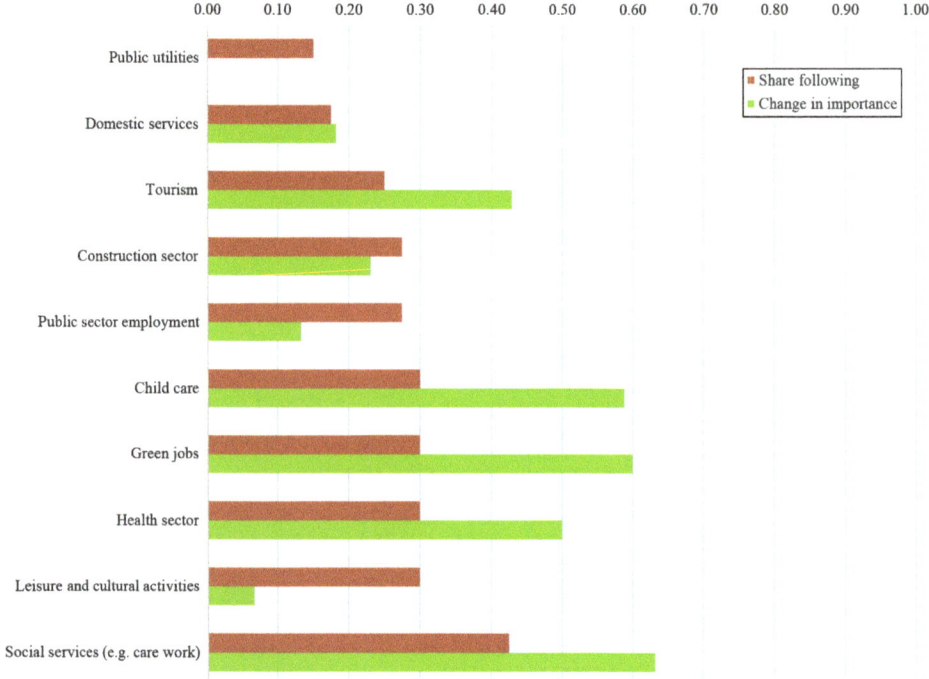

Figure 7-6 Share of Pact/LEIs with sector strategies and change of importance in these sector strategies (Share following: share of PES organisations following sector strategy; change in importance: average score on a scale from 1: increased in importance to −1: reduced in importance)

7.3 Conceptual framework and hypotheses

In sum, the trends towards increasing regional autonomy and the increasing importance of policy networks have continued to be of relevance since 2008. Furthermore, in the light of mounting labour market problems in recent years, both regional PES organisations as well as Pact/LEIs have increasingly concentrated on their core competencies. These developments, however, also differed substantially across different PES organisations and Pact/LEIs. From a policy perspective, it may thus be of relevance to conduct a deeper analysis of this heterogeneity to better understand the links between different factors driving the stakeholders and objective structure of PES organisations and the factors affecting the emergence and organisation of Pact/LEIs.

The conceptual framework on which we base this analysis (see Figure 7-7) starts from the assumption that both the organisation as well as the objectives of regional PESs and Pact/LEIs are on the one hand determined by a number of regional, national, and EU-wide framework conditions. This is strengthened by several research results (ECOTEC 2002; Ludovica Gambaro, Simona Milio, and Marco Simoni 2004; Robert Strauss 2005; Bachtler and McMaster 2008; Francesca Froy et al. 2011; Mosley 2011). These may, for instance, consist of legal stipulations, the specific labour market problems of a region or country, the resources available to conduct certain policies, or national or EU-wide support for certain policies. On the other hand, different elements of the organisation and objective structure of Pact/LEIs and PES organisations also interact. This interaction may be within an organisation or across organisations. Thus, within organisations, the degree of autonomy of regional PES organisations may influence the size and structure of their stakeholder network. This is either because more autonomous PES organisations are more interesting for a larger range of stakeholders or because more autonomous PES organisations also look for larger stakeholder networks to help plan and coordinate their activities. Similarly, a PES's or Pact/LEI's objective structure may depend on its autonomy and stakeholder network, if for instance stakeholders or partners use their voice or expertise to influence the priorities of a PES or Pact/LEI, or by defining the activities that can be undertaken by these organisations. In addition, the two organisations influence each other, for example by the autonomy of the regional PES defining the political space in which the Pact/LEI can cooperate or by facilitating or hampering the conditions for the emergence of a Pact/LEI or the inclusion of certain partners in the Pact/LEI partnership.

Clearly many links between variables can be considered within this general conceptual framework. In this study, we are primarily interested in three such links. The first is that between a PES organisation's autonomy and its stakeholder structure. This is of particular relevance as it provides evidence on the interrelation of devolution of power and formation of policy networks concerning labour market policy at the local or regional level. A number of authors (Sylvain Giguère and Francesca Froy 2009; Rodríguez-Pose and Tijmstra 2009) have argued that to design adequate regional labour market policies, organisations at the regional level on the one hand need to involve a large number of stakeholders and on the other hand need to have some autonomy in designing, implementing, administrating as well as monitoring and controlling regional labour market policies. Second, we focus on the link between a PES organisation's autonomy and stakeholder network and

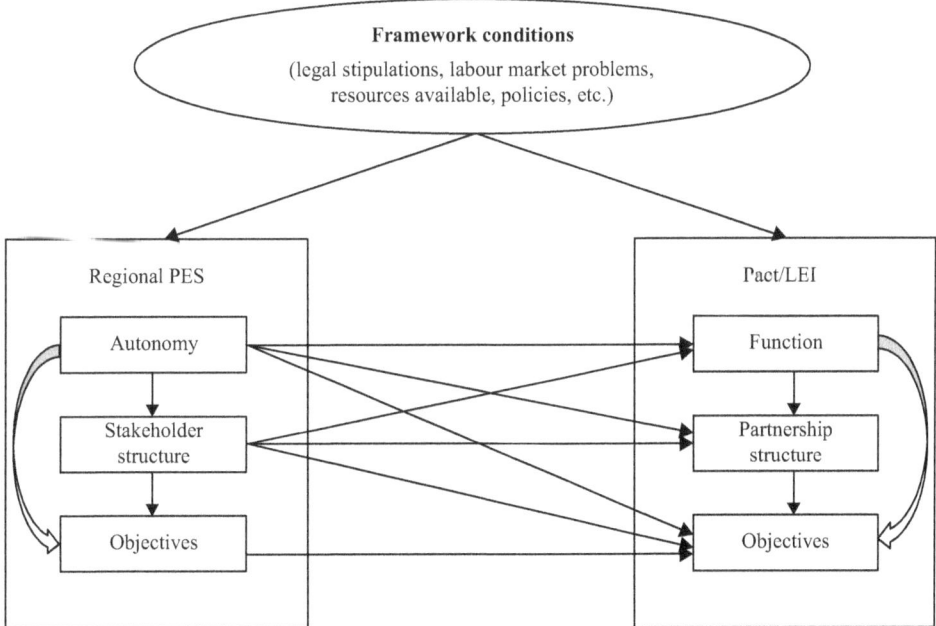

Figure 7-7 Conceptual framework of the study on labour markets

its target groups as well as its responsiveness to new policy challenges. This is of importance, because it has often been stated that more autonomous organisations based on large partner or stakeholder networks are also likely to react more flexibly to new situations. Finally, we also focus on the link between the stakeholder networks with type I multilevel governance organisations of the regional PES and the emergence and development of type II organisations such as Pact/LEIs. This is particularly relevant because such linkages provide information to policymakers on what factors contribute to the emergence of a Pact/LEI in a city and how the structure of this partnership and its objectives interacts with the organisation of the regional PES.

7.3.1 Autonomy and stakeholder structure

With respect to the relationship between the autonomy of a PES and its stakeholder structure, we hypothesise that regional PES organisations enjoying more autonomy should be more capable of forming large stakeholder networks than organisations that only have limited autonomy. This is because more autonomous PES organisations will require more external competencies to conduct and design their policies and may have greater possibilities to recruit such external expertise. Moreover, such PES organisations may also be more interesting for stakeholders seeking to influence the design of labour market policies on account of their greater competencies and larger financial resources (see Henry Buller 2000). Similarly, regional labour market policy organisations (PES or Pact/LEIs) serving cities of different sizes could face rather different preconditions for cooperation with other partners. With respect to this variable, two opposing forces may be at work. On the one hand, such organisations serving larger cities – because these cities host a larger number of competent potential stakeholders – could face more favourable conditions for building large stakeholder networks. On the other hand, in smaller cities – on account of smaller cities providing for more accessible and denser informal networks – such organisations could also find more favourable conditions for building networks. These two countervailing tendencies would lead us to expect a nonlinear relationship between city size and size of stakeholder networks, with medium-sized cities being disadvantaged in particular.

Furthermore, certain types of autonomy may have different impacts on the probability of cooperation of certain potential partners with the regional PES and thus on the structure of the partnership and stakeholder networks of Pact/LEIs or PES organisations. Following the above logic, social partners and NGOs could for instance have a particularly high propensity to cooperate with regional PES organisations with high budgetary autonomy (or in Pact/LEIs coordinating policy), since such cooperation could potentially make accessible substantial funds for the clientele of these organisations. Education institutions and enterprises, by contrast, might be more interested in cooperation with regional PES organisations with high autonomy to subcontract, because cooperation with such organisations may allow them to obtain additional subcontracts. In addition, the age and function of a Pact/LEI may impact on the formality of the network, because older Pact/LEIs should also have more formal partnerships, on account of them having had more time to build and formalise their partnership. Pact/LEIs that have the function of a platform for the exchange of information may require less formal (and potentially also smaller) partnerships than Pact/LEIs whose aim is to formally coordinate labour market policies.

7.3.2 Autonomy, stakeholder networks, and policy changes

The autonomy and the stakeholder structure of a regional PES organisation may also have an impact on their objective structure. In this respect, it has been argued that a greater degree of autonomy with respect to budget allocation, designing programmes, and defining target groups[10] as well as a more varied stakeholder structure[11] may lead to the better adaptation of regional labour market policies to regional needs. It may also provide for a higher responsiveness to the changing needs of their respective regional labour markets (Giguère and Eberts 2009).

We would therefore expect PES organisations with more autonomy (in particular with respect to budget allocation, designing programmes, and defining target groups) and with a larger number of stakeholders to follow a larger number of target groups, objectives, and sector strategies. Similarly, we would also expect such organisations to have been more responsive to the labour market challenges posed by the post-crisis years. This would imply that such organisations have experienced a larger number of changes of importance of target groups, objectives, and sector strategies than organisations with less autonomy and a smaller stakeholder network.

7.3.3 Interaction of regional PES and Pact/LEI organisations

With respect to the third relationship of interest, a number of authors have argued that Pact/LEIs are formed in order to overcome gaps or deficits in the policy of a particular region (ECOTEC 2002; Buchegger-Traxler, Roggenkamp, and Scheffelt 2003; OECD 2004). This could lead one to expect that the form of organisation of regional PES may have an impact on the Pact/LEI in that region. This impact could be on a number of levels. A first one is whether a Pact/LEI is organised at all. This could be influenced by the size of the stakeholder network of the regional PES. If a large network of regional stakeholders is collaborating within the regional PES, this may make the organisation of a further network by a Pact/LEI unnecessary. The existence of such a large network may also reduce the set-up costs for a new network and thus facilitate the creation of a Pact/LEI. Similarly, the emergence of a Pact/LEI may also be affected by the autonomy of the regional PES organisation. If a Pact/LEI is a means for regional actors to overcome institutional deficits in labour market policymaking in a region, Pact/LEIs should have a high probability of emerging in regions where the regional PES has few competences or little autonomy. By contrast, lacking autonomy to finance regional Pact/LEIs by the regional PES may be an impediment to the emergence of a Pact/LEI.[12]

A further channel through which the regional PES could affect the organisation of the Pact/LEI could be through the purpose fulfilled by the Pact/LEI and through the PES organisation's influence on the Pact/LEI's partnership structure. For instance, in regions where the PES has few stakeholders or is under the particularly strong influence of central organisations, regional policymakers may be keen to construct larger and potentially more formal networks and may also be keen to construct Pact/LEIs with a strong role in implementing and designing policies. In such regions however, regional policymakers may also lack the autonomy or competencies to construct such Pact/LEIs. This may lead to more informal Pact/LEI partnerships that are restricted to the exchange of information in such regions.

Finally, a last such interaction would be on the level of objectives. Here, if Pact/LEIs indeed complement PES organisations, one would expect that Pact/LEIs in regions where the regional PES follows a more diverse set of target groups or sector strategies would have more narrowly defined objectives. Similarly, one may also expect that Pact/LEIs operating in territories where the regional PES organisation has shown a higher responsiveness in terms of policy changes since 2008 may have experienced a lower necessity to respond to new labour market challenges.

7.4 Results from forty European cities

7.4.1 The stakeholder structure of PES organisations

Predictors of stakeholder network size

We conduct two kinds of analysis to assess whether the hypotheses with respect to the impact of the autonomy of a PES on its stakeholder network find empirical support in our data. In the first, we aim to explain the number of stakeholders involved in a PES organisation (both in total as well as for national, regional, and other stakeholders) by a regression of this variable on indicator variables for city size (which may be medium and large cities with the base category being small cities) and measures of its autonomy (an indicator variable if a PES organisation is part of a ministry, the share of its budget decided on autonomously as well as the indices of autonomy for various subfields discussed above). Following our hypotheses, the latter variables should have a positive impact on the stakeholder network size of a regional PES, while city size should be nonlinearly related to the stakeholder network size. In addition, we also include control variables for whether a regional PES serves a territory corresponding to the administrative city boundaries and for the European region in which the city is located. These variables are included to control for any distortions of estimates that could arise from a PES organisation serving a territory differing from the administrative city limits (and thus incorrectly measuring the size of the territory covered by the PES) and to minimise the omitted variable bias from not measuring any of the institutional details not accounted for in our data.

Table 7-3 shows a number of regression results. In the first two rows of this table, we focus on specifications in which the share of autonomously decided budget is included in the regression. However, these results are based on only very few observations because of the low response rate to the question on the autonomously decided budget share. Thus, in columns (3) and (4), we exclude this variable to increase the number of observations. Furthermore, to assess the impact of potential missing variable bias resulting from not controlling for country-specific characteristics in columns (2) and (4), country group dummy variables are included, while in columns (1) and (3) they are excluded.

The results of these specifications are largely consistent with our hypotheses. They suggest that the share of the budget autonomously decided on by the PES as well as greater autonomy in allocating budgets and greater autonomy in outsourcing statistically significantly increases the size of the stakeholder network. By contrast, PES organisations that are part of a ministry as well as regional PES organisations that have a higher index of autonomy for defining target groups have a statistically significantly smaller stakeholder network. In addition, PES organisations located in medium-sized cities have the smallest network size throughout, while the network size of large cities is significantly smaller than that of small cities when focusing on the specification including the autonomous budget share and excluding region controls, but statistically insignificantly different from small cities in all other specifications. Finally, the control variables (i.e. European region

Table 7-3 Regression results for the number of stakeholders involved in a PES organisation

	(1)		(2)		(3)		(4)	
	Coef.	Std. Err.	Coef.	Std. Err.	Coef.	Std. Err.	Coef.	Std. Err.
Medium city	-8.49**	3.32	-8.13**	3.34	-7.11**	3.41	-6.78**	3.36
Small city	-6.75**	3.33	-3.25	4.05	-0.67	2.53	-0.23	2.94
Large city	Base category		Base category		Base category		Base category	
Territory corresponds to city limit	3.67	2.77	3.97	2.79	1.20	2.03	1.06	2.14
Part of ministry	-7.18**	2.87	-8.63**	-6.69	-6.36	2.04	-6.27	4.83
Autonomous budget share	0.09***	0.03	0.10**	0.03				
Aut. in designing programs	7.78	6.05	6.80	6.43	5.01	5.46	4.89**	2.01
Aut. in allocating budget	10.48**	4.53	10.07**	4.65	12.71***	3.35	12.44***	3.09
Aut. in defining target groups	-7.17*	3.96	-8.65**	3.94	-6.14**	3.10	-6.41**	3.28
Aut. in monitoring	4.51	4.88	5.04	4.96	0.01	4.16	-0.47	4.35
Aut. in administration	5.63	4.09	8.14	4.73	2.11	3.72	2.36	4.14
Aut. in outsourcing	16.84**	6.54	14.27**	6.57	12.70**	5.82	11.95*	6.26
Eastern Europe			Base category				Base category	
Northern Europe			0.11	6.55			-2.49	5.48
Southern Europe			-1.54	6.88			-1.71	5.45
			-5.83	5.59			-3.37	4.49
Constant	6.14**	2.5	7.31	6.93	6.03**	2.29	8.70	5.76
Observations	28		28		40		40	
R²	0.60		0.69		0.33		0.36	

Note: Coef. = estimated coefficient, Std. Err. = Standard Error; ***, **, and *signify significance at the 1%, 5%, and 10% levels, respectively.
Source: WWWforEurope questionnaire

dummies and the indicator variable for PES organisations serving a territory of the same size as the administrative city limits) are statistically insignificant. This suggests that, after controlling for autonomy, the effects of unmeasured region-specific effects on network size cannot be reliably identified and that (also after controlling for autonomy and other variables) the measurement error with respect to the size of the territory serviced by a PES organisation is of minor importance for results.

Probability of individual stakeholders being part of the network

In the second analysis, we extend on these results by focusing on the probability of a particular stakeholder being part of the stakeholder network of a regional PES organisation, while leaving the explanatory variables unchanged.[13] The results of these regressions (in Table 7-4) in their majority are consistent with our hypotheses. PES organisations that are part of a ministry have a lower probability of involving all partners, but this lower probability is statistically significant (at the 5 per cent level) only for national and regional social partner organisations as well as for education institutions and national social policy actors. Thus, PES organisations that are part of a ministry are particularly unlikely to have these organisations as a stakeholder. Greater budget autonomy (statistically significantly) increases the probability of social partner institutions, national employment policy actors, regional and national regional policy actors, committees for EU structural funds assistance as well as enterprises and education institutions being stakeholders. Furthermore, regional and national social partner organisations are significantly more often stakeholders in regional PES organisations that have more competencies in allocating budgets. This suggests that social partners and other often less considered partners are more often stakeholders in PES organisations with high budgetary autonomy. Finally, PES organisations with more competencies in outsourcing have a statistically significantly higher probability of having (both national and regional) NGOs, enterprises, and education institutions as well as regional policy actors among their stakeholders. This may be an indication that these organisations are particularly likely to profit from subcontracts of a regional PES.

Moreover, the results suggest that higher administrative autonomy is a significantly positive predictor of the probability of regional and national social partner organisations being stakeholders and that competencies in defining target groups are statistically negatively correlated with the probability of enterprises and committees for EU structural fund assistance being stakeholders, while more competencies in designing programmes are also statistically positive predictors of enterprises being partners. More interestingly, the U-shaped relationship between stakeholder network size and city size found above is strongly associated with a U-shaped probability of having national and regional social policy actors and committees for EU structural funds assistance as stakeholders, while the probability of having both national and regional social partner institutions and NGOs as stakeholders uniformly falls with city size. This may indicate that PES organisations in large cities face particular problems in attracting social policy actors to participate in the stakeholder networks.

7.4.2 Determinants of the target groups and sector strategies of PES organisations

To analyse the interaction between the number of target groups and sector strategies followed as well as the responsiveness of the PES organisation to new policy challenges, we construct a number of indicators on the diversity of the objective structure of a PES

Table 7-4 Regression results for the probability of a stakeholder to be involved in a PES organisation

				National actors				
	PES	Social policy	Employment policy	Regional policy	NGOs	Social partners	Committees for EU structural assistance	Municipalities
Small city				Base category				
Medium city	-0.716	-1.094***	-0.420	-0.457	-0.197	-0.760**	-0.950***	0.390
Large city	-0.443	-0.806***	-0.113	-0.035	-0.267	-0.971**	-0.317	-0.551
Ter. corresponds to city limits	0.192	0.681**	-0.145	-0.092	0.102	0.227	0.341	0.531
Part of ministry	-0.395	-0.712**	-0.425	-0.519	-0.091	-0.750**	-0.487	-0.515
Autonomous budget share	0.005	0.003	0.006**	0.006**	0.002	0.008***	0.006**	0.003
Aut. in designing programs	-0.147	0.608	0.577	0.599	0.026	0.328	1.089*	-0.556
Aut. in allocating budget	0.645	0.555	0.911	0.787	0.764	1.054**	0.750*	0.399
Aut. in defining target groups	-0.370	-0.608	-0.426	-0.449	-0.209	-0.474	-0.823**	0.444
Aut. in monitoring	0.399	0.880*	-0.164	-0.452	-0.163	0.155	0.357	0.334
Aut. in administration	-0.004	0.031	0.239	0.412	0.534	0.946**	0.417	0.216
Aut. in outsourcing	0.510	0.479	0.472	1.213	1.933**	0.938	0.546	0.583
Constant	1.012	0.975***	0.953***	0.689	-0.054	0.672**	0.454*	0.320

(Continued)

Table 7-4 (Continued)

	Social policy	Employment policy	Regional policy	NGOs	Social partner	Private actors	Education institutions	Research institution
				Regional and other actors				
Small city	Base category							
Medium city	−0.731**	−0.040	−0.616	−0.560	−0.425	−0.357	−0.271	−0.550
Large city	−0.365	−0.151	−0.312	−0.886**	−0.717**	−0.113	−0.256	−0.399
Ter. corresponds to city limits	0.228	−0.131	0.237	0.358	0.630**	0.106	0.296	0.217
Part of ministry	−0.265	−0.002	−0.519*	−0.616	−0.652**	−0.330	−0.425	−0.562
Autonomous budget share	0.004	0.004	0.008**	0.004	0.006**	0.006***	0.004**	0.006
Aut. in designing programs	0.569	0.165	0.673	0.424	0.448	1.401**	0.437	0.950
Aut. in allocating budget	0.152	0.103	0.854	0.862	0.839**	0.528	0.737	−0.608
Aut. in defining target groups	−0.449	−0.240	−0.836	−0.015	−0.091	−1.152***	−0.241	−0.623
Aut. in monitoring	0.661	0.480	0.446	0.361	0.308	0.326	0.494	0.286
Aut. in administration	−0.195	−0.043	0.218	0.496	1.074***	−0.192	0.485	0.494
Aut. in outsourcing	1.020	0.624	1.518**	1.112	0.887	1.485**	1.683***	1.274
Constant	0.254	0.194	0.278	0.324	0.083	0.157	−0.238	0.076

Note: Coef. = estimated coefficient, Std. Err = Standard Error; *** and ** signify significance at the 1% and 5%, levels, respectively.

Source: WWWforEurope questionnaire

organisation as well as on the changes in the importance of target groups and sector strategies since 2008. To measure the diversity of the objective structure, we divide the target groups into 'core target groups' and 'less considered target groups' of the PES. The former are target groups considered to be important by more than 80 per cent of the PES organisations (i.e. elderly, people with disabilities, youths, and the long-term unemployed). The latter are target groups considered by less than 40 per cent of the PES organisations (men, older employed, employed, large enterprises, women on child leave, the short-term unemployed, and women returning from child leave). All other target groups are collected into an intermediate group. Based on these groups, we count the proportion of target groups considered important by each PES in these groups, so as to derive a measure of how strongly a PES emphasises 'core', 'intermediate', and 'less considered' target groups. Furthermore, as two further measures of the diversity of the objective structure of PES organisations, we consider the total number of target groups (relative to the maximum number of target groups) considered important by each of the PES organisations and the total number of sector-specific strategies (relative to the maximum number of sector-specific strategies) followed by the regional PES organisations. To measure the responsiveness of PES organisations, by contrast, we construct a proxy variable, which measures the proportion of target groups or sector strategies where the importance has changed (i.e. either increased or decreased) in the total number of target groups or sector strategies as a dependent variable, for each of the groups discussed above.

The top panel of Table 7-5 shows the results of a regression analysis for specifications, including the share of autonomously decided budgets, in which each of the indicators of the diversity of the objective structure is regressed on the indicator variables for city size and autonomy as well as the control variables already used in the previous analysis (territory serviced by the PES relative to city size and location of the PES) and on measures of stakeholder network size. According to our hypotheses, the autonomy of the PES as well as its number of stakeholders should increase the diversity of target groups and sector strategies. These hypotheses only meet partial support. In particular, the diversity of target groups followed is positively correlated to the autonomy of a regional PES organisation in designing programmes, while other aspects of autonomy (such as the autonomous budget share and autonomy in monitoring) are significant only in the case of sector strategies when focusing on the specification including the share of autonomously decided budget. Thus, only PES organisations that have greater autonomy in designing programmes have a robustly statistically significantly more varied number of target groups for all indicators of target group heterogeneity. Furthermore, the number of stakeholders is only statistically significantly positively correlated to the number of less considered target groups and sector strategies. This implies that PES organisations with a broader stakeholder network, while – as hypothesised – considering a broader range of target groups, do so only for less considered target groups and sector strategies.

Interestingly, however, the results also suggest that the primary variable predicting target group and sector strategy diversity of a PES is city size. Relative to small cities (which are the base category in all regressions), both medium-sized and large cities have a statistically significantly smaller set of target groups irrespective of whether the core, less considered, or intermediary target groups or all target groups are considered. In addition, PES organisations in large cities also follow a statistically significantly lower number of sector-specific strategies than small cities.[14]

The bottom panel of Table 7-5 shows the results of a regression analysis in which we use the intensity of change in (core, less considered, intermediary, and total) target groups

Table 7-5 Determinants of share of target groups and sector strategies followed by PES organisations and change in importance of target groups and sector strategies

Dependent variable	Core target group		Less considered target groups		Intermediate target groups		All target groups		Sector strategies	
	Coef.	Std. Err.	Coef.	Std. Err.	Coef.	Std. Err.	Coef.	Std. Err.	Coef.	Std. Err.
	Dependent variable: share of target group and strategies followed									
Medium city	−0.346***	0.090	−0.393**	0.168	−0.427**	0.168	−8.795***	2.903	−1.607	1.086
Large city	−0.315**	0.112	−0.706***	0.211	−0.632**	0.211	−13.226***	3.645	−4.101***	1.364
Part of ministry	−0.155	0.188	−0.178	0.354	−0.396	0.354	−5.997	6.111	−4.508*	2.286
No of stakeholders	0.002	0.007	0.020*	0.012	0.004	0.014	0.124	0.234	0.232**	0.088
Aut. budget share	0.000	0.001	−0.003	0.002	0.000	0.002	−0.019	0.033	0.021*	0.012
Aut. in designing programs	0.435**	0.194	0.562**	0.264	0.677*	0.364	13.006**	6.286	−1.049	2.352
Aut. in def. target groups	−0.302**	0.127	0.071	0.238	−0.100	0.239	−1.632	4.116	0.165	1.540
Aut. in monitoring	0.074	0.138	−0.058	0.259	−0.133	0.260	−1.500	4.480	3.159*	1.676
Aut. in administration	0.223	0.145	−0.181	0.273	0.206	0.273	1.504	4.717	−3.984	1.764
Aut. in outsourcing	0.214	0.176	0.084	0.331	−0.153	0.331	−0.001	5.717	−3.149	2.139
Eastern Europe	0.242	0.193	−0.515	0.363	−0.410	0.363	−7.255	6.271	−9.179***	2.346
Northern Europe	0.198	0.201	0.076	0.377	0.016	0.378	1.558	6.514	−4.284	2.437
Southern Europe	0.083	0.166	0.181	0.311	0.112	0.312	2.900	5.376	−3.085	2.011
Constant	0.832***	0.205	0.657*	0.385	0.889**	0.386	17.472***	6.653	10.111***	2.489
Observations	28		28		28		28		28	
R2	0.77		0.68		0.66		0.71		0.78	

Dependent variable: share of target groups and strategies with a change in importance

	Coef.	Std. Err.	Coef.	Std. Err.	Coef.	Std. Err.	Coef.	Std. Err.
Medium city	−0.269	0.159	−0.085	0.170	−0.136	0.180	−0.141	0.148	−0.162*	0.079
Large city	−0.486**	0.200	−0.155	0.214	−0.247	0.226	−0.257*	0.146	−0.262**	0.099
Part of ministry	−0.591	0.336	0.126	0.359	−0.207	0.380	−0.156	0.312	−0.246	0.167
No of stakeholders	0.016	0.013	−0.002	0.014	−0.008	0.015	−0.002	0.012	0.022**	0.006
Aut. budget share	−0.002	0.002	−0.002	0.002	−0.001	0.002	−0.002	0.002	−0.003**	0.001
Aut. in designing programs	−0.119	0.345	0.003	0.369	−0.164	0.390	−0.095	0.321	−0.059	0.171
Aut. in def. target groups	0.096	0.226	0.198	0.242	0.096	0.256	0.133	0.210	0.024	0.112
Aut. in monitoring	0.275	0.246	0.191	0.263	0.204	0.278	0.212	0.229	0.214*	0.122
Aut. in administration	−0.225	0.259	−0.118	0.277	0.126	0.293	−0.027	0.241	−0.173	0.129
Aut. in outsourcing	0.056	0.314	0.015	0.336	−0.109	0.355	−0.034	0.292	0.089	0.156
Eastern Europe	−0.429	0.345	−0.083	0.368	−0.259	0.390	−0.226	0.321	−0.511**	0.171
Northern Europe	−0.592*	0.318	0.028	0.382	−0.164	0.405	−0.172	0.333	−0.204	0.177
Southern Europe	−0.223	0.295	0.033	0.316	−0.109	0.334	−0.078	0.275	−0.095	0.146
Constant	1.271**	0.366	0.195	0.391	0.599	0.413	0.574*	0.340	0.460**	0.181
Observations	28		28		28		28		28	
R²	0.508		0.386		0.313		0.347		0.778	

Note: Table presents regression results; Coef. = estimated coefficient, Std. Err. = Standard Error of the estimate; *** and ** signify significance at the 1% and 5% levels, respectively.

Source: WWWforEurope questionnaire

as well as in sector strategies and control for the same variables as in the previous analysis. These results provide only weak evidence for the view that more autonomous PES organisations and/or PES organisations with a larger stakeholder network are generally more responsive to new labour market challenges. The hypothesised determinants of changes in importance of target groups are statistically insignificant for all types of target groups (except when considering the autonomy in monitoring and the autonomous budget share for the specification including the autonomously decided budget share), and the number of stakeholders only attain significance for sector strategies. Once more, however, the results in many specifications suggest that small cities have been more responsive to new labour market challenges than large cities since 2008 (in particular with respect to core target groups and sector strategies).

7.4.3 The interaction of PES organisations and Pact/LEIs

Formation of a Pact/LEI

Finally, for the set of hypotheses referring to the interaction of PES organisations and Pact/LEIs, we conduct three types of analysis. In the first, using a logit model, we regress a dependent variable that takes the value of 1 if a Pact/LEI exists in the city under consideration and 0 otherwise, on the set of variables already used in the previous analyses (city size indicators, dummy variables for the European region, the size of the stakeholder network of the regional PES as well as indicators measuring the autonomy of the regional PES organisation). Table 7-6 presents the results of five different variants of this specification. In the first, we exclude the various indices of regional autonomy and the controls for the region of location of the city but include the autonomous budget share. The second excludes the share of budget decided autonomously from the regression but includes the various indices of regional autonomy in the other fields, while the next two re-estimate the first two but include the family of dummy variables indicating the European region in which the city is located. Finally, the fifth specification includes only those variables that were significant in at least one of the first four specifications.

While our hypotheses suggest that both PES autonomy and stakeholder network size could either have a positive or a negative impact on the probability of observing a Pact/LEI in a region, the results (in Table 7-6) indicate that, in particular, a higher budgetary autonomy and a larger number of national stakeholders in the regional PES is positively correlated to the probability of observing a Pact/LEI in a region. Thus, according to all specifications (except for when we include the autonomous budget share as well as controls for the region in which a city is located, which is the specification with the lowest number of degrees of freedom), a larger number of national stakeholders of a regional PES organisation is significantly positively correlated to the probability of observing a Pact/LEI in the region, while a larger number of regional stakeholders is mostly negatively correlated with this probability, with this effect only being significant in the last of these specifications. Similarly, greater autonomy in allocating budgets of the PES also significantly increases the probability of a region having a Pact/LEI in all specifications in which this variable is included, while greater autonomy in designing programmes has a weakly significantly negative impact on this probability only when also controlling for the region in which a city is located.

In addition, these results indicate that the probability of observing a Pact/LEI is statistically significantly lower in medium-sized and large cities than in small cities (as the

Table 7-6 Logit regression results for probability to observe a Pact/LEI in a region

	(1)		(2)		(3)		(4)		(5)	
	Coef.	Std. Err.	Coef.	Std. Err.	Coef.	Std. Err.	Coef.	Std. Err.	Coef.	Std. Err.
Medium city	−3.419*	1.997	0.682	1.290	0.421	1.527	−4.714**	2.361	−0.324	0.964
Large city	−4.140**	2.067	−1.520	1.342	−0.391	1.670	−5.904**	2.935	−1.900*	1.055
Part of ministry	−1.580	1.652	1.750	1.156	1.774	2.465	1.090	3.002		
No. national PES stakeholders	0.329*	0.171	0.636*	0.367	0.806*	0.475	0.369	0.487	0.467*	0.259
No. regional PES stakeholders	−0.232	0.226	−0.297	0.245	−0.493	0.328	−0.259	0.296	−0.301*	0.166
Autonomous budget share	0.003	0.012					0.008	0.020		
Aut. in designing programs			−4.230	2.825	−7.110*	3.928			−1.073	2.006
Aut. in allocating budget			4.632**	2.134	6.313**	2.597			2.654**	1.320
Aut. in defining target groups			2.303	1.658	2.280	1.720				
Aut. in monitoring			0.677	2.039	2.463	2.764				
Aut. in administration			0.168	1.793	0.557	2.098				
Aut. in outsourcing			−4.827	3.507	−3.827	3.641				
Eastern Europe					1.695	2.465	1.178	3.002		
Northern Europe					1.597	2.465	1.536	3.002		
Southern Europe					1.390	2.465	1.349	3.002		
Territory corresponds to city lim.					0.428	1.102	1.919	1.502		
Constant	4.972*	2.593	−1.369	1.674	−1.805	2.465	−0.727	3.002	0.111	1.194
No. Obs.	28		40		40		28		40	

Note: Coef. = estimated coefficient, Std. Err. = Standard Error; *** and ** signify significance at the 1%, (5%) levels, respectively.

Source: WWWforEurope questionnaire

baseline) in all specifications where the European region in which the city is located is not controlled for. This thus suggests that, in addition to PES organisations with large national stakeholder networks and high budgetary autonomy, small cities may have an advantage in organising Pact/LEIs, with this latter effect potentially being due to smaller cities providing for more accessible and denser informal networks.

Correlations of the functions and partnerships of a Pact/LEI

In the second analysis, we explore to what degree regional characteristics and the organisational features of the regional PES are correlated with the function a Pact/LEI fulfils and the size of the partnership (see Table 7-7). Since the low number of observations on Pact/LEIs precludes a multivariate analysis in this case, we focus on the correlation of these variables with all the variables included in the regressions above (i.e. city size, indicator variables for PES organisations that are part of a ministry, budgetary autonomy, and indices of autonomy) as well as a set of Pact/LEI characteristics. When focusing on the function of the Pact/LEI, this is the age of the Pact/LEI; when focusing on the number of partners, these are the age and indicator variables for the function of the Pact/LEI.

In contrast to our hypotheses, the size of the stakeholder network of a PES is uncorrelated to both the function of and the number of formal and informal partners involved in a Pact/LEI, and also the link between the function and the size of a partnership of a Pact/LEI and the autonomy of the regional PES applies only to certain aspects of the autonomy of a regional PES. Here in particular, cities in which the regional PES has more autonomy in designing programmes and administration (statistically only weakly significant) more rarely have Pact/LEIs that serve as an information exchange platform between different actors, and Pact/LEIs located in cities where the PES is a part of a ministry or has greater autonomy in designing programmes have significantly fewer formal partners.

By contrast, our hypotheses relating to the impact of the age function of a Pact/LEI on the size and structure of its partnerships are corroborated by this analysis as younger Pact/LEIs (with a later year of founding) have fewer partners in total (mainly on account of having fewer informal partners) and as Pact/LEIs serving the coordination of policies have more partners, while those serving as a platform for exchange have fewer.

Interaction at the level of the diversity and intensity of change of objectives and sector strategies

Finally, in an analogous way to the indices of diversity and flexibility of the PES, we construct similar indices for the Pact/LEIs. In these, to measure the diversity of their objective structure and their sector-specific strategies, we consider the total number of objectives considered important by each Pact/LEI (as a percentage of all objectives) and the total number of sector strategies followed by the regional PES organisations to measure the diversity of a Pact/LEI's objective structure. In addition, we also use the proportion of objectives or sector strategies whose importance has changed (i.e. either increased or decreased) in the total number of objectives or sector strategies to measure the responsiveness of Pact/LEIs to changed labour market conditions since 2008. Finally, we correlate these measures with the variables already used in the analysis of the partner structure of Pact/LEIs but augment this with additional indicators on the number of formal and informal partners in Pact/LEIs.

Table 7-7 Correlation of Pact/LEI functions and partnership size with regional and PES characteristics

	Function of the Pact/LEI			Number of partners of Pact/LEI		
	Co-ordination	Design	Information platform	Total	Formal partners	Informal partners
Part of ministry	0.199	−0.028	−0.138	−0.428***	−0.477***	0.151
No national PES stakeholders	−0.100	−0.053	0.056	0.012	−0.029	0.051
No regional PES stakeholders	−0.155	−0.054	0.088	−0.213	−0.245	−0.067
Autonomous budget share	0.034	−0.013	0.330	−0.186	−0.087	−0.188
Aut. in designing programs	−0.293	−0.008	−0.329*	−0.179	−0.298**	0.046
Aut. in allocating budget	0.027	−0.129	−0.164	0.012	0.024	−0.008
Aut. in defining target groups	−0.213	0.062	0.013	−0.092	−0.146	0.016
Aut. in monitoring	−0.117	−0.157	−0.024	−0.059	−0.131	0.050
Aut. in administration	−0.155	0.033	−0.353*	0.117	0.045	0.135
Aut. in outsourcing	−0.065	−0.207	−0.086	−0.018	−0.068	0.047
Territory corresponds to city lim.	−0.064	−0.145	−0.044	−0.180	−0.140	−0.130
Year of founding of pact	−0.142	−0.036	0.086	−0.309*	−0.373*	0.013
Coordination of policy measures of partners				0.278*	0.389**	−0.062
Designing and implementing policies				0.005	0.212	−0.197
Exchange platform for strat. and plans of regional actors				−0.363*	−0.130	−0.280

Note: Table presents pair wise correlation coefficients; *** and ** signify significance at the 1% and (5%) levels, respectively.

Source: WWWforEurope questionnaire

Table 7-8 Correlates of the share of target groups and sector strategies followed and the share of target groups and sector strategies with a change in importance since 2008

	Share of objectives followed	Share of sector strategies followed	Share of objectives with change in importance	Share of sector strategies with change in importance
	Diversity and intensity of change of PES objectives			
Diversity of targets groups of PES	0.249	0.352*	0.365*	0.339*
Diversity of sector strategies of PES	0.023	0.125	0.144	−0.105
Change in importance of target groups of PES	0.231	0.124	0.265	0.242
Change in importance of sector strategies of PES	0.023	0.201	0.079	−0.029
	Other PES characteristics			
PES corresponds to territory	0.119	0.220	0.400**	−0.027
Part of ministry	0.095	0.291	0.070	0.291
Autonomous budget share	0.348*	0.517**	0.445**	0.277
Aut. in designing programs	0.125	0.352**	0.331*	0.096
Aut. in allocating budget	0.236	0.248	0.523**	−0.099
Aut. in defining target groups	0.192	0.255	0.224	0.264
Aut. in monitoring	0.155	0.111	0.103	0.025
Aut. in administration	0.080	0.343*	0.151	0.093
Aut. in outsourcing	0.384*	0.263	0.546***	0.130
No. of stakeholders in PES	−0.142	0.394**	0.076	0.068
No. of nat. stakeholders in PES	−0.295	0.264	−0.202	0.083
No. of reg. stakeholders in PES	−0.018	0.385*	0.236	0.050

(Continued)

	Share of objectives followed	Share of sector strategies followed	Share of objectives with change in importance	Share of sector strategies with change in importance
	Pact/LEI characteristics			
Year of founding of pacts	−0.305*	−0.193	−0.549***	−0.250
Coordination of policy measures of partners	−0.214	−0.059	−0.172	0.141
Designing and implementing policies	−0.266	0.196	−0.116	0.032
Exchange platform for strat. and plans of regional actors	−0.033	−0.225	−0.007	0.038
No. partners in Pact/LEI	0.071	0.108	−0.070	0.245
No. formal partners in Pact/LEI	−0.065	0.127	−0.108	0.092
No. informal partners in Pact/LEI	0.141	−0.001	0.026	0.185

Note: Table presents correlation coefficients; *** and ** signify significance at the 1% and (5%) levels, respectively.

Source: WWWforEurope questionnaire

The results (Table 7-8) remain inconclusive for the correlation between diversity of the target groups and sector strategies followed by the PES and the diversity of the objectives followed by Pact/LEIs, as both these correlations are statistically insignificant. Similar observations apply to the correlation between the change in importance of both objectives and target groups between the two organisations. The results, however, also indicate a statistically weakly significant positive correlation between the diversity of sector strategies followed by a Pact/LEI and the diversity of the target groups of a PES in a region as well as a positively significant correlation between the change in importance of sector strategies and the diversity of the target groups of a PES. Thus, while – in contrast to our prior expectations – the evidence for an interaction of the diversity of objective structure and intensity of change of objective between the regional PES and Pact/LEIs remains rather limited, Pact/LEIs operating in regions where the regional PES has a more diverse objective structure developed more sector-specific strategies and also experienced more change in the objective structure in the period from 2008 to 2013.

Results also suggest only very few links between PES and Pact/LEI characteristics and the objectives of a Pact/LEI, since most of the correlations are statistically insignificant. The only exceptions with respect to the diversity of objectives are a weakly significant positive correlation with the region's PES's budget autonomy and autonomy in outsourcing and a negative one with the year of founding of the Pact/LEI. This indicates that older

Pact/LEIs, but also Pact/LEIs in regions where the PES has more budget autonomy and autonomy in outsourcing, tend to have a more diverse objective structure.

With respect to the diversity of the sector strategies followed and the changes of importance in objectives, by contrast, more variables are significant. These suggest that Pact/LEIs operating in regions where the PES has more budget autonomy, greater autonomy in administrative tasks, and a larger number of (in particular regional) stakeholders have a larger diversity in sector strategies. Results also suggest that the intensity of change in importance of Pact/LEI objectives has been largest in regions where the territory covered by the PES corresponds to the administrative city limits, where the budget autonomy and also the autonomy of the PES in outsourcing and designing programmes is high, and where the Pacts/LEI is older.

7.5 Summary and policy conclusions

In regional labour market policy debates, decentralisation of tasks and/or devolution of decision powers to regional actor networks is often seen as a possibility to guarantee tailor-made labour market policies that take account of the specifics of a region, promote innovation in and efficiency of labour market policy, improve accountability, and raise awareness of 'missing' policy elements in regional labour markets. Increasingly it is also recognised in this debate that decentralisation alone is not a sufficient condition to guarantee efficient policymaking on a regional level but that decentralisation has to be accompanied by sufficient horizontal coordination between different policy actors and capacity building at the regional level to achieve its full potential (Eberts 2009). The result of this recognition has been a parallel move towards increased networking among regional policy actors in recent years.

Institutionally, this development has taken different forms. On the one hand, it has resulted in the decentralisation and devolution of decision powers to, as well as increased involvement of, additional stakeholders in regional PES organisations, which are classical 'top-down' organisations of labour market governance, with a countrywide and rather stable architecture of nonintersecting multi-tier organisations. On the other hand, it has resulted in the development of a set of 'bottom-up' organisations, commonly referred to as Territorial Employment Pacts or Local Employment Initiatives (Pact/LEIs), which, in contrast to regional PES organisations, are more flexible in design and may even have intersecting membership.

The current study takes stock of the preconditions for conducting partnership-based local labour market policies in an urban context and analyses the development of both regional PES organisations as well as Pact/LEIs in the time since the economic crisis of 2008.

We find that the trend towards increasing autonomy of regional labour market policy and the increasing importance of policy networks, in which actors in various policy fields interact in the provision of public services in a partnership-based approach, have continued to be of relevance since 2008. In particular, the vast majority of the regional PES organisations in all types of cities of Europe considered in this study experienced an increase in all aspects of their autonomy. Likewise, the vast majority of the PES organisations reported that most of their regional, national, and other stakeholders have become increasingly important in their decision-making in the last five years.

We, however, also find that in the face of mounting labour market problems, both regional PES organisations as well as Pact/LEIs have reacted by focusing their objectives on their core target groups (such as combating youth and long-term unemployment).

While most PES organisations and Pact/LEIs report an increased importance of almost all of their target groups, sector strategies, and objectives, these increases were substantially more pronounced for the 'core' objectives and target groups than for those that are less often considered. This suggests that while trends in the change of governance structure were less affected by the crisis of 2008–2009, objective structures have become more concentrated. This may be a disadvantage from the perspective of the objectives of regional development initiatives that focus on linking different policy fields and the breaking out of policy silos (Froy et al. 2011).

The most outstanding feature with respect to all indicators analysed in this chapter is the vast heterogeneity in the governance of regional labour market policies in Europe. This heterogeneity applies to all analysed preconditions for regional policymaking such as the autonomy of PES organisations, their stakeholder structure as well as to their target groups and sector strategies and even more strongly to the partnership and objectives as well as sector-specific strategies followed by Pact/LEIs. In order to allow policymakers to assess the differences in the challenges faced in designing partnership-based regional labour market approaches, this chapter therefore also explores the sources for this heterogeneity by considering the interaction of different aspects of the organisation and objective structure of PES and Pact/LEI organisations within a region.

The results indicate that in particular budgetary autonomy of the regional PES – and potentially also other aspects of autonomy – plays an important role for network sizes of regional PES organisations. Thus we find a positive correlation between budgetary autonomy and autonomy in outsourcing and a negative one with the regional PES being part of a ministry with network size. In addition, there is a nonlinear impact of city size on the size of a PES organisation's stakeholder network. This suggests that PES organisations located in medium-sized cities tend to have smaller stakeholder networks than PES organisations located in both small and large cities.

We also find some – albeit admittedly weaker – links between the diversity of the objectives of a PES and the responsiveness of these objectives and its autonomy and stakeholder structure. In general, PES organisations that have more autonomy in designing labour market programmes as well as PES organisations in small cities have a significantly more diverse target group structure, while PES organisations with a larger number of stakeholders include less considered target groups and sector strategies more often. By contrast, PES organisations that have more competences in monitoring and with a larger number of stakeholders experienced more change in importance of sector strategies, but PES organisations that have more budgetary autonomy experienced less change of such strategies (probably on account of facing lower budgetary constraints).

While these results are based on a small sample of observations only, from a policy perspective they suggest that increasing the different aspects of the autonomy of a PES does have a predictable impact on both the stakeholders and the objective structure of PES organisations as well as on the responsiveness of these organisations to new policy challenges. This may be indicative of how decentralisation and devolution of decision powers to the regional-level impact the participation of institutions in stakeholder networks and on the objective structure of PES organisations. Greater autonomy of PES organisations (in particular budgetary autonomy) increases both the likelihood of these organisations involving a larger stakeholder network and of following a more diverse spectrum of objectives. In addition, involving a larger spectrum of partners may further increase the spectrum of objectives followed by regional labour market policy organisations (in particular with respect to less often considered objectives), while both a larger partnership structure and more autonomy in monitoring results improves – potentially on account of improved access to information – the responsiveness of the organisation to new policy challenges with respect to these less considered objectives.

Furthermore, the study also explores how regional PES organisations and Pact/LEIs interact at the level of their organisation and objectives. We find that cities' PES organisations that have more national stakeholders and more autonomy in allocating budgets are also the more likely to have a Pact/LEI. In addition, Pact/LEIs are also significantly less likely to exist in large cities. Similarly, Pact/LEIs located in regions where the regional PES has greater autonomy in designing programmes and where the PES is a part of a ministry have fewer particularly formal partners. This thus indicates that changes in the organisation and autonomy of regional PES organisations may also influence the probability of a Pact/LEI forming in the city and could affect its chances of winning a larger stakeholder network.

With respect to the policy objectives followed, by contrast, our evidence suggests that rather than the Pact/LEIs 'filling gaps' in regional policies, they follow rather similar policies to the regional PES organisations. In particular, if one of the institutions follows a particular sector strategy, the probability increases that the other institution in the same region also follows this strategy. At the same time, when for one of the institutions the importance of a sector strategy increases, then the other one also faces a higher probability of an increasing importance of this sector strategy. Similarly, the diversity of objectives followed in Pact/LEIs and PES organisations are also either uncorrelated or positively correlated. This suggests that the close relationship between Pact/LEIs and PES organisations often leads to these organisations focusing on similar objectives and that care therefore needs to be taken to guarantee additional value from Pact/LEIs relative to PES organisations.

Although our data contains too few observations to allow for a more detailed analysis of these stylised facts and the causal effects underlying them, these results suggest that the most effective measures to foster partnership-based regional labour market approaches in the EU would consist of increasing budgetary autonomy on the regional level of labour market policy institutions, aligning their competencies to the results that are expected from them, and investing in the development of partnerships both in terms of the number of actors as well as their structure.

Given the substantial heterogeneity in regional labour market policy institutions and the few formal competencies in labour market policy of the EU, the European Commission could best support such an approach by

a) raising awareness among national and regional policymakers of the benefits of decentralisation and devolution for regional labour market policy;
b) providing know-how and tools sufficiently flexible to accommodate the widely varying needs of different local initiatives in terms of data generation, monitoring, and evaluation; and
c) providing funding schemes which are flexible enough to cope with the heterogeneity of approaches that are likely to be developed by local bottom-up initiatives such as Pact/LEIs.

Notes

1 For instance, in Linz, the unemployment rate amounted to 3.6 per cent, according to EUROSTAT sources, in 2010, and in Valencia, to 22.3 per cent.

2 In the vast majority of cases, however, this is also organised at the national level and only has regional suborganisations (see http://ec.europa.eu/social/main.jsp?catId=105&langId=en for a description of PES organisations in Europe).
3 This is confirmed by a regression analysis that controls for city size group, country group, and independence of PES organisations. Among these variables for budgetary autonomy, city size is significant, as is the control for independence of the PES organisation. For the other indicator variables, country groups (for allocating budget, monitoring and evaluating, and outsourcing) and the dummy for independent PES organisations (for allocating budgets, defining target groups, monitoring and evaluating as well as administration) are significant.
4 This is consistent with Hugh Mosley (2011), who finds that Eastern European PES organisations have high levels of managerial decentralisation.
5 The differences in results for the question on the share of budget allocated autonomously and the question on budgetary autonomy are due to the low response rate to the former question. In both questions, however, small cities experienced almost no increase in budgetary autonomy, while large cities experienced a substantial one.
6 In all subsequent analyses, we refer to regional stakeholders as municipalities, regional social partner organisations, regional NGOs and regional social policy, employment policy, and regional policy actors; national stakeholders as national social partner organisations, national NGOs and national social policy, employment policy, and regional policy actors as well as EU structural funds committees; and other stakeholders as private actors, research and education institutions, and actors in neighbouring regions.
7 This analysis is weakened by the fact that we do not observe stakeholders that were part of the network before the crisis but have withdrawn since.
8 This is supported by a correlation analysis and applies both to the 'levels' and the 'dynamic' interactions between Pact/LEIs and PES organisations (Huber 2014).
9 This is corroborated by correlations between the importance of individual target groups in 2013 and the change in their importance in the period from 2008 to 2013. This is a statistically significantly positive correlation, indicating that more important target groups in 2013 also experienced a larger increase in importance in the time period since 2008.
10 Such autonomy allows for a regional variance in the objective structure.
11 This increases the competencies of regional PES organisations or Pact/LEIs in fields outside their core activities.
12 The latter line of reasoning is particularly relevant in the context of the results of a set of questions in our questionnaire, in which the regional PES organisations were asked if and in what form the PES interacts with the Pact/LEI. The answers suggest that this interaction is rather close in most cases. Thirty-six per cent of the interviewed PES organisations state that the regional PES operates and finances at least one Pact/LEI in the region. In another 28 per cent of the cases, the regional PES is a partner in a Pact/LEI, and in a further 4 per cent (each), the regional PES contributes financially or through consultancy to a Pact/LEI, and in 20 per cent, the regional PES cooperates informally with the Pact/LEIs in its territory.
13 To save on space here, we only report results of the first specification in Table 7-3.
14 In addition, according to the results in Table 7-5, sector strategies are significantly less often followed in Eastern European countries and in PES organisations that are part of a ministry.

Chapter 8

Institutional diversity

Stephanie Barnebeck, Yannick Kalff and Thomas Sauer

This chapter sums up the empirical research results and evaluates the findings in the light of institutional diversity. It is obvious that the different cases analysed throughout this book have different aspects in ongoing institutional diversification. Therefore, the four topics cannot be compared on the same level. Whilst urban resource pools are the most common examples of self-organised usage terms, the case of labour markets is far more difficult to understand than the self-organised approach. Commonly, labour market policies are an aspect of national policymaking. Their special feature is their form of market that actively pronounces the classic distinction between markets and governments. Whereas self-organisation is a specific institutional setting beyond this paradigmatic dichotomy, labour markets are one side of this distinction. However, the endeavour of labour market policies indicates that governmental interventions sustain and support the market itself. This is commonplace for any market that is in a dependent relationship with state structures. Above all, the state has to ensure the market's survival by frameworks and by rulesets. At this point, it becomes understandable that, whilst self-organised resource systems are an institutional alternative to markets or hierarchies, the labour market is – after all – a market. Therefore, the research evaluates different institutional settings for a market-based system.

On the one hand, institutional diversity refers to the currently ongoing socio-ecological transition that restructures urban resource use. Here the focus lies on alternatives to the current system. On the other hand, regarding labour markets, institutional diversity and diversification mean assessing alternatives within the existing system. This chapter therefore compares the three resource systems separately. The fourth issue of labour markets is analysed in its own right. A dimension for comparison is the spatial attribute of these institutional settings: Self-organisation refers to local and regional levels, while the policy shifts we discuss in labour markets concern a transformation from 'place-blind' to 'place-based' policies. Spatial attributes become visible and significant in the development of specific policies, and thus change the institutional settings in which labour markets are embedded.

8.1 Urban resources: energy, green spaces, and water

This first part of the chapter takes a closer look at the first three empirical analyses that focused the urban resource systems. In the light of Elinor Ostrom's work, this research argues that a shift of institutional settings can produce stable equilibria for the use of resources (Ostrom 1990, 2005). Moreover, the possibility of a self-organised approach is higher than expected in commonplace economics that for a long time followed Garrett Hardin's dictum of a 'tragedy of the commons' (Hardin 1968). However, not every resource system is equal to the others. The first step is a thorough comparison of the three researched urban resource systems to assess their similarities and differences.

8.1.1 Comparison of the resource systems

In the preceding chapters on energy, green spaces, and water, the three urban resource systems were examined separately by answering the first six research questions raised in chapter 3.2.7 on the *transition observed, self-organisation, actors and factors, lessons learned, norm adoption,* and *local decision-making*. Preconditions and status of the transition differ between these resource systems and between the regions as well. Thus, the emergence of new institutional arrangements affects these resource systems to different extents and in different ways. In this section, a short comparison of the resource systems will be presented. It is structured alongside these six research questions.

Scope rules, concerning the basic issues and time horizons, are the first rule set to be inquired into. The energy system is generally perceived as the most important resource system for sustainability enhancement. Clean energy and public transport are the central leverages for the socio-ecological transition of the cities. For example, particulate matter reductions through alternative mobility concepts as well as renewable energies have been discussed intensely over the last years. This also shows in the questionnaire, where the government sector rated public transport as the most important aspect for defining a future strategy for sustainability in the cities. Civil society representatives in general find diverse aspects – like climate change, clean energy, citizens' consumption behaviours, production patterns of local enterprises, or the management of land resources and green spaces – more relevant than business and government respondents do. However, all groups agree that these aspects are highly important. There are in general differences between the regions. Climate change and clean energy are assessed as less important in Eastern Europe, where 'less abstract' issues – like the management of local land and water resources, education, and labour markets – are perceived as more relevant. The Northern and Western European regions seem to be a step ahead in many issues. Social objectives for sustainability most frequently named in the North were 'values and lifestyle' issues, such as more free time, respect of public goods, healthiness, and awareness of sustainability matters. 'Empowerment' – such as the participation of citizens and the third sector in decision processes, encouragement of small entrepreneurship, and the strengthening of the city's autonomy – were frequently named in the East. 'Social care and integration' seems to be an important topic in the South and West. Examples are intergenerational fairness, social justice, public service accessibility, and equal conditions of participation. 'Youth employment' is furthermore an important issue in Southern Europe, and 'affordable housing', in the West. The roles of social and ecological aspects are considered equally important. Even if sustainability issues are perceived differently depending on sector and region, they are important for all respondents. There is a common understanding on sustainability transition across all resource systems, sectors, and regions.

Information rules, affecting the level of information available to the different actors, are basic to self-organisation as a transition driver. Collaboration between government and civil society is generally poor, and since there is not much cooperation, there are few conflicts. Still there are visible cases with good cooperation. The real level of cooperation is hard to assess, but participation is often misunderstood as the obtaining of acceptance and the assessment depends on the actor's view. Government actors on average consider the degree of cooperation higher than civil society respondents do.

Civil society groups are in general not common in the cities, especially not in the water and energy system. Nevertheless, in the energy system, NGOs sometimes show medium leadership concerning energy efficiency and the development of renewable energy. There are various civil society activities in green spaces, differing in size and responsibilities. The green spaces system is the only urban resource system observed where self-organisation has even become a transition driver in some cities.

Payoff rules concern the possible returns and motivation for the diverse actors. The actors and factors driving the transition of the local resource systems are quite different. Concerning energy consumption, the retrofitting of buildings had the strongest influence on the decrease in the past ten years. Behaviour and cultural habits influence both energy and water consumption. Education and lifestyle factors strongly determine energy and water consumption, which is difficult to observe on the individual level – like the energy use for single electronic devices or for the heating of water for a bath – apart from the monitoring of the overall consumption of a household or building through water or energy meters. Thus, awareness is needed to reduce energy and water consumption. The price has a stronger influence on water consumption and plays no big role in energy consumption, where rebound effects (cf. chapter 4) also play a role. The potential to save water is possibly still higher than the potential to save energy, or habits of use could be changed faster – also as the replacement of equipment with low energy efficiency would demand higher investment – or more effectively by rising costs. It is in some way more visible if water runs out of the tap without being used than how much energy is lost by stand-by devices and there are no rebound effects. Energy and water poverty are very relevant phenomena in this context. Some social groups are not able to pay rising prices for water and energy. Sustainability transition, for example by introducing renewable energy production and new water technologies, is expected to create extra costs for the users. Economically weak people thus fear being excluded from or harmed by the use of these 'clean' resources. Thus, sustainability can become a segregation attribute or a privilege of wealthier groups. A major issue for social sustainability in connection with the energy system therefore is energy poverty. A sincere effect is visible in Greece, where due to the current socio-economic crisis energy consumption patterns have changed drastically. Illegal wood clearing and the burning of cheap and low-quality oil has created rising pollution and CO_2 emissions.

Generally, there have been financial capabilities for the existence, maintenance, and use of green spaces, but in a scenario with ongoing urbanisation, further financial gaps of the municipalities, and privatisation, existing green spaces could be less well maintained, reduced, or privatised, meaning that it could become a privilege of solvent citizens to use parks. To prevent these tendencies, an active civil society has started self-organising in this resource system (cf. chapter 5).

In some aspects, the three urban systems are likely to compete for scarce resources. The local stock of unbuilt land is one factor potentially relevant for all three of them. In any event, it has so far not been a constraint for the availability of green spaces or the development of renewable energy in the last ten years. Conflicts over water use concerning green spaces irrigation in times of drought have come up regularly. Grey water used for irrigation instead of drinkable water could be one solution to this conflict.

The national regulatory framework is very important for the development of renewable energies in the region. In contrast, green spaces systems are mostly governed on the local level. Local regulations tend to be important for both renewable energy and green spaces.

In the energy and the green spaces system, many diverse actors play important roles. These are for example the mayor and politicians of the majority, government administration, and environmental NGOs. In the energy system, universities and the utility providers also take an important position. In contrast, in the water system, only the two main actors (water provider and government administration) were named, whereas other potential actors play a minor role. The levels of participation and self-organisation are highest in green spaces management, and some activities can be observed in the energy system. Thus, the assumption that diverse actors could be obstructing self-organisation cannot be confirmed. More likely, technological characteristics of the urban resource system influence both the number of actors and the level of self-organisation. Expensive and complex technology with a long economic lifetime makes self-organisation unlikely – like in the water system – and limits the number of actors, whereas tangible, easily convertible topics that create manageable costs – like urban gardening – invite numerous actors to contribute. Renewable energy production takes an inclined position, as diverse actors are involved, but only a few self-organised arrangements can be observed.

Green spaces systems are highly influenced by social movements that arise around the demands for emancipative and democratic participation and self-organisation in urban areas, like 'Right to the City' or 'transition towns' (cf. section 1.2). The movement demands access to urban decision-making for several topics, including green spaces, housing, and sustainable economy, through creative forms of protest and disobedience like guerrilla gardening, squatting, alternative forms of close economy, and so on. This can be seen as an emancipative formation of an active civil society that is interested in actively seizing opportunities to get involved in urban agendas – if only for subcultural niches of a rather politically leftist culture.

Position rules determine authorised actors, related to their reputation. The lessons learned and reputations gained from leadership in the management of the local resource systems are quite different in the three systems, but some groups are relevant for all. The political majority and the mayor are important leaders in all three systems. More or equally important are utility providers for water and energy. In green spaces and energy management, NGOs, cooperatives, and civil society associations play an important role, too. In the water system, they could not build up much reputation. Local universities are quite important in the energy system, but – surprisingly – not much in water. Being very technical and facing many challenges, research is of more importance to the water system, but may face challenges in funding or technological lock-ins that complicate scientific inquiry. In green spaces management, local community groups play a major role compared to the other resource systems. Only minor difficulties can be observed for the actors in defining a joint strategy in green spaces and water management. Nonlocal factors and missing local capacities are still problems in the energy system.

The EU is perceived as an important external leader for water management, but not as the proper policy level for the energy system and green spaces. It can only be speculated why this assessment was made by many respondents. Possibly, the discussion about the privatisation of resources plays a role as well as the high dependence of many cities on EU funding in the modernisation of water systems. Privatisation rates are very different in the resource systems. About 40 per cent of the interviewed (local) energy providers are private or partially private companies. About 15 per cent of the interviewees in the water questionnaire stated that water had been recently privatised or would be within the next 10 years. In green spaces, the quantitative data does not reveal a privatisation trend, whereas the qualitative data sheds light on examples of privatisation from several cities.

The question for transitional socio-ecological norm adoption towards trust and cooperation concerns *boundary rules* defining entrance and exit of actors to the system.

1. The boundaries of the local water and green spaces systems are clear-cut and well understood. This does not apply to the energy system, where for example the proportion of primary energy supplied by local actors is not well known and not subject to local regulation.
2. The rights of local actors to make their own rules concerning all resource systems are rather *not* recognised by the higher levels of government.
3. Most actors affected by the local resource system are *not* authorised to participate in making and modifying the system's rules. This takes effect for all resource systems.
4. Nonlocal actors do not undermine local governance in the water and the green spaces systems, but they do undermine the energy system's governance.
5. The water system and urban green spaces are relatively autonomous subunits of larger resource systems. The energy system is in general not such an autonomous subunit.
6. In general, reputable persons or agencies monitor the contribution and benefit levels of actors involved in the local energy and water systems, but still not very intensely on average. Monitoring of the quality, use, and resource characteristics are generally good, yet better in the water system than for green spaces.
7. There are different prices or cross-subsidies amongst water and energy users, for example for households, administration, and industry.
8. Increasing sanctions for violations of the local resource regimes – starting very low but becoming stronger if an actor repeatedly violates a rule – exist for the water system and by tendency also for the energy and green spaces systems.
9. Rapid, low-cost local arenas for resolving conflicts among actors in the local resource system exist for water and green spaces, but do not exist for energy-related conflicts.

Aggregation rules define the actors' degree of communication and depend on the level of local decision-making autonomy. To what extent local decision-making matters in socio-ecological transition processes depends on the resource system observed. In green spaces, the local level is perceived as best suited for governing the resource system. For the urban water system, it is the local as well as the subnational level. In the energy system, the national level seems most appropriate. In green spaces and water management, the local government has high autonomy. In the energy system's governance, the local government is important but severely constrained by its mandate and human and financial capacities.

8.1.2 Delegated power and citizen control

Regarding *choice rules*, it depends on the system's characteristics to what extent citizens have equal access to the governance of urban resource systems – in terms of delegated power and citizen control. Institutional diversification in the sense of an increasing third sector of self-organisation and citizens' participation grows with the tangibility and clarity of the subject.

In the energy system, the main topic is the decentralisation of energy production. New technology must be efficient but no longer needs to be large-scale and centralised. This technological transition entails an institutional transition. Cooperative, decentralised, and small-scale organisational forms should be further supported and developed. Nevertheless, the urban spatial limitation makes the energy system's size larger than the urban expansion of one city, since for instance wind power or biodigesters need considerable space and are complex to install. Thus, an energy transition cannot be related alone to the urban system. Cities need to connect and collaborate at least with neighbouring rural regions – with larger spaces for energy production – to cover their energy demand. In other words, an urban–rural linkage is needed. Since the steering of the energy system is complex, a certain level of centrality is required. Smart grids and virtual power plants help to synchronise production of and demand for energy. Citizen-controlled and delegated power can be complementary in this resource system. Still, the infrastructure needed for energy supply requires a certain amount of centralised control.

The urban green spaces system serves as a good example of emerging institutional arrangements based on self-organisation and citizen control. The high tangibility and the strong local context support citizen involvement. Projects can be realised within a relatively short time horizon, without complex technological requirements, and with low financial commitment. Local autonomy is essentially given, and the cities can create proper legal frameworks. Delegated power is not as important in this resource system, as self-organised citizens could make many operational decisions, as long as the legal framework allows them to do so and the quality of the space is retained. Nevertheless, the municipalities should still assume their responsibility, and privatisation and enclosure should be avoided. The related topic of *boundary rules* is quite visible here, as entrance to and the size of a group play a major role for the possibility to self-organise on the local level.

In the example of the urban water system, the impact of complex technology, long time horizons of investments, and the system's indivisibility lead to strong technological and institutional constraints. Citizens value 'social aspects' of drinking water supply – like affordability and access – very highly but mostly lack the ability and scope to participate in planning processes. Thus, the governance of the resource system is typically delegated to the local, national, or European representatives, and citizen control plays a minor role. Nevertheless, citizens want their representatives to act in accordance to their needs and use their influence through public opinion formation. This probably explains the strength of the first European Citizen's Initiative, which was directed against the privatisation of water utilities that would have severely constrained the citizen control on this resource system.

8.1.3 The role of institutional arrangements in the socio-ecological transitions

The answer to the initial research question, 'What is the transformative role of institutional diversification and innovation in the governance of core urban common-pool resources?' is a complex one and has to consider the variety of the different resource systems. Our empirical inquiry and our conducted interviews show that there are individual traits and differences in the various countries and cities as well as explicit convergences. However, a central role for changing institutional arrangements lies in degrees of local autonomy, coherent legal frameworks, and activities of civil society.

The energy system is affected especially by the degree of local autonomy and the influence of other governmental levels, like regional, national, or European governments. In the process of a socio-ecological transition, the spatial attributes of the resource systems are changing as well. This means that another dimension of complexity lies in the spatial recoupling of energy production and consumption. For this step, a shift in regional or national decision-making towards local decision-making autonomy is necessary, since local energy production has to be installed, maintained, and handled by the local users. Therefore, a central point to support socio-ecological transitions towards sustainability in the energy sector lies in the empowerment of the local level, directly influenced by the resource system. In the progress of norm adaption, several actors from different cities have stated that the most productive way to achieve this lies in legal frameworks that make certain sustainability standards mandatory but allow individual implementation on the local level. These frames and rules have to *enable* people and politics alike, rather than imply punitive measures. High levels of national administrative centralisation interfere with the possibilities of such an approach and need to be considered in coherent legislation. In addition, several actors stated that the sole legislative power for sustainability issues should lie with the European Commission and thus relieve the national levels, especially concerning emissions and legal standards. This also affects national decision-making in energy questions like in Germany or France and has to be restructured accordingly. In the end, the overall framework has to be open for participation and self-organising capabilities, since decisions come from and affect the local level. If institutionalised participatory processes in common political proceedings are anchored, the possibility to take control of issues in close vicinity is tangible. This also applies to alternatives *outside* of these common political structures; both under the premise that sustainability criteria are met.

The green spaces sector is the most vivid example of an active civil society and attempts to introduce alternative institutional arrangements. The approach to self-organising local urban green spaces for manifold uses in recreational aspects, to increase biodiversity, or for producing food is growing in several European cities. One reason is the close relationship this movement shares with a broader politically motivated movement about urban social problems. Issues addressed by this (heterogeneous) movement are perceived as especially urgent by a younger generation. The dynamics of social conflicts and of conflicts evolving around political rights to take part in decision processes relating to urban spaces are considerable driving forces. However, this does not come without considerable potential for conflicts. In general, the questions 'how do we want to live?' and 'in what kind of city do we want to live?' are deeply connected and one major factor for civil activism. For the question about the role that new institutional arrangements can play, the insights are fruitful. The example of green spaces indicates that one opportunity lies in an emancipatory aspect of civil society to create an urban space compatible with diverse aspects of social and ecological sustainability. This view is tempting, since our assumption has been from the beginning that any socio-ecological transition is a movement that concerns society as a whole.

The urban water system is an individual and interesting case that shows distinct differences to the energy systems. Here, the complexity of the resource system shows itself in several aspects. In contrast to the energy system, nearly no cooperatives were found in our empirical research. This can be traced to the diverse features that influence the face of the resource system. It is sensitive to biological, technological, ecological, and economic aspects, and it is an indivisible natural monopoly, all of which make a participatory or self-organised approach difficult. Being organised, for example in a cooperative form, requires an extensive understanding of the resource system – expert knowledge. Empirically, we find this in the fact that we could not find any cooperative forms dealing with urban drinking water. However, a common approach lies in city-owned public utility providers that are socialised and assemble the necessary experts' knowledge. Civil society can participate in decisions on the resource system to an extent that does not need in-depth knowledge of the resource system. For example, the citizens' response to initiatives to privatise the European water suppliers was overwhelming. In addition, self-organisation does exist when it comes to the preservation of natural water basins like lakes or rivers. However, our research only focused on human-made water infrastructure. Concerning infrastructure, another factor becomes visible. Water systems are organised in long timespans: Concession rights easily last 70 years. While this factor also hinders the possibility to participate or to self-organise in the resource system, it provides a long-term planning horizon with adequate room for long-term strategies for sustainable developments. Where complex in-depth participation is nearly impossible, the integration of citizenry must remain on a more superficial level and concern the local handling of the water suppliers. However, a critical awareness of the importance of the resource system is present and evolving.

To conclude our research at this point, new institutional arrangements do play a significant role for socio-ecological transitions. However, their part in different resource systems has to be evaluated separately. The individual features of a resource system have different results on the reach of these new forms. An in-depth evaluation of the distinct traits of these systems has to consider the several unique dimensions that are entangled with the structural aspects of the resources as well as with the degree civil society can be and is informed about them. Where a socio-ecological transition heavily relies on expert knowledge and professionalism, the interventions of civil society face difficult hindrances. However, this must not hide the fact that professionalism and expertism can be misused to restrict access to influential positions in the resource system.

8.2 Labour markets: respecting spatial dimensions

The introduction of this chapter already explained the differences between the three resource systems and labour markets. Since the research on the resource systems focuses on potential institutional alternatives to markets or hierarchies, this section focuses on an alternative policy foundation for (labour) markets. Thus, it remains in the traditional distinction between markets and states. However, this dichotomy is – to some extent – counterintuitive. Markets are not phenomena that appear out of nothing. Moreover, social relations and legal acts establish and sustain them. This means in specific terms that they emerge because of governmental policies. Polanyi (1944) points out that the market is embedded in societal practices and is fostered by rituals. He speaks of the social embeddedness of markets. This view is furthered by sociological approaches towards economy that – for example – argue for the social embedding of transactions. No market transaction is sterile and in a vacuum. It is part of a social system that encloses those parties who *interact* on a market (Mark Granovetter 1985).

Labour markets have a distinct role in contemporary societies. They allow individuals to participate and strive for employment. The emergence of labour markets is a complex historical development that set people free from the medieval social order of the three estates (clergy, nobility, and commoners). Therefore, the citizens were able to *choose* their employment and their career instead of following their predetermined professions, which were mostly bound to their estates and their ancestors' professions. With this newly gained freedom for a self-determined biography, new ambivalences arose. Especially the necessity to interact on labour markets and to appraise one's own labour force is a new pressure that is exerted when jobs are scarce and the oversupply of work force is sensible. However, at this place, labour markets act as a generator for individual freedom, in the sense of providing positions for individual societal integration by employment. Labour markets at this point though are also a mode to organise scarceness of workplaces or work force. They "structure [the] allocation of individuals to jobs of differential desirability" (Wolfgang Streeck 2005, 254).[1]

Where a socio-ecological transition relies on a paradigmatic shift in institutional settings, labour market policies are also affected by policy shifts, especially when these concern multilevel governance concepts (Hooghe and Marks 2001, 2010). While the focus remains on a market-driven mechanism, the focus of these policies becomes more aware of spatial attributes.

8.2.1 Place-blind versus place-based policies

The initial starting points to study regional labour market policies are the huge regional unemployment rate disparities in the European Union and the fact that previous studies have – depending on the authors – emphasised two very different potential explanations for these (cf. chapter 7). On the one hand, some analysts have blamed rigid national labour market institutions that impede regional mobility and regional labour market flexibility in the EU. According to proponents of this view, this makes European labour markets incapable of adjusting to region-specific shocks to labour demand. This causes huge and long-lasting disparities in regional unemployment rates. On the other hand, a second view, which has been forcefully argued in a number of publications of the OECD LEED programme, sees regional unemployment problems as deeply rooted in the economic and institutional specifics of each region.

The proponents of these two views also come to rather different conclusions with respect to the adequate policy responses to regional unemployment rate disparities. For proponents of the first view, combating regional unemployment rate disparities requires (uniform) institutional labour market reforms at the national level to strengthen regional adjustment mechanisms to labour market disparities. Their typical policy recommendations therefore are a reduction of trade union power and the generosity of European welfare states, to increase search incentives for the unemployed. For proponents of the second view, by contrast, tailor-made, region-specific policies are needed that (on account of lacking information of central policymakers on region-specific problems) have to be designed by regional actors in a partnership-based approach to address the relevant issues.

The discussion around regional or local market policies points out that resulting labour market policies are fitting better to local specialities. The basic principle is comparable to the restructuring of institutional settings in the resource systems. The focus lies on decentralising and the devolution of decision-making capabilities. Where place-blind strategies are installed by the national level, local or regional authorities initiate place-based options. In general, this conforms with the principle of subsidiarity, which distributes responsibility to the affected governmental level. Therefore, place-based policies guarantee a more thorough regard of actually appearing local problems. However, any decentralised approach that is bound to local and regional uniqueness bears dangers of failing in its own complexity. Therefore, the central aspect that must be met is a horizontal linkage of involved and concerned stakeholders. Potential ways to meet these criteria are institutionalised networks that connect stakeholders and provide a way to communicate.

The primary interest is the interaction between the general-purpose jurisdictions with systemwide and durable architecture. These are nonintersecting in membership and organised in a limited number of levels. These are type I multilevel governance according to Liesbet Hooghe and Gary Marks (2010), such as Public Employment Services (PES). Opposing are task-specific jurisdictions that have a rather flexible design and in principle can have intersecting memberships and no limits to the number of jurisdictional levels (type II multilevel governance) such as Territorial Employment Pacts and/or Local Employment Initiatives (Pact/LEIs) in regional labour market governance (Hooghe and Marks 2010).

A further factor impeding on both the development of local initiatives and place-based policies are situations with spillover effects to other regions. For instance, in the case study on the governance of urban resource systems, respondents repeatedly refer to the fact that in the management of water and energy systems, major parts of the resource system evade regional control. This precludes developing regional strategies. Particularly the involvement of other (neighbouring) regional governance systems still seems to be in its infancy in most European regions. This is evidenced by the case study on regional labour market governance, where it was found that only a very small proportion of both the PES and Pact/LEI organisations involve actors from regions outside their own region.

8.2.2 Institutional diversification in labour markets

European labour market policies are also a particularly interesting example to study the evolution of two salient trends in EU governance. These are, first, the increased dispersion of formal competencies from central states to regional and local authorities (Hooghe and Marks 2001; Rodríguez-Pose and Tijmstra 2009; Schakel, Hooghe, and Marks 2015) and, second, the increasing importance of policy networks in particular at the regional and local level (OECD 2004). European labour market policy is mainly based on a soft (open) method of coordination because of lacking formal competencies of the European Commission. With EU authorities having only little coercive powers to influence labour market policy directly, European initiatives in the field of labour market policies have been aimed at encouraging more region-based approaches to employment and labour market policy (López-Santana 2006). At the same time, this empowerment has also resulted in the creation of large and diverse networks conducting labour market policy that include national and regional social partner organisations, NGOs, educational institutions, individual companies, as well as potential further actors as members or stakeholders (OECD 2009b).

The empirical results for regional labour market governance, by contrast, indicate that (uniform) national institutional reforms are unlikely to be helpful in reducing regional unemployment rate disparities in the EU. Among 16 indicators measuring national labour market institutions,[2] only two – net replacement rates and the generosity of health benefits – are robustly positively correlated to unemployment rate disparities within OECD countries. By contrast, other institutions seem to work in the direction of increasing regional inequality rather than decreasing it. Countries with higher centralisation of wage bargaining, more generous minimum wages, and more generous old age benefits as well as higher effective tax rates of moving from unemployment to employment robustly have lower regional unemployment rate disparities than countries with lower centralisation of wage bargaining, less generous minimum wages and old age benefits, or lower effective tax rates of moving from unemployment to employment. More centralised wage bargaining systems, but also more generous minimum wages and old age benefit systems (probably through making early retirement in depressed regions more attractive) and higher tax progressivity (as a proxy for welfare state development in a country), therefore seem to reduce regional unemployment rate disparities rather than increase them. Only (uniform) national reforms of the health and unemployment insurance systems appear to have a positive impact on the search incentives of the unemployed.

At the same time, these results suggest an important role for explanations based on regional productivity differences and differences in natural and human-made amenities between regions. Countries with higher disparities in regional productivity levels as well as with higher disparities in terms of cultural, recreational, and natural amenities robustly have higher regional unemployment rate disparities irrespective of the measure of regional disparities considered and of the method used to test for their impact on regional disparities. Region-specific factors therefore seem to be more important determinants of regional unemployment rate disparities. This supports the case for more place-based policies to combat regional unemployment rate disparities and questions the efficiency of institutional reforms in reducing regional labour market disparities.

These results are also reflected in the inquiry in the labour market policy case study. The questionnaire conducted among regional Public Employment Services (PES) as well as among more 'bottom-up' organisations in regional labour market policies (such as Territorial Employment Pacts and Local Employment Initiatives) was used. Regional labour market policy actors were highly discontent with central government and EU-wide support for such labour market policies. In particular, these actors consider the targets set by national and EU actors as well as the general distribution of competencies as rather unhelpful in conducting effective regional labour market policies.

In sum, the case studies suggest that the perceptions of the role of the EU and national governments by regional actors depend very strongly on a) the policy field considered and b) the concrete function of the higher-tier governance structure considered. On a very general level, this therefore suggests that reforms of the multilevel governance systems of the EU will have to take a 'case-by-case' approach that considers both sector as well as functional criteria.

Regional actors, however, are also aware of the limits to place-based cooperative policies. These arise in cases where the regional level does not have the relevant information to conduct such policies sensibly. Thus, for instance in the study on the governance of urban resource systems, a number of actors clearly state that they lack the information to assess the situation of the respective resource system. In the labour market case, the high importance of developing regional information and evaluation systems for regional labour market policy as well as the emphasis of the value-added of cooperation with various local actors suggest that lack of information on the local economy is a major impediment to the development of effective region-based approaches to labour market policy.

Furthermore, such limits arise in cases where the regional level simply does not have sufficient resources or legal competences to conduct place-based policies. In this respect, the economic and financial crisis since 2008 seems to have substantially impeded the feasibility of place-based approaches in particular in fields where major investments are necessary. Thus, in particular in the case study on urban resource systems, the interviewed experts repeatedly stress the strained financial situation of many urban administrations prevents the improvement of public infrastructure (Peter Huber 2013a, 2013b, 2014).

8.3 Institutional diversity in a socio-ecological transition

This chapter discussed different diversifications of institutional settings in a socio-ecological transition. On the one hand, the self-organisation of resource systems in European cities affects existing choice rules. In the work of Elinor Ostrom, these potential structures delegate local decision-making and autonomy to the local level. Specifically, civil society actors in collaboration with other local stakeholders from governments or economy can engage and interact in a self-organised resource cultivation that meets sustainability criteria.

For labour markets, the picture is a bit more diffuse. First, the institutional setting still refers to a rather 'traditional' form of organisation – that of markets. The diversity of institutional settings here refers to the distinction between place-blind or place-based alternatives. The study has shown that the picture is rather diffuse. On the one hand, place-based policies are fruitful – but they need to be complemented by place-blind aspects as well. On the other hand, regionally organised wage bargaining shows that place-based policies can produce unemployment rate disparities as well. Therefore, place-based policies do not genuinely oppose place-blind approaches. Moreover, they allow a supplement in efficiency.

For the self-organisation of resource systems, this can be sensed to some extent as well. Especially the interaction of national or EU frameworks with place-specific policies creates an institutional arrangement that efficiently guides the local socio-ecological transition and links it with different governance levels.

Notes

1 Nonetheless, labour markets are not the only institutional setting that allows thinking of individual freedom. It has been a central assumption that especially capitalist market societies are granting this liberty and are, above all other constellations, bound to individual rights. The fundamental argument for this is the nondiscriminating nature of markets: Anyone can and is allowed to exchange on markets. However, this neglects potential institutional restrictions and is highly idealised. Above all, it is a simple contingency, as discussions around basic income try to point out.
2 These were wage bargaining institutions and trade union organisations, labour and product market regulation, the generosity of minimum wages and national social security systems as well as on active labour market policies.

Chapter 9

Governing the multilevel transition

Cristina Garzillo and Stefan Kuhn

9.1 Governance and local transitions

In recent years, the role of local governments in enabling local sustainability has been increasingly emphasised. Local governments play an influential role in a city's life, reaching out to promote dialogue with other actors such as municipally owned and private companies, interest groups such as nongovernmental organisations, media, or other authorities and citizens. All this may be broadly conceived as the process of governance. "Governance . . . is the sphere of public debate, partnership, interaction, dialogue and conflict entered into by local citizens and organisations and by local governments" (Bob Evans et al. 2005, 3).

This chapter aims to reflect upon the nexuses between government, governance, and local sustainability, as they emerged in the research. As such, it illustrates how governments manage a transition towards local sustainability through governance processes outside the scope of traditional governmental activities (Yvonne Rydin 2010, 47). Local governments have become involved in networks to ensure the realisation of activities that pertain to the public interest. Although local governments are key agencies for initiating changes, many decisions cannot be addressed by local political actors alone. This means welcoming alliances with external agencies and other levels of government and explains the diversity of governance approaches that has emerged, as evidenced by the extensive range of terms that are in use: networked governance, integrated governance (Benoît Lévesque 2013, 32), and multilevel governance.

The Committee of the Regions has established a commitment to recognise and promote multilevel governance in Europe "based on coordinated action by the European Union, the Member States and regional and local authorities according to the principles of subsidiarity, proportionality and partnership" as presented in the charter for multilevel governance in Europe (Committee of the Regions 2014, 3). In this resolution, the creation of networks (networked governance) between political bodies and administrations from the local to the European levels, and vice versa, is seen as a necessary precondition to foster interconnection and interaction between the political, economic, associative, and cultural spheres. This latter allows room for integrated governance – meaning that various forms of expertise built up over time must work together to create holistic solutions. The integrated perspective is also fostered in the White Paper on Multilevel Governance (Committee of the Regions 2009). It points out the "added value of an integrated approach, particularly in terms of enhancing, in accordance with the subsidiarity principle, the synergies between the EU's sustainable development strategy and the Europe 2020 strategy and the use of structural funds for energy investments" (Committee of the Regions 2012, 67). At the local level, this means explicitly considering all issues and framing them with existing plans, priorities, and programmes.

Governance and local sustainability go hand in hand. Local sustainability initiatives – as explored in this research – take many forms and reflect the self-defined goals of local communities, who often define sustainability in different ways according to their values and priorities (ICLEI 2012, 11). However, there is a high degree of consensus about the importance of the concepts of sustainable development and local sustainability (Paul Fenton 2014, 19). Still, there is a contradicting consensus that economic development is an indicator of vitality for regions – this is coupled with labour market performance. These two factors need to be dealt with in terms of economic sustainability.

After a short introduction, this chapter starts with a reflection on the common model of local sustainability and analyses how the traditional three pillars of sustainable development are functionally interrelated. Subsequently, the chapter reports on the DISCUS project (2001–2004), examining the principal research question: *What are the factors and conditions that permit good governance for sustainable urban development?* The section aims at stimulating a discussion to consider if what worked more than ten years ago still fits the reality and forms the basis for the consequent key observations on sustainability transition governance.

The role of local governments in the last two decades of global action for sustainable development is then highlighted in the international preparatory process for the United Nations Conference on Sustainable Development in 2012, also known as the Rio+20 Conference. One of the fundamental conclusions of the Local Sustainability Study 2012 (ICLEI 2012, 81) is that: *Sustainable development needs a multilevel governance system with a multisectoral approach.*

This in turn leads to analysing cities as laboratories of transitions towards sustainability. An increasing number of articles and documents discussing how to accelerate sustainability transitions on the local level have emerged – including the current research. Section 9.4 presents an overview of approaches used in European research projects on managing transitions, along with the specific themes and topics addressed.

Key observations from the city sample follow. These are the key issue of this chapter and illustrate the processes of government and governance in the cities, reflecting upon how stakeholders and local government perceive their relationship in the field of sustainability.

Following the observations, a short outlook reflects upon the potential for further contributions and policies that may enhance local sustainability and looks into future needs and trends such as the role of civil society self-organisation, the role of information and communication technologies in governing local society and managing infrastructure, and a potentially refined understanding of multilevel governance.

9.2 Governing sustainable cities

9.2.1 Changing economic practices

The majority of literature about sustainable development refers to the three dimensions or three pillars of sustainability, composed of environment, economy, and society. However convincing this 'magic triangle' may appear at first sight, its operationalisation has been problematic right from the start of the sustainability debate in the early 1990s. In addition, the findings from the interview material of the current research place heavy emphasis on institutional capacity and governmental aspects for sustainable development policy achievements, suggesting that good governance is central to sustainability. In order to understand how current practices need to change to initiate transition processes of the socio-ecological systems on the local level, the different characters of the distinct, yet linked, sustainability dimensions need to be highlighted. The international network ICLEI – Local Governments for Sustainability has developed a helpful alternative model that focuses on the functional interrelations between them (ICLEI 2012, 60):

- What is often referred to as 'the environment' is in fact the stock of natural resources and the capacity of natural systems to recover and replenish themselves. Any overexploitation of these systems will inevitably lead to reduced availability of ecosystem services, with severe implications for the ability of humans to organise their daily lives. Keeping our use of these natural systems and resources within their physical self-recovery boundaries may therefore be considered the non-negotiable reference point of the sustainable city.
- Key aspects of the social pillar refer to an aggregation of cultural patterns; functional systems such as legal, political, educational, and societal systems; and physical infrastructure to satisfy basic needs such as shelter, mobility, safety, and food. Together they are embedded in a socio-structural and cultural web that is correlated to what we could call quality of life. They are based on the use of natural resources, and on a number of societal consensuses and norms that can in principle change and be changed over time.
- Economic practices are performed by businesses, governments, and civil society (non-profit) organisations as well as by ordinary citizens at all levels and by any individual person. Every act of production, service provision, and purchase entails a certain degree of consumption of natural resources in order to improve quality of life. Even under the condition that societal systems and norms remain unchanged over longer periods of time, changes in economic practices may modify the input–output ratio of natural resources and quality of life immediately.

Finally, this process of constant interrelation between human economic activity, resource use, and quality of life is embedded in management and governance rules, which themselves influence how the mechanism described above works.

Figure 9-1 illustrates the functional relationship between natural resources, economic activity, and quality of life. It is important to keep in mind that when talking about sustainable cities we implicitly refer to changes in economic practices, which may lead to changes in societal consensus and systems, with the aim of leading human utilisation of natural systems back to within their limits of self-recovery.

9.2.2 Success factors for governing local sustainability transition processes

Already a decade prior to the field research this book is based on, another research project cofunded by the European Commission investigated how cities in Europe are "Developing Institutional and Social Capacities for Urban Sustainability" (DISCUS, 2001–2004). As in the recent research, 40 cities across Europe were visited by fieldworkers; however, DISCUS cities had been chosen based on their reputation as forerunner cities, evidenced by awards they had won or by frequent reference as good practice cases in the area of sustainable urban development. The basic assumption was that successful local policies for sustainable development are rooted in higher levels of capacity of the local citizenship to

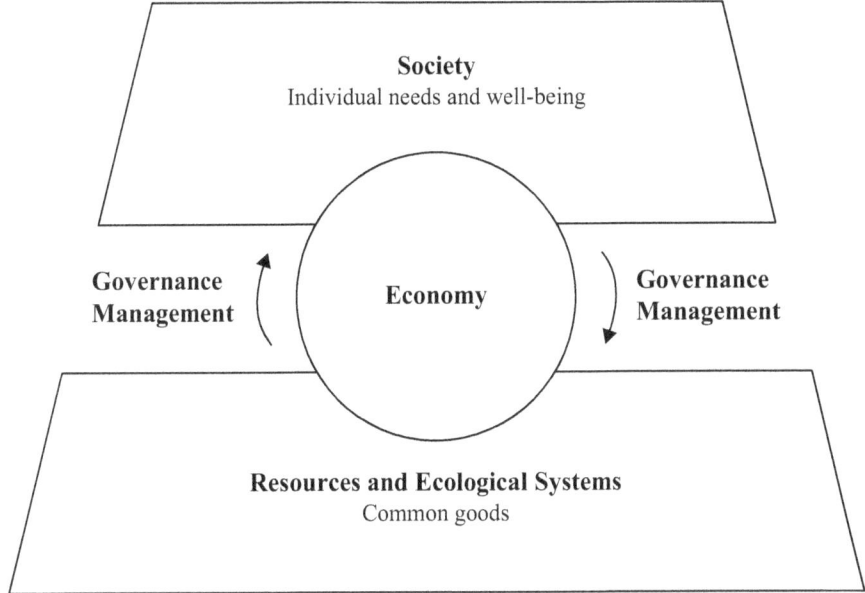

Figure 9-1 Interrelations among the three sustainability pillars

support and self-organise sustainability action and of the local government to manage complex long-term processes and cooperate with external actors. "The 'art' of governing sustainable cities is thus to create competent local governments that, in interaction with a highly responsible (and responsive) civil society, apply a form of governing that brings about the most sustainable solutions" (Evans et al. 2005, ix). At the time of the DISCUS research, the authors of its report conceded that this might be "a straight contradiction to the current paradigm of individualism and enhanced competition" (Evans et al. 2005, ix). However, as the results of current research show, ten years later, we can see indications of a changing attitude of citizens towards a shared responsibility for the common goods, and higher levels of self-organisation, maybe further supported by the revolution in information and communication technologies the last decade has seen.

In order for local governments to "undergo a process of innovation and even transformation ... to govern sustainable cities in the future" (Evans et al. 2005, 117), the DISCUS researchers identified the following ten key success factors, which have also been published as 'The Fano Guidelines – Building Capacity for Local Sustainability' (DISCUS Project 2005):

1 *Learning as an organisation:* Investment in training on sustainable development for both officers and politicians builds capacity within local governments.
2 *Moving away from 'policy silos' within local governments:* The complexity of sustainable development requires a response that combines knowledge from all policy areas, and utilises the maximum resources available.
3 *Making alliances with people and organisations:* Businesses, organisations, and individuals are all sources of influence and knowledge for sustainable development.
4 *Facilitating the process and developing credible leadership:* Setting an example in sustainability management and activities builds up trust and credibility within civil society.

5 *Encouraging creativity and innovation in policymaking:* Creative people within and outside local government are key to answering new challenges.
6 *Communicating to make a difference:* Within a knowledge-based society, communication is central to raising awareness of the changes in behaviour that sustainable development demands.
7 *Catalysing action through raising environmental awareness:* Winning people's interest in sustainable development issues can be promoted through raising environmental awareness.
8 *Maintaining commitment to achieving the long-term vision:* Action for sustainability needs to be systematic whilst guided by the long-term vision.
9 *Sharing experience with peers:* Networking with other cities and towns creates a common cause for the reorientation of local development.
10 *Influencing all levels of government:* Working with other levels of government increases the opportunities for local-level considerations to be included in national legislation and strategies for the promotion of sustainable development.

Ten years after the identification of these success factors for sustainable urban development and the publication of the Fano Guidelines, most of the key issues they address are still debated widely – however, they have found their way out of the research arena and into the realm of policymaking and administrative reform. As the next section will show, when talking about transition processes, it is important to understand that local government is only one out of a long list of key players that design our society's future.

9.2.3 Initiating local transition processes

As the Fano Guidelines in the section above show, the DISCUS research was led by the idea that local government needs to be the driving force behind the initiation of a local transition process towards sustainability. This approach followed well the original mandate given to local governments in chapter 28 of Agenda 21 (UN 1992), the outcome document of the United Nations Conference on Environment and Development 1992 in Rio de Janeiro. This was however never purely the case, as ICLEI's Global Review 'Local Sustainability 2012 – Taking stock and moving forward', revealed (ICLEI 2012). Twenty years after the original Rio mandate to local governments to develop a 'Local Agenda 21', the network reviewed local sustainability processes worldwide with the intention of creating a geography of Local Agendas, identifying process types according to world regions (such as the African Local Agenda compared to the European Local Agenda). Surprisingly, similarities of local sustainability processes emerged between countries as far away from each other as France and South Korea, India and Poland, or Germany and Brazil. The explanation for these unforeseen similarities was that the kind of initial driver of a local process defines the character of the process much more than its geographical location. The study thus identified five main types of local sustainability processes, characterised by the political level and the type of organisation that initiated them:

1 *Local Government Strategy:* This first type comes closest to the ideal underlying the previously described Fano Guidelines in that departments or individuals from a local government start the process of moving local development towards sustainability. The motivation for this strategy can simply be benefits the initiators see for their city, or it can be a reaction to a local (often economic) problem or crisis.

2 *Civil Society Initiative:* The second type already reflects some of the ideas and assumptions made in this book about local self-organisation of civil society in governing and managing common goods. Civil-society-based local processes are typically characterised by a high level of creativity and openness to new solutions but sometimes lack a clear link to the 'official' policymaking arena.
3 *Concerted Action:* The third type of local process is based on the initiative of national and/or international local government networks and associations. Particularly in countries where national government engagement for sustainability is poor, their support and capacity-building programmes unite and instruct local processes and their actors.
4 *National Policy:* The fourth type constitutes the rather rare case that national government runs a full-fledged programme for local sustainability processes, providing financial support, local and national recognition, guidance, and monitoring/reporting schemes.
5 *International Cooperation:* The fifth type occurs where local development is predominantly defined by the financial support and political objectives of international donor organisations. Cities receiving such support are often instructed 'through the back door' to set up sustainability strategies together with local stakeholders as a precondition for receiving funds for local development projects.

The most important finding of the Local Sustainability 2012 review is that the five types of different actors initiating local transition processes together constitute an ideal instruction set for the multilevel governance of the transition of socio-ecological systems. Each of the initial drivers of local processes has its particular strengths, which, combined, can unfold a powerful alliance:

> An ideal local sustainability process will thus combine as many as possible of the properties of each of the five types identified, and be laid down in a local strategy, rooted in a civil society initiative, linked with others as part of a concerted action, embedded in a national policy, [and] enriched by international partnership at the same time.
>
> (ICLEI 2012, 76)

9.3 The governance of transitions

This section reflects upon some of the issues related to local sustainability outlined above by looking in detail at the cities as laboratories of transitions with particular reference to recent developments at EU level. There are good grounds for doing so. There is a growing lack of trust in government. Democratic engagement and citizenship in many countries are shrinking. At the same time, transition processes are taking place in many urban systems, and opportunities are visible in new social movements, new technologies, other civil society groups, and networks. Particularly cities and networks of cities play an important role in this process.

Many projects and research activities attempt to understand and explain the dynamics of fundamental, long-term societal change. This new perspective outlines that transitions, rather than being managed, can be influenced, supported, and accelerated. By allowing openness, exchange, stimulation of differences, and contradictory conditions to occur at the same time, city officials can play into existing societal dynamics.

The European MUSIC project (Mitigation in Urban Context, Solutions for Innovative Cities, 2010–2015) manual details a theoretical framework and a practical process to support the transition of cities towards sustainability: the transition management approach. The approach was applied in five European cities, which shared the ambition of meeting or even going beyond the European 2020 climate targets: Aberdeen (UK), Montreuil (France), Ghent (Belgium), Ludwigsburg (Germany), and Rotterdam (Netherlands). These cities aimed to realise their ambitions by finding fundamental new ways of thinking, working, planning, and organising.

The transition management theory looks at different system levels and interactions: Niches are confined spaces where novel artefacts (technology, processes, business, models, social practices, etc.) are implemented, nurtured, and experimented with. Depending on the experiences gained, these artefacts may later be scaled up and may evolve to form a new regime or alter the incumbent regime in an incremental way (Holger Berg et al. 2014a). Transition experiments are projects that take a societal challenge as a starting point to develop alternative practices at a feasible scale; the transition arena is a temporary setting that provides an informal and well-structured space to a small group of change agents from diverse backgrounds (businesses, government, research institutes, NGOs, and citizens), going beyond current interests and daily routines and developing a shared transition agenda, which provides a starting point for involving a wider group and instigating new activities, networks, and collaborations and develops transition pathways to realise the vision (Chris Roorda et al. 2014, 11).

Obviously, a transition management approach does not replace the need for other policy interventions. While the notion that transition management and other governance activities can be pursued simultaneously is increasingly being advocated, there are also some important trade-offs to be aware of when developing strategies. For example, the *system analysis* to explore the state of the city and its dynamics can be built on an existing CO_2 baseline study, and the transition agenda can inspire policy formulation (Roorda et al. 2014, 11). Therefore, in this perspective, transition management and other governance activities are complementary. However, city officials can create significant political capital on the CO_2 issue, whereas addressing transitions requires a different kind of leadership, engaging a wider group of actors, and opening up for more creative approaches (see subsection 3.2.1 for a brief critique of transition management).

The European TRANSITION (Transnational Network for Social Innovation Incubation 2014–2016) project aims at scaling up nationally, regionally, or internationally 300 social innovations, as well as extending their impact and replicating in new territories. London (UK), Paris (France), Bilbao (Spain), Milan (Italy), Tampere (Finland), and Galway (Ireland) are the six scaling centres that have used their collective expertise to design a common support framework for finding, supporting, and scaling 300 models of social innovation. Each centre will follow a so-called *social innovation journey* and methods to scale up these models.

Other projects focus on specific themes, which nevertheless call for collaboration across a range of areas of activities and disciplines. For example, Transition Cities (Transition Cities Consortium 2014) identifies three main areas of activity in buildings, energy, and mobility where consolidating activity could move cities away from a narrow, isolated project approach. This means that local governments may look at such themes from different perspectives instead of delegating them to one specific sector; local governments may also work on short-term projects that tend to be too focused and generate discontinuity and fragmentation of commitments. The development of multi-actor clusters in these areas enables cities to articulate better their needs and challenges as well as undertake pilots and experiments.

There are several areas where research into transitions towards sustainability is particularly timely and urgent and the clustering of existing and new projects could be beneficial:

- Transition to a renewable energy society. According to the Transition Cities project, hundreds of imaginative and innovative low-carbon projects are underway. Yet currently the general picture is that these projects remain isolated initiatives, lacking in strategic coherence and with no agreed perspective on where to focus investment and how to scale them up. Hence, the achievement of the targets is in doubt. The new opportunities for transitions in the energy system call for concerted visions, strategies, and actions between the economy, the policy system, civil society, media, and science. Cities and regions play an important role in this process, and more integrated approaches are needed between energy, climate systems, and land use options (Pathways 2014).
- Land use transition. There is a need to promote multifunctional and sustainable pathways of the land system. Under this theme, European projects (e.g. VOLANTE; Pathways) investigate the socio-economic and ecological processes that shape land use transitions and the innovative visions that can be formulated for future sustainable resource management and land use policy development. Modelling tools can make important contributions to the assessment of critical thresholds for resource management with reference to land use change and ecosystem services. According to the European Commission, a clearer picture of the linkages between the process of land degradation and inefficient use on the one hand and key socio-economic variables on the other is a necessary condition for a better integration of land use efficiency into EU and national policy instruments.
- New media and information and communication technologies (ICT) connectivity. The explosion of new forms of communication and networking and the amount of information associated with computing, the Internet, and new media is one of the biggest transformations in information and technology. There is a need to understand the role of ICT within physical city assets and explore how to take advantage of it. Citizens and enterprises apply new ICT to economise time, improve individual mobility, facilitate access to information and services, and participate in urban decision-making processes (Klaus Kunzmann 2014, 12).
- Smart urban governance. Cities need to be more adaptive, strategic, innovative, and so on. However, many forms of governance are slow, inefficient, and obsolete (Joe Ravetz 2013). ICT-based cities are only a part of the change happening in local communities. Citizens' initiatives, networks, and community structures and their synergies with local governments, spatial planning, and the built environment can improve urban governance.

Initiatives and actions that occur across the city sample address many of the themes above. What is apparent from the Compendium of Case Studies (Garzillo and Ulrich 2015) is that these can clearly be seen as part of the story of progress and value-added in the transition towards sustainable development.

9.4 Key issues of urban transition governance

9.4.1 The city sample in the research

This section draws together the key observations on sustainability transition governance that have emerged from the city sample of the energy, green spaces, and water systems' transitions towards sustainability and a shift towards place-based policies for labour markets. It provides insights into the real-world practice of governance and local sustainability, as observed by politicians, city officials, and stakeholders and reported by the field researchers.

It may not always be possible to make comparisons between cities from different countries. Particular types of cities may share similar framework conditions; others may be significantly different – in terms of factors such as size, geographical context, climate, activities, urban management, population, legal and political framework, and so on.

Similar challenges are evident when analysing cities within a single national context (Fenton 2014, 8). Although the legal framework is standardised, there may be significant differences in the constellations of stakeholders, opportunities for citizen participation, social inclusion, responsiveness of decision-making, and the ways in which local governments interact with their civil societies. The ease of doing business also varies between cities within countries as a result of differences in the way national regulations are implemented (European Commission 2014b, 127). In some cases, similarities occur more between cities located in very different parts of Europe, finding appropriate forms of connectivity between cross-border regions.

The material for this section is derived from case study reports of the field researchers on the 40 cities under investigation and the analysis of empirical material in chapters 4 to 7 of this book, interviews, questionnaires, and field researcher summary reports[1] (Garzillo and Ulrich 2015). Analysis of such material allows us to highlight some necessary elements of initiating and managing challenging transition initiatives.

9.4.2 Local government autonomy

European Local Governments have become more autonomous over the past 50 years. However, there are different ways to define and frame autonomy and numerous challenges related to how autonomy is operationalised. In general, the degree of administrative decentralisation directly influences the degree of independent decision-making. In special cases, EU policies and programmes may also influence the level of autonomy, especially in countries that are under fiscal control and subjected to austerity politics.

Analysis of recent trends in subnational finances shows that these budgets were reduced significantly by the crisis (European Commission 2014b). The need for financial resources is clearly present in order to increase autonomy and local decision-making, as well as general investments and procurement activities.

Local government autonomy varies between countries, and these differences are important to take into account when assessing governance. In the discussion of the findings, what emerges is that

- due to the municipal right to self-administration ('Kommunales Selbstverwaltungsrecht'), German local governments have a very high degree of autonomy;

- the autonomy of the local level seems to be highly respected in Swiss cities and cantons, due to the federal organisation of the state;
- the level of autonomy increased substantially in recent years in Eastern countries and Greece but remained nevertheless relatively low;
- Greece had to undergo an administrative reform to comply with imposed objectives of austerity politics, enforcing decentralisation of administration and shifting decision-making capabilities to the lower levels;
- in Romania, a new law on regional administration, allowing more decision-making to take place at the subnational level, is in the process of being approved;
- in Poland, local governments are dependent on the central government's decisions, even though the degree of self-organisation increased in the last years. However, due to the principle of subsidiarity and solidarity ('Janosikowe'), financial resources retained in cities are limited in amount; the rest is directed to central government and then redistributed by the Ministry of Finance.

It was noted that centralised states undermine local-level autonomy (e.g. Larissa, Strasbourg, Rennes, Istanbul[2]). France is a highly centralised state, which can be seen in energy politics but also in general in the local decision autonomy, where "local authorities have nothing to say" (Nice, a2, 101).

Likewise, the Turkish administrative system is highly centralised. Central government has increased its control over regional and local authorities. Municipalities face serious problems due to the limited autonomy; they have been granted no power but have responsibilities concerning the rapid increase in built-up areas and huge transformations taking place in their own territories. Moreover, the rapid transformation process managed at the national level is often not going hand in hand with adequate efforts on societal and ecological issues.

In addition to governmental challenges, the role and influence of economy and business actors on local decision autonomy is important. Particularly the interests of business actors coming from the economic logic – realising profits and prevailing on the market – fosters competitive behaviour. The influence of market-oriented policies, prioritising the private sector and profit seeking, can be felt in local decisions in cities (e.g. Rome).

Capital cities have different governance systems due to their dimension, complexity, and higher status. For example, in Rome, the institution of the 'Capital Rome' local authority grants more powers to the city. The 'Greater London Authority' is a strategic authority with powers over transport, policing, economic development, and fire and emergency planning and has the aim of improving the coordination between the local authorities in Greater London. 'Grand Paris' was created for the definition and implementation of metropolitan action and coordinates efforts of Paris and its neighbouring cities in a coherent structure.

It was generally reported by most cities that the progress towards decentralisation is slow because of routine operations, bureaucratic inertia and ineffectiveness, and the resistance of long-established routines and structures to change. Constitutional problems and decisions on the national level obstruct the progress, while the financial dependence of the subnational levels on the central state also delays procedures. In Greece, for example, the central government still has the general supervision on the elaboration of regional/urban master plans, statutory town plans, environmental protection programmes, public investments, integrated development programmes, and so on (Erika Nagy et al. 2008).

9.4.3 Reconfigured boundaries

Cross-sector, cross-border, and intergovernmental coordination is necessary but difficult in practice. The constellation of actors involved in transitions is large, and their interests need to be aligned. It is clear that a complex and multifaceted process like a socio-ecological transition can be realised neither solely by individuals (officials or politicians or figures with charisma and motivation), nor by national or local governments alone.

A framework for joint action and policy exchanges between European, national, regional, and local actors is needed. Cities, regions, nation states, and Europe as a whole can benefit from this connectivity, including many forms of linkages (Labaeye and Sauer 2013). The effects of the interrelationships are presented below.

Regional and national influences

Local governments report that often they are significantly constrained by the national government. In some countries (e.g. Romania), national instability has a negative impact on the local level; constitutional problems, heavy bureaucracy, and contradictory decisions at the national level often obstruct progress. In some other cases, the national level is felt to be completely missing and thereby hindering by its absence the proper realisation of specific sustainability processes at the local level, as reported in Milan, Trieste, and Barcelona.

The lack of legislation concerning sustainability topics hindered proper collaboration with other levels of governance (e.g. Naples). In some countries, such as Greece, actors noted that the central government still has the general supervision on the elaboration of regional/urban master plans, statutory town plans, environmental protection programmes, public investments, and integrated development programmes. However, a slow decision-making process, badly organised public consultations, a focus on short-term electoral gains, and frequent changes in policies and priorities tend to undermine progress.

Overall, constitutional problems and decisions on the national level obstruct the progress while the financial dependence of the subnational levels on the central level also delays procedures.

European influences

The perception of how the European policies affect the way local governments operate and perform varies among the countries.

The given legal frameworks have their own influences on socio-ecological transitions. In particular, the degree of local autonomy is directly connected to the impact of national administrative frames and European directives – thus, the state of decentralisation is an essential indicator for the overall independence of the local level and its possibility to enact a transition.

The European level is perceived by actors in Southern and Eastern Europe as proposing the general framework, which is not provided by the state, and European policies are mentioned to be more forward thinking and outpacing than the national law, as reported in Kiel, Germany.

The perception of European influence is also diverging among actors. Some actors expressed concerns about the nonflexibility of European or national constraints, even those aimed at protecting the environment (Nice). On the other hand, European directives, mandatory at the local level, are equally considered to be helpful. Therefore, according to many, a fiercer environmental legislation on the national/EU level is needed with more solid and clearer rules whose noncompliance on the local level is also consistently sanctioned (e.g. Lodz, Timisoara, Madrid, Lugano).

It was said that "regulation pressure always makes things move" (Strasbourg, a3, 50), although an actor states that (national) governmental instances do not necessarily follow EU policies (Thessaloniki).

Further propositions include the alignment of EU funding schemes along regions instead of nations, pointing to the fact that cities' situations can be very different within a nation but similar to others in the same region, yet not belonging to the same state (e.g. Naples). The challenges faced by cities cut across national boundaries; thus, cooperation at an appropriate territorial level is needed.

Regarding the installed and maintained frameworks, consideration might differ: Either frameworks on European, national, or local levels are helpful and productive to initiate campaigns (Rennes), or governmental institutions can slow down and delay processes, such as in bureaucratic organisations with long and complex official channels (Potsdam).

Overall, it is clear that legal frameworks exist to guide and standardise efforts towards sustainability accordingly. However, it is crucial for local governments to influence national and European framework conditions in order to successfully implement their transition strategies.

Urban–rural linkages

In many European regions, the differences between rural and urban life get blurred, partly due to the existence of infrastructure that makes the daily mobility or instant communication (Internet) between areas easier (Global Europe 2012, 124).

Appropriate urban–rural linkages are in some cases missing. These territories are often the site of conflict and rivalry concerning the use and control of space between the urban and the surrounding areas. The general pattern can be explained by neighbouring developments with new urban expansions typically located at the fringes of existing urban areas and merging into the rural landscape. Especially labour market institutions show this effect, which can be traced to the complex urban–rural linkage where urban areas provide employment, especially in industry, and the service sector and rural areas provide the necessary workforce (cf. subsection 7.2.1 and note 6 in chapter 7). Further, the case of energy systems has shown that spatial issues in high-density cities occur. Thus, an urban–rural linkage is necessary to allow a productive energy provision.

In Greece the situation is politically difficult and highly problematic since the rural hinterland – rural areas surrounding the peri-urban areas, but within the urban–rural region (Annette Piorr, Joe Ravetz, and Iván Tosics 2011, 24) – is very important for the overall, collective development of the region. In general, this calls for new governance challenges in the peri-urban situation, alongside new forms of integrated cooperation.

Long-term visions

Visions influence the extent to which politicians and leaders are willing to change or modify systems, regulations, and norms that pose barriers to action. Long-term visions can unify even diverse groups, generate new ideas and experiments, and serve as a compass for the daily work (InContext 2013, 1). In some cases, cities have a clear and easy-to-understand vision, while in other cases local governments are focused on short-term electoral gain and therefore concentrated only on daily decisions.

It was stated that Polish and Romanian cities have lacked a long-term vision of development, causing inefficiencies in city management. The lack of distant, long-term objectives may be due to political instability and high turnover in strategic management positions, the relatively poor condition of infrastructure, and a deficit of financial resources for sustainability projects.

Most policies tend to be short term, reactive, and ad-hoc, instead of proactive and long term, particularly when little progress can be shown.

9.4.4 Local governments and citizen participation

As mentioned above, democratic engagement and citizenship is shrinking in many countries. In response, active community groups are emerging that work on a wide range of issues, primarily on green spaces as well as on social inclusion and migrants' rights.

The range of citizen participation varies according to local context, as well as to the particular problem, issue, and policy at hand. Attention tends to be more focused on green spaces, allotment gardens, urban food strategies (Leeds), urban regeneration (Glasgow), and local neighbourhood planning, and less on heavy infrastructure such as metro expansion, energy, and water (Copenhagen, Leeds, Istanbul). Local civil society can hardly be observed on drinking water, maybe due to the complexity of the issue and new governance networks involved in water systems.

Participation is more on "ideas, visions; whereas the substantial decisions are made by the big companies and politicians" (Innsbruck, a2, 79). In some cases, there is a very good relationship between the groups and the local council (Birmingham). In other cases, citizens feel that most decisions are already made and that there is no substance behind the dialogue (Gothenburg) and that community groups are not always content with their relations with the council (Glasgow).

Sometimes the initiatives are local-authority-led and steered from above. For example, the city of Aalborg established a green council where nonprofit organisations are taken into account and invited to participate in strategies about spatial planning. A few cities have the so-called civil society and citizens' interests' office belonging directly to the Lord Mayor (e.g. Dortmund) and have a long tradition of forming associations and advocacy groups (Basque country; Freiburg).

In Italy, many municipalities are trying to increase the level of participation in the decision-making process because they recognise this as the first step in enforcing brave and innovative policies. The need and will of citizens to participate noticeably increased after several cases of corruption in the managing of common resources. Therefore, citizens' participation is perceived as a way to grant the openness and legality of the process (for example waste emergencies in Naples).

While expectations are rising, the involvement of citizens and community groups in many places is falling. Participation does not have a strong tradition in cities in the Czech Republic (e.g. Jihlava) and in Romania (for example in Giurgiu only a very small number of nonprofit associations exist). The legitimacy of a large range of stakeholders must be recognised, and appropriate means must be found for obtaining their participation.

In Poland (Lodz), only a few of the registered NGOs are widely recognisable and active. In some cities, existing participatory tools have been badly managed by the administration and citizens are now tired of them, diminishing trust in public services (e.g. Bilbao).

In France, local power still benefits from a good level of legitimacy among the public. This may help explain the scarcity of bottom-up initiatives and the strong and leading presence of public institutions.

A special case is that of Swiss cities. There are virtually no bottom-up initiatives in the cities analysed in the research. This might be explained by the highly centralised but well-working services provided by the government and by its bodies, coupled to the possibility for all citizens to influence government decisions through referendums.

Finally, the Turkish political structure does not contribute to citizens' lively participation and bottom-up actions; active participation in decision-making processes is strongly discouraged.

9.4.5 Trust

One important prerequisite and benefit of participation is that it increases trust between the citizens and the government. Balancing the needs and fears of different community groups creates trust in political leadership towards sustainability. On the other hand, lack of participation and low-quality governance create a vicious cycle, in which trust in government breaks down. Trust and effective interpersonal relationships seem to be at the heart of the information that is most valued by cities. However, missing trust in public institutions is mentioned in every region except in the Western countries. The results of the Standard Eurobarometer survey conducted in November 2013 (European Commission 2013a) show that trust in national political institutions continues to decrease and Europeans still perceive the current economic situation at national and European levels as bad.

Missing or low levels of trust might be a result of experienced (sometimes illegal) entanglement between the public and the private sector and many administrative opportunities for discretionary behaviour. Citizens refrain from joining associations, stop caring about the common good (e.g. Milan), and might not trust association leaders any more if they were led by personal interests in the past (Larissa) or influenced by recent political scandals or by the local financial and economic situation as well as by the inefficiency of the legal system (Jihlava).

In particular, the issue of personal trust is fundamental to effective connectivity between research and policymaking. Implicit is the idea that only through strong personal relationships with trusted professional contacts can actors access information and foster innovation approaches.

Trust, common understanding, and also a 'willingness to step out of the box' are obviously central elements for the success of transition processes.

9.4.6 Networking between local governments

Twenty years after the adoption of Agenda 21, the Rio+20 Final Declaration "The Future We Want" takes note of the unprecedented success of this movement and contains a reference to cities and regional and local governments as major actors for sustainable development. In particular, it "encourage[s] regional, national, sub-national and local authorities as appropriate to develop and utilize sustainable development strategies as key instruments for guiding decision-making" and "recognise[s] that partnerships among cities and communities play an important role in promoting sustainable development" (UN 2012, 26).

Such initiatives, and others, are regarded as an important channel for knowledge sharing on sustainability and potentially play an important role in the learning process at the subnational level. As a matter of fact, many of these networks and campaigns have the ambition to build the capacity of their members to engage in sustainable development (Labaeye and Sauer 2013).

Transnational local government networks – such as ICLEI and Eurocities – are important according to many cities (e.g. Birmingham) because they facilitate the exchange of information and experiences and provide access to expertise and external funding as well as political strength to promote sustainability internally (Labaeye and Sauer 2013). In addition, schemes such as the Covenant of Mayors permit exchanges on sustainable energy topics, as reported in Naples and Bilbao.

National networks and partnerships can also evolve at multiple scales. In some countries, for example Italy or Sweden, new municipal associations or networks have been created that focus specifically on sustainable development issues.

At more regional and provincial scales, partnerships have proved to be critical in building the resources and capacities of municipal governments to address local sustainability. For example, the Network of Valencian Municipalities towards Sustainability composed of the Provincial Council of Valencia, the municipalities, interested public and private entities, and the Advisory Council for Sustainable Development of Catalonia (CADS) was created in 1998 to collaborate with local governments, networks, and other entities on matters of the environment and sustainable development.

To conclude, it seems obvious that networking with other cities can open local governments up to good practice and experience elsewhere. This raises questions on the possibilities of fostering a competitive advantage of Europe by strengthening networks of cities (Ravetz 2013) and increasing their flexibility, resilience, and adaptation to responding to change.

9.4.7 Horizontal coordination

The crosscutting nature of governance and local sustainability means that various forms of expertise must work hand in hand. Elaborated networks that institutionalise collaboration are particularly important. Within these collaboration networks, extended numbers of actors bringing socio-ecological transitions forward are involved, such as NGOs, education, trade unions, ethnic groups, faith groups, and so forth, especially to address economic and social topics.

In the field of energy in particular, cooperation spans a diverse set of actors that nearly everywhere include politics and administration as well as business associations, technology companies, and utilities and local providers (e.g. Aalborg and Dortmund).

Very interesting is the role of local universities and scientific institutes that provide knowledge and technical assistance or uphold a counter-discourse for sustainability issues (St. Gallen, Dortmund, Freiburg, Copenhagen, Umea). In particular, Freiburg constitutes a vivid example where the university and research institutes are integrated in a public discourse on sustainability both grounded in an understanding of the real world and remaining focused on improving lives.

Sometimes the (often informal) presence of influential scientists can be instrumental in establishing local sustainability on the political agenda (Aalborg, Nice), and above that, networks between practitioners and researchers/academics can foster the integration of social innovations (Leeds, Rennes).

9.5 Outlook

9.5.1 Future needs

It is clear from the previous sections that a variety of connective processes acting on different scales are fundamental attributes for cities. Links and flows between political/institutional, economic, and socio-cultural dimensions need to be explored to advance transitions.

Meanwhile, information and communication technologies (ICT) have profoundly changed many aspects of life, including the nature of entertainment, work, communication, education, health care, industrial production and business, social relations, and conflicts. They have had a radical and widespread impact on our moral lives and on contemporary ethical debates (Luciano Floridi 2013).

The Digital Agenda for Europe aims to help citizens and businesses to get the most out of digital technologies. It is the first of seven flagship initiatives under Europe 2020, the EU's strategy to deliver smart, sustainable, and inclusive growth. In addition, the European Commission has already funded a number of research and development projects through the 7th Framework Programme for Research and Technological Development (FP7) and the Competitiveness and Innovation Programme (CIP) on themes such as Smart Buildings, ICT Systems for Energy Efficiency, Smart Data, Energy Efficient Manufacturing, Smart Grids, Climate Change Management with ICT, and ICT for Water Management.

Currently, Horizon 2020, the new EU Framework Programme for Research and Innovation (2014–2020), supports the development of ICT in science, industrial leadership, and societal challenges.

Of particular interest are the contributions in ICT in 'Societal Challenges' covering the following issues: health, demographic change, and well-being; secure, clean, and efficient energy; smart, green, and integrated transport; climate action, environment, resource efficiency, and raw materials; Europe in a changing world – innovative, inclusive, and reflective societies; and secure societies – protecting the freedom and security of Europe and its citizens.

It is clear that much attention has been posed by European research and projects on ICT-based and smart cities. However, ICT can have a profound effect only if taking into account structures of governance (Committee of the Regions 2011). The question of governance becomes critical to influencing transitions. Cities are often locked in unsustainable patterns due to a mix of different factors. There are institutional and economic factors; there are levels of corruption and administrative burden; there are problems of ownership or control of land and resources; there are private behaviours motivated by self-interest.

Decision-makers need to go beyond the short timescale within which they operate, to overcome the need to act within nested hierarchies of governance structures and the spatial scale of their jurisdiction. There is a need to change the way of thinking about cities considering their interdependencies and interactions and enhancing the spaces of flows (Manuel Castells 1996) as well as the circulation of people, capital, resources, and identities.

The European Union's Committee of the Regions through the charter recognised the importance of improving the relation among different levels of government for multilevel governance (Committee of the Regions 2014). The charter calls public authorities of all levels of governance (local, national, and European) to use and promote multilevel governance in their future undertakings. This includes experiments with innovative policy solutions in adherence with principles of subsidiarity, proportionality, and partnership, and promotion of the use of multilevel partnerships and instruments for joint policy action.

9.5.2 Future trends

With a shrinking population and stagnating economic growth rates, Europe is forced to apply the ecological principle of keeping within the limits of resource systems' capacities to recover its national and local economies as well. This means that the logic of closed loops will no longer only be an ecological mandate but also an economic paradigm. Quality of life will thus be oriented more and more towards social cohesion and inclusion and towards guaranteeing the satisfaction of basic societal needs rather than redistributing growth. For a civil society, this means that self-organisation within and outside the profit sector will cover many services that up to now have been provided by public administration.

ICT will be the technological backbone of civil society self-organisation, giving practically everyone access to information and participation at any time via mobile devices and networks. New forms of shared use or reuse of goods, spontaneous conventions of people, co-creation, and crowd sourcing and funding, to name but a few, will add to the former trends of individualisation and competition.

At the same time, ICT will constitute the urban operation systems based on which decentralised energy production and distribution as well as control over buildings and mobility systems can take place. One obvious challenge related to this will be the governance of data ownership and managing the resilience of such highly complex systems against disasters or attacks. As of this writing, 'Smart City' approaches yet have to prove that they can increase quality of life for more than just an elite social milieu and at the same time contribute to considerable reductions in the use of natural resources.

Finally, the often-quoted multilevel governance of transition processes will undergo some redefinition. As the section on initial driving forces above has shown, each level has its particular strengths, and only if these strengths are wisely combined will they mutually support each other and develop more power together than each level alone. However, for example in the energy sector, part of this combination might factually consist of shifts of power from one level to another. The systemic changes necessary for a transition of socio-ecological systems will thus affect the architecture of current multilevel governance, and it is unlikely that the related shifts in responsibility and power will just occur without conflicts and resistance.

Notes

1 The following sections refer to cities and their development according to insights gained by field researchers. These cities are referenced in parentheses and refer to the observatory case studies in Garzillo and Ulrich (2015), which can be accessed online.
2 References to cities or countries in chapter 9 without further specification originate from Garzillo and Ulrich (2015).

Chapter 10

Mobilising the citizens for the socio-ecological transition

Susanne Elsen and Judith Schicklinski

It is the central assumption of this chapter that any strategy developed to enhance the socio-ecological transition is unlikely to yield strong results unless the resources of regional and local actors are mobilised and the complex interactions between central policy initiatives and their regional and local implementation are taken into account. Local actors operate in the political, economic, and civil society realm of society. Although innovation is not restricted to civil society actors, this chapter follows the thesis that a socio-ecological transition is not feasible without realising and incorporating civil society's innovative potential.

Thus, leading questions of this contribution are: What is the innovative potential of civil society for the socio-ecological transition? Who are the new local and regional actors, and how do they organise? How can a new interplay between connected realms, levels, and actors be enabled? What are the basic conditions for civil society action to evolve, and which obstacles exist? How can local knowledge for sustainability be produced cooperatively?

10.1 Social innovation and the significance of civil society actors for socio-ecological transitions

Socio-ecological problems are highly complex, uncertain, and shaped on a multilevel scale. They affect different actors and institutions, characterised by diverse kinds of knowledge, interests, and values. The fundamental aim of the socio-ecological transition is to arrive at sustainability. The complexity of the socio-ecological transition requires the concept of sustainability (cf. section 1.1) to be lived and thus transformed into habits and action (Susanne Elsen 2013). Sustainable development has to meet the needs of individuals and society while protecting the natural environment. A major concern is the equitable distribution of resources between present and future generations.

Stephen Viederman (1994) provides a comprehensive definition of sustainability as a participatory process, in which a community respects and makes prudent use of its resources – for example natural, human, human-created, social, cultural, and scientific ones. Accordingly, sustainability is perceived as the present generation's possibility of attaining a high level of economic security and of realising democracy while maintaining the resilience of the ecological system on which all life and all production depends.

These definitions bring out that living within the limits of the natural environment is a major precondition for achieving long-term sustainability. The equitable distribution of resources and opportunities within the same generation and between succeeding generations is a common characteristic of most definitions of sustainability. Since these concepts are constructed and interpreted by humans, sustainability entails multiple ways of knowing. Sustainable action strongly depends on actors' knowledge, attitudes, and competences, and on their options and restrictions within the respective context (Charles Redman 2014). Hence, a practical implementation "has to incorporate the inherent conflicts between the values, ambitions and goals of a multitude of stakeholders" (Derk Loorbach and Jan Rotmans 2006, 188).

As a result, approximating sustainability becomes a complex task. The considerations illustrate that transforming the concept of sustainability into socio-ecological action and creating a common basis for decision processes involving politics, civil society, and economy is only conceivable as a broad societal learning process. It depends on the placement of new actors, the design of new institutional arrangements, and the participatory management of knowledge and common resources. The societal innovation described here has some core characteristics: decentralisation, reflexive localisation, participation, self-organisation, and knowledge production for responsible citizenship and resilient communities. The relevance of local commons regimes and designing their management are core issues of socio-ecological development.

Participation as the main principle of social innovation (cf. section 1.1) is defined here as a process in which individuals, groups, and organisations take an active role in making decisions on questions affecting them (Enquete-Kommission "Zukunft des Bürgerschaftlichen Engagements" 2002; Mark S. Reed 2008; see also subsection 3.1.1). De facto, participatory development and civic self-organisation have increased since the turn of the millennium. This seems to be contradictory in light of complaints about declining participation in political elections. Colin Crouch developed the concept of 'post-democracy' to designate a society in which, despite democratic mechanisms like elections still in place, a more egalitarian society remains out of reach. This is because political processes are mainly determined by economic lobbyists, whereas the majority of citizens only assume a passive recipient position (Crouch 2004, viii, 4). While we agree with Crouch's analysis up to this point, we consider, in contrast to him, the so-called disenchantment with politics as nothing but a paradigm shift. The existing crisis of representative democracy expressing itself in decreasing participation levels in elections goes along with increasing and diverse forms of participation and self-organisation. This is a form of democracy that goes beyond the voting right. Citizens ask for more codetermination and for a different culture of political participation. Civic engagement is much more than volunteer work within predefined boundaries. It is a bottom-up reaction to the aforementioned tendencies and can thus be considered as political action.

Regarding citizens' motivation to participate and self-organise, different scholars have identified a whole range of them. Besides carving out altruistic motives of actors within humanitarian and social projects, they defined individual ones like the desire for meaningful activities and contentedness or the wish to get in contact with others. In our context, those actors, driven by the desire to solve both their own and common problems and to look for new arrangements and self-efficacy, are the change agents of a new equilibrium (Enquete-Kommission "Zukunft des Bürgerschaftlichen Engagements" 2002, 114). Civil society actors have entered the political and economic arenas. The grassroots level and project-based way of working, the orientation towards network structures, and the disposition towards civic self-organisation represent a new participatory culture affecting state and market. Civil society actors take over responsibility for questions regarding their life and the concerns of the community. For example, cooperative associations created in civil society try to find answers to unemployment, transgressing the boundaries of market and state. The interference of civil society actors in these systems inserts their rationalities as corrective, complementary, or alternative drafts. Good examples of citizens' actions causing social innovation in the governance of European cities are mainly drawn from chapter 5. This is due to the fact that citizens more easily participate and self-organise in the green spaces resource system than in water or energy, not to mention labour markets. For an explanation of this phenomenon cf. chapter 8.1.2. Nevertheless, citizens do not remain inactive in the other two resource systems, as for example the numerous citizens' initiatives against the privatisation of water utilities in Italy (cf. chapter 6) as well as the foundation of energy cooperatives in Germany (cf. chapter 4) show.

Right Livelihood Award laureate Nicanor Perlas has high hopes for civil society's cultural power on the local and global level: "Civil society, in its present form, is the most important social innovation of the 20th century. Its significance equals that of the establishment of nation states in the early 17th century, or the emergence of modern market economies in the 18th century" (Nicanor Perlas 2000, 19). He defines civil society as one dimension of the socio-cultural lifeworld, which represents specific roles, norms, practices, relationships, and competencies. According to him, norms and practices of civil society association, self-organisation, and organised communication are not restricted to individual spheres of society but take effect in political, social, and economic contexts. He regards the growing strength of civil society as a balancing third agency and speaks of a new redistribution of power between state, market, and civil society. The conception is not that of competing sectors but of an integrative cooperation between politics, economy, and civil society based on civic engagement that advocates the concerns of society and nature.

The shifting balance of power and the diversification of rationalities cause a process of democratisation in the sense of 'rule of people' in all societal sectors. A central aspect of this process can be seen in civil society's corrective and countervailing power (Archon Fung and Erik O. Wright 2003). The rationality is that of lifeworld concerns, and the coordination principles are association, interpersonal communication, cooperation, and the coordination of diversity. The hybrid structures of movements, initiatives, and associations within this realm emerge in multifaceted forms. Especially in the initial stage, these associations are highly informal and strongly focused on the common issue. Hybrid forms of organisations "pursue social and ecological as well as economic aims, operate in the economic system, yet are part of organised civil society" (Susanne Elsen 2007, 45). The hybridity of the structure enables flexible adaptations to different needs and options.

According to Jürgen Habermas (1981b; 1981a), the patterns of acting in a civil society context are strongly connected with internal processes of communication and understanding. In this context, his Theory of Communicative Action implies a reference to the sources of social innovation. The basic differences between the acting logics of the market and state systems in contrast to those of civil society carry the potential of new institutional arrangements and solutions. While market processes are governed by the rationalities of capital and competition and state processes by law and power, civil society actors, driven by common interest, coordinate their affairs by communication in a lifeworld context. It is not only these differences that cause social evolution. The communicative rationality and the reciprocal interaction between different reasons, processes of differentiation, or new combinations, for example in the development of socio-ecological economies, are drivers of social innovation. This is due to their function as "centers of concentrated communication" (Jürgen Habermas 1985b, 364) rooted in direct lifeworld concerns. The logic of these 'centers of concentrated communication' can "develop into autonomous public spheres" (Habermas 1985b) with the potential to draw attention to and to counter two important phenomena of modern times: the 'uncoupling' of system and lifeworld logics and the colonisation of lifeworld by the imperatives of systems (Stephen Kemmis 2001, 96).

Habermas and Ostrom overlap in at least two main points. Both emphasise the importance of communicative rationalities for negotiation and conflict management as well as the significance of socially embedded and interconnected institutions, and both are convinced that "forms of self-organization strengthen the collective capacity for action" (Habermas 1985b, 364–65). Ostrom (2009) showed that the aforementioned aspects build the basis for sustainable commons management. According to her, the overuse of common goods due to users' selfish behaviour can only be prevented if the evolvement of communication between their users is allowed and fostered. This is the precondition for social capital to be built up, leading to cooperation between users. Elinor Ostrom and Toh-Kyeong Ahn (2003, xiv) define social capital "as an attribute of individuals and of their relationship that enhances their ability to solve collective action problems", and they name three types of social capital with particular relevance to collective action: "(1) trustworthiness, (2) networks, and (3) formal and informal rules or institutions" (Ostrom and Ahn 2003, xiv). Social capital is created by interaction and negotiation processes between local actors. Two of Ostrom's design principles for a successful governance of the commons are the participation right of the users to jointly define working rules and the existence of local institutionalised arenas for conflict regulation (Ostrom 1990). To be able to do so "individuals need to invest in those working rules in the form of devising, revising, monitoring, and sanctioning" (Ostrom and Ahn 2003, xxiii). This continuous process is only conceivable in an 'autonomous public sphere' as conceptualised by Habermas.

Besides gaining political influence, civil society actors have also entered the economic sphere. New forms of economic self-organisation in order to secure livelihood and adequate supply on the local and regional level can be regarded as civic experiments to reclaim basic civil rights to social, political, and economic participation. The objectives span beyond the interests of particular groups, taking on a new political dimension. For example, civic economies generate social capital and improve resilience through cooperation and the joint management of commons. They follow an independent logic of economic action with social objectives. This counterbalances the dominance of profit and competition as the main control instruments for economic activities.

10.2 Self-organisation and the 'third sector'

Citizen participation and self-organisation are important drivers of social innovation, even though they also constitute a challenge for the actors themselves and for their respective counterparts. Self-organisation means any form of associative effort of civil society actors to organise common concerns. An important distinction between participation and self-organisation is the question of initiative-taking. In the case of participation it lies with public authorities, whereas in the case of self-organisation it rests with members of civil society (Boostra and Boelens 2011, 109), who not only define the aims but also the process to achieve them (cf. subsection 3.1.1).

Indeed, we need to draw on a differentiated definition of citizens' self-organisation when talking about social innovation and the formation of socio-ecological solutions, since Mafia organisations, radical vigilance committees, or organisations of fundamental bigots are also civil-society-driven forms of self-organisation. What we mean are approaches of democratic solutions and the realisation of basic rights of citizens beyond predefined goals and processes. This requires defining the common good or general interests as well as rights, freedoms, and responsibilities for social and ecological justice.

The associative realm of self-organised citizens' concerns is an important base of self-governance in different societal spheres. "Without sustaining a certain self-governing capacity, societal governance is an altogether impossible task (as the history of many totalitarian regimes has shown)" (Jan Kooiman and Maarten Bavinck 2013, 21). Associative self-organisation is an expression of a strong civil society and is to be seen as a pool of social innovation. It arises informally and spontaneously to answer concrete lifeworld needs. The rationality of this hybrid realm is not unequivocal but multifaceted, and that implies its transformative potential. Social innovation is the result of new combinations, of links between elements that have previously been separated, or of the replacement of single aspects of a unit. It is particularly caused by the participation of actors that previously were not involved. Civil society actors entering political, economic, or societal institutions have their own rationalities; challenge routines of politics, administration, and economy; and insert new perspectives into the sectors in which they act, sometimes provoking broader paradigm shifts. This comprehension is attributed to the Austrian economist Joseph Schumpeter (1911).

The so-called third sector gains high attention in connection with the question of societal transition and social innovation. It is defined by the delineation from the political and the economic system, even if third sector organisations act within political and economic fields. The basic difference lies in the specific context of formation following concrete citizens' needs and in a distinct rationality (Enquete-Kommission "Zukunft des Bürgerschaftlichen Engagements" 2002, 482–92). Furthermore, this realm is characterised by its specific coordination principles such as cooperation, mutuality, and solidarity. However, these civil-society-based associative constructs are open to the systems of market and state and frequently act like incubators, transforming informal into formal solutions or formal into community-based ones.

Particularly in the initial phase, associations are highly informal and not organised as legal units. Most of the self-organised initiatives in urban agriculture, as discussed further below, are informal and spontaneous citizens' initiatives, at least in their initial phase. The stable management of resources, however, requires the formation of a suitable organisational structure. If for example an urban food initiative tries to develop distributional systems, it will move to a food cooperative and enter the formal economic sector with a distinct, not primarily profit-orientated, rationality. The negative definition, which is characterised by the fact that profit is not the main aim of these economies, is that of a nonprofit organisation (NPO). The positive definition as social and solidarity economy is based on the aim and on the specific coordination principles. As equivalent, civil-society-based third sector organisations, acting in realms that concern public or common interests, are negatively defined as nongovernmental organisations (NGOs) in order to distinguish them from political or general administrative structures. Twenty years ago, Jeremy Rifkin described the reasons for the rapid global growth of the 'third' sector. The withdrawal of the state-run as well as the economic sector from local communities and their concerns leaves a crucial vacuum (Jeremy Rifkin 1995, 275–93). This vacuum is filled by civil society actors taking over responsibility for social, cultural, and ecological matters and for the rebuilding of community.

In his notable analysis of the 'third' sector's societal function, Wolfgang Seibel describes its role in a historical perspective as steering reserve for societal change. The formation of free associations was an important move towards the political emancipation of the bourgeoisie and the working class. The new discussion, following Seibel, is dominated by the reasoning that 'third' sector organisations compensate for failures of market and state (Wolfgang Seibel 1994, 40–50). According to Hazel Henderson, up to 65 per cent of productive work worldwide is achieved within the 'third' sector (Hazel Henderson 1997, 364). The 'third' sector contains a variety of formal and informal organisational structures. Besides clubs, foundations, and mutual societies, it includes cooperatives able to manage commons in a sustainable way. Innovation opportunities arise within the broader context of the 'third' sector and are embedded in civil society. The 'third' sector has the capacity to bring up new options for people and communities as well as to be a step in the direction of sustainability. For example, a neighbourhood initiative to redesign the space around its housing area can become the driver of social and ecological innovation in the quarter. The processes can be characterised by the extended rationality of action and of actors' motivation and by the effect that civic engagement has on people's lives as well as on common concerns.

This can be called the potential of 'as-well-as' in contrast to the 'either-or' logic that coins the systems of market and state. Civil-society-based associations have social, ecological, and economic objectives. They act within the economic sector, are embedded in civil society, and challenge ecological, social, or labour market issues. Hence, they penetrate the systems of market and state and effectuate integration as an alternative draft to externalisation and dysfunctional differentiation. Sliding transitions from the informal to the formal sector are possible, and the mixture of multiple activities and roles is innovating by the pluralisation of perspectives. The democratic and nonhierarchic structures up to the cooperative principle of 'one person, one vote' require and enable a broader perspective of participants in a learning context for active citizenship.

The capability of individuals and groups to self-organise and to represent their own and common concerns depends on personal, social, economic, and political preconditions. This capability is the core competence of active citizenship. However, it follows the social mechanism of silent selectivity, varying along the demarcation line of social inequality (Elsen 2007). The theory of social capital developed by Pierre Bourdieu (1985) is helpful to understand the intrinsic and sociocultural depth effects of a lack of cultural and social capital. Having such capital is a precondition for individuals' active and self-confident participation in all societal sectors. Therefore, having it makes the emergence of participation and self-organisation more probable. However, all civil society actors, also those who are not adept at articulating their needs and opinions in public, must have adequate options to participate. Involving citizens in societal steering and problem-solving does not only promote efficiency and effectiveness and does not only enhance the results but also effects empowerment and social change (Chandra K. Pradeep and Terry L. Cooper 2005). Consequently, new forms of direct democracy and public participation as well as opportunities for social learning need to be provided to foster civic self-organisation, especially of disadvantaged groups. If we want these groups to participate in democratic processes, it is important to create spaces for social innovation characterised by openness and an enabling political culture. The activation and facilitation of civic engagement can be supported by intermediaries, operating as facilitators and change agents.

10.3 Reflexive localisation, democratisation, and polycentric governance

One of the implications of globalisation is the increasing importance of communities and the endeavour to decentralise and regionalise. The traditional concept of subsidiarity, which encompasses the priority of smaller and true-to-life units against more general and larger ones, has been renewed in communitarian concepts against the background of globalisation. Against the abstractness, impersonality, and unswayable realities of modern societies, the rediscovery of community is linked with the desire for identity, self-efficacy, and participation (Ulrich Beck 2000). This phenomenon can also be explained by the above-described shift in the balance of power between politics, economy, and civil society.

Societal challenges of socio-ecological transition are interconnected, cutting across different levels, sectors, and areas of society. Therefore, the transition process has to undergo multiple changes. How can the institutional settings of multilevel European governance be improved to achieve a maximum of coherence between regional, national, and EU policies, and what does this imply for the role of regional EU policies in successfully advancing the socio-ecological transition? The answers to this complexity are systemic, synergetic, and integrative approaches transgressing different sectors and areas in comprehensive and participatory ways and involving relevant actors. Following Ostrom (2009), for polycentric governance to succeed, social capital is essential. Regarding citizens as pivotal actors and involving them accordingly as well as establishing networks between actors across different levels, sectors, and areas of society seems to be the prerequisite for social capital to evolve. The importance of multilevel governance was strongly underlined by the European Parliament and the Committee of the Regions in the 'Cities of Tomorrow' report (European Commission 2011b, 93). According to its conclusions, European, national, regional, and local policies need to operate in a multiscalar governance framework (see chapter 9).

Thus, confronting socio-ecological challenges requires adequate preparation of enabling and responsible units. The national level alone does not seem to be suitable either for ensuring participatory democracy and quality of life on the local level or for guaranteeing the political frame to face global challenges. Regionalisation, localisation, and new subsidiarity are guidelines for sustainable development. They enable integrative approaches, an efficient use of resources, and local–regional value-added circuits (Elsen 2007, 153). The setting-up of regional units in diversity (Paul Raskin et al. 2002) across the European Union promises to be the right way. It offers a great coherence between local, regional, national, and EU policies, with which cities and communities can develop integrative solutions based on democracy and the participation of relevant actors in the political and administrative, economic, and civil society sectors. The involvement of different stakeholders, their capacity and creativity, and their different perspectives and common interests can lead to new forms of communication and decision-finding at all levels and in and across sectors. It can create new institutional arrangements, capable of answering specific local questions in a sustainable way.

Examples of actors generating such a change while again being changed by it are found across the cities that were investigated. In Lugano citizens fight to safeguard remaining undeveloped mountains around the city from construction. An institutionalised hearing process was realised and allows participation in the planning procedure. This consists of informative meetings with all stakeholders involved and is led by an external facilitator (cf. subsection 5.2.2). In Copenhagen, high pressure from nongovernmental organisations on local authorities led to the official involvement of civil society actors in local politics, for example in committees. In these cases, actors have provoked institutional changes by entering the action area. They now interact with other actors already present in the arena according to newly created or renegotiated rules which retroact and alter in turn their initial behaviour.

Localisation and the global protection of localities do not tend to reimplement protectionism but does tend to foster local resilience and a greater independence from global economic and cultural processes. Their aim is to create a safe base for local development to meet the needs of local people (Bernd Hamm et al. 1996, 359). According to E.M. DuPuis and David Goodman (2005), we refer to the concept of reflexive localisation focusing on social inclusion, economic innovation, the common good, and the valuation of entrepreneurship and diversity. Local participation does more than create self-confident citizens and share out political power. It also contributes to a culture of democracy throughout society (Stuart Weir and David Beetham 1999). It seems to be impossible to discuss localised democracy without referring to the concept of local autonomy. Since Alexis de Tocqueville (1835), the idea of local self-government has been a central component of a broader concept of participatory democracy. The European Charter of Local Self-Government considers local freedom from central government interference as a fundamental aspect of local democracy. Decision-making for public policies should be conducted by those authorities that are closest to the citizens (Council of Europe 1985, article 4.3). This communal idea is not new. It was the basis of the Greek polis and other city-states all over the world (Györy Széll 2013).

Local autonomy must go hand in hand with the application of the principle of connexity. If tasks are handed down to the local level without providing the financial resources to fulfil them, local authorities see themselves forced to further reduce public spending to a minimum. Then, they often do not shrink back from more drastic options like selling off public land to private (foreign) investors, so that even basic public services such as the maintenance of public green spaces cannot be sustained any more. This aggravates the already severe situation of local public budgets, especially in countries such as Greece and Italy, where the room for manoeuvre for local authorities was already radically curtailed by drastic demands for budget cuts due to postcrisis austerity policies (cf. chapter 5).

Several empirical examples show that a high degree of local autonomy is generally conducive to the involvement of citizens and to the advancement of the socio-ecological transition, provided that it goes along with a shift of financial resources from higher government levels to the local one. For example, Danish local authorities are amongst those with the highest degree of local autonomy. Operating in a clearly set legal framework, they are granted a wide scope of autonomous management with a concomitant high degree of responsibility and human and financial resources to try out innovative options.

John Dewey (1927, 142) argued that citizen participation on the level of local communities is possible and constitutes the base of a strong democracy: "Without communication the public will remain shadowy and formless." Following Dewey, communication in local community can also create a greater community. However, new localism and a high degree of local autonomy are only necessary but not sufficient conditions for local democracy, which also has to be seen in a broader democratic frame. Lawrence Pratchett (2004) underlines the difference between local autonomy and local democracy and between 'freedom from' and 'freedom for'. Local autonomy can first be defined as freedom from higher authorities and second as freedom for innovative solutions such as socio-ecological priorities. This distinction is useful "because its use draws parallels with the autonomy of the individual. Autonomy is about liberty, whether of the individual person or the individual organization. In contrast, democracy is a collective process through which conflicts and differences are articulated and resolved" (Pratchett 2004, 372). He also points out that subcentral or local democracy is a cornerstone of a broader participatory democracy. "It is at the local level that the relationship between representative democracy and widespread citizen participation makes most sense" (Pratchett 2004, 361). This calls for a communalisation process with a shifting of competences and resources to the local level in order to achieve, along with civic engagement that can most easily unfold on this level, an influential and sustainable change (Roland Roth 2000, 350).

Already in 1970, the Italian region of Emilia Romagna developed within its programme for regional autonomy an elaborated model of decentralised governance of local units based on neighbourhood councils and meetings through which citizens could express their common needs directly (Max Jäggi, Roger Müller, and Sil Schmid 1977). This model is remarkable, because neighbourhood councils facilitate bottom-up structures within the governmental framework. Experiments to realise models of a local and participatory state are nowadays being conducted in numerous cities in the world, following the pioneer city of Porto Alegre (Carsten Herzberg 2009). Citizens take over responsibility for the planning and management of green spaces, public mobility, cultural and social institutions, and so forth, based on a citizens' budget and following transparent rules of target definition and decision-making. Sustainability strategies as expressed in the Agenda 21 document or the Aalborg Charter are based on these integrative local approaches, involving citizens and relevant actors and fostering bottom-up solutions (UN 1992; Aalborg Charter 1994).

The qualitative data of our research shows that in all regions individuals coming from all sectors are highly influential and can become key change agents. They often have a known reputation, for example a dedicated mayor driving forward sustainability issues (Sibiu, a2, 69). Highly driven individuals working as civil servants in the Environment Department can be decisive (Gothenburg, a4, 46). The same applies for well-informed leading figures from civil society that are good networkers launching innovative ideas, for example in the field of urban food production (Leeds, a4, 31). In addition, the position of the city's semi-public companies on sustainability issues influences the city's orientation towards sustainability (Copenhagen, a2, 57–58; Saarbrücken, a4, 33).

The local level seems to be a narrow frame for transition activities. However, it enables widespread, synergetic, and participatory solutions and can be a laboratory for politics of possibilities from below. Indeed, these bottom-up policies and top-down structures have to be interlinked as enabling and supporting conditions. Local democracy also provides the base for strong national and regional democratic institutions. A subcentral and polycentric governance plays a key role in providing a political frame for socio-ecological innovation and for a more sustainable lifestyle (W. Neil Adger and Andrew Jordan 2009).

Strengthening the local level has to be realised within a model of political steerage and redistribution on different levels – from local to global. In a world in which risks are globalised, socio-ecological responsibilities cannot be delegated to the national, regional, or local level alone. Yet decentralised and democratic organisations and decision-making processes as well as new institutional arrangements at the local level are the base of socio-ecological development. A conscious policy would allow and facilitate the influence of civil society to unfold. In this sense, political actors can even become transition drivers, interacting with other actors from a proactive administration, economy, and civil society (Aalborg, a4, 43).

10.4 Interactive community governance

Following the central thesis of a new balance of power between politics, economy, and civil society, the governance of local units is based on the combined efforts of actors from these three realms. This brings up the question of governing roles and cross-sectoral interaction. We share a special interest in civil society's contribution to governance and agenda-setting processes and assume that it accounts for inserting societal concerns and effecting social innovation. Parts of sections 10.4 and 10.5 have been taken from Judith Schicklinski (2015, 39–63).

Regarding new models of steering the particularity and at the same time interconnected complexity of local units, there are different approaches of community governance that aim at closeness to citizens, their actions, and their concerns. Gerry Stocker (2004, 24) developed the networked community governance model "to facilitate the achievement of community objectives. Its role is to lead the debate, develop shared visions and help to ensure that appropriate resources – both public and private – are found and blended together to achieve common objectives." This is a new understanding of the interplay of elected representatives and other actors in the community. Networked governance has "to provide the basis for learning, to drive the search for collective solutions to complex and shared problems" (Stocker 2004, 26).

Incipient stages of networked governance are found in several cities in the field of green spaces, where, often out of financial needs, local authorities opt for assigning the management of public green spaces to associations as well as to private companies. This adoption scheme does not work perfectly yet but is one example of the collaboration of local actors across sector boundaries to find, via a joint learning process, innovative solutions to local shared problems (for example Milan, Madrid, Naples, Rome, Thessaloniki; cf. chapter 5).

In Leeds, there is a high degree of cross-sector cooperation around the topic of urban food production. Numerous activities are going on in cooperation with local authorities, schools, the university, and civil society and economic actors. This is partly thanks to well-informed leading figures from civil society who are good networkers implementing innovative ideas. For example, initiatives were started after an activist had contacted the councillor, who then realised that interacting actors from different realms can bring benefits to the city. Now, all actors are connected in a very vivid, loose local network. There is lively communication, and via the foundation of an autonomous committee, contact to the council is institutionalised (Judith Schicklinski 2015, 40).

Interesting coalitions have been formed in Istanbul, a city suffering greatly from persisting economic growth logic. Here, local nongovernmental organisations collaborate with local district politicians to fight against construction plans on public green spaces, mobilising numerous residents. Actions range from demonstrations to legal proceedings (cf. chapter 5).

If collaboration between government representatives and the governed is initiated by the local government, it is also known as interactive policymaking, opening options of democratic participation 'from above' mostly within the limits defined by the elected local government but also within dynamics of opening this predetermined frame under the influence of other stakeholders in response to public needs. Interactive governance "emphasizes solving societal problems and creating opportunities through interaction between civil, public and private persons and organizations" (Kooiman and Bavinck 2013, 9). Governance following this model is based on communication and negotiation between actors, representing different values, aims, and rationalities. It is a process of social innovation by cooperative learning. Where basic approaches of interactive governance are visible, political and administrative actors can even become transition drivers, then interacting with other actors from a proactive administration, economy, and civil society. Urban innovation can be launched by bottom-up actors, yet can also be initiated by political actors in power. The initiation of networks by political or administrative actors can stabilise the collaboration between heterogeneous local stakeholders and make the emergence of social innovative projects more probable (cf. chapter 4).

The mayor of Sibiu is described as dedicated to driving forward sustainability issues. In Jihlava, the mayor has composed a heterogeneous team consisting of local policy experts but also of nonlocal ones experienced with neither local policymaking nor with local social structures and not even dependent on re-election.

Examples of urban innovation initiated from within the local administration come from Copenhagen and Saarbrücken. In Copenhagen, there is a palpable feeling of entrepreneurship in the municipality. Civil servants are very motivated and even passionate about their work, and they are given resources and the allowance and space to realise their innovative ideas: "It is easier to be an employee in the City of Copenhagen than in other municipalities in the world... [it] is less bureaucratic... there are better options for 'entrepreneurship' in the municipality... some really good innovative people... who are really passionate about what they do – and they are allowed to do so" (Copenhagen, a3, 52). In Saarbrücken, the creativity of the head of the green spaces' department makes it possible to continuously promote sustainability aspects in green spaces management even with fewer resources. An active civil society can support such innovations emerging in the state sector by collaborating with them, and options for this need to be provided 'from the top', as for example in Aalborg, where individuals and association representatives are involved in different councils. In Larissa, a municipal vegetable garden was founded by local authorities, giving citizens with no or an insufficient income the option to cultivate food for self-consumption. The garden has met so much demand that it has already been enlarged (cf. section 5.3). In Thessaloniki and Naples, citizens monitor the local budget, increasing transparency and trust. In Germany, the nature conservation associations have long been actively involved in landscape planning and the designation of conservation areas, cooperating with and providing expert knowledge to local authorities from the local and regional level.

The Theory of Communicative Action (Habermas 1981b, 1981a), referring to the sources of social innovation, is getting concrete in these models of interactive governance. The communicative rationality and the reciprocal interaction between different actors cause new combinations and solutions. Societal structure refers to different actors within their respective frameworks, and it points to the specific natural, geographic, economic, and cultural conditions on site as well as to those of higher-level systems. Social ecology points out that actors continuously generate changes within these social-ecological frames while continuously being changed by them (Peter L. Berger and Thomas Luckmann

1967). This explains the dynamic process of permanent societal changes affecting actors and their frameworks as well as actors' influence on the frames.

This reciprocal interaction process can be noticed in cities in which the sustainability topic has been brought up by citizens' movements, and then was taken up by politicians. High pressure from nongovernmental organisations on local authorities can lead to the official involvement of civil society actors into local politics, for example in committees. Collaboration with nongovernmental organisations can then have a spillover effect to also involving individual citizens, for example via local councils (Copenhagen, a2, 54–55).

In the complex and diverse context of different actors from diverse realms operating within interactive government processes, uncertainties and unforeseeable effects emerge, which need to be recognised as an enormous challenge. The model of interactive governance is a project for a learning society and needs flexible forms of governing, procedural paths, the clarification of roles and responsibilities, and first of all a facilitating political culture. It has to take into account the societal structures of inequality and has to invest in the capacities of the silent majority.

Creating such a facilitating political culture has been tried in Freiburg with the foundation of a sustainability council in 2006, which is composed of lay experts from the local Agenda 21 movement, de facto experts for specific topics, administrative experts from the local government for certain specialist subjects, and members of the city council. This council for example elaborated in a participatory process the local sustainability goals.

Examples of investing in the capacities of the silent majority come from Saarbrücken, where the community work offices are very active and supported by the local government. The community association 'People for Malstadt' promotes citizens' initiatives in cooperation with the district's community work office and runs another project in cooperation with the department of green spaces to commonly improve existing open green spaces. In another district, the community work office is supported by a nongovernmental organisation and subsidised amongst others by the city, enabling it to run several projects in the field of community work, sustainability, and community enterprises.

10.5 Civic economies: new alternative urban spaces

Since the 1980s the so-called social and solidarity economy has been rapidly growing. It originates in civil society, transgressing the boundaries of the state and the market. The field includes formal organisations like cooperatives, social enterprises, mutual societies, associations, and foundations but also informal ones like exchange networks of complementary currencies, initiatives of urban agriculture, time banks, or community-supported agriculture (Elsen 2007). The concept is not a standardised position in economic sciences. Its occurrence is both normative and a phenomenon that has emerged in a variety of ways in the past and is appearing in various shapes and forms across the globe.

There are different conclusions one can draw from the emergence of socio-economic activities and networks: Not least, they are a sign of two phenomena. First, they signal the transfer of participatory democracy to the economic sector. Second, they show the consequences responsible citizens are drawing from having realised the following: The dependencies and weaknesses of politics and the irresponsibility of the economic system require a line to be drawn and complementary alternative economic structures to be provided.

Social and solidarity economies are characterised by voluntariness, cooperation, democratic organisation, association, self-organisation, and a focus on the common good as their principles of action. In the international discourse, they are related to the 'third' sector. Their potential lies, as described above, in an extended logic of action following specific needs and in the effect that citizens' engagement has on people's lives as well as on common concerns. Social and solidarity economies can be better understood if placed in the wider conceptual framework of 'diverse economy', coined by Gibson-Graham (1996). In the international discourse, this framework is able to attract public attention, since it offers alternatives and complementary structures to current economic practice, which is increasingly subject to crises. Regardless of diverse forms and contexts from which they have emerged, they show distinct similarities, and the attempts to conceptualise them make clear that they constitute a civil-society-based complementary structure to meet the needs of communities.

The normative premises of social and solidarity economy are, at the same time, some kind of strategic behaviour. The following criteria are common to social and solidarity economy movements around the world:

1 Democratic organisational culture (one person, one vote)
2 Inclusive ownership
3 Drivers are specific needs (not primarily focused on profit)
4 Democratically decided profit appropriation (for commonly defined purposes)
5 Social integration

These organisational principles set out by the international movement for cooperatives 150 years ago are the basis for an instinctual economic culture. The concept is also based on an extended interpretation of labour, incorporating a broader perspective on meaningful work, which covers neighbourhood work, family work, barter, subsistence economies, work in cooperatives, gainful employment, and forms of civic engagement.

The hybridity of organisational forms and the plurality of action and rationalities characterise this alternative space. Social and solidarity economies pursue social and ecological as well as economic goals. They act economically but are actually part of organised civil society. Well-established delimitations between private and public, political and social, or cultural and economic are challenged by these forms of appropriation and intervention.

Apart from informal economic activities that arise from adversity, it is important to pay attention to those that emerge as a reflected alternative to social distortion or as a responsible step towards sustainability. They are characterised by their actors' motivation and build an experimental ground for a new kind of local economy. They are part of the alliance of "growth critics' dissidence", described by Jürgen Habermas (1985a, 156), that aims to strengthen the vital foundations of lifeworlds against administrative powers and money through forms of self-organisation at the grassroots level.

As mentioned above, movements for the appropriation and the self-determined use of urban spaces and for reactivating subsistence options in cities are emerging. The trend towards urban agriculture and community gardening for social, cultural, local economic, and ecological purposes can be seen in almost all regions of the world, and even in Europe, urban food production is not only a field of collective self-realisation but also an answer to new poverty. In some European cities, food security is becoming an issue again. Empirical examples show that especially after the multiple crises from 2008 onwards and subsequent austerity policies being enforced in several European countries, urban food production has again in some places, mostly in Southern Europe, become a means to mitigate private and public poverty.

In Milan, the local administration continues to follow the idea of giving allotments to families with lower incomes (Milan, a3, 47). In Thessaloniki, the local government plans to increase the number of allotments, which do not have a strong tradition in Greece (Thessaloniki, a3, 79). In Larissa, the local administration initiated a municipal vegetable garden in 2011, which gives citizens with a low or no income the possibility to grow food for self-consumption. The demand is high, and the garden has already been expanded.

Particularly in the field of urban food production or repair and reuse initiatives, innovative ideas have evolved that could be developed further as social and solidarity economy options providing complementary and alternative economic spaces to meet local needs as well as being steps to sustainable communities. These niches and their actors start to gain influence on land use, urban planning, or the prevention of speculation.

Across European cities, urban commons are increasingly used for food production, which is a self-organised activity in most cases. For example, in Copenhagen, the 'Copenhagen Food Community' initiative is only one out of many in the city (Copenhagen, a4, 39). In Potsdam, a nonprofit association, undertaking many different sustainability projects, is a major player in the city in the network of community gardens. There is also a trend of young people renting an allotment together, thus blurring the boundary between private and community food production. Indeed, allotment gardens have been experiencing an increased interest since the end of the last millennium. For example, in Dortmund, there are more than 120 allotment associations (Dortmund, a4, 42). In Milan, the owner of an inner-city plot started a pilot project renting 60 allotments to families. There are more than 350 families on the waiting list, and this is without ever placing an advertisement (Milan, a3, 58–59). He is trying to obtain land from the city to be administered in the form of a cooperative in order to enlarge the existing allotments. Then everyone interested in producing food could become a cooperative member by buying a share, and he hopes that the city will acknowledge this management of green space in the city development plan as well. By letting a cooperative manage a piece of inner-city agricultural land, its abandonment will be prevented, and thus it will also be withdrawn from financial building speculation interests, thus countering land speculation and prevailing profit orientation in land use policy.

The theory of social and solidarity economy as an answer to state and market failure is becoming concrete in some of these empirical examples. The solutions, created under circumstances of need or crisis, open up future prospects for sustainable urban spaces and ideas for a complementary local social policy based on productive options. The assignments of public spaces to citizens as well as the appropriation of productive spaces by citizens also seem to be reactions to the rising problems of public and private poverty within European cities. Indeed, the positive ecological effects also seem to have been recognised.

Community food production often makes use of fallow land. In Strasbourg, inhabitants started to plant tomatoes on a public green space (Strasbourg, a4, 88–90), and in Aalborg, a project to make use of fallow public land was successfully started, with one of the developed initiatives being urban gardening (Aalborg, a4, 61). In Madrid, the urban gardens' network was created as a citizens' initiative without support from the city council (Madrid, a3, 58–59), transforming for example parts of the *Casa de Campo*, a big park in the heart of the city into an urban garden (Madrid, a4, 45). Most neighbourhood associations operate on appropriated abandoned public space, which was foreseen for building development, in order to do urban gardening (Madrid, a3, 59). In Milan, an association has reclaimed an abandoned park, which led to the uncovering of illegal activities taking place there. They have converted parts of the park for allotments and farming (Milan, a4, 52).

In Thessaloniki, due to lack of action on the part of public authorities and the municipality's insufficient management of green spaces, there have been several actions to use public space for food production: "Therefore, on the one hand we observe the poor management of the municipality and on the other the beautiful, self-organised initiatives of the civil society" (Thessaloniki, a3, 85). Strong initiatives have emerged. The first and biggest citizens' urban agriculture initiative is called 'Periastikes Kalliergies' (PER.KA, peri-urban agriculture), operating on a former military camp. It was formed after the concession of the spaces from the district municipalities to these self-organised citizen groups, in order for them to cultivate vegetables and fruits for self-consumption. Meanwhile, the initiative has yielded numerous similar subinitiatives in other parts of the city, always on abandoned military camps (Thessaloniki, a3, 45–46). Particularly the first PER.KA has a "unique development in terms of citizen participation" (Thessaloniki, a3, 45–46).

In the same city, even dumping sites were used to start urban gardening. In two dumping sites, a citizens' initiative was started by a large group of urban farmers, starting to cultivate fruits and vegetables, cleaning, embellishing, and making the spaces available for food production designated for self-production (Thessaloniki, a3, 78, 85). This happened because the ongoing transformation of the former military camp into a composting site undertaken by city employees was suddenly stopped due to the economic crisis and consequent budget problems. The staff was dismissed, and the place turned into an illegal dumping ground (Thessaloniki, a3, 84–85). Here, citizens reacted to the city's difficulty in providing sufficient management of public green spaces by self-organising.

In Strasbourg, the movement 'Incroyables Comestibles' tries to raise awareness about inner-city food production by bringing back fruit trees as well as agriculture into the city and to reintroduce native species (Strasbourg, a4, 82–86). In Potsdam, the intercultural garden founded by an NGO has created an orchard, which is open to everyone (Potsdam, a4, 173). In Saarbrücken the "Saarbrücken – Edible City" movement was founded by some individuals who started to grow vegetables on public ground without official permission by local authorities. It was supported by a local NGO – for example via lecture events – and subsequently also by the city. Meanwhile growing continues on a second spot, this time private space, with the owner's permission – the church. The movement is judged by a respondent as a successful example of self-organisation, although it has to be seen whether it is more than a temporary trend (Schicklinski 2015, 39–41).

10.6 Obstacles to and basic conditions for citizen participation and self-organisation

A shifting balance of power and the requested significance of civil society for controlling, correcting, and complementing politics and the economic system from below or for generating social innovation requires several processes of change. These are processes of learning for active citizenship, empowering people, and enabling particularly disadvantaged groups, as well as accepting social innovation beyond rhetorical declarations. A fundamental shift is needed to overcome the obvious knowledge–behaviour gap to open up arenas where unconventional bottom-up initiatives and top-down approaches can meet to approve and enable societal innovations. In particular, the political and administrative systems are challenged to come to a new culture of interplay with civil society actors to demonstrate that they consider civic engagement to be "more than a political residual" (Roth 2000, 350). Roth criticises that instead of drawing on the diverse forms of civic engagement that are evolving because citizens are increasingly aware of their competence, "political democracy is still enclosed representatively and colonised by the political parties" (Roth 2000, 350).

Some of the following obstacles and basic conditions were already identified in a remarkable European study about local development and employment initiatives (European Commission 1995, 23–24). After more than 20 years of efforts to foster locally embedded 'bottom-up' strategies, these obstacles are as effective as before. Furthermore, on the one hand, advanced public poverty and the pressure for cutbacks and the privatisation of public services and commons tend to impede citizens' action for public interests. On the other hand, our case studies show that some cities, as a consequence of increasing public and private poverty, delegate for example the responsibility for the maintenance of public green spaces to local citizens (cf. chapter 5).

Nevertheless, citizen participation and self-organisation are more than an emergency solution. They require a fundamental change in local politics and administration:

1. Public administration commonly follows a sector-specific rationality, not considering the holistic, broad, and integrative view of civil society actors driven by concrete local problems and interests. Their objectives always have a sector-overlapping character.
2. Public funding rarely provides long-term support for integrative and holistic local development projects but follows the sector-specific logic and a short-term perspective.
3. Financial support and facilitating intermediary actors are necessary to initiate processes of development and change, especially in disadvantaged areas, to produce learning processes of all actors and sustainable effects.
4. Election periods and the dependency on the economic system create specific dynamics for political actors. They tend to avoid unpopular topics such as socio-ecological priorities, rules, and restrictions and to align their action with the interests of powerful actors from the economic sphere.
5. After more than 30 years of efforts to decentralise and open administration and politics for citizen participation and self-organisation, the holistic view of civil society actors and their 'horizontal-type methods' still tend to be regarded as disturbing the apparent routines and implicitness of administrative and political processes and actors.
6. Continuous learning processes of all actors are the most important basic condition for successful citizen participation. Public authorities not only have to recognise that citizen participation and citizens' self-organisation are the constituent part of democracy, but they also have to ensure that it leads to better and sustainable results in all planning and development processes.
7. Not only persons but also legal systems often appear to militate against new, creative, and unconventional citizens' activities. Yet these activities require a political culture of enabling and facilitating legal, administrative, and political frameworks that are keen to experiment and to produce supportive regulations.

10.7 Cooperative knowledge production for active citizenship and social innovation

Coping with the challenges of growth up- and downturns and generating sustainable solutions depend on the creative potential and the willingness of citizens and decision-makers. The challenges require a methodology suited to mobilising, initiating, attending, and coshaping processes of social, political, and economic development and transformation. "Reflexivity arises because meanings have to be constructed and attributed to social actions" (Helga Nowotny, Peter Scott, and Michael Gibbons 2001, 44).

The local development approaches of community education, community organising, and community development include a broad variety of activating methods and instruments (Susanne Elsen 1998; Elsen 2007). They are the globally most widespread strategies of participatory innovation and planned change on the local level in cooperation with concerned people (Herbert J. Rubin and Irene Rubin 2008). As the example of Saarbrücken shows (cf. section 10.6), community workers activate and facilitate community-based social-ecological transition, involving citizens, especially socially disadvantaged people, and other relevant actors. As many examples show, this is the basis of a planned change towards sustainable communities.

The empirical data reveals that universities and other research institutes are increasingly drawn on for their expertise by decision-makers in the sustainability discourse (cf. chapter 4). However, very few examples could be found that equally involve citizens' 'lay' expert knowledge and connect it to the 'official' one. This constitutes a forfeited opportunity since innovative and realistic solutions to local problems cannot emerge without taking into consideration the knowledge of the persons concerned. Therefore, local knowledge production systems have to develop self-organising capacities in order to link up with other sites of local systems, for example with universities. If this does not happen, knowledge cannot be stabilised (Nowotny, Scott, and Gibbons 2001, 48). Combining activating community approaches with those of action research, especially in the context of urban and rural planning and in international development cooperation, is not new (Elsen 1998). Yet, in the light of socio-ecological transition, these approaches gain new significance. Hence, the rediscovery of democratic and participatory action research, frequently based in community settings, is not surprising. Especially approaches that underline the significance of cooperative knowledge production with local people, based on an egalitarian relationship between scientific and nonscientific actors, also have to be regarded as the democratisation of the scientific sector. Civil society actors also bring about change in this realm.

Critical action research's inherent aim is "to see what kind of collaborative social action might be necessary to transform things for the better" (Kemmis 2001, 93). Action research is defined by its design consisting of three recurring stages: inquiry, action, and reflection (Kurt Lewin 1947). Through multiple cycles of these stages, improvements in knowledge and understanding of those involved in the inquiry lead to social action. Reflection on action leads to new understanding and to the opening up of new areas of inquiry (Uwe Schneidewind 2013). The transition cycle is based on four consecutive steps of inquiry: 1. problem assessment, 2. vision development, 3. experiments, 4. learning and upscaling (Loorbach and Rotmans 2006). It is aimed at system knowledge, future knowledge, and transformation knowledge.

Research for sustainability implies the alteration of at least two of these forms (system and future knowledge) that methodologically have to be considered and reflected, whereas practice for sustainability in particular has to be confronted with transformative knowledge. These steps cut across the typical phases of the community-development approach that indeed takes also the next step of participatory implementation. Preconditions for and the basis of this kind of community-based action research and development are the deep understanding of the specific lifeworlds of the concerned people (Susanne Elsen 2014, 260).

10.8 Conclusion

The complexity and uncertainty of socio-ecological problems can only be dealt with in a broad societal participatory learning process. In this process, civil society has increasingly been recognised as a creative, steering, and corrective power in society and in the economic, political, and scientific systems. It is also a discrete societal actor, following the needs of the lifeworld. The main thesis of this chapter, following Habermas and other scholars, is that of a new power balance between economy, politics, and civil society. Shifting balances become visible within processes of social innovation and democratisation and approaches to socio-ecological development especially on the local level.

This chapter dealt with the question of how already existing processes of socio-ecological transition can enter political decision-making and direct the latter into reinforcing the transition and how citizens' will formation and presence can be core drivers of problem-solving and social innovation. Civil society actors take over responsibility for social, cultural, and ecological matters and for the rebuilding of community. Both Habermas and Ostrom emphasise the importance of communicative rationalities for negotiation and conflict management as well as the significance of socially embedded and interconnected institutions, and both acknowledge the transformative potential of associative self-organisations. The rise of the social and solidarity economy signals the transfer of participatory democracy to the economic sector and provides complementary alternative economic structures. These economies pursue social, ecological, and economic goals. They generate social capital by acting economically while still being part of organised civil society.

The second focus was on opening opportunities to citizens' self-organisation in urban development and local economy. The capability of individuals and groups to self-organise and to represent their own and common concerns depends on personal, social, economic, and political preconditions. New forms of direct democracy and public participation as well as opportunities for social learning need to be provided to foster civic self-organisation, especially of disadvantaged groups. In particular, the local level enables widespread, synergetic, and participatory solutions and can be a laboratory for politics of possibilities from below. As our research has shown, cities most advanced in the transition draw on the potential of civil society actors by opening up two-way information channels and by providing concrete options for citizens to participate in local governance processes as well as spaces and support for self-organisation. With such a cross-sectoral interactive networked governance style, the possibility of incorporating all actors' knowledge for jointly advancing the sustainability cause in a process of constant, not conflict-free, negotiation of interests is highest.

Chapter 11

Cities as places of a new, shared prosperity

Thomas Sauer, Susanne Elsen and Cristina Garzillo[1]

11.1 Laboratories for new ways of producing, distributing, and consuming goods

The inquiry into 40 European cities explored possible seeds for new ways of producing, distributing, and consuming goods in the urban context, which respect the boundaries of the planetary ecosystems and the human striving for well-being at the same time. It was motivated by the assumption that the simultaneous pursuit of these goals would collide with the goal of ever-growing market income and increasing purchasing power at the global scale. Analysing the data of the past four decades, the strong ties between world income growth and world greenhouse gas emissions show no signs of relaxation. Economic growth endangers other global ecosystems as well, as current studies indicate (Jørgen Randers 2012; Will Steffen et al. 2015). Thus, a worldwide search is underway for new forms of economic activity that are independent of the imperative of ever-growing market income. There is a wealth of concepts on offer, all claiming to solve the same problem of resource overconsumption: green growth, de-growth, post-growth, and others. They coincide in their joint rejection of 'brown growth', which is based on the burning of fossil fuels. Yet even the question of whether the use of nuclear power is part of the problem or part of the solution is controversial (cf. chapter 4). Their joint criticism of the mainstream focus on market income growth in respect of its negative ecological and social effects is relevant. But it is doubtful whether alternatives to the still prevailing brown growth paradigm should be defined – with different prefixes – in terms of growth at all. Expressions like *prosperity, sustainability*, or *resilience* are instead more useful to overcoming the general obsession with economic growth.

Using the concept *prosperity* instead overcomes the idea that growth is an end in itself. Talking about prosperity redirects the focus of the debate from the means towards the ends of human activities: prospering in the sense of blossoming or flourishing. It is worth having a look at relevant meanings of prosperity. Following Amartya Sen's proposal, at least three different concepts of prosperity can be distinguished: opulence, utility, and capability to flourish (Jackson 2009, 37). *Opulence* denotes the overall material wealth the human population can dispose of, for example as fruits harvested or grown, or goods produced by humans. In a somewhat narrower definition, opulence could also be defined as the surplus of human economic activities beyond the means necessary for the producers' subsistence and the reproduction of the other factors of production. The term *utility* labels the fact that results of human activities are appreciated by humans as serving specific ends, whose appreciation is expressed by payments in kind or in money, or by the acceptance as a gift.

According to Jackson's interpretation of Sen, the *capability to flourish* entails "the right to choose whether or not to participate in society, to work in paid employment and perhaps even whether to live a healthy life" (Jackson 2009, 44). A society able to guarantee the preconditions for its citizens' rights to choose their way of living could be labelled as prosperous. With regard to the intertemporal aspect of sustainability, the *capability to flourish* requires the maintenance of the preconditions for a prosperous life for future generations as well – the social and the biophysical ones.

Introducing the maintenance of a prosperous life for future generations requires to inclusion of the *capability to practical reason* (Martha C. Nussbaum 2006), in a modern sense, the capability to think in terms of systems. Regarding the sustainability issues considered here, this would include the capability of practical reasoning on the coevolution of social and ecological systems – in abbreviated form, the *capability to co-evolve* – as a new element of prosperity. The second new element of prosperity is the *common-pool resource view* regarding the governance of these socio-ecological systems, which requires the *capability to diversify institutionally* the governance of common-pool resources. This kind of capability to diversify excludes lopsided institutional solutions for the provision of services of general interest (SGI):

> SGI are services that public authorities of the Member States classify as being of general interest and, therefore, subject to specific public service obligations (PSO). The term covers both economic activities . . . and non-economic services. The latter are not subject to specific EU legislation and are not covered by the internal market and competition rules of the Treaty.
>
> (European Commission 2011a, 3)

Institutional diversification paves the way for experimenting with new, cooperative, and self-organised institutional arrangements for the governance of ecological resource systems such as water, energy, and green spaces. A basic assumption of such institutional diversification processes is the nonexistence of a panacea for the governance of such ecological resource systems. The third new element of the overall capability to flourish is the *capability to participate for all citizens (up to the level of citizens' control)*. To summarise, prosperity is to be considered as *shared* if it entails the triple capabilities to coevolve, to diversify institutionally, and to participate.

For such a *participative, diversifying, and co-evolutionary regime of shared prosperity* to become true, a steady stream of social innovation is required. These social innovations have to meet the social needs considered here as a better and sustainable organisation of key ecological resource systems and to improve the capabilities of all citizens to take part in prospering. Such social innovations can be found most notably at places where people interact, where they lead to new products, services, models, markets, processes, and so forth, which are serving the community on multiple levels. This kind of social innovation would change everyday behaviour.

Thus, the focus of this inquiry was directed towards institutional factors responsible for the framing of human behaviour: institutions organising and structuring the everyday interactions of people. Considering multilateral approaches as rather ineffective pathways for the solution of global ecological problems, this study shifts the research interest towards bottom-up approaches as possible game changers. It looks at the everyday activities of people that are relevant for the sustainability of interactions between the social system on the one hand and the ecological resource system on the other. Formal and informal norms are guiding them. New kinds of technology, knowledge, ambition, and power have the potential to change these relations between the social and ecological system – and thus to change the norms guiding these interactions and, hopefully, to induce transitions towards a stronger regime of sustainability.

Whether socio-ecological or sustainability transitions are happening or not essentially depends on the learning processes of human actors at the local level. Here, two bodies of knowledge are opposing each other, because "there is beyond question a body of very important but unorganized knowledge which cannot possibly be called scientific in the sense of knowledge of general rules: the knowledge of the particular circumstances of time and place" (Friedrich A. v. Hayek 1945, 521). On the one hand, complex global problems like climate change can be analysed with the help of a wide range of approaches from different scientific disciplines. But, on the other hand, only with the help of involved actors' tacit knowledge of the particular circumstances of time and place will the consequences deduced from this scientific knowledge be implemented successfully at the local level. If this complementarity with local actors' tacit knowledge is given, they are capable of absorbing the scientific knowledge on global ecosystems and to change their everyday behaviour as well as the norms guiding it accordingly.

11.2 Cities as laboratories of sustainability transition

Cities are advantageous places for studying the co-evolution of behaviour and institutions locally. Besides being made of stone, bricks, and concrete, cities are built on a foundation of rights and rules for their citizens. This legal foundation has governed communal life from the early beginnings: Rights are claimed by citizens and sometimes granted by a sovereign; rules are regulating the urban life – like the use of resources such as public spaces, water, and land. Introducing societal rules into the human use of ecological resource systems creates urban socio-ecological systems: The institutional setting – consisting of strategies, norms, and rules – governs the interaction of the ecological resource system with the societal system. This institutional setting is not fixed for all time but dependent, as already mentioned, on the evolution of technology, knowledge, human ambition, and power. The balance of power and its dynamics are important for understanding institutional change: "Institutions are not necessarily or even usually created to be socially efficient; rather they, or at least the formal rules, are created to serve the interests of those with the bargaining power to create new rules" (Douglass C. North 1993).

From this point of view, the probable outcome of such institutional bargaining is very much predetermined by the endowment of the participating players with such power resources. An example of this is the disastrous outcome of the Copenhagen Conference on Climate Change in 2009: Some veto players were able to block an agreement on limits for greenhouse gas emissions binding for all parties. The most prominent resources for this veto power were legitimacy, dependency, and living standards. It appeared to be legitimate for the governments of less-developed countries to demand the same 'right to pollute' for their citizens as the inhabitants of early industrialised countries already had during their long history of greenhouse gas emissions. It seemed to be easy for economies with huge reserves of fossil fuels to veto by using the dependency of economies without sufficient capacities to substitute the import of fossil fuels with renewable energy sources – at least in the short term. Interest groups from early industrialised countries successfully made the point that the transition from 'brown growth' to 'green growth', i.e. from fossil to renewable energy sources, would endanger the living standards of ordinary people. According to this narrative, such energy transition would increase costs for producers and consumers, simultaneously induce a loss of international competitiveness, and harm the real purchasing power of the domestic middle classes in the short and long term.

Such veto players, keen to impede the introduction of new rules conflicting with their vested interests, are to be expected on all levels of human interaction – from the international level down to the national and the local level as well. Nevertheless, at the local level, it is in many cases much easier to challenge the positions of the bargaining parties: The tacit knowledge of the particular circumstances of time and place is here by definition more accessible and more equally distributed between the negotiating parties. This, as well as the concentration of creative classes (Richard Florida 2002) and social conflicts (Harvey 2008) in urban areas, could be considered as the main reasons to expect the bulk of social innovations to emerge in cities rather than in villages (Jin Xue 2014).

In this sense, cities could be considered – at least potentially – as laboratories for proving competing prosperity concepts and their implementation locally. Urban activities that are relevant for the *capabilities of flourishing* approach to prosperity in terms of their environmental impact are to be found in the fields of land use planning, transport, building, energy, waste, and water (OECD 2013a, 16). Some of these activities are directly related to the interaction of societal and ecological resource systems: labour, energy, water, and land use. They were of special importance in the study here.

11.3 Solving the trade-off between complexity and participation

The field research brought forward a significant trade-off between the complexity of the resource systems considered and the opportunities for urban citizens to participate in their governance. Regarding the local water system, a misled understanding of participation as 'private monitoring' of water quality was observed, while prices for drinking water and the possible privatisation of the local water utilities were considered as social issues with high priority. It was difficult (and even impossible) to create awareness and civic commitment for the invisible, underground part of the aquifer.

In contrast, the resource system of green spaces was considered the outstanding example of civil society involvement and social innovation: Here participation and self-organisation emerge more easily and more often than in the governance of water or energy systems. Sometimes civil society actors fought for this right to cogovern the green spaces, sometimes this right was granted to them by the local government. Compared to the other resource systems, it was much easier for them to get support from local authorities and to become active players in urban governance.

The concepts of participation and self-organisation in the governance of the energy system are highly contested and sometimes problematic. Mostly they were reduced to information provision for the citizens and excluded them from participating in any decision-making concerning the provision of electric energy. This could be explained at least partly by the high technological complexity of the energy system and the history of political priorities for more or less centralised and spatially remote systems of electric energy provision, located far from the city limits. Further research on the instruments and institutional settings that could grant citizens a direct influence on remixing the energy in favour of renewable sources from the supply side is needed.

Our case studies revealed that transition is a multilevel endeavour. This point was particularly stressed by the experts on energy issues: Both the EU and the national levels are very much appreciated for providing guidelines, instruments, and financing for fostering the energy transition. Such financial aid and legal frameworks could assist local-level actors in pushing forward for the local use of renewable energy sources. In contrast, real long-term plans for local water resources are mostly missing. Interestingly, regarding the governance of green spaces, local governments are the key actors. This is particularly true if they are advanced in developing their own sustainability strategies. In this case, they are mostly ready to allow innovative experiments on public green spaces and to scale them up if these experiments are successful. The same is true for local labour market policy: Only the responsibility for deciding on active labour market policy budgets, designing passive labour market policies, and monitoring the success of active labour market policy are significantly positively correlated with the share of the autonomously decided budget.

To conclude, the complementarity of the different governance levels has to be recognised. This is particularly important for the energy system, because the framework for the energy transition is very much defined on the national level, which is sometimes prone to servicing the vested interests of energy providers in favour of fossil or nuclear energy sources. Thus, pressure from the European level in favour of institutional diversification could help the local level to break up such corporatist conservativism in favour of new actors and to overcome the bargaining power of the related vested interests in favour of renewable-friendly institutions. The transfer of knowledge generated by successful experiments with community energy like in the UK (Gill Seyfang, Jung J. Park, and Adrian Smith 2013; Department of Energy and Climate Change 2014) could enhance the cooperative capital needed for decentralised approaches to the energy transition, driven by civil society actors.

11.4 Stepping stones towards urban sustainability transitions

The field research showed a growing lack of trust in government. In many countries, democratic engagement and citizenship are shrinking. At the same time, transition processes are taking place in many urban systems, and opportunities are visible in new social movements, new technologies, and other civil society groups and networks (cf. chapter 10). Cities and networks of cities play a particularly important role in this process, as well as bottom-up initiatives emerging from citizenry in response to the urgent transition needs (cf. chapter 9).

Varieties of connective processes acting on different scales are fundamental attributes for cities. A concerted strategy is needed to make things possible. It is supportive in ensuring institutional rules in favour of local sustainability, enabling access to technologies and allowing their impact on the status quo in which cities operate. It allows governments to act in pursuit of change. Stimulating community-led bottom-up approaches, including a self-organising community of interest among residents, landowners, infrastructure companies, businesses, social enterprises, NGOs, and community organisations are key factors to this.

In the course of finding new institutional arrays with which to govern local urban common-pool resources, different actors are equally important. In self-organising these resource systems in a sustainable way, the interaction and negotiation between government, business actors, and civil society is vital to providing a healthy socio-ecologic transition for the well-being of all.

This new perspective of collective changing and (re-)aligning institutional settings shows that transitions, rather than being managed, can be influenced, supported, and accelerated. By allowing openness, exchange, stimulation of differences and contradictory conditions to occur at the same time, local urban actors can play an important part in these dynamics. Their insight and knowledge of their local urban features allow for a thorough assessment and promotion of socio-ecological transitions. According to the socio-ecological transition approach developed in chapter 3, a sequence of norm adaption should be considered as steps towards strong sustainability.

Table 11-1 sums up the main findings of our research. The issues presented pertain to different areas of possible action like politics or self-organisation. Stepping stones to commence with actions to change rules and norms and encourage a transition process to stronger sustainability are listed in the third column. The following sections will discuss these eight options one by one. Examples are often given for the energy transition, as the energy system is commonly understood as the foremost leverage towards a stronger sustainability because of its key role in creating CO_2 emissions and affecting climate change. Special focus will be on the role and perspectives for civil society to be proactive in sustainability transition.

Table 11-1 Findings and recommended stepping stones

Issue	Area	Stepping stone
Tangibility of resource systems and influences on it	All	A common understanding of sustainability is required to allow a collective undertaking towards set-out goals in congruent timeframes.
Complex constitution of the resource system	Participation, self-organisation, politics	A holistic approach is necessary and, with it, transparent information as well as education. Open access to transparent information is a basis for involvement.
Individual responsibility for transition	Politics, education, participation, self-organisation	Seeing SET as individual responsibility negates its complexity. Communal solutions must be collective efforts. Local cooperation strengthens mutual and individual benefits.
Lack of education, awareness, and understanding, as well as lack of trust	Cooperation, communication	Complex processes are hard to grasp. To create an understanding of SET, education is important. It is not an expert topic and concerns everybody. Everybody should be able to comprehend the basic concepts. Cooperation produces mutual trust and reputation for further developments in the long term.

Issue	Area	Stepping stone
Spatial limitation for socio-ecological transition	Planning, self-organisation	Urban areas cannot be decoupled from close rural areas. Production (and thus labour) need to be in the vicinity and still decentralised. In addition, production and consumption need to be efficient enough to optimise the ratio of production to spatial size.
Coherent legal frameworks for a maximum of local autonomy and bottom-up governance	Governance, politics, laws	To enforce a SET to sustainability, a binding overarching legal framework is necessary that guarantees decision-making processes at the local level. National political decisions and laws cannot interfere with local-level politics. Rather, governance must be thought as 'bottom-up'.
Sustainable socio-ecological transition needs an active public sphere	Participation, self-organisation, public discourse	Transitions cannot be enacted; they need a broad coalition, involving all affected actors. These actors need to be empowered to act as transition players.
Social cohesion	Politics	To prevent the effects of gentrification and rising living costs due to sustainability processes, a coherent social policy is needed. Labour markets are one pillar of it.

11.4.1 Moving targets: develop a common understanding of sustainability transition

According to the sequential sustainability transition model developed and explored by the field research (cf. chapters 3–7), the common understanding of the scope and time horizon of sustainability is the alpha and omega of every transition strategy. Every human action starts within a contextual horizon defined by its lifeworld and natural habitat, but every effective action changes the lifeworld and natural habitat of humans as well. Thus, permanent feedback can be assumed between the social and ecological systems, driven by the human motivations, actions, learning processes, and norm adoptions. As a result, sustainable development goals are moving targets, and the speed of this move depends on the speed of human learning.

To achieve a socio-ecological transition, the approach needs to consider the city and its resources in a comprehensive, holistic way. Complex resource systems and transitions towards sustainability themselves can only be grasped in a way that reflects manifold influencing aspects. Especially social aspects cannot be neglected when dealing with a transition. By interfering with one resource system, feedbacks are created that emit to other systems and induce side effects. Interdependencies exist between ecological resources as well as between ecological and social systems. Cities are a complex ecology where changes in one feature provoke resonance in others. Coherent policies must reflect this complex entangled field and cannot be restricted to one resource system; they have to include the city as a unity.

Thus, the recently adopted UN Post-2015 Agenda and universal Sustainable Development Goals (UN 2012, 2014b, 2014c) are a good starting point for defining such sustainability objectives at the European, national, subnational, and local levels as well. They are available measures at the level of the EU member states and should be broken down to the ground (local) level as well. This is a highly participatory and not simply administrative task, because these objectives and the measurement of their implementation will only guide everyday behaviour if everybody has a voice in formulating them.

The time horizon of goal attainment influences the extent to which politicians and citizens are willing to change or modify systems, regulations, and norms that pose barriers to actions. Long-term visions can unify even diverse groups, generate new ideas and experiments, and serve as a compass for the daily work (InContext 2013, 1). Strengthening science–policy–society interfaces and citizens' engagement are important elements of transition processes (EEA 2015). The lack of distant, long-term objectives reported in particular by many Eastern European cities (Barnebeck and Kalff 2015, chapter 2) may be due to political instability and high turnover in strategic management positions, relatively poor infrastructure conditions, and deficits of financial resources for sustainability projects. A long-term perspective is essential to guide sustainability transition processes. Political decision-making has to realise and surpass the one-dimensional logics of single sectors and provide an integrating narrative.

Another issue in defining the scope of transition is to agree in Europe on the key sustainability objectives. An example is the definition of a sustainable European energy strategy. In order to empower the decisive local action level, it should be entirely clear that a 'low-carbon' strategy is not enough. Neither a fossil nor a nuclear-driven energy policy is the appropriate instrument to facilitate the responsible co-creation of sustainable energy services at the local level. Substantial endeavours to reduce carbon emissions by investing in renewable energy systems are implemented locally. However, currently, the general picture is that these projects remain isolated initiatives, lacking in strategic coherence and lacking an agreed perspective on where to focus investment and how to scale them up. The new opportunities for transitions in the energy system call for concerted visions, strategies, and actions between the economy, the policy system, civil society, media, and science focusing on the accelerated implementation of renewable energy systems – being an important leverage for an SET. Cities and regions play an important role in this process, and more integrated approaches are needed between energy systems, climate systems, and land use options (Holger Berg et al. 2014b). Coherent strategies that are 'translated' into local action plans significantly aid this process. This also relates to the necessity of a holistic view, integrating all elements of sustainability and bringing together different relevant resources and other aspects.

11.4.2 Smart inclusion: improve the information basis for everyone

A close monitoring of the attainment of commonly agreed sustainability objectives at the local level as well as open access to that data for every citizen is an essential precondition for the democratic, participative steering of local transition processes. At the same time, new forms of communication and networking are emerging, and the amount of information manageable is one of the biggest transformation challenges. Citizens and enterprises could benefit from an extended economisation of time, improved individual mobility, and facilitated access to information and services, which simplify participation in the urban decision-making process by opening up new communication channels, and by creating and promoting an aware public (Kunzmann 2014, 12).

Against this backdrop, the accelerated integration and miniaturisation of ICT (information and communication technologies) could become a valuable instrument of civil society's self-organisation, giving practically everyone access to information and participation. New forms of shared use or reuse of goods, spontaneous conventions of people, co-creation, and crowdsourcing and crowdfunding, to name just a few, will add collaboration and cooperation to the former trends of individualisation and competition – and could counterpoise them.

Thus, ICTs bear a potential for supporting self-organising bottom-up initiatives as well as allocating financial resources via crowdfunding. A broad aspect of informing citizens is already realised. However, 'Smart City' approaches have yet to prove that they are socially inclusive, including both the increasing proportions of elderly people and the less affluent. They can increase participation for more than just an elite social milieu and at the same time contribute to considerable reductions in the use of natural resources.

However, many forms of governance are still slow, inefficient, and obsolete (Joe Ravetz 2011). ICT-based cities are only part of the change happening in local communities. Citizens' initiatives, networks, community structures and their synergies with local governments, spatial planning, and the built environment can improve urban governance. From some cities surveyed by the ROCSET project came the urge to adapt 'sustainable governance structures', meaning that urban governance needs to evolve to a coherent twenty-first-century form of city planning and politics. In addition, coherent sustainable government structures foster socio-ecological transitions by providing adequate representation of local actors from all sectors and resource systems. Involvement and transparency though require engagement – in terms of time and other resources – from civil society actors. Participation channels must not be seen as one-way channels. Available information should be used in an appropriate way by these local actors.

11.4.3 Equal payoff: motivate the striving for transitions towards strong sustainability

Transition justice is a crucial issue, because social heterogeneity is a severe impediment for the public support of sustainability transformations. The envisaged socio-ecological transition will only happen if 'no one is left behind', and with regard to the rules of social inclusion. Therefore, for example, electricity prices for private households could easily be manipulated and used as an instrument for the mobilisation against the transition to renewable energy, if social heterogeneity is high and energy poverty a severe issue. In a well-developed welfare regime, it appears to be much easier to distribute the gains of self-organised investments in urban socio-ecological systems in an equal way and thus to make the high returns of cooperation visible and accessible to everyone.

Furthermore, socio-ecological transition justice is also an issue of regional cohesion. It became apparent that the cities in the EU13 member states had different priorities regarding sustainable development, compared to the EU15 member states, with their significantly lower income level. The provision of the basic services of general interest took a higher priority than safeguarding climate stability and the transition to renewable energy sources. This could lead to lock-in effects, freezing a conventional energy policy in these countries as well as in the EU.

Finally yet importantly, socio-ecological transition in Europe will only happen if inter-temporal justice in this transition is taken into consideration considering all resources (cf. section 1.1). This excludes European energy strategies that were built on the use of nuclear energy. The operative security of nuclear plants is not guaranteed, even in advanced industrial countries, as the Fukushima disaster has demonstrated, and the problem of the permanent disposal of nuclear waste is not solvable. Thus, shifting these problems to future generations is not a sustainable option. A transition towards renewable energy sources is inevitable in this context. Sustainable options must take into consideration their impact on future generations.

11.4.4 Transformative learning: develop trust and reputation in joint transitions

One important benefit of a co-creative approach to a sustainability transition is that it increases trust between citizens and the government. Balancing the needs and fears of different community groups establishes reputation and trust in political leadership towards sustainability. In contrast, lack of participation and low-quality governance create a vicious circle in which trust in government breaks down. At this point, self-organisation might substitute for civil society's otherwise insufficient influence on political processes. However, the interactions of effects are complex. Our research shows that there is a significant lack of participation above the level of becoming informed. Top-down decision-making usually excludes citizens and civil society and thus hinders trust-building in politics. Particularly with a continuing crisis and rejection of institutionalised politics, this is considerably harmful. Thus, European sustainability policies have to focus on emancipative forms of politics, which enable the citizens to take control of these transition processes.

The role of local universities and scientific institutions is substantial in providing knowledge and technical assistance or upholding a counter-discourse for sustainability issues. The connection between scientific research and local-level issues and practices must be advanced; science should play a transformative role and assist local practitioners in the transition at hand. Scientific and academic expertise serves to promote knowledge and exemplary pilot projects for other transition processes. However, community and scientific initiatives will usually remain limited in scope and impact without the partnership of local government, regardless of their innovative potential. Partnerships between science, civil society, government, and business should be encouraged and fostered.

In addition, partnerships and networks among cities and communities play a significant role in promoting sustainable development and are regarded as an important channel for knowledge-sharing on sustainability. The knowledge brokerage processes are part of contemporary governance (Joas et al. 2013). Potentially, these partnerships play a decisive role in the learning process at the subnational level and are needed to join forces to increase pressure on the national and EU level. In fact, many of these networks and campaigns have the ambition to build the capacity of their members to engage in sustainable development (Labaeye and Sauer 2013). While networks support knowledge exchange and the sharing of practical experiences, they also foster the specific collaboration of cities and regions and act as intermediaries or linkage agents. The cross-cutting nature of governance and local sustainability means that various forms of expertise must work hand in hand. Elaborate networks that institutionalise collaboration are particularly important. Within these collaboration networks, extended numbers of actors bringing socio-ecological transitions forward are involved, such as NGOs, educational institutions, trade unions, ethnic groups, faith groups, and so on, especially to address ecological and social topics. Forms of local representation of affected actors are necessary to initiate dialogue, discussion, and cooperation on an institutionalised level. Policies should consider infrastructures for local exchange as well as communication between cities.

11.4.5 Congruent boundaries: bringing in line social and ecological systems in urban spaces

There is a strong need to readjust the boundaries of social and ecological systems to secure a better spatial overlap between them. This is particularly true for the transition towards renewable energy resources, which could technologically enable such spatial recoupling of energy production and energy use. Such a recoupling includes the co-creation of a new, sustainable energy system by the close interaction of providers and users of this resource system at the local level. Whether this becomes true or not is neither a purely technological nor a purely economic decision, but a matter of socio-ecological performativity (Donald A. MacKenzie 2006; Donald A. MacKenzie, Fabian Muniesa, and Lucia Siu 2007; Egan-Krieger, Tanja v. 2014). In other words, a participatory bottom-up decision process will deliver different results than a top-down decision, ignoring the potential of decentralised renewable energy systems. More generally, what is needed is a new way of thinking about their interdependencies and interactions, enhancing the spaces of flows (Castells 1996) as well as the circulation of people, capital, resources, and identities. Beyond that, the decision-making process has to be opened up for local actors that are affected by these local decisions. Existing power structures are not easily overcome, as established large corporations will not just give up their positions and citizens are often not willing to accept changes in their lifeworld and environment. Public approval for infrastructure projects, for example for pumped-storage power plants or high-voltage transmission lines, affecting their own neighbourhood is already diminishing in many regions. This makes the structures in which decisions on issues affecting the local community are made locally all the more important. Transition is never thinkable only in technical terms; power structures, and thus rules as well as habits, need to be considered – and changed – as well.

11.4.6 Participatory transitions: thinking and doing bottom-up governance

Democratic engagement and citizenship is shrinking in many countries. Simultaneously, active community groups are emerging that are working on a wide range of issues, primarily on green spaces as well as on social inclusion and migrants' rights. The range of citizen participation varies according to local context, as well as to the particular problem, issue, and policy at hand.

European local governments have become more autonomous over the past 50 years. However, there is still a variety of ways to define and frame autonomy and numerous challenges related to how autonomy is operationalised. Most cities reported that progress towards decentralisation is slow because of routine operations, bureaucratic inertia, ineffectiveness, and the resistance to change of long-established routines and structures. Reducing bureaucracy and making official procedures easier and more accessible positively influences socio-ecological transitions. Thus, the degree of administrative decentralisation directly influences the degree of independent decision-making. It should be supported by a significant enhancement of local financial autonomy as well.

It has been shown in the research that participation is a vital goal of European policies. However, the implementations on the different levels are not always consistent and show different understandings of participation as a political concept. The major problem is the lack of room for participation in its institutional settings. Furthermore, arguing for self-organisation in urban contexts exceeds the request of participation. Local urban resources being regarded as common-pool resources imply a shift in governance principles. The main point is that bottom-up governance must be defined accordingly to allow the local level a coherent and stringent approach towards self-organisation. Further, the shift has to include not only the 'thinking of' but also the 'doing of' bottom-up governance. This term implies that civil society governance 'has to be done' in practice. It must not remain a hypothetical aspect of civil society involvement; it is an ongoing process that is formed and sustained *in its process*. The structural frame cannot predetermine the process as a whole – the process may find its own way and its own obstacles that are dealt with while trying to self-organise. Therefore, there is no best practice: Every attempt results in a solution cut out for the individual local case.

More broadly, participation is a means to involve citizens in existing institutional settings, grant them access to information and decision-making, and give them voicing options. A process is tied closer to the existing institutions and can parallel self-organisation. However, it is as contested as self-organisation and the autonomy of the local decision-makers. Local participation has to be fostered and has to exceed mere opportunities to become informed about decisions. The right to participate in decisions about local-level resources should be institutionally anchored and should concern every stage of the political decision-making process. Hence, local government autonomy does not mean autonomy from citizens. It should reflect possibilities to make local decisions independently of economic interests or political agendas from higher levels – in consensus with all affected actors.

Creating and nourishing a socio-ecological transition has to come from the bottom. The institutional framework has to fit the specific necessities and allow autonomy for the local actors, but in the end, participation or self-organisation rely on people, civil society, and actors in general that effectively take part in the process. There needs to be 'talk' about a socio-ecological transition as well as 'action'. Therefore, 'doing' the transition towards sustainability is equally important.

11.4.7 Citizen control: empowering the transition agents

A proactive state with extended opportunities for participation is correctly understood elsewhere as a crucial precondition for a Great Transformation towards sustainability (WBGU 2011). This is not only about enhancing the legitimacy of decisions via delegated power, but about enhancing direct citizen control over central issues of socio-ecological transition, such as the enabling of and the support for the introduction of decentralised systems of renewable energy sources by energy cooperatives or the provision of innovative governance structures for urban green spaces in cooperation with community groups. This also entails a preference for realising the economies in the scope of urban co-creation structures in the use of ecological resource systems, instead of favouring privatised technological structures, for instance prevailing in the fossil and nuclear energy systems, which have blocked citizen control in the past.

Citizen control therefore is a vital alternative to the existing property system of resources and resource distribution. As has been stated in the point above, self-organisation in a special sense and participation in a broader sense may rely on different forms of ownership, since resource systems need to be in public possession. The 'tragedy of the commons' is evitable. Thus, institutional diversification beyond simple nationalisation or privatisation of public utilities is feasible, and cooperative and self-organised forms of governing common-pool resources work, if the local level acquires the resource systems and decides on their usage. This frames a certain picture: Rendering the fate of the local resource systems to the local-level civil society in an alliance with local government and local business, supported by the superior level, empowers the local level as a whole – and first of all the urban citizens.

However, the empowerment cannot only affect the civil society but must include other important transition agents as well. Speaking of a broad alliance conveys the idea that only a well-working network of different actors can realise a transition towards sustainability in urban contexts. Even when important positions are held by the citizens themselves, their role must be extended, and they need to be enacted and engaged. This is easily proposed but argues against a political and philosophical understanding that relies heavily on the individuation and separation of people. Against any form of collective action, the proposition of the last decades has been the singularity of individual existence.

Civil society and citizens need to take a crucial role. This is an active role that exceeds by far a stance that indulges them an active consumption choice as a means to an end in affecting a socio-ecologic transition towards sustainability.

11.4.8 The European urban agenda: sustainability transition is the key issue

With the installment of a European Urban Agenda, the EU multilevel governance of transition processes will undergo a significant redefinition (European Commission 1997, 2013c, 2015). Each level has its particular strengths, and only if these strengths are wisely combined will they mutually support each other and develop more power together than each level on its own. The importance of improving relations between different levels of government was recognised by the European Union's Committee of the Regions through the Charter for Multilevel Governance, calling public authorities of all levels of governance (local, national, and European) to use and promote multilevel governance in their future undertakings (cf. chapter 9). This includes experiments with innovative policy solutions in adherence to principles of subsidiarity, proportionality, and partnership, and the promotion of the use of multilevel partnerships and instruments for joint policy action.

However, for example in the energy sector, part of this combination might factually consist of shifts of power from one level to another, breaking up remainders of close corporate connections, as it has been stated above. The systemic changes necessary for a transition of socio-ecological systems will thus supplement the architecture of current multilevel governance by introducing the urban level, and it is unlikely that the related shifts in responsibility and power will occur without conflict or resistance. The Urban Agenda, which has been discussed for the past couple of years, tries to empower the urban local level with specific policies designed for urban spaces. This is sensible when looking at the different kinds of sustainability strategies that are implemented in different cities (Barnebeck and Kalff 2015, 15–18). Assessing the existing strategies reveals potentials to improve socio-ecological transitions towards sustainability in many cities. The strength of an Urban Agenda lies in a coherent framework that allows the distribution of responsibility to the local level, where the knowledge and problem-solving capability fits best to the challenges at hand.

However, the European Urban Agenda is not without contradiction. Especially in the consultation's discussions, the principle of subsidiarity is referred to as the basic political principle that on the one hand guarantees responsibility on the respective governance levels but on the other hand limits the efficiency of any EU policy. Further, Barnebeck and Kalff (2015) have shown from the consultation documents that a substantial part in this consultation comes from political actors and thus shapes the policy-development path in a direction where the political participation of citizens is not mentioned once.

While the Urban Agenda can be a formidable approach to granting agency to the local level and to civil society, the dangers lie in the bureaucratisation of the policy development process. Allowing a rather technocratic influence in the design of policies, even one that concerns urban systems, the institutional settings are narrowed down to 'conservative' ones. It is obvious that a successful socio-ecological transition must endorse a broad public alliance of competent, interested, and empowered actors. Such a coalition is a consolidation that fosters action and responsibility for the local resource systems, and other aspects of local live or societal integration.

Note

1 Kindly supported by *Judith Schicklinski, Stefan Kuhn, Stephanie Barnebeck,* and *Yannick Kalff.*

References

2000-Watt Gesellschaft. n.a. *Die 2000-Watt-Gesellschaft*. http://www.2000watt.ch/ (accessed 1 September 2015).
Aalborg Charter. 1994. Charter of European Cities & Towns Towards Sustainability. As approved by the participants at the European Conference on Sustainable Cities & Towns in Aalborg, Denmark, on 27 May 1994. http://ec.europa.eu/environment/urban/pdf/aalborg_charter.pdf (accessed 1 September 2015).
Adascalitei, Dragos. 2012. "Welfare State Development in Central and Eastern Europe. A State of the Art Literature Review." *Studies of Transition States and Societies*, 4(2): 59–70.
Adger, W. Neil and Andrew Jordan. 2009. *Governing Sustainability*. Cambridge, UK, and New York, NY: Cambridge University Press.
Aidukaite, Jolanta. 2011. "Welfare Reforms and Socio-Economic Trends in the 10 New EU Member States of Central and Eastern Europe." *Communist and Post-Communist Studies*, 44(3): 211–19.
Allard, Jenna, Carl Davidson, and Julie Matthaei. 2008. *Solidarity Economy. Building Alternatives for People and Planet; Papers and Reports from the U.S. Social Forum 2007*. Chicago, IL: ChangeMaker Publications.
Alvesson, Mats and Hugh Willmott. 1992. "Critical Theory and Management Studies. An Introduction." In *Critical Management Studies*, ed. Mats Alvesson and Hugh Willmott, pp. 1–20. London, UK, Newbury Park, CA, and New Delhi, India: Sage Publications.
Alvesson, Mats and Hugh Willmott. 1996. *Making Sense of Management. A Critical Introduction*. 4th ed. London, UK, Thousand Oaks, CA, and New Delhi, India: Sage Publications.
Amable, Bruno. 2003. *The Diversity of Modern Capitalism*. Oxford, UK, and New York, NY: Oxford University Press.
Andersen, Mikael S. 2010. "Europe's Experience with Carbon-energy Taxation." *S.A.P.I.EN.S*, 3(2): 1–11.
Arin, Tülay. 2002. "The Poverty of Social Security. The Welfare Regime in Turkey." In *The Ravages of Neo-Liberalism. Economy, Society, and Gender in Turkey*, ed. Nescan Balkan and Sungur Savran, pp. 73–91. Huntington, WV: Nova Science.
Arnstein, Sherry R. 1969. "A Ladder of Citizen Participation." *Journal of the American Planning Association*, 35(4): 216–24.
Arthur, Sue and James Nazroo. 2003. "Designing Fieldwork Strategies and Materials." In *Qualitative Research Practice. A Guide for Social Science Students and Researchers*, ed. Jane Ritchie and Jane Lewis, pp. 109–37. London, UK, Thousand Oaks, CA, and New Delhi, India: Sage Publications.
Arts, Wil and John Gelissen. 2002. "Three Worlds of Welfare Capitalism or More? A State-of-the-art Report." *Journal of European Social Policy*, 12(2): 137–58.
Bachtler, John and Irene McMaster. 2008. "EU Cohesion Policy and the Role of the Regions: Investigating the Influence of Structural Funds in the New Member States." *Environment and Planning C: Government and Policy*, 26(2): 398–427.
Barnebeck, Stephanie and Yannick Kalff. 2015. "Urban Agenda and Urban Sustainability Strategies. Taking Stock of Policy Implementation and Policy Discussion." WWWforEurope. Working Paper 103. http://www.foreurope.eu/fileadmin/documents/pdf/Workingpapers/WWWforEurope_WPS_no103_MS224.pdf (accessed 1 September 2015).

Barthel, Stephan, John Parker, and Henrik Ernstson. 2013. "Food and Green Space in Cities. A Resilience Lens on Gardens and Urban Environmental Movements." *Urban Studies*, 52(7): 1321–38.

Bauer, Michael W. 2002. "The EU 'Partnership Principle'. Still a Sustainable Governance Device across Multiple Administrative Arenas?" *Public Administration*, 80(4): 769–89.

Baycan-Levent, Tüzin, Ron Vreeker, and Peter Nijkamp. 2009. "A Multi-Criteria Evaluation of Green Spaces in European Cities." *European Urban and Regional Studies*, 16(2): 193–213.

Beck, Ulrich. 2000. *What Is Globalization?* Cambridge, MA: Polity Press.

Berg, Holger, Johannes Buhl, Laura Echternacht, Josephine Wohlrab, and Andries Hof. 2014a. "Criteria for Analysis of Case Studies According to the Different Approaches of Analysis." PATHWAYS Project: Exploring Transition Pathways to Sustainable, Low Carbon Societies. Deliverable D3.1. http://pathways-project.eu/sites/default/files/D3_1_Criteria%20Analysis%20Case%20Studies_28July_FinalVersion.pdf (accessed 1 September 2015).

Berg, Holger, Johannes Buhl, Laura Echternacht, Josephine Wohlrab, and Andries Hof, ed. 2014b. PATHWAYS Project. Exploring Transition Pathways to Sustainable, Low Carbon Societies Criteria for Analysis of Case Studies According to the Different Approaches of Analysis. http://pathways-project.eu/sites/default/files/D3_1_Criteria%20Analysis%20Case%20Studies_28July_FinalVersion.pdf (accessed 1 September 2015).

Berger, Peter L. and Thomas Luckmann. 1967. *The Social Construction of Reality. A Treatise in the Sociology of Knowledge*. Garden City, NY: Doubleday.

Bergh, Jeroen van den. 2015. "Green Agrowth as a Third Option. Removing GDP-Growth Constraint on Human Progress." WWWforEurope Policy Paper 19. http://www.foreurope.eu/fileadmin/documents/pdf/PolicyPapers/WWWforEurope_Policy_Paper_019.pdf (accessed 1 September 2015).

Bergh, Jeroen van den and Miklos Antal. 2014. "Energy Rebound due to Re-spending. A Growing Concern." WWWforEurope. Policy Paper 9. http://www.foreurope.eu/fileadmin/documents/pdf/PolicyPapers/WWWforEurope_Policy_Paper_009.pdf (accessed 1 September 2015).

Bergh, Jeroen van den and Giorgios Kallis. 2012. "Growth, A-Growth or Degrowth to Stay within Planetary Boundaries?" *Journal of Economic Issues*, XLV(4): 909–19.

Bettini, Yvette, Rebekah R. Brown, Fjalar J. de Haan, and Megan Farrelly. 2014. "Understanding Institutional Capacity for Urban Water Transitions." *Technological Forecasting and Social Change*, 94(May): 65–79.

Binder, Claudia R., Jochen Hinkel, Pieter W.G. Bots, and Claudia Pahl-Wostl. 2013. "Comparison of Frameworks for Analyzing Social-ecological Systems." *Ecology and Society*, 18(4): 26.

Biswas, Asit K. 2004. "Integrated Water Resources Management. A Reassessment." *Water International*, 29(2): 248–56.

Blomquist, William A., Edella Schlager, and Tanya Heikkila. 2004. *Common Waters, Diverging Streams. Linking Institutions to Water Management in Arizona, California, and Colorado*. Washington, DC: Resources for the Future.

Boeckenfoerde, Markus, Philipp Dann, and Verena Wiesner. 2007. "Max Planck Manual on Different Forms of Decentralization." https://www.academia.edu/3354254/Max_Planck_Manual_on_Different_Forms_of_Decentralization (accessed 1 September 2015).

Bogner, Alexander, Beate Littig, and Wolfgang Menz, ed. 2009. *Interviewing Experts. Methodology and Practice*. Basingstoke, UK, and New York, NY: Palgrave Macmillan.

Bohle, Dorothee and Béla Greskovits. 2007. "Neoliberalism, Embedded Neoliberalism, and Neocorporatism. Paths Towards Transnational Capitalism in Central-Eastern Europe." *West European Politics*, 30(3): 443–66.

Böhlke, John-Karl. 2002. "Groundwater Recharge and Agricultural Contamination." *Hydrogeology Journal*, 10(1): 153–79.

Bollier, David, and Silke Helfrich. 2012. *The Wealth of the Commons. A World beyond Market and State*. Amherst, MA: Levellers Press.

Boostra, Beitske and Luuk Boelens. 2011. "Self-organization in Urban Development. Towards a New Perspective on Spatial Planning." Urban *Research & Practice*, 4(2): 99–122.

Bourdieu, Pierre. 1985. "The Social Space and the Genesis of Groups." *Theory and Society*, 14(6): 723–44.
Brandes, Oliver M. 2005. "At a Watershed. Ecological Governance and Sustainable Water Management in Canada." *Journal of Environmental Law & Practice*, 16(1): 79–97.
Bringezu, Stefan, Helmut Schütz, Walter Pengue, Meghan O'Brian, Fernando Garcia, Ralph E.H. Sims, Robert W. Howarth, Lea Kauppi, Mark Swilling, and Jeffrey Herrick. 2014. *Assessing Global Land Use. Balancing Consumption with Sustainable Supply*. Nairobi, Kenya: United Nations Environment Programme (UNEP).
Broomfield, Mark. 2012. "Support to the Identification of Potential risks for the Environment and Human Health arising from Hydrocarbons Operations Involving Hydraulic Fracturing in Europe." European Commission DG Environment. ED57281 Issue Number 17c. http://ec.europa.eu/environment/integration/energy/pdf/fracking%20study.pdf (accessed 1 September 2015).
Bryman, Alan and Emma Bell. 2011. *Business Research Methods*. 3rd ed. Oxford, UK, and New York, NY: Oxford University Press.
Buchegger-Traxler, Anita, Martin Roggenkamp, and Elke Scheffelt. 2003. "Territoriale Beschäftigungspakete. Erfolgschancen und institutionelle Rahmenbedingungen im europäischen Vergleich." In *Die Zukunft der Arbeit in den Städten. Kommunale Bündnisse für Arbeit aus Akteurs- und Forschungssicht*, ed. Leo Kißler and Elke Wiechmann, pp. 93–107. Baden-Baden, Germany: Nomos.
Buller, Henry. 2000. "Re-Creating Rural Territories: Leader in France." *Sociologica Ruralis*, 40(2):190–99.
Carballa, Marta, Francisco Omil, Juan M. Lema, Maria Llompart, Carmen Garcia-Jares, Isaac Rodriguez, Mariano Gomez, and Thomas Ternes. 2004. "Behavior of Pharmaceuticals, Cosmetics and Hormones in a Sewage Treatment Plant." *Water Research*, 38(12): 2918–26.
Carlowitz, Hans C. 1713. *Sylvicultura oeconomica. oder haußwirthliche Nachricht und Naturmäßige Anweisung zur wilden Baum-Zucht*. Leipzig, Germany: Johann Friedrich Braun.
Castells, Manuel. 1996. *The Information Age: Economy, Society and Culture*. 3 Vols. Vol. 1, *The Rise of the Network Society*. Cambridge, MA: Blackwell.
Chardas, Anastassios. 2012. "Multi-level Governance and the Application of the Partnership Principle in Times of Economic Crisis in Greece." http://eprints.lse.ac.uk/43382/ (accessed 1 September 2015).
Christians, Clifford G. 2005. "Ethics and Politics in Qualitative Research." In *The SAGE Handbook of Qualitative Research*. 3rd ed., ed. Norman K. Denzin and Yvonna S. Lincoln, pp. 139–64. Thousand Oaks, CA, London, UK, and New Delhi, India: Sage Publications.
Clegg, Stewart R. 1990. *Modern Organizations. Organization Studies in the Postmodern World*. London, UK, Newbury Park, CA, and New Delhi, India: Sage Publications.
Colding, Johan, Stephan Barthel, Pim Bendt, Robbert Snep, Wim van der Knaap, and Henrik Ernstson. 2013. "Urban Green Commons. Insights on Urban Common Property Systems." *Global Environmental Change*, 23: 1039–51.
Committee of the Regions. 2009. "The Committee of the Regions' White Paper on Multilevel Governance." European Union. CONST-IV 020. http://web.cor.europa.eu/epp/Ourviews/Documents/White%20Paper%20on%20MLG.pdf (accessed 1 September 2015).
Committee of the Regions. 2011. "Urban Governance in the EU. Current Challenges and Forward Prospects." European Union. http://espas.eu/orbis/sites/default/files/generated/document/en/Consolidated%20version%20-%20Urban%20Goverance%20-%20final.pdf (accessed 1 September 2015).
Committee of the Regions. 2012. "Opinion of the Committee of the Regions on 'Building a European Culture of Multilevel Governance: Follow-up to the Committee of the Regions' White Paper'." European Union 2012/C 113/12. http://eur-lex.europa.eu/legal-content/EN/TXT/PDF/?uri=CELEX:52011IR0273&from=EN (accessed 1 September 2015).
Committee of the Regions. 2014. "Resolution of the Committee of the Regions on the Charter for Multilevel Governance in Europe." European Union. RESOL-V 012. http://cor.europa.eu/en/activities/governance/Documents/mlg-charter/en.pdf (accessed 1 September 2015).
Council of Europe. 1985. "European Charter of Local Self-Government." http://conventions.coe.int/treaty/en/treaties/html/122.htm (accessed 1 September 2015).

Council of the European Union. 2006. "Review of the EU Sustainable Development Strategy (EU SDS). Renewed Strategy." Council of the European Union. http://www.mzp.cz/C125750E003B698B/en/renewed_eu_sds/$FILE/KM-EU_SDS_eng-20060615.pdf (accessed 1 September 2015).

The Covenant of Mayors. 2015. "Committed to Local Sustainable Energy." http://www.covenantofmayors.eu/about/covenant-of-mayors_en.html (accessed 1 September 2015).

Crouch, Colin. 2004. *Post-Democracy*. Cambridge, MA: Polity Press.

Davies, Anna and Julie Simon. 2013. "Engaging Citizens in Social Innovation. A Short Guide to the Research for Policy Makers and Practitioners." FP7-project: 290771 (TEPSIE). http://siresearch.eu/sites/default/files/5.4_final.pdf (accessed 1 September 2015).

Department of Energy and Climate Change. 2014. "Community Energy Strategy. Full Report." Department of Energy and Climate Change. https://www.gov.uk/government/uploads/system/uploads/attachment_data/file/275163/20140126Community_Energy_Strategy.pdf (accessed 1 September 2015).

Dewey, John. 1927. *The Public and Its Problem*. Chicago, IL: Swallow Press, (Orig. pub. 1927).

DiMaggio, Paul J. and Walter W. Powell. 1983. "The Iron Cage Revisited. Institutional Isomorphism and Collective Rationality in *Organizational* Fields." *American Sociological Review*, 48(2): 147–60.

DISCUS Project. 2005. "Building Capacity for Local Sustainability." The Fano Guidelines. http://localcapacity21.iclei-europe.org/ (accessed 1 September 2015).

DuPuis, E.M. and David Goodman. 2005. "Should We Go "Home" to Eat? Toward a Reflexive Politics of Localism." *Journal of Rural Studies*, 21(3): 359–71.

Ebenhöh, Eva and Claudia Pahl-Wostl. 2008. "Agent Behavior between Maximization and Cooperation." *Rationality and Society*, 20(2): 227–52.

Eberts, Randal W. 2009. "The Role of Labour Market Policy in Horizontal Co-ordination." In *Local Economic and Employment Development (LEED), Flexible Policy for More and Better Jobs*, ed. Sylvain Giguère and Francesca Froy, pp. 103–48. Paris, France: OECD Publishing.

The Ecologist. 1994. "Whose Common Future. Reclaiming the Commons." *Environment and Urbanization*, 6(1): 106–30.

ECOTEC. 2002. "Thematic Evaluation of the Territorial Employment Pacts." http://ec.europa.eu/regional_policy/sources/docgener/evaluation/doc/tep_report1.pdf (accessed 1 September 2015).

EEA. 2015. "The European Environment – state and outlook 2015: Synthesis Report." European Environment Agency. http://www.eea.europa.eu/soer/#pdf-choice-synthesis (accessed 1 September 2015).

Egan-Krieger, Tanja v. 2014. *Die Illusion wertfreier Ökonomie. Eine Untersuchung der Normativität heterodoxer Theorien*. Frankfurt am Main, Germany, and New York, NY: Campus Verlag.

Elsen, Susanne. 1998. *Gemeinwesenökonomie – eine Antwort auf Arbeitslosigkeit, Armut und soziale Ausgrenzung? Soziale Arbeit, Gemeinwesenarbeit und Gemeinwesenökonomie im Zeitalter der Globalisierung*. Neuwied, Germany: Luchterhand.

Elsen, Susanne. 2007. *Die Ökonomie des Gemeinwesens. Sozialpolitik und Soziale Arbeit im Kontext von gesellschaftlicher Wertschöpfung- und - verteilung*. Weinheim, Munich, Germany: Juventa.

Elsen, Susanne. 2013. "Nachhaltigkeit." In *Handbuch, Handbuch Soziale Arbeit. Grundlagen der Sozialarbeit und Sozialpädagogik*, ed. Hans-Uwe Otto, pp. 1079–90. Munich, Germany: Ernst Reinhard Verlag.

Elsen, Susanne. 2014. "Soziale Innovation, ökosoziale Ökonomien und Community Development." In *Brixener Studien zu Sozialpolitik und Sozialwissenschaft, Social Innovation, Participation and the Development of Society. Soziale Innovation, Partizipation und die Entwicklung der Gesellschaft*, ed. Walter Lorenz and Susanne Elsen, pp. 231–63. Bozen, Germany: Bozen University Press.

Enquete-Kommission "Zukunft des Bürgerschaftlichen Engagements". 2002. *Drucksache*. 14/8900, *Bürgerschaftliches Engagement. Auf dem Weg in eine zukunftsfähige Bürgergesellschaft*. Opladen, Germany: Leske + Budrich.

EPSU. 2011. "EPSU Welcomes the Result of the Italian Water Referendum!" http://www.epsu.org/IMG/pdf/PR_2011_14_06_water_referendum.pdf (accessed 1 September 2015).

Esping-Andersen, Gøsta. 1990. *The Three Worlds of Welfare Capitalism*. Cambridge, MA: Polity Press.

Esping-Andersen, Gøsta. 1996. "Welfare States without Work. The Impasse of Labour Shedding and Familialism in Continental European Social Policy." In *Welfare States in Transition. National Adaptions in Global Economies*, ed. Gøsta Esping-Andersen, pp. 66–87. London, UK, Thousand Oaks, CA, and New Delhi, India: Sage Publications.

Esping-Andersen, Gøsta. 1997. "Hybrid or Unique? The Japanese Welfare State between Europe and America." *Journal of European Social Policy*, 7(3): 179–89.

Esping-Andersen, Gøsta. 1999. *Social Foundations of Postindustrial Economies*. Oxford, UK, and New York, NY: Oxford University Press.

ESPON. 2005. "Spatial Scenarios and Orientations in Relation to the ESDP and Cohesion Policy." http://www.espon.eu/export/sites/default/Documents/Projects/ESPON2006Projects/CoordinatingCrossThematicProjects/Scenarios/2.ir_3.2-full.pdf (accessed 1 September 2015).

European Commission. n. a. "Public Employment Services." http://ec.europa.eu/social/main.jsp?catId=105&langId=en (accessed 1 September 2015).

European Commission. 1995. *Local Development and Employment Initiatives. An Investigation in the European Union: Internal Document*. Luxembourg: EUR-OP.

European Commission. 1997. "Towards an Urban Agenda in the European Union." Communication from the Commission 197. http://ec.europa.eu/regional_policy/sources/docoffic/official/communic/pdf/urban/urban_197_en.pdf (accessed 1 September 2015).

European Commission. 1999. "Guide to Territorial Employment Pacts." http://ec.europa.eu/regional_policy/archive/innovation/innovating/pacts/down/pdf/pactfin_en.pdf (accessed 1 September 2015).

European Commission. 2010. "Europe 2020. A Strategy for Smart, Sustainable and Inclusive Growth." http://eur-lex.europa.eu/LexUriServ/LexUriServ.do?uri=COM:2010:2020:FIN:EN:PDF (accessed 1 September 2015).

European Commission. 2011a. "A Quality Framework for Services of General Interest in Europe." Communication from the Commission COM (2011) 900 final. http://ec.europa.eu/services_general_interest/docs/comm_quality_framework_en.pdf (accessed 1 September 2015).

European Commission. 2011b. "Cities of Tomorrow. Challenges, Visions, Ways Forward." http://ec.europa.eu/regional_policy/sources/docgener/studies/pdf/citiesoftomorrow/citiesoftomorrow_final.pdf (accessed 1 September 2015).

European Commission. 2011c. "Roadmap to a Resource Efficient Europe." http://eur-lex.europa.eu/legal-content/EN/TXT/PDF/?uri=CELEX:52011DC0571&from=EN (accessed 1 September 2015).

European Commission. 2013a. "Public Opinion in the European Union." http://ec.europa.eu/public_opinion/archives/eb/eb80/eb80_first_en.pdf (accessed 1 September 2015).

European Commission. 2013b. "The EU Emissions Trading System (EU ETS)." http://ec.europa.eu/clima/publications/docs/factsheet_ets_en.pdf (accessed 1 September 2015).

European Commission. 2013c. "The Urban and Regional Dimension of the Crisis. Eigth Progress Report on Economic, Sozial and Territorial Cohesion." EC European Commission. http://ec.europa.eu/regional_policy/sources/docoffic/official/reports/interim8/interim8_en.pdf (accessed 1 September 2015).

European Commission. 2014a. "Background Annex for Discussion in the Forum 'CITIES— Cities of Tomorrow: Investing in Europe'. Brussels 17–18 February 2014." http://ec.europa.eu/regional_policy/sources/conferences/urban2014/doc/issues_paper_annex.pdf (accessed 1 September 2015).

European Commission. 2014b. "Investments for Jobs and Growth. Promoting Development and Good Governance in EU Regions and Cities." European Commission. Report on Economic, Social and Territorial Cohesion 6. http://ec.europa.eu/regional_policy/sources/docoffic/official/reports/cohesion6/6cr_en.pdf (accessed 1 September 2015).

European Commission. 2014c. "Issues Paper for Discussion in the forum 'CITIES— Cities of Tomorrow: Investing in Europe'. Brussels 17–18 February 2014." http://ec.europa.eu/regional_policy/sources/conferences/urban2014/doc/issues_paper_final.pdf (accessed 1 September 2015).

European Commission. 2015. "Results of the Public Consultation on the Key Features of an European Urban Agenda." Commission Staff Working Document SWD (2015) 109 final/2. http://ec.europa.eu/regional_policy/sources/consultation/urb_agenda/pdf/swd_2015.pdf (accessed 1 September 2015).

European Environment Agency. 2012. *EEA report. 2/2012, Urban Adaptation to Climate Change in Europe. Challenges and Opportunities for Cities together with Supportive National and European Policies.* Luxembourg: EUR-OP.

European Environment Agency. 2014. "Public Participation. Contributing to Better Water Management." Experiences from Eight Case Studies across Europe. EEA report 3. http://www.eea.europa.eu/publications/public-participation-contributing-to-better/at_download/file (accessed 1 September 2015).

Eurostat. 2004. *Urban Audit. Methodological Handbook.* Luxembourg: Office for Official Publications of the European Communities.

Eurostat. 2009. *Sustainable Development in the European Union. 2009 Monitoring Report of the EU Sustainable Development Strategy.* Luxembourg: Office for Official Publications of the European Communities.

Eurostat. 2011. *Sustainable Development in the European Union. 2011 Monitoring Report of the EU Sustainable Development Strategy.* 2011st ed. Luxembourg: Publications Office of the European Union.

Eurostat. 2013a. *Sustainable Development in the European Union. 2013 Monitoring Report of the EU Sustainable Development Strategy.* Luxembourg: Publications Office of the European Union.

Eurostat. 2013b. "European Demography. EU28 population 505.7 million at 1 January 2013." http://ec.europa.eu/eurostat/documents/2995521/5167222/3-20112013-AP-EN.PDF (accessed 1 September 2015).

Eurostat. 2014. "GDP per Capita in PPS." http://ec.europa.eu/eurostat/tgm/table.do?tab=table&init=1&language=en&pcode=tec00114&plugin=1 (accessed 1 September 2015).

Evans, Bob, Marko Joas, Susan Sundback, and Kate Theobald. 2005. *Governing Sustainable Cities.* London, UK: Earthscan.

Evers, Adalbert and Jean-Louis Laville, ed. 2004. *The Third Sector in Europe.* Cheltenham, UK, and Northampton, MA: Edward Elgar Publishing.

Falkenmark, Malin and Johan Rockström. 2004. *Balancing Water for Humans and Nature. The New Approach in Ecohydrology.* London, UK: Earthscan.

Fenger, H.J. Menno. 2007. "Welfare Regimes in Central and Eastern Europe. Incorporating Post-communist Countries in a Welfare Regime Typology." *Contemporary Issues and Ideas in Social Sciences,* 2(3): 1–30.

Fenton, Paul. 2014. "Five Factors for Urban Sustainability. Exploring Influences on Municipal Strategic Planning." Linköping Studies in Science and Technology – Licentiate Thesis n. 1646, Linköping University. Linköping, Sweden.

Ferge, Zsuzsa. 2008. "Is There a Specific East-Central European Welfare Culture?" In *Culture and Welfare State. Values and Social Policy in Comparative Perspective,* ed. Wim van Oorschot, Michael Opielka, and Birgit Pfau-Effinger, pp. 141–61. Cheltenham, UK, and Northampton, MA: Edward Elgar Publishing.

Ferguson, Briony C., Rebekah R. Brown, Niki Frantzeskaki, Fjalar J. de Haan, and Ana Deletic. 2013. "The Enabling Institutional Context for Integrated Water Management. Lessons from Melbourne." *Water Research,* 47(20): 7300–14.

Fernihough, Alan and Kevin H. O'Rourke. 2014. "Coal and the European Industrial Revolution." University of Oxford. Discussion Papers in Economic and Social History 124. http://www.economics.ox.ac.uk/materials/papers/13183/Coal%20-%20O%27Rourke%20124.pdf (accessed 1 September 2015).

Flick, Uwe. 2011. *Introducing Research Methodology. A Beginner's Guide to Doing a Research Project.* London, UK, Thousand Oaks, CA, and New Delhi, India: Sage Publications.

Florida, Richard. 2002. "The Economic Geography of Talent." *Annals of the Association of American Geographers,* 92(4): 743–55.

Floridi, Luciano. 2013. *The Ethics of Information.* Oxford, UK, and New York, NY: Oxford University Press.

Fortenau, Bénédicte, Nancy Neamtan, Frederick Wanyama, Leandro Pereira Morais, and Mathieu de Porter. 2010. *Social and Solidarity Economy. Building a Common Understanding.* In support of the First edition of the Social and Solidarity Economy Academy, 25–29 October 2010, ITC ILO, Turin, Italy.

Fournier, Valérie. 2013. "Commoning. On the Social Organisation of the Commons." *M@n@gement*, 16(4): 433–53.

Franz, Hans-Werner, Josef Hochgerner, and Jürgen Howaldt, ed. 2012. *Challenge Social Innovation. Potentials for Business, Social Entrepreneurship, Welfare and Civil Society*. Berlin and Heidelberg, Germany: Springer.

Frohlich, Norman and Joe A. Oppenheimer. 2001. "Choosing. A Cognitive Model of Economic and Political Choice." University of Manitoba, Faculty of Management. Working Papers. http://www.ibrarian.net/navon/paper/Choosing__A_Cognitive_Model_of_Economic_and_Polit.pdf?paperid=1213055 (accessed 1 September 2015).

Froy, Francesca and Sylvain Giguère. 2009. "Which Countries Have Most Flexibility in the Management of Labour Market Flexibility? An OECD Comparison." In *Local Economic and Employment Development (LEED), Flexible Policy for More and Better Jobs*, ed. Sylvain Giguère and Francesca Froy, pp. 35–58. Paris, France: OECD Publishing.

Froy, Francesca, Sylvain Giguère, Lucy Pyne, and Donna E. Wood. 2011. "Building Flexibility and Accountability into Local Employment Services. Synthesis of OECD studies in Belgium, Canada, Denmark and the Netherlands." OECD Publishing. OECD Local Economic and Employment Development (LEED) Working Papers 2011/10. http://www.oecd-ilibrary.org/docserver/download/5kg3mkv3tr21.pdf?expires=1436429714&id=id&accname=guest&checksum=A4507AE2227D2ABDBD33F5070AAC8200 (accessed 1 September 2015).

Fung, Archon and Erik O. Wright. 2003. *Deepening Democracy. Institutional Innovations in Empowered Participatory Governance*. The Real Utopias Project IV. London, UK, and New York, NY: Verso.

Gambaro, Ludovica, Simona Milio, and Marco Simoni. 2004. "Partnerships for Development. Studies on Territorial Employment Pacts in Italy." International Institute for Labour Studies Discussion paper DP/155/2004. http://www.ilo.org/wcmsp5/groups/public/—-dgreports/—-inst/documents/publication/wcms_193622.pdf (accessed 1 September 2015).

Garmendia, Eneko and Sigrid Stagl. 2010. "Public Participation for Sustainability and Social Learning. Concepts and Lessons from Three Case Studies in Europe." *Ecological Economics*, 69(8): 1712–22.

Garzillo, Cristina and Peter Ulrich. 2015. "Annex to MS94: Compilation of Case Study Reports. A Compendium of 40 Case Study Reports from Cities in 14 European Countries." WWWforEurope. Working Paper 94. http://www.foreurope.eu/fileadmin/documents/pdf/Workingpapers/WWWforEurope_WPS_no094_MS94_Annex.pdf (accessed 1 September 2015).

Geddes, Michael. 1998. *Local Partnership. A Successful Strategy for Social Cohesion? European Research Report*. Dublin, UK, and Lanham, MD: European Foundation for the Improvement of Living and Working Conditions.

Geels, Frank W. 2011. "The Multi-Level Perspective on Sustainability Transitions. Responses to Seven Criticisms." *Environmental Innovation and Societal Transitions*, 1(1): 24–40.

Gerring, John. 2007. *Case Study Research. Principles and Practices*. Cambridge, UK, and New York, NY: Cambridge University Press.

Gibson-Graham, J.K. 1996. *The End of Capitalism (As We Knew It). A Feminist Critique of Political Economy*. Minneapolis, MN, and London, UK: University of Minnesota Press, (Orig. pub. 1996).

Giguère, Sylvain and Randal W. Eberts. 2009. "Effects of Decentralisation and Flexibility of Active Labour Market Policy on Country Level Employment Rates." In *Local Economic and Employment Development (LEED), Flexible Policy for More and Better Jobs*, ed. Sylvain Giguère and Francesca Froy, pp. 59–72. Paris, France: OECD Publishing.

Giguère, Sylvain and Francesca Froy. 2009. "A new framework for labour market policy in a global economy." In *Local Economic and Employment Development (LEED), Flexible Policy for More and Better Jobs*, ed. Sylvain Giguère and Francesca Froy, pp. 17–34. Paris, France: OECD Publishing.

Goel, Prem. K. 2006. *Water Pollution. Causes, Effects and Control*. 2nd ed. New Delhi, India: New Age International.

Goulas, Dimitrios S. and Georgia N. Kontogeorga. 2013. "How Did the Economic Crisis in Greece Affect the Steps in Applying E-Government at the First Degree Self Government of Greece." *Journal of Governance and Regulation*, 2(4): 7–12.

Granovetter, Mark. 1985. "Economic Action and Social Structure. The Problem of Embeddedness." *American Journal of Sociology*, 91(3): 481–510.

Greening, Lorna A., David L. Greene, and Carmen Difiglio. 2000. "Energy Efficiency and Consumption – the Rebound Effect – A Survey." *Energy Policy*, 28(6–7): 389–401.

Grepperud, Sverre and Ingeborg Rasmussen. 2004. "A General Equilibrium Assessment of Rebound Effects." *Energy Economics*, 26(2): 261–82.

Grin, John, Jan Rotmans, and Johan Schot. 2010. *Transitions to Sustainable Development. New directions in the Study of Long Term Transformative Change*. London, UK, and New York, NY: Routledge.

Gutzwiller, Lukas. 2006. 21. "Exkurs. 2000-Watt-Gesellschaft." http://www.2000watt.ch/fileadmin/user_upload/2000Watt-Gesellschaft/de/Dateien/weitereInformationen/Exkurs_2000-Watt-Gesellschaft.pdf (accessed 1 September 2015).

Haan, Fjalar J. de, Briony C. Ferguson, Rachelle C. Adamowicz, Phillip Johnstone, Rebekah R. Brown, and Tony H. Wong. 2014. "The Needs of Society. A New Understanding of Transitions, Sustainability and Liveability." *Technological Forecasting and Social Change*, 85(June), 1: 121–32.

Habermas, Jürgen. 1976. *Legitimation Crisis*. London, UK: Heinemann.

Habermas, Jürgen. 1981a. *The Theory of Communicative Action. Reason and The Rationalisation of Society*. 2 Vols. Boston, MA: Beacon Press, (Orig. pub. 1981).

Habermas, Jürgen. 1981b. *The Theory of Communicative Action. Lifeworld and System: A Critique of Functionalist Reason*. 2 Vols. Boston, MA: Beacon Press, (Orig. pub. 1981).

Habermas, Jürgen. 1985a. *Kleine Politische Schriften. V, Die Neue Unübersichtlichkeit*. Frankfurt am Main, Germany: Suhrkamp.

Habermas, Jürgen. 1985b. *The Philosophical Discourse of Modernity. Twelve Lectures*. Cambridge, MA: Polity Press, (Orig. pub. 1985).

Habermas, Jürgen. 1989. *The Structural Transformation of the Public Sphere. An Inquiry into a Category of Bourgeois Society*. Cambridge, MA: MIT Press.

Häikiö, Liisa. 2012. "From Innovation to Convention. Legitimate Citizen Participation in Local Governance." *Local Government Studies*, 38(4): 415–35.

Hall, Peter A. and David Soskice. 2001. "Introduction." In *Varieties of Capitalism. The Institutional Foundations of Comparative Advantage*, ed. Peter A. Hall and David Soskice, pp. 1–68. Oxford, UK, and New York, NY: Oxford University Press.

Hamm, Bernd, Ingo Neumann, Peter Suska, and Gabi Gotzen. 1996. *Siedlungs-, Umwelt- und Planungssoziologie. Ökologische Soziologie*. Opladen, Germany: Leske + Budrich.

Hardin, Garrett. 1968. "The Tragedy of the Commons." *Science*, 162: 1243–48.

Harvey, David. 2008. "The Right to the City." *New Left Review*, 53: 23–40.

Harvey, David. 2012. *Rebel Cities. From the Right to the City to the Urban Revolution*. London, UK: Verso.

Hayek, Friedrich A. v. 1945. "The Use of Knowledge in Society." *American Economic Review*, XXXV(4): 519–30.

Heberer, Thomas. 2002. "Tracking Persistent Pharmaceutical Residues from Municipal Sewage to Drinking Water." *Journal of Hydrology*, 266(3–4): 175–89.

Heinonen, Jukka, Mikko Jalas, Jouni K. Juntunen, Sanna Ala-Mantila, and Seppo Junnila. 2013a. "Situated Lifestyles. I. How Lifestyles Change Along with the Level of Urbanization and What the Greenhouse Gas Implications Are – A Study of Finland." *Environmental Research Letters*, 8(2): 025003, 1–13.

Heinonen, Jukka, Mikko Jalas, Jouni K. Juntunen, Sanna Ala-Mantila, and Seppo Junnila. 2013b. "Situated Lifestyles. II. The Impacts of Urban Density, Housing Type and Motorization on the Greenhouse Gas Emissions of the Middle-Income Consumers in Finland." *Environmental Research Letters*, 8(3): 035050, 1–10.

Helfrich, Silke, ed. 2012. *Commons. Für eine neue Politik jenseits von Markt und Staat*. 1st ed. Bielefeld, Germany: Transcript.

Henderson, Hazel. 1997. "Macht beide Seiten zu Gewinnern! Oder Leben jenseits des globalen ökonomischen Krieges." In *Grenzen-los? Jedes System braucht Grenzen, aber wie durchlässig müssen diese sein?*, ed. Ernst U. von Weizsäcker and Rainer Klüting, pp. 348–75. Berlin, Germany, and Boston, MA: Birkhäuser.

Herring, Horace and Steve Sorrell, ed. 2009. *Energy, Climate and the Environment Series, Energy efficiency and Sustainable Consumption. The Rebound Effect*. Basingstoke, UK, and New York, NY: Palgrave Macmillan.

Herzberg, Carsten. 2009.*Von der Bürger- zur Solidarkommune. Lokale Demokratie in Zeiten der Globalisierung*. Hamburg, Germany:VSA-Verlag.

Hooghe, Liesbet and Gary Marks. 2001. *Multi-level Governance and European Integration*. Lanham, MD, Boulder, CO, New York, NY, Toronto, Ontario, and Oxford, UK: Rowman & Littlefield Publishers.

Hooghe, Liesbet and Gary Marks. 2010. "Types of Multi-level Governance." In *Handbook on Multi-level Governance*, ed. Henrik Enderlein, Sonja Wälti, and Michael Zürn, pp. 17–31. Cheltenham, UK, and Northampton, MA: Edward Elgar Publishing.

Huber, Peter. 2005. "Schwerpunkt 6: Territoriale Beschäftigungspakte." In *Evaluierung Europäischer Sozialfonds 2000–2006. Ziel 3 — Österreich*, ed. Hedwig Lutz and Helmut Mahringer, pp. 1–156. Vienna, Austria: Austrian Institute of Economic Research, WIFO (eigenverlag).

Huber, Peter. 2013a. "Labour Market Institutions and Regional Unemployment Disparities." WWWforEurope. Working Paper 29. http://www.foreurope.eu/fileadmin/documents/pdf/Workingpapers/WWWforEurope_WPS_no029_MS95.pdf (accessed 1 September 2015).

Huber, Peter. 2013b. "The Impact of Networks, Segregation and Diversity on Migrants' Labour Market Integration." WWWforEurope. Working Paper 22. http://www.foreurope.eu/fileadmin/documents/pdf/Workingpapers/WWWforEurope_WPS_no022_MS100.pdf (accessed 1 September 2015).

Huber, Peter. 2014. "The Institutional Pre-conditions for Regional Labour Market Policy Making in the EU. Case Studies and Policy Conclusions." WWWforEurope. Working Paper 70. http://www.foreurope.eu/fileadmin/documents/pdf/Workingpapers/WWWforEurope_WPS_no070_MS96_MS97.pdf (accessed 1 September 2015).

Human Right to Water. 2014. "Press Release – Commission Lacks Ambition in Replying to First European Citizen's Initiative." http://www.right2water.eu/news/press-release-commission-lacks-ambition-replying-first-european-citizens%E2%80%99-initiative (accessed 1 September 2015).

ICLEI, ed. 2012. *Local Sustainability 2012. Taking Stock and Moving Forward*. Global Review. Bonn, Germanny: ICLEI – Local Governments for Sustainability.

InContext. 2013. "Going Out of the Town Hall. The Benefits and How They Can Be Achieved." Ecologic Institute. Policy Brief. http://www.incontext-fp7.eu/sites/default/files/D5.3_Out%20of%20the%20townhall-final.pdf (accessed 1 September 2015).

Inhetveen, Katharina. 2012. "Translation Challenges. Qualitative Interviewing in a Multi-Lingual Field." *Qualitative Sociology Review*, 8(2): 28–45.

IPCC. 2014. "Summary for Policy Makers." In *Climate change 2014. Mitigation of Climate Change*, ed. Ottmar Edenhofen, Ramón Pichs-Madruga, Youba Sokona, Jan C. Minx, Ellie Farahani, Susanne Kadner, and Kristin Seyboth, pp. 1–30. Cambridge, UK, and New York, NY: Cambridge University Press.

Jackson, Tim. 2009. *Prosperity without Growth. Economics for a Finite Planet*. London, UK: Earthscan.

Jäggi, Max, Roger Müller, and Sil Schmid. 1977. *Red Bologna* London, UK: Writers and Readers.

Joas, Marko, Kate Theobald, David McGuinnes, Cristina Garzillo, and Stefan Kuhn, ed. 2013. *Informed Cities. Making Research work for Local Sustainability*. London, UK, and New York, NY: Routledge.

Johnson, Harry. 1958. "Demand Theory further Revisited or Goods are Goods." *Economica*, 25 (May):149.

Kalff, Yannick. 2015. "Alvesson, Mats/Willmott, Hugh (1996): Making Sense of Management: A Critical Introduction." In *Schlüsselwerke der Organisationsforschung*, ed. Stefan Kühl, 55–59. Wiesbaden, Germany: SpringerVS.

Kasozi, Anthony S. 2004. "Towards a Taxonomy of Institutions in Economic Development." https://www.ashridge.org.uk/Media-Library/Ashridge/PDFs/Publications/TowardstaxonomyPaper.pdf (accessed 1 September 2015).

Kato, Yuki, Catarina Passidomo, and Daina Harvey. 2014. "Political Gardening in a Post-Disaster City. Lessons from New Orleans." *Urban Studies*, 51(9): 1833–49.

Kawano, Emily, Thomas N. Masterson, and Jonathan Teller-Elsberg. 2009. *Solidarity Economy I. Building Alternatives for People and Planet; Papers and Reports from the 2009 U.S. Forum on the Solidarity Economy*. Amherst, MA: Center for Popular Economics.

Kemmis, Stephen. 2001. "Exploring the Relevance of Critical Theory for Action Research. Emancipatory Action Research in the Footsteps of Jürgen Habermas." In *Handbook of Action Research. Participative Inquiry and Practice*, ed. Peter Reason and Hilary Bradbury, pp. 91–102. London, UK, Thousand Oaks, CA, and New Delhi, India: Sage Publications.

Knight, Daniel M. 2014. "A Critical Perspective on Economy, Modernity and Temporality in Contemporary Greece through the Prism of Energy Practice." Hellenic Observatory. Hellenic Observatory Papers on Greece and Southeast Europe, GreeSE Paper 81. http://www.lse.ac.uk/europeanInstitute/research/hellenicObservatory/CMS%20pdf/Publications/GreeSE/GreeSE-No-81.pdf (accessed 1 September 2015).

Kolberg, Jon E. and Gøsta Esping-Andersen. 1992. "Welfare States and Employment Regimes." In *The Study of Welfare State Regimes*, ed. Jon E. Kolberg, pp. 3–36. New York, NY: M. E. Sharpe.

Kooiman, Jan and Maarten Bavinck. 2013. "Theorizing Governability – The Interactive Governance Perspective." In *Governability of Fisheries and Aquaculture. Theory and Applications*, ed. Maarten Bavinck, Ratana Chuenpagdee, Svein Jentoft, and Jan Kooiman, pp. 9–30. Dordrecht, Netherlands: Springer.

Krasny, Elke. 2012. *Hands-on Urbanism 1850–2012. The Right to Green*. Hong Kong: MCCM Creations.

Kropp, Cordula. 2011. "Gärtner(n) ohne Grenzen. Eine neue Politik des 'Sowohl-als-auch' urbaner Gärten?" In *Urban Gardening. Über die Rückkehr der Gärten in die Stadt*. 4th ed., ed. Christa Müller, pp. 76–87. Munich, Germany: Oekom.

Kunze, Conrad and Sören Becker. 2014. "Energy Democracy in Europe. A Survey and Outlook." http://rosalux-europa.info/userfiles/file/Energy-democracy-in-Europe.pdf (accessed 1 September 2015).

Kunzmann, Klaus. 2014. "Smart Cities. A New Paradigm of Urban Development." *CRIOS*, (7): 9–19.

Labaeye, Adrien and Thomas Sauer. 2013. "City Networks and the Socio-ecological Transition. A European Inventory." WWWforEurope. Working Paper 27. http://www.foreurope.eu/fileadmin/documents/pdf/Workingpapers/WWWforEurope_WPS_no027_MS89.pdf (accessed 1 September 2015).

LABGOV. 2014. "Regulation on Collaboration between Citizens and the City for the Care and Regeneration of Urban Commons." http://www.comune.bologna.it/media/files/bolognaregulation.pdf.

Lakshmi, Geeta. 2011. "Water for Commons~Disparity in Chennai." In *Vocabulary of Commons*, ed. Foundation for Ecological Security, pp. 313–30. Bangalore, India: Judge Press.

Latour, Bruno and Vincent A. Lépinay. 2009. *The Science of Passionate Interests. An Introduction to Gabriel Tarde's Economic Anthropology*. Chicago, IL: Prickly Paradigm Press.

Lefebvre, Henri. 1990. *The Urban Revolution*. Minneapolis, MN, and London, UK: University of Minnesota Press, (Orig. pub. 1990).

Lefebvre, Henri. 1996. *Writings on Cities*. Oxford, UK: Blackwell.

Lenzen, Manfred. 2008. "Life Cycle Energy and Greenhouse Gas Emissions of Nuclear Energy. A Review." *Energy Conversion and Management*, 49(8): 2178–99.

Lévesque, Benoît. 2013. "Social Innovation in Governance and Public Management Systems. Toward a New Paradigm?" In *The International Handbook on Social Innovation. Collective Action, Social Learning and Transdisciplinary Research*, ed. Frank Moulaert, Diana MacCallum, Abid Mehmood, and Abdelillah Hamdouch, pp. 25–39. Cheltenham, UK, and Northampton, MA: Edward Elgar Publishing.

Lewin, Kurt. 1947. "Frontiers in Group Dynamics. Concept, Method and Reality in Social Science." *Human Relations*, 1(2): 143–53.

Lewis, Jane and Jane Ritchie. 2003. "Generalising from Qualitative Research." In *Qualitative Research Practice. A Guide for Social Science Students and Researchers*, ed. Jane Ritchie and Jane Lewis, pp. 263–85. London, UK, Thousand Oaks, CA, and New Delhi, India: Sage Publications.

Lidström, Anders. 2003. *Kommunsystem i Europa [Local Government Systems in Europe]*. Malmö, Sweden: Liberförlag.

Littig, Beate. 2011. "Interviews, Expert." In *International Encyclopedia of Political Science*, ed. Bertrand Badie, Dirk Berg-Schlosser, and Leonardo Morlino, pp. 1343–46. London, UK, Thousand Oaks, CA, and New Delhi, India: Sage Publications.

Lloyd, William Forster. 1833. *Two Lectures on the Checks to Population*. Delivered before the University of Oxford in Michaelmas term 1883. Oxford, UK: unknown.

Long, J. Scott and Jeremy Freese. 2006. *Regression Models for Categorical Dependent Variables using Stata*. 2nd ed. College Station, TX: Stata Press.

Loorbach, Derk and Jan Rotmans. 2006. "Managing Transitions for Sustainable Development." In *Environment & policy, Understanding Industrial Transformation. Views from Different Disciplines*, ed. Xander Olsthoorn and Anna J. Wieczorek, pp. 187–206. Dordrecht, Netherlands: Springer.

López-Santana, Mariely. 2006. "The Domestic Implications of European soft Law. Framing and Transmitting Change in Employment Policy." *Journal of European Public Policy*, 13(4): 481–99.

Lund, Henrik. 2007. "Renewable Energy Strategies for Sustainable Development." *Energy*, 32(6): 912–19.

MacKenzie, Donald A. 2006. *An Engine, Not a Camera. How Financial Models Shape Markets*. Cambridge, MA: MIT Press.

MacKenzie, Donald A., Fabian Muniesa, and Lucia Siu, ed. 2007. *Do Economists Make Markets? On the Performativity of Economics*. Princeton, NJ: Princeton University Press.

Mantino, Francesco. 2011. "Developing a Territorial Approach for the CAP." Discussion Paper, Institute for European Environmental Policy. http://mpra.ub.uni-muenchen.de/49298/ (accessed 1 September 2015).

Marlow, David R., Magnus Moglia, Stephen Cook, and David J. Beale. 2013. "Towards Sustainable Urban Water Management: A Critical Reassessment." *Water Research*, 47(20): 7150–61.

Martinez-Fernandez, Cristina, Pawel Chorazy, Tamara Weyman, and Monika Gawron. 2011. "A Local Approach for Local Jobs?" OECD Publishing. OECD Local Economic and Employment Working Papers 2011/23. http://www.oecd.org/cfe/leed/49318562.pdf (accessed 1 September 2015).

Mason, Jennifer. 2002. *Qualitative Researching*. 2nd ed. London, UK, Thousand Oaks, CA, and New Delhi, India: Sage Publications.

McCarty, Perry L., Jaeho Bae, and Jeonghwan Kim. 2011. "Domestic Wastewater Treatment as a Net Energy Producer – Can This Be Achieved?" *Environmental Science & Technology*, 45(17): 7100–6.

McGinnis, Michael and Elinor Ostrom. 2010. "IAD and SES Dynamic Flows. Introducing the Program in Institutional Analysis of Socio-Ecological Systems (PIASES) Framework". Paper presented at the Workshop in Political Theory and Policy Analysis, Indiana University, Bloomington, IN, 24 March 2010.

Medema, Wietske, Brian S. McIntosh, and Paul J. Jeffrey. 2008. "From Premise to Practice. A Critical Assessment of Integrated Water Resources Management and Adaptive Management Approaches in the Water Sector." *Ecology and Society*, 13(2): 29.

Ménard, Claude and Aleksandra Peeroo. 2011. "Liberalization in the Water Sector. Three leading Models." In *International Handbook of Network Industries: The Liberalization of Infrastructure*, ed. Matthias Finger and Rolf W. Künneke, pp. 310–28. Cheltenham, UK, and Northampton, MA: Edward Elgar Publishing.

Mieg, Harald A. and Klaus Töpfer, ed. 2013. *Institutional and Social Innovation for Sustainable Urban Development*. London, UK, and New York, NY: Routledge.

Mosley, Hugh G. 2009. "The Trade-off between Flexibility and Accountability in Labour Market Policy." In *Local Economic and Employment Development (LEED), Flexible Policy for More and Better Jobs*, ed. Sylvain Giguère and Francesca Froy, pp. 73–101. Paris, France: OECD Publishing.

Mosley, Hugh G. 2011. "Decentralisation of Public Employment Services." European Commission. http://zielonalinia.gov.pl/upload/epsz/Decentralisation_PES.pdf (accessed 1 September 2015).

Moulaert, Frank and Oana Ailenei. 2005. "Social Economy, Third Sector and Solidarity Relations. A conceptual Synthesis from History to Present." *Urban Studies*, 42(11): 2037–54.

Mulgan, Geoff, Simon Tucker, Rushanara Ali, and Ben Sanders. 2007. "Social Innovation. What It Is, Why It Matters and How It Can Be Accelerated." Working Paper. http://eureka.bodleian.ox.ac.uk/761/1/Social_Innovation.pdf (accessed 1 September 2015).

Nagy, Erika, Gábor Nagy, Judit Timár, Kirsten Mangels, Nadine Schrader-Bölsche, and Janez Berdavs. 2008. "Transnational Comparison of National Policies and Planning Systems." South east Europe Transnational cooperation programme. Integrated Urban Development of Vital Historic Towns as Regional Centres in South East Europe. http://www.southeast-europe.net/document.cmt?id=474 (accessed 1 September 2015).

Nordhaus, William D. 1994. *Managing the Global Commons. The Economics of Climate Change*. Cambridge, MA: MIT Press.

North, Douglass C. 1990. *Political Economy of Institutions and Decisions, Institutions, Institutional Change and Economic Performance*. 27th ed. Cambridge, UK, and New York, NY: Cambridge University Press, (Orig. pub. 1990).

North, Douglass C. 1993. "Prize Lecture. Economic Performance through Time." http://www.nobelprize.org/nobel_prizes/economic-sciences/laureates/1993/north-lecture.html (accessed 1 September 2015).

Nowotny, Helga, Peter Scott, and Michael Gibbons. 2001. *Re-thinking Science. Knowledge and the Public in an Age of Uncertainty*. 2nd ed. Cambridge, MA: Polity Press, (Orig. pub. 2001).

Nuclear Energy Institute. n. a. Life-Cycle Emissions Analyses. http://www.nei.org/Issues-Policy/Protecting-the-Environment/Life-Cycle-Emissions-Analyses (accessed 1 September 2015).

Nussbaum, Martha C. 2006. *The Tanner Lectures on Human Values, Frontiers of Justice. Disability, Nationality, Species Membership*. Cambridge, MA: Belknap Press of Harvard University Press.

OECD, ed. 2004. *New Forms of Governance for Economic Development*. Paris, France: OECD Publishing.

OECD. 2009a. "Coping with the Crisis at Local Level. Policy Lessons from the OECD Programme on Local Economic and Employment Development." OECD Publishing. internal working document CFE. https://www.oecd.org/cfe/leed/42965605.pdf (accessed 1 September 2015).

OECD. 2009b. "Flexible Policy for More and Better Jobs." OECD. http://browse.oecdbookshop.org/oecd/pdfs/product/8409021e.pdf (accessed 1 September 2015).

OECD. 2013a. *OECD Green Growth Studies, Green Growth in Cities*. Paris, France: OECD Publishing.

OECD. 2013b. "Local Job Creation. How Employment and Training Agencies Can Help, United States." OECD Publishing. OECD Local Economic and Employment Development (LEED) Working Papers 2013/10. http://www.oecd-ilibrary.org/docserver/download/5k44zcpz25vg.pdf?expires=1436526999&id=id&accname=guest&checksum=EC898EB13C5E99C12A549F531F3FBE48 (accessed 1 September 2015).

Olson, Mancur. 2000. *Power and Prosperity. Outgrowing Communist and Capitalist Dictatorships*. Cambridge, MA: Harvard University Press.

Oorschot, Wim van, Michael Opielka, and Birgit Pfau-Effinger, ed. 2008. *Culture and Welfare State. Values and Social Policy in Comparative Perspective*. Cheltenham, UK, and Northampton, MA: Edward Elgar Publishing.

Osborne, Stephen P. 2008. *The Third Sector in Europe. Prospects and Challenges*. London, UK, and New York, NY: Routledge.

Ostrom, Elinor. 1990. *Governing the Commons. The Evolution of Institutions for Collective Action*. Cambridge, UK, and New York, NY: Cambridge University Press.

Ostrom, Elinor. 2005. *Understanding Institutional Diversity*. Princeton, NJ: Princeton University Press.

Ostrom, Elinor. 2007. "A Diagnostic Approach for going Beyond Panaceas." *Proceedings of the National Academy of Sciences*, 104(39): 15181–87.

Ostrom, Elinor. 2009. "A Polycentric approach for Coping with Climate Change." Policy Research Working Paper 5095. http://www-wds.worldbank.org/servlet/WDSContentServer/WDSP/IB/2009/10/26/000158349_20091026142624/Rendered/PDF/WPS5095.pdf (accessed 1 September 2015).

Ostrom, Elinor and Toh-Kyeong Ahn. 2003. "Introduction." In *Foundations of Social Capital*, ed. Elinor Ostrom and Toh-Kyeong Ahn, pp. xi–xxxix. Cheltenham, UK, and Northampton, MA: Edward Elgar Publishing.

Ostrom, Elinor and Charlotte Hess. 2007. "A Framework for Analyzing the Knowledge Commons." In *Understanding Knowledge as a Commons. From Theory to Practice*, ed. Charlotte Hess and Elinor Ostrom, pp. 41–81. Cambridge, MA: MIT Press.

Ostrom, Elinor, Roger B. Parks, and Gordon P. Whitaker. 1978. *Patterns of Metropolitan Policing*. Cambridge, MA: Ballinger.

Parker, Martin. 2002. *Against Management. Organization in the Age of Managerialism*. Cambridge, MA: Polity Press.

Parker, Martin, Valérie Fournier, and Patrick Reedy. 2007. *The Dictionary of Alternatives. Utopianism and Organisation*. London, UK, and New York, NY: Zed Books.
Parks, Louisa. 2014. "Framing in the Right2Water European Citizen's Initiative." Paper prepared for presentation at the ECPR general conference, 3–6 September 2014. http://www.right2water.eu/sites/water/files/Conference%20paper%20Right2Water%20by%20Louisa%20Parks.pdf (accessed 1 September 2015).
Perlas, Nicanor. 2000. *Die Globalisierung gestalten. Zivilgesellschaft, Kulturkraft und Dreigliederung*. Frankfurt am Main, Germany: Info-3.
Phills, James A., Jr., Kriss Deiglmeier, and Dale T. Miller. 2008. "Rediscovering Social Innovation." *Stanford Social Innovation Review* (Fall): 36–43.
Piketty, Thomas. 2014. *Capital in the Twenty-first Century*. Cambridge, MA: Belknap Press of Harvard University Press.
Piorr, Annette, Joe Ravetz, and Iván Tosics. 2011. "Peri-urbanisation in Europe. Towards a European Policy to Sustain Urban-Rural Futures." PLUREL. Synthesis Report. http://www.plurel.net/images/Peri_Urbanisation_in_Europe_printversion.pdf (accessed 1 September 2015).
Polanyi, Karl. 1944. *The Great Transformation. The Political and Economic Origins of Our Time*. 2nd ed. Boston, MA: Beacon Press, (Orig. pub. 1944).
Poteete, Amy R., Marco A. Janssen, and Elinor Ostrom. 2010. *Working Together. Collective Action, the Commons, and Multiple Methods in Practice*. Princeton, NJ: Princeton University Press.
Powell, Walter W. 1990. "Neither Market nor Hierarchy. Network Forms of Organization." *Research on Organizational Behavior*, 12: 295–336.
Pradeep, Chandra K. and Terry L. Cooper. 2005. "Democratizing the Administrative State. Connecting Neighborhood Councils and City Agencies." *Public Administration Review*, 65(5): 559–67.
Pratchett, Lawrence. 2004. "Local Autonomy, Local Democracy and the 'New Localism'." *Political Studies*, 52(2): 358–75.
Prats-Monne, Xavier. 2004. "The Role of the European Union in Local and Regional Development." OECD. Paper presented at the World Bank Institute City Round. http://www.oecd.org/regional/leed/27917034.pdf (accessed 1 September 2015).
Purcell, Mark. 2003. "Excavating Lefebvre. The Right to the City and its Urban Politics of the Inhabitant." *GeoJournal*, 58: 99–108.
Pyke, Frank. 1998. "Local Development Initiatives and the Management of Change." Employment and Training Department, ILO. Employment and Training papers 31. http://www.oit.org/wcmsp5/groups/public/@ed_emp/documents/publication/wcms_120331.pdf (accessed 1 September 2015).
Randers, Jørgen. 2012. *2052. A Global Forecast for the Next Forty Years; A Report to the Club of Rome Commemorating the 40th Anniversary of The Limits to Growth*. White River Junction, VT: Chelsea Green.
Raskin, Paul, Tariq Banuri, Gilberto Gallopín, Pablo Gutman, Al Hammond, Robert Kates, and Rob Swart. 2002. *Great Transition. The Promise and Lure of the Times Ahead*. SEI PoleStar series report. no. 12. Boston, MA: Stockholm Environment Institute.
Rauschmayer, Felix, Tom Bauler, and Niko Schäpke. 2015. "Towards a Thick Understanding of sustainability Transitions – Linking Transition Management, Capabilities and Social Practices." *Ecological Economics*, (109): 211–21.
Ravetz, Joe. 2011. "Urban Synergy Foresight." In *Urban Governance in the EU. Current Challenges and Forward Prospects*, pp. 31–44. Brussels, Belgium: EU Committee of the Regions.
Ravetz, Joe. 2013. "New Futures for Older Ports. Synergistic Development in a Global Urban System." *Sustainability*, 5(12): 5100–18.
Redman, Charles. 2014. "Should Sustainability and Resilience Be Combined or Remain Distinct Pursuits?" *Ecology and Society*, 19(2): Art. 37.
Reed, Mark S. 2008. "Stakeholder Participation for Environmental anagement. A Literature Review." *Biological Conservation*, 141(10): 2417–31.

Regalia, Ida. 2008. "Territorial Pacts and Local Level Concertation in Europe. A Multi-level Governance Perspective." University of Milan. NEWGOV-New modes of governance. http://www.eu-newgov.org/database/DELIV/D18bD05b_Territorial_Pacts_and_Local_Level_Concertation_in_Europe.pdf (accessed 1 September 2015).

Reinstaller, Andreas. 2013. "An Evolutionary View on Social Innovation and the Process of Economic Change." WWWforEurope. Working Paper 43. http://www.foreurope.eu/fileadmin/documents/pdf/Workingpapers/WWWforEurope_WPS_no043_MS51.pdf (accessed 1 September 2015).

REScoop.EU. 2013. "Charter of REScoop.eu." http://rescoop.eu/sites/default/files/charter_rescoop_eu.pdf (accessed 1 September 2015).

Rietzler, Katja. 2014. "Anhaltender Verfall der Infrastruktur. Die Lösung muss bei den Kommunen ansetzen." Institut für Makroökonomie und Konjunkturforschung in der Hans-Böckler-Stiftung. Report 94. http://www.boeckler.de/pdf/p_imk_report_94_2014.pdf (accessed 1 September 2015).

Rifkin, Jeremy. 1995. *The End of Work. The Decline of the Global Work-Force and the Dawn of the Post-Market Era*. New York, NY: Putnam Publishing, (Orig. pub. 1995).

RIPESS. 2013. "Differences and Convergences in Social Solidarity Economy Concepts, Definitions and Framework." RIPESS Working Paper. http://ripess.eu/wp-content/uploads/2014/06/Differences-and-Convergences-in-Social-Solidarity-Economy-Concepts.pdf (accessed 1 September 2015).

Ritchie, Jane, Jane Lewis, and Gillian Elam. 2003. "Designing and Selecting Samples." In *Qualitative Research Practice. A Guide for Social Science Students and Researchers*, ed. Jane Ritchie and Jane Lewis, pp. 81–108. London, UK, Thousand Oaks, CA, and New Delhi, India: Sage Publications.

Rockström, Johan, Will Steffen, Kevin Noone, Åsa Persson, F.S.I. Chapin, Eric Lambin, Timothy M. Lenton, Marten Scheffer, Carl Folke, Hans J. Schellnhuber, Björn Nykvist, Cynthia A. de Wit, Terry Hughes, Sander van der Leeuw, Henning Rodhe, Sverker Sörlin, Peter K. Snyder, Robert Costanza, Uno Svedin, Malin Falkenmark, Louise Karlberg, Robert W. Corell, Victoria J. Fabry, James Hansen, Brian Walker, Diana Liverman, Katherine Richardson, Paul Crutzen, and Jonathan Foley. 2009. "Planetary Boundaries. Exploring the Safe Operating Space for Humanity." *Ecology and Society*, 14(2). http://www.ecologyandsociety.org/vol14/iss2/art32/ (accessed 3 July 2014).

Rodríguez-Pose, Andrés and Sylvia Tijmstra. 2009. "On the Emergence and Significance of Local Economic Development Strategies." http://scioteca.caf.com/handle/123456789/200 (accessed 9 July 2015).

Rohracher, Harald. 2008. "Energy Systems in Transition. Contributions from Social Sciences." *International Journal of Environmental Technology and Management*, 9(2/3): 144–61.

Roorda, Chris, Julia Wittmayer, Pepik Henneman, Frank van Steenbergen, Niki Frantzeskaki, and Derk Loorbach. 2014. "Transition Management in the Urban Context. Guidance Manual." DRIFT, Erasmus University Rotterdam. http://www.drift.eur.nl/wp-content/uploads/2014/10/DRIFT-Transition_management_in_the_urban_context-guidance_manual.pdf (accessed 1 September 2015).

Roth, Christian and Josef Schmid. 2000. "Multi-level governance in the European Employment and Labour Market Policy." *German Policy Studies*, 1(1), 92–130. http://www.spaef.com/file.php?id=815 (accessed 1 September 2015).

Roth, Roland. 2000. "Bürgerschaftliches Engagement – Formen, Bedingungen, Perspektiven." In *Engagierte Bürgerschaft. Traditionen und Perspektiven*, ed. Annette Zimmer and Stefan Nährlich, pp. 25–48. Opladen, Germany: Leske + Budrich.

Rotmans, Jan, Derk Loorbach, and René Kemp. 2007. Transition Management. Its Origin, Evolution and Critique. http://repub.eur.nl/pub/37240/Metis_125563.pdf (accessed 1 September 2015).

Rubin, Herbert J. and Irene Rubin. 2008. *Community Organizing and Development*. 4th ed. Boston, MA: Pearson.

Rutherford, Jonathan and Olivier Coutard. 2014. "Urban Energy Transitions. Places, Processes and Politics of Socio-technical Change." *Urban Studies*, 51(7): 1353–77.

Rydin, Yvonne. 2010. *Governing for Sustainable Urban Development*. London, UK: Earthscan.

Saller, Raymond. 2005. "Local Employment Initiatives of European Cities." City of Munich. Department for Labor and Economic Development 107.

Samuelson, Paul A. 1954. "The Pure Theory of Public Expenditure." *The Review of Economics and Statistics*, 36(4): 387–89.

Sandberg, Audun. 2008. "Collective Rights in a Modernizing North. On Institutionalizing Sámi and Local Rights to Land and Water in Northern Norway." *International Journal of the Commons*, 2(2): 269–87.

Sauer, Thomas. 2012. "Elemente einer kontextuellen Ökonomie der Nachhaltigkeit. Der Beitrag Elinor Ostroms." In *Ökonomie der Nachhaltigkeit. Grundlagen, Indikatoren, Strategien*, ed. Thomas Sauer, pp. 135–60. Marburg, Germany: Metropolis.

Savenije, Hubert H. 2002. "Why Water Is Not an Ordinary Economic Good, or Why the Girl Is Special." *Physics and Chemistry of the Earth, Parts A/B/C*, 27(11–22): 741–44.

Schakel, Arjan H., Liesbet Hooghe, and Gary Marks. 2015. "Multilevel Governance and the State." In *The Oxford Handbook of Transformations of the State*, ed. Stephan Leibfried, Evelyne Huber, Matthew Lange, Jonah D. Levy, Frank Nullmeier, and John D. Stephens, chap. 14. Oxford, UK, and New York, NY: Oxford University Press.

Schicklinski, Judith. 2015. "Civil Society Actors as Drivers of Socio-ecological Transition? Green Spaces in European Cities as Laboratories of Social Innovation." WWWforEurope. Working Paper 102. http://www.foreurope.eu/fileadmin/documents/pdf/Workingpapers/WWWforEurope_WPS_no102_MS223.pdf (accessed 1 September 2015).

Schipper, Lee and Michael Grubb. 2000. "On the rebound? Feedback between Energy Intensities and Energy uses in IEA countries." *Energy Policy*, 28(6–7): 367–88.

Schlager, Edella and William A. Blomquist. 2008. *Embracing Watershed Politics*. Boulder, CO: University Press of Colorado.

Schmidt, Johannes, Martin Schönhart, Markus Biberacher, Thomas Guggenberger, Stephan Hausl, Gerald Kalt, Sylvain Leduc, Ingrid Schardinger, and Ervin Schmid. 2012. "Regional Energy Autarky. Potentials, Costs and Consequences for an Austrian Region." *Energy Policy*, 47: 211–21.

Schneidewind, Uwe. 2013. "Transformative Literacy. Gesellschaftliche Veränderungsprozesse verstehen und gestalten." *GAIA – Ecological Perspectives* for *Science and Society*, 22(2): 82–86.

Schüle, Ralf. 2007. JET-SET. Die Einführung von Emissionshandelssystemen als sozial-ökologischer Transformationsprozess; Abschlussbericht; Berichtszeitraum: 2003–2006 = Joint emissions trading as a socio-ecological transformation. http://edok01.tib.uni-hannover.de/edoks/e01fb09/599804114.pdf (accessed 1 September 2015).

Schumpeter, Joseph A. 1911. Social Science Classics Series, *The Theory of Economic Development. An Inquiry into Profits, Capital, Credit, Interest, and the Business Cycle*. New Brunswick, NJ: Transaction Books, (Orig. pub. 1911).

Seibel, Wolfgang. 1994. *Funktionaler Dilettantismus. Erfolgreich scheiternde Organisationen im "Dritten Sektor" zwischen Markt und Staat*. 2nd ed. Baden-Baden, Germany: Nomos.

Seley, John E. 1983. Politics of Planning Series, *The Politics of Public-facility Planning*. Lexington, KY: Lexington Books.

Sellers, Jeffrey M. and Anders Lidström. 2007. "Decentralization, Local Government, and the Welfare State." *Governance: An International Journal of Policy, Administration, and Institutions*, 20(4): 609–32.

Sennett, Richard. 1976. *The Fall of Public Man*. Cambridge, UK, and New York, NY: Cambridge University Press.

Sennett, Richard. 1992. *The Conscience of the Eye. The Design and Social Life of Cities*. New York, NY: W. W. Norton.

Seyfang, Gill, Jung J. Park, and Adrian Smith. 2013. "A Thousand Flowers Blooming? An Examination of Community Energy in the UK." *Energy Policy*, (61): 977–89.

Sheskin, David. 2000. *Handbook of Parametric and Nonparametric Statistical Procedures*. 2nd ed. Boca Raton, FL: Chapman & Hall.

Shove, Elisabeth and Gordon Walker. 2007. "CAUTION! Transitions Ahead. Politics, Practice, and Sustainable Transition Management." *Environment* and *Planning A*, 39(4): 763–70.

Shucksmith, Mark. 2000. "Endogenous Development, Social Capital and Social Inclusion. Perspectives from LEADER in the UK." *Sociologia Ruralis*, 40(2): 208–18.

Sims, Ralph E.H., Hans-Holger Rogner, and Ken Gregory. 2003. "Carbon Emission and Mitigation Cost comparisons between Fossil Fuel, Nuclear and Renewable Energy Resources for Electricity Generation." *Energy Policy*, 31(13): 1315–26.

Sinn, Hans-Werner. 2007. "Public Policies against Global Warming." CESifo Working Paper. CESifo Working Paper 2087. http://www.cesifo-group.de/pls/guestci/download/CESifo%20Working%20Papers%202007/CESifo%20Working%20Papers%20August%202007/cesifo1_wp2087.pdf (accessed 1 September 2015).

Sofianou, Eleni, Dimitrios S. Goulas, Georgia N. Kontogeorga, and Kassiani Droulia. 2014. "Evaluation of the First Outcomes of Decentralization Reform with 'Kallikratis Plan' in Greece. The Case of Ilida's Municipality." *Journal of Governance and Regulation*, 3(2): 7–13.

Späth, Philipp and Harald Rohracher. 2010. "'Energy Regions'. The Transformative Power of Regional Discourses on Socio-technical Futures." *Research Policy*, 39(4): 449–58.

Spencer, Thomas, Oliver Sartor, and Mathilde Mathieu. 2014. "Unconventional Wisdom. Economic Analysis of US Shale Gas and Implications for the EU." Institute for Sustainable Development and International Relations. Studies 2. http://www.iddri.org/Publications/Collections/Syntheses/PB0514.pdf(accessed 1 September 2015).

Steffen, Will, Katherine Richardson, Johan Rockström, Sarah E. Cornell, Ingo Fetzer, Elena M. Bennett, R. Biggs, Stephen R. Carpenter, Wim de Vries, de Wit, Cynthia A, Carl Folke, Dieter Gerten, Jens Heinke, Georgina M. Mace, Linn M. Persson, Veerabhadran Ramanathan, B. Reyers, and Sverker Sörlin. 2015. "Planetary Boundaries. Guiding Human Development on a Changing Planet." *Science*, 1–16.

Stocker, Gerry. 2004. *Transforming Local Governance: From Thatcherism to New Labour*. Basingstoke, UK, and New York, NY: Palgrave Macmillan.

Strauss, Robert. 2005. "The Local Dimension of the European Employment Strategy." Japan Institute for Labor Policy and Training. http://www.jil.go.jp/english/events/documents/20050209/chapter4.pdf (accessed 1 September 2015).

Streeck, Wolfgang. 2005. "The Sociology of Labour Markets and Trade Unions." In *The Handbook of Economic Sociology*. 2nd ed., ed. Neil J. Smelser and Richard Swedberg, pp. 254–83. Princeton, NJ: Princeton University Press.

Széll, Györy. 2013. "Historical Perspectives on Participation." In *The Communal Idea in the 21st Century*, ed. Eliezer Ben-Rafeal, Yaacov Oved, and Menachem Topel, pp. 131–45. Boston, MA: Brill.

Tapia, Carlos, Iraxte Peña, Efren Feliu, Rasmus O. Rasmussen, Ryan Weber, Gunnar Lindberg, Anna Berlina, Klaus Spiekermann, Mike Dokter, Ruslan Zhechkov, Ellen Baltzar, and Anders C. Hansen. 2013. "GREECO. Territorial Potentials for a Greener Economy." ESPON. http://www.espon.eu/export/sites/default/Documents/Projects/AppliedResearch/GREECO/FR/GREECO_FR_-_Vol_1.2_Main_Report.pdf (accessed 1 September 2015).

Tarde, Gabriel de. 1902. *Psychologie économique. Tome premier*. Paris, France: Felix Alcan.

Taylor, Richard G., Bridget Scanlon, Petra Döll, Matt Rodell, Rens van Beek, Yoshihide Wada, Laurent Longuevergne, Marc Leblanc, James S. Famiglietti, Mike Edmunds, Leonard Konikow, Timothy R. Green, Jianyao Chen, Makoto Taniguchi, Marc F.P. Bierkens, Alan MacDonald, Ying Fan, Reed M. Maxwell, Yossi Yechieli, Jason J. Gurdak, Diana M. Allen, Kevin Hiscock, Pat J.-F. Yeh, and Ian Holman. 2013. "Ground Water and Climate Change." *Nature Climate Change*, 3: 322–29.

Tocqueville, Alexis de. 1835. *Democracy in America*. London, UK: Fontana, (Orig. pub. 1835).

Tosics, Iván. 2011. "Multilevel Government Systems in Urban Areas." In *Multilevel Urban Governance or the Art of Working Together. Methods, Instruments and Practices*, ed. Mart Grisel and Van de Waart, Frans, pp. 26–35. Hague, Netherlands: European Urban Knowledge Network.

Tosics, Iván and Joe Ravetz. 2011. "Managing Growth." In *Synthesis Report, Peri-urbanisation in Europe. Towards a European Policy to sustain Urban-Rural Futures*, ed. Annette Piorr, Joe Ravetz, and Iván Tosics, pp. 80–87: University of Copenhagen, Denmark: Academic Books Life Sciences.

Transition Cities Consortium. 2014. "Transition Cities." http://www.climate-kic.org/projects/transition-cities/ (accessed 1 September 2015).

UN. 1992. Agenda 21. "Programme of Action for Sustainable Development." https://sustainabledevelopment.un.org/content/documents/Agenda21.pdf (accessed 1 September 2015).

UN. 2010. "Classification of Countries by Major Area and Region of the World." http://esa.un.org/wpp/Excel-Data/country-classification.pdf (accessed 1 September 2015).

UN. 2012. "The Future We Want." http://www.uncsd2012.org/content/documents/727The%20Future%20We%20Want%2019%20June%201230pm.pdf (accessed 1 September 2015).

UN. 2014a. "Millennium Development Goal Indicators." http://unstats.un.org/unsd/mdg/Data.aspx (accessed 1 September 2015).

UN. 2014b. "Report of the Open Working Group of the General Assembly on Sustainable Development Goals." United Nations (UN) A/68/970 (accessed 1 September 2015).

UN. 2014c. "The Road to Dignity by 2030: Ending Poverty, Transforming All Lives and Protecting the Planet. Synthesis report of the Secretary-General on the post-2015 sustainable development agenda." United Nations (UN) A/69/700 (accessed 1 September 2015).

UNRISD. 2013. "Potential and Limits of Social and Solidarity Economy." http://www.unrisd.org/80256B3C005BCCF9/%28httpAuxPages%29/5936F8772AFB3780C1257BBE0056F0F9/$file/01%20-%20SSE%20Event%20%28final%20pdf%20for%20web%29.pdf (accessed 1 September 2015).

Veldhuizen, Harry van, Mark C.M. van Loosdrecht, and Sef J.J. Heijnen. 1999. "Modelling Biological Phosphorus and Nitrogen Removal in a Full Scale Activated Sludge Process." *Water Research*, 33(16): 3459–68.

Victor, Peter A. 2008. *Advances in Ecological Economics, Managing without Growth. Slower by Design, not Disaster*. Cheltenham, UK, and Northampton, MA: Edward Elgar Publishing.

Viederman, Stephen. 1994. "The Economics of Sustainability. Challenges." Paper presented at The Economics of Sustainability workshop, Fundacao Jaquin Nabuco, Recife, Brazil (accessed 1 September 2015).

Walsh, Adrian. 2011. "The Commodification of the Public Service of Water. A Normative Perspective." *Public Reason*, 3(2): 90–106.

WBGU. 1997. *World in Transition. Ways Towards Sustainable Management of Freshwater Resources*. Berlin and Heidelberg, Germany: Springer.

WBGU. 2011. *World in Transition. A Social Contract for Sustainability*. Berlin, Germany: Wissenschaftlicher Beirat der Bundesregierung Globale Umweltveränderungen (WBGU).

Weber, Gabriel and Ignasi Puig-Ventosa. 2013. "Market Based Instruments in Water Supply and Waste Management. A Form of Transforming Commons into Private Goods?" Paper presented at Seminar on Theories and Perspectives on Political Ecology. University of Manchester, 18–22nd February 2013 (accepted in *Spanish* translation in Revista Ecología Política) (accessed 1 September 2015).

Weber, Max. 1978. *Economy and Society. An Outline of Interpretative Sociology*. Berkeley, CA: University of California Press.

Wei, Xinchao, Roger C. Jr. Viadero, and Shilpa Bhojappa. 2008. "Phosphorus Removal by Acid Mine Drainage Sludge from Secondary Effluents of Municipal Wastewater Treatment Plants." *Water Research*, 42(13): 3275–84.

Weir, Stuart and David Beetham. 1999. *Democratic Audit of the United Kingdom, Political Power and Democratic Control in Britain. The Democratic Audit of the United Kingdom*. London, UK, and New York, NY: Routledge.

World Bank, United Cities and Local Governments. 2009. *Decentralization and Local Democracy in the World. First Global Report by United Cities and Local Governments, 2008*. Washington, DC: World Bank, United Cities and Local Governments.

The World Commission on Environment and Development. 1987. *Our Common Future*. Oxford, UK, and New York, NY: Oxford University Press.

Wright, Michael T., Hella von Unger, and Martina Block. 2010. "Partizipation der Zielgruppe in der Gesundheitsförderung und Prävention." In *Prävention und Gesundheitsförderung, Partizipative*

Qualitätsentwicklung in der Gesundheitsförderung und Prävention, ed. Michael T. Wright, pp. 35–52. Bern, Switzerland: Huber.

Xue, Jin. 2014. "Is Eco-village/urban village the Future of a Degrowth Society? An Urban Planner's Perspective." *Ecological Economics*, 105: 130–38.

Yin, Robert K. 2003. *Case Study Research. Design and Methods*. 3rd ed. Thousand Oaks, CA, London, UK, New Delhi, India, and Singapore: Sage Publications.

Young, Oran R. 2012. "Navigating the Sustainability Transition. Governing Complex and Dynamic Socio-ecological Systems." In *Global Environmental Commons. Analytical and Political Challenges in Building Governance Mechanisms*, ed. Éric Brousseau, Tom Dedeurwaerdere, Pierre-André Jouvet, and Marc Willinger, pp. 80–101. Oxford, UK, and New York, NY: Oxford University Press.

Young, Pauline. 1939. *Scientific Social Surveys and Research*. New York, NY: Prentice Hall.

Zalasiewicz, Jan, Mark Williams, Will Steffen, and Paul Crutzen. 2012. "The New World of the Anthropocene." *Environmental Science and* Technology *Viewpoint*, 44(7): 2228–31.

Index

Page numbers for figures and tables are in boldface.

Aalborg 27–8, 61–2, 64–5, 68, 70, 74, 76, 78, 81–3, 86, 94, 96, 98–100, 102–3, 106, 107, 110, 113, 118–9, 216, 218–19, 229–31, 234
Aalborg Charter 229
action research 237
action situation 47–55, 105, 116, 118
active citizenship 226, 235, 236
actor: actor sample 15, 30, 61; key actor 15, 26, 30, 35, 61, 243; *see also* expert
administration 36, 44, 64, 69, 76, 85, 87, 90, 97, 99, 102, 105–6, 111, 113, 115, 119–20, 122, 134–5, 149, **164**, 196, 218, 225; actors of administration 67, 72, 94, 109, 113, 127, 230–1; administration in network 204; administrational reform 208 (*see also* reform); autonomy in administration 175, **16, 177–8, 180–1, 183**, 184, **185–6**; city administration 15, 67, 79, 88, 100, 119, 154, 156, 203, 217; decentralisation of administration 116, 213, 236 (*see also* decentralisation); government administration 68, 89, 139, 150, 195; local administration 16, 30, 71, 75, 85–6, 91, 108, 109, 112, 138, 150, 155, 231–4, 236; local and national administration 146, 148; PES administration 162 (*see also* PES); public administration 22, 24, 36, 42, 135, 139, 220, 236; self administration 18, 212; *see also* institution
Advisory Council for Sustainable Development of Catalonia 218
Agenda 21 61, 74, 83, 89, 208, 217, 229, 232
aggregation rules 51–2, 54, 56, 105, 196
Ahn, T. K. 224
Amable, B. 23
anthropocene 1, 39
Antipodean Fourth World 20
appropriation: appropriation and self-determined use of urban spaces 233; appropriation of productive spaces 234; appropriation of urban green spaces 103; democratically decided profit appropriation 233; (re)appropriation of public green spaces 103
Architekturzentrum Wien 7
Arin, T. 20
Arnstein Ladder of Citizen Participation **42**, 55
Arnstein, S. 42
association: business association 72, 218; cooperative association (*see* cooperatives); citizens' associations 102, 110, 123; civil society association 195, 223, 226; community association 69, 232; local association 119, 138, 150; neighbouhood associations 50, 112, 234, 50; nonprofit association 216, 234; private association 41; *see also* IAP2
austerity policies 104, 122, 228, 233
Austria 9, **16, 18, 19, 21–3**, 28, 128, 130, 141, 143, 153, 225
autonomous public sphere 224
autonomy 22, 34, 54, 83, 84, 87, 90, 108, 112, 119, 153, 160, 162–4, 171–4, 176, 179, 182, 184, 188–90, 193, 212–13, 229, 249; decision-making autonomy 13, 39, 56, 58, 80, 84–8, 90, 116, 119, 146, 151, 153–4, 196, 198, 250 (*see also* decision making); financial autonomy 84, 86–8, 153, 163, 172, 176, 182, 184, 187–90, 250; local autonomy 18, 61, 72, 77, 83–4, 87, 90, 97, 107–8, 113, 119–24, 149, 196–8, 203, 212–14, 228–9, **245**, 250; local collective-choice autonomy **49, 52, 54**; local decision autonomy 61, 66, 69, 85–8, 90, 213; regional autonomy 170–1, 182, 184, 188, 229
awareness 63, 67, 69, 71, 74, 76, 80, 82, 87, 89, 91, 97–8, 106, 111, 113, 115, 124, 126–8, 131, 133, 139, 143–5, 147, 150, 155, 156, 158–9, 188, 190, 193–4, 299, 208, 235, 242, **244**

Barcelona 28, 61, 63, 65–7, 69, 71, 76–7, 80, 82, 87, 127, 129, 131, 133–6, 139, 143–7, 150–3, 214

Barnebeck, S. 252; *see also* Urban Agenda
barriers 6, 83, 106–7, 215, 246
Bauler, T. 46
behaviour 4, 9, 49–50, **62**, 63–4, 71–89, 128, 131, 134, 146, 193–4, 208, 213, 217, 219, 224, 228, 233, 235, 240–1, 246
Belgium 22, 210
benefit 9–10, 33, 47–8, 50–**1**, 53, 79, 89, 93–4, 106, 112–13, 123, 125, 131, 144, 146, 148–9, 152, 155, 168–9 190, 196, 201–2, 208, 214, 217, 230, **244**, 246, 248
Berlin 29
Bettini, Y. 155
Bilbao 27–8, 63, 65, 69, 71, 74, 76, 78, 82–3, 87, 94, 95–6, 98, 100, 103, 107, 112–13, 115, 118, 120, 210, 217, 218
biodiversity 1, 3, 93–4, 96–7, **108**, 113–14, 118, 123, 198
Birmingham **29**, 61, 63–4, 68, 73–4, 76, 79, 83–4, 87, 89, 127–9, 132–7, 141–7, 149, 153, 216, 218
'bottom-up' 63, 202, 236, 245; bottom-up actor 84, 124, 103, 188, 202, 231; bottom-up approach 4, 17, 143, 159, 240, 243; bottom-up initiative 19, 30–2, 71, 84, 91, 106, 112, 115, 117, 122, 123, 160, 190, 217, 222, 229, 235, 247, 249–50; bottom-up project 69; bottom-up transition 66; relationship of top down and bottom-up approaches 143
boundary 234; *boundary rules* 51, 54, 56, 65, 111, 119, 196–7; planetary boundaries 1, 3, 5–6, 39–40; reconfigured boundary 214
Bourdieu, P. 226
Brazil 208
Brundtland Commission 1
budget 34, 68, 87–8, 95, 99, 102–4, 106, 112, 118, 120–4, 142, 153, 155, 162–3, 172–90, 212, 228–9, 231, 235, 243
building and infrastructure development 95, 100, 103
Bulgaria 9, 21
bureaucracy 85, 89, 107, 123, 146, 152, 214, 249
business 7, 41, 60, 84, 88, 94, 96, 102, 104, 113–16, 122, 136–9, 141–2, 148, 150, 152–3, 155, 193, 206–7, 210, 212, 218–19, 248; business actor 31, 61, 74–5, 86, 96, 104, 108–9, 111–12, 127, 134, 138, 213, 243; business companies 72, 74; business representative 35, 68, 146; business sector 6, 15, 30, 33–4, 98, 110, 119, 124; local business 74, 79, 98, 251; *see also* association

capability: *capability to co-evolve* 240; *capability to diversify institutionally* 240; *capability to flourish* 239, 240, 242; *capability to participate* 240; *capability to practical reason* 240; sanctioning capabilities **50**, **52**; *self organisation capabilities* 14, 31, 34, 66–71, 89, 94–109, 124, 127, 133–8, 226; *see also* sustainability
capacity 64, 94, 107–**8**, 112, 129, 158, 188, 205, 206–7, 209, 218, 224–7, 248
capital 5–6, 53, 210, 219, 223; capitalistic 19–20; human capital 132, 134, 243; norms social capital **49**, **52**; social capital 22, 226–7, 238; 'varieties of capitalism' 23
'Capital Rome' 213
carbon 8, 59, 60, 94; carbon taxes 1, 2; carbon intensity 2–3, decarbonisation of the energy system 10; 'low carbon' strategy 211–12; *see also* CO2 emission
Casa de Campo 234
change **2**, 4, 9, 20, 34, 39, 44–6, 50–1, 53, **55**, 63, 65–6, 69, 71, 75–7, 79–80, 89, 91, 96–7, 99–100, 105, 109, 114, 116, 118, 125, 128, 132, 134, 143–6, 150–1, 163–8, 170, 173, 179, 182, **186**–91, 204, 206, 208–11, 220, 226, 229, 231–2, 236–7, 243, 245, 247, 249, 251; change agents 222, 227, 229; institutional change 13, 40, 50, 54, 97, 228, 241 (*see also* institution)
Charter for Multilevel Governance in Europe 204, 251
CIP 219
cities *see* city
citizens' 10, 41–2, 44, 56, 58, **62**, 65–9, 71, 73–6, 78, 80, 89, 91, 96, 98, 100, 102–15, 118–20, 123, 127–8, 131–46, 151–2, 155–6, 193–4, 196–7, 199–200, 204, 206–7, 210–11, 216–17, 219, 221–3, 225–38, 240–2, 246–52; citizens' budget 118, 229; citizen control **42**, **55**, 57–8, 196–7, 250–1; citizens' initiative 69, 71, 103, 110, 127, 135–**7**, 155, 211, 223, 225, 232, 234–5, 247; citizens' movements 70, 103, 108, 110–11, 232; citizen participation 41–**2**, 56–7, 66, 68, 69, 71, 103, 106, 113, 115, 118, 139, 196, 212, 216, 224, 228–9, 235–6, 249
citizenship 19, 56; active citizenship 137, 226, 235–6
city: cities and transitions 14; cities and urbanisation 91; cities in network 79; 'Cities of Tomorrow' 8–12, 227; city selection 14–16, 23, 26–**8**; "class city" 76; climate–resilient cities 93; definition 9; post-industrial cities 65, 73, 76
City Statistics *see* Urban Audit
civic engagement 222–3, 22–7, 229, 233, 235
civil society 6–8, 10, 12, 15, 30–4, 41, 46, 52–3, 61, 67–8, 71–2, 74–5, 79, 83, 89, 91, 94, 96–104, 107–16, 119–20, 122–4, 127–8, 134–9, 141, 143, 150, 152–6, 193–5, 197–9, 203, 205–7, 209, 211, 216, 220–33, 235–8, 242–4, 246–8, 250–2
climate change 4, 59, **62**, 83, 93, 97, 100, 125, 130, 155, 193, 194, 241, 244; *see also* global warming

Index

Climate Change Management 219
climate-resilient cities 93
co-decision making 102; *see also* participation
CO2 emission **2**, 3, 59–60, 63, 73, 82–3, 90, 194, 210, 244
collaboration 73, 76, 79, 102, 104, 109–12, 115, 119–21, 123, 139–41, 144, 146, 193, 203, 210, 214, 218, 230–2, 247–8
collective changing and (re-)aligning institutional settings 244
commitment 1, 15, 111, 112, 120, 143–4, 159, 197, 204, 208, 211, 242
commodification 124, 156, 157
commoning 92
common-pool resource 8–10, 13, 23, 39, 40, 43–**4**, 51, 53–6, 197, 240, 243, 250–1; *see also* commons
commons 3–4, 40, 92, 103, 224, 226, 236; commons goods 43–4; urban commons 8–9, 12, 44, 112, 234; *see also* common pool resources; tragedy of the commons
communication 29, 40, 50, **52**–3, 56, 94, 106, 131–2, 137, 196, 215, 223, 224, 227–8, 230–1, **244**, 246, 249; communication channel 113, 120, 134, 247; cross-sector communication 99, 119; *see also* Dewey, J.; ICT
communicative rationalities 224, 238
community 89, 96, 108, 114, 133, 228, 238, 240, 247–50; community development 237; community education 237; community energy 243; community gardening 7, 233–4; community governance 230; community organising 237; community-supported agriculture 232–3; rediscovery of community 227
comparative research 13
complexity 55, 63, 66, 68–9, 78, 87, 97, 105–6, 111, 115–16, 155, 160, 198, 201, 207, 213, 216, 221, 227, 230, 238, 242, **244**
conflict 11, 41, **70**, 73, 84, 90–1, 93–5, 97, 99–100, 102–4, 106, 111, 115, 118, 135–6, 143, 147–9, 193–4, 196, 198, 204, 215, 219–20, 222, 224, 229; conflict resolution **52**, 81
cooperative 7, 39, 50, 55–6, 119, 197, 199, 202, 240, 243, 251; cooperative knowledge production 236–7; cooperative management 123–4, 234; non-cooperative 40, 49
cooperative learning 231
cooperatives 6–8, 10, 39, 41, 50, 55–6, 70, 112, 119, 123–4, 133, 195, 197–9, 202, 223, 225, 226, 231–4, 236–7, 240, 243, 250–1
construction development 96, 99, 119; *see also* development
consultation *see* participation
Copenhagen 27, **28**, 61, 63–4, 69, 73, 76, 83, 94, 97, 98, 100, 102, 105, 106, 108–11, 113, 115, 119–20, 162, 216, 218, 228–9, 231–4, 241

Copenhagen Conference on Climate Change 241
'Copenhagen Food Community' 234
Country 2, 13, 18, 21, 23, 69, 118 country sample 17, **19**, 26–9; country selection 16–18, 23
Covenant of Mayors 63, 74, 79, 218
Cracow 27, **28**, 94–6, 98, 100, 102, 103–4, 107, 109, 113, 117, 122
Crouch, C. 91, 222; *see also* Post-Democracy
crises: economic and financial crises 7–8, 22, 65–6, 98, 104, 112, 118, 120, 122, 145, 151–2, 155, 161, 188, 194, 203, 208, 212, 222, 234–5, 248; post crises austerity polices 228
Croatia **7**
crowdfunding 247
'culture-debating' to 'culture consuming' 91; *see also* Habermas, J.
Czech Republic 16–17, 19–21, **28**, 142–3, 216
Cyprus **7, 21**

decarbonisation of the energy system 10
decentralisation 13, 19, 22–3, 53, 77, 84–5, 158–9, 188–91, 197, 212–14, 222, 249; 'decentralised revolution' 71–2; decentralised states **21**–2
de-commodification 19–20
delegated decision-making 102
democratic engagement 209, 216, 243, 249
democratisation 91, 223, 227, 237–8
demographic changes **62**, 219
Denmark 9, **16**, **18**–**19**, **21**, **23**, **28**, 127–8, 162
densification 96, 139
development *see* local development; sustainable development
Dewey, J.: communication in local community 228
Digital Agenda for Europe 219
disadvantaged groups 226, 235, 237–8
DISCUS project 205–8
diversification 40, 47, 50, 203, 223; institutional diversification 4, 12, 39, 192, 196–7, 201, 240, 243, 251
Dortmund **28**, 61, **62**, 66, 69, 73–4, 76–7, 79, 81–2, 84, 87, 94, 216, 218, 234
DuPuis, E.M. 228

Earth Summit in Rio de Janeiro 1, 62, 208
East Asia 20
ecological resource system 4–6, 11, 40–1, 55, 57, 240–2, 250
ecology 63, 76, 128, 231, 245
economy: 4, 6, 20, 23, **24**, 68, 71–2, 74, 76, 82, 84, 86, 97, 120, 128, 146, 151, 157, 195, 199, 202–3, 205, **207**, 211, 213, 222–3, 227, 230–1, 246; circular economy 64; civic economy 224, 232; community economy 7; diverse economy, green economy 39, 233; integrated economy 64;

social and solidarity economy 7, 225, 232–4, 238
ecosystem 43, **48**, 90, 97, 125, 129, 147, 156, 239, 241; ecosystem services 97, 206, 211
ECOTEC 159, 160, 162
EDF 86
education 24, **62**, 64, 72–4, 76–7, 89, 99, 106–7, 113, 115, 122, 127, 131, 141, 165, 169, 172, 176, 178, 193–4; educational institution 139, 159, 201, 249; *see also* community
Emilia Romagna 229
emission *see* CO2 emission
Emission Trading System 2
EMPA 76
employment 6, **24**, 84, 94, 107, 159, 164–7, 176–8, 193, 199–202, 215, 233, 236, 240; employment policy 164–5, **176–8**; *see also* LEI; Pacts; Pacts/LEI PES; TEP
empowerment 55, 56, 112, 135, 159, 193, 198, 201, 226, 251
energy: energy demand 65, 197; energy efficiency 59, 64, 67–**8**, 71, 73–4, 79–81, 86, 89, 132, 143, 194, 219; energy in sustainability transition 59–60, 125–7, 245–6
energy market 86, 88
energy system 10, 53, 59, 69, 71, **81**, **82**, 86, 91, 123, 125–27, 155, 193–8, 201, 211, 215, 242–4, 246, 249–50
engagement 46, 87, 102, 209, 216, 222–3, 225–7, 229, 233, 235, 243, 246–7, 249
EPSU 145
ERDF 83
Esping-Andersen, G. 19, 20
ESPON 21
EU-15 **21–2**
EU-27 COUNTRIES 21
EU-28 9
EU funding 195, 215
EU Framework Programme for Research and Innovation (2014–2020) 219
EU policy 11, 79, 82, 84, 132, 151, 212, 215, 227, 252
Eurobarometer 217
European Charter of Local Self-Government 228
European Citizen's Initiative 197, 155, 127, 10, 8
European Commission 8, 93, 127, 146, 159, 190, 198, 201, 206, 211, 219
European Committee of the Regions 204, 220, 227, 251
European MUSIC project 210
European TRANSITION project 210
European Union's Committee of the Regions 204, 220, 251
Europe 2020 61, 63–4, 93, 204, 219
EU 2020 strategies 11, 61, 63–4, 93, 204, 210, 219

Expert: expert knowledge 15, 105, 120, 199, 231, 237
explanatory parsimony 20
EXPO 74
externalities 2–3, 98, 106, 118, 123

factors: success factors 106, 112, 206–8; transition factors 35–6, 61, 76–7, 113, 115, 140
"familiarism" 20
'Fano Guidelines- Building Capacity for Local Sustainability', the 207–8
federal states **21–2**
Fenger, H.J.M. 20
field research 16, 26–7, 29–30, 32–3, 35–7, 48, 88, 94, 206, 212, 242–3, 245
Finland **7**, **21**, 210
food production 103–5, 109, 111–12, 116, 151, 155–6, 225, 229–30, 233–5
food security 112, 233
fossil **2**, 3, 10, 59–60, 129, 239, 241, 243, 246, 250
framework 12, 21, 40, 47–8, 57, 61, 68, 74, 82, 84, 87, 89, 108, 120, 123, 137, 143, 146, 158, 170–1, 192, 195, 203, 210, 219, 229, 231–3, 236, 243, 250, 252; *see also* IAD framework; legal framework; SES framework
France 9, **16**, **18–19**, **21–3**, **28**, 84–6, 145, 198, 208, 210, 213, 217
Freiburg **28**, 60–1, 63–4, 71–3, 76, 79, 83–4, 127, 128, 129–35, 138–9, 143, 145, 153–4, 216, 218, 232
Fukushima disaster 248
funding 66, 71, 74, 77, 79, 82–3, 86–8, 90–1, 99, 106, 112–13, 115, 118, 120, 122, 131, 135–6, 142, 144, 151–2, 155, 190, 218, 220, 236; *see also* crowdfunding; EU funding
future generations 1, 63, 77, 118, 221, 240, 248
"Future we want", the 217; *see also* Earth Summit in Rio de Janeiro

GDP 2–3, 13, 17–**18**, 22, 26, **28–9**
Germany 9, **16**, **18–19**, **21–3**, 72, 75, 79, 84–5, 162, 198, 208, 210, 214, 223, 231
Gerring, J. 15
Gibson, G. 233
Giurgiu **28**, 61, 73–4, 77, 84, 102, 127–9, 131–9, 142–4, 146–7, 151, 153–4, 216
Glasgow **29**, 61, 64–5, 69, 73, 76, 78, 82, 94–5, 97–100, 107, 119
global commons 4
global ecological system 6
global warming 1–3, 59
Goodman, D. 228
goods: 8, 40, 43, **44**, 132, 146, 193, 220, 239, 247; common goods 115, 132, 146, **207**, 209, 224; goods and commons, the difference 43; private goods 43–4; public goods **44**, 193; tool goods **44**

Goteborg 28
governance: bottom-up governance 245, 249–50;
 governance levels 41, 50, 58, 71, 131, 203, 243,
 252; Labour Market governance 158, 160,
 188, 201; multilevel governance 153, 158, 172,
 200–2, 204–5, 209, 220, 227, 251; polycentric
 governance 120, 227, 229; *see also* sustainable
 governance
government: local government 19, 22–3, 29–30,
 41, 55, 59, 72, 87, 89, 102, 104, 107–9, 111–16,
 119, 121–3, 135–7, 139, 142, 150, 153, 155–6,
 196, 204–5, 207–18, 230–4, 242–3, 247–51;
 see also administration
Grammar of Institution 14
'Grand Paris' 213
'Greater London Authority' 213
Greece **16, 18–23, 28**, 84, 86, 90, 112, 127, 136,
 143, 161, 194, 213–15, 228, 234
Greek polis 228
"Green Agrowth" 6
green economy *see* economy
greenhouse gas 1, 3, 60, 239, 241
green roofs 96
green spaces 5, 7–8, 10, 12, 14, **30–2**, 33–5,
 39, 41, 53, 55–7, **62**, 90–1, 93–105, 107–17,
 119–24, 126–7, 131–2, 155, 192–8, 212, 216,
 223, 228–32, 235–6, 240, 242–3, 249–50
"Green university" 76
grid 60, 92, 197, 219
groundwater 40, 43, **44**, 94, 125–6
growth 1, 3, 5–6, 12, 43, 60, 98, 106, 143, 146,
 155, 219, 225, 233, 236 239; economic growth
 7, 16, 39, 80, 86, 97–8, 103–4, 123–4, 220, 230,
 239; GDP growth 3, 26, **28–9**; green growth
 8, 239, 241; growth logic 124; growth rates 13,
 123, 139, 220; postgrowth logic 98

Habermas, J. 91, 223–4, 231, 233, 238
habit 98, 134, 139, 142–3, 150, 156, 194,
 221, 249; cultural habits 194; transport
 habits 75
habitat 94, 125, 245
Hardin, G. 40, 193
Henderson, H. 226
Hess, C. 46
heterogeneity 9, 11, 13, 54, 63, 160, 170, 247;
 heterogeneity in benefits and costs 50;
 heterogeneity of European Labour Markets
 160–2, 179, 189–90; heterogeneity of
 participants **52**, 54, 56
holistic 62–3, 80, 89, 91, 131, 156, 204, 236,
 244–6
holocene 1
Hooghe, L. 158–9, 201
Hungary **7, 21**
hybrid forms of organisations 223, 233

IAD framework14, 46–7, 49, 61
IAP2 42–**3**
ICLEI 16, 29, 205–6, 208, 218
ICT 211, 219–20, 247
impact **31**, 40, **50**–1, **52**, 54, 59, 72, 77–8, 87–8,
 123, 197, 210, 214, 219, 242–3, 248; impact
 and green spaces 93, 97, 99, 100, 114, 116, 118;
 impact and labour market 160–1, 163, 172–4,
 182–4, 189, 202; impact and water system
 125–6, 130, 132, 136–**7**, 149, 155
income 3, 6, 9, 18, 23–**4**, 60, 112, 122, 142, 231,
 234, 239, 247
income growth 3, 5–6, 239
India 208
indicators 23, 49, 53, 106, 137, 162–3;
 environmental indicators 26; indicators of
 citizens involvement 55–6; indicators of PES
 162–5, 179, 182, 184, 189, 201; indicators on
 water system 135; Urban Audit indicators
 24, 26
information 26, 29, 37, 40, **43**, 48–54, 56, 63–4,
 66–7, 69, 78–9, 87, 102, 106, 131–2, 137, 139,
 159, 185, 200, 202, 238, 242, **244**, 247; access
 to information 116, 155, 190, 202, 211, 217,
 220, 250; information about water 134, 156;
 information and awareness- raising 111, 144;
 information and communication (*see* ICT);
 information basis 246; information campaigns
 74, 113; information exchange 74, 172–3, 184,
 218; information rules 51, 53, 56, 106, 193
influences: European influences 76, 214; national
 influences 214
infrastructure 8, 10, 55, 60, 65, 84, 96, 103–4,
 118, 197, 199, 203, 205–6, 215–16, 243, 249;
 infrastructure development 95, 100, 103, 124;
 water infrastructure 125–6, 129–31, 135, **137**,
 140–2, 144, 153, 155, 199
innovation 65, 83, 110, 158–9, 188, 217, 219, 221,
 226, 231, 237; governance innovation 124, 143,
 197, 207–8; technological innovation 46; urban
 innovation 231; *see also* social innovation
Innsbruck **28**, 61, 63, 66–8, 74, 78, 81, 86, 94, 98,
 100, 103, 111–12, 127–9, 131–3, 139–40, 146,
 151–3, 216
Institute for Applied Ecology 76
institution: IAD 47, 49, 61; national labour market
 institutions 10, 200–1; *see also* institutional
institutional: institutional arrangements 3–8,
 11, 34, 39, 41, 56, 127, 135, 144, 154–6, 193,
 197–9, 222–3, 230; institutional change (*see*
 change); institutional setting 6, 8, 11–12, 14,
 19, 23, 40, 43, 47, 53, 58, 105, 192, 200, 227,
 241–2, 244, 250, 252
institutional diversity 4, 10, 14–16, 33, 123,
 192–203
institutionalism: neoinstitutionalism 19

interaction: Interactive Community Governance 230; interactive governance 231–2, 238
intercultural garden 235
interview 13–16, 27–9, 31–8, 60–2, 67, 69, 71, 73, 75, 79, 82–3, 85–91, 94, 96–7, 113, 116, 118–19, 120, 127, 134–5, 138, 145–6, 153, 155–6, 162–6, 168, 191, 195, 197, 203, 205, 212
invasive species 93, 100
involvement 18, 19, 36, 46, 56, 72, 78, 106, 111, 131, 156, 201, **244**, 247, 250; civil society involvement **101**, **108**, 110, 127, 154, 216, 228, 232, 242; citizens' involvement 123, 197, 228; participation and involvement 135; stakeholders involvement 164, 188, 227 (*see also* stakeholders)
Ireland **7, 21**
isomorphism 19
Istanbul **16**, 18, 26, **29**, 61, 66, 69, 79, 83, 85, 94–100, 102, 104, 106–7, 109, 115–16, 118, 120, 127–9, 132–6, 139, 143–4, 146–7, 150–1, 213, 216, 230
Italy **16**, **18–19**, 20, **21–3**, **28**, 86, 122, 127, 141, 145, 210, 216, 218, 223, 228

Janssen, M. A. 15, 46, 48, **49–50**, **52**, 54, 116
Jihlava **28**, 61, 67–8, 74, 94, 102, 107, 111, 116, 216–17, 231
justice *see* social justice

Kalff, Y. 252
Kallikratis *see* reform
keyholder 16, 29–30, 35
Kiel **28**, 60–1, 63, 67–9, 73, 76, 79, 83–4, 86, 127, 129, 131–3, 135, 138–9, 144, 148, 151–3, 214
know-how *see* knowledge
Knowledge: local knowledge 98, 103, 221, 237; citizens' 'lay' expert knowledge 237; citizens' local expert knowledge 105
Kruskal-Wallis equality-of population pank test 34
Kyoto Protocol 1, 3

laboratory 48, 229
labour market 4–6, 8, 10, 12, 14, **30**, **32–4**, **62**, 158–61, 163, 165–6, 168, 170–4, 182, 184, 188–90, 192–3, 199–203, 205, 212, 215, 223, 226, 243, **245**; European labour market 159–60, 200–1; labour market policies 4, 6, 10, 38, 158–88, 192, 200–3, 243; local labour market 5, 14, 160, 188, 243; *see also* institution
land consumption 93, 115, 117
land use 25, 53, 86, 93, 97, 111, 118, 124, 211, 234, 242, 246
Larissa **28**, 61, 63, 67, 69, 71, 74–5, 80, 85–6, 94–6, 98, 102–3, 107, 111–13, 118, 120, 213, 217, 231, 234

Latvia **7, 21**
leadership **49**, **52**, 54, 56, 58, **67–8**, 78, 82–3, 90, 107–10, **134**, 136–9, 194–5, 207, 210, 217, 219, 248
Leeds **29**, 61, 64, 66, 69, 71, 73–4, 79–80, 83, 87–8, 94–7, 100, 103, 106, 109, 110–13, 115, 118, 121–2
legal framework 69, 76–7, 79, 81, 86, 90, 97, 99, 102, 112–13, 116, 117, 121, 124, 127, 148, 150, 153, 197–8, 212, 214, 215, 228, 243, **245**
LEI **32**, 159, 188, 201–2; *see also* Pact/LEI
lessons learned 56, 58, 71, 138, 193, 195
Lidström, A. 22–3
lifeworld 223–5, 233, 237–8, 245, 249
limitation 33, 81, 197, 233
Linz **28**, 60–1, 63–4, 67, 73, 76, 78–9, 82–3, 86, 94–6, 98, 104, 106, 108, 110, 112–13, 116, 121
Lisbon Agenda 61
Lithuania **7, 21**
local decision-making 13, 56, 58, 66, 80, 84–6, **88**, 100, 116–22, 146, 153, **154**, 193, 196, 198, 203, 212
local development 118, 132, 208–9, 228, 236–7
localisation 227–8
local private households 72
Local Sustainability Study 2012 205, 209
Lodz **28**, 61, 74, 81, 83, 94, 96, 99, 102, 104, 107, 109–10, 113, 117–19, 127–8, 131, 135, 140, 142, 146, 152, 215, 217
London 26, **28**, 127–9, 131–3, 136–7, 139, 143–5, 151–4, 210, 213
Lublin **28**, 61, 64, 79–80, 94, 96–7, 99–100, 102, 106–7, 110, 117, 120, 127–9, 131, 134, 146, 151–2
Lugano **29**, 61, 63, 66, 68–9, 71, 76–7, 80, 84–5, 94–5, 97–9, 102–4, 106–7, 110, 113, 115, 118–19, 121, 215, 227
Luxemburg 9

Madrid **28**, 61, 63, 65, 67, 69, 71, 73, 80, 94–6, 98–100, 102, 104, 107–8, 112, 114–15, 118, 122, 215, 230, 234
Malta **7, 21**
management: *autonomous management* 120; *city management* 99; *Critical Management Studies* 45; environmental management system 76, 118; governance management **207**; management of green spaces 62, 100, 104–**5**, 108, 110–12, 123–4, 195–6, 231, 235; transition management 44–6, 210; *see also* water
market *see* labour market; water
market-state dichotomy 11
Marks, G. 158–9, 201
MaxQDA (VERSION 11) 35
meaningful work 233
"Mediterranean Countries" 20

mental model **49**, 99
methodology 13–14, 36–7, 236
Migration **62**, 94
Milan **28**, 61–2, 66, 68, 71, 73–5, 80, 82–3, 87, 94, 96–100, 102, 107, 111–13, 121, 210, 214, 217, 230, 234
mitigation and adaptation capacities 93
MLP multilevel perspective 46
mobilisation 247
monitoring 34, 49, **52**–3, 56, 80–1, 103, 107–**8**, 115–16, 127, 134, 194, 209, 224, 246; monitoring labour market 163–4, 171, 175, 177–8, **180**–90, 243; water monitoring 133–4, 137, 139–40, 143, 149–50, 242
motivation 15, 36, 53, 56, 63, 69, 72, 80, **105**, 115, 133, 137, 194, 208, 214, 222, 226, 233, 245
movement for urban agriculture 10
multilevel governance *see* governance

Napoleonic system 22
Naples **28**, 61, 74, 79–80, 83, 86–7, 94–6, 98–9, 102–3, 105–7, 109, 111, 118, 120–2, 214–16, 218, 230–1
neo-institutionalism 19
Netherlands 9, **21**
network: network size 174, 176, 179, 182, 189; *see also* Stakeholder networks
networked community governance 230
networked governance 204, 230, 238
networking *see* network
Network of Valencia 218
NGO *see* organisation
Nice **28**, 61–4, 67, 74–5, 78–9, 82–3, 85, 127–33, 135, 138, 144–5, 147, 151, 153, 213–14, 219
NIMBY 109
no net loss 97, 118
non-EU cities 18
norms: norm adoption 33, 47, 50–1, 56, 58, 61, 80, 84, 113, 116, 119, 123, 146, 151, 193, 196, 245
not-for-profit 6–7
nuclear 60, 73, 239, 243, 246, 248, 250
NUT3/city level 26

objectives: objective structure 34, 166, 170–1, 173, 176, 179, 184, 187–9
OECD 159, 173, 200–1
opulence 239
organisation: NGO 30–2, 35–6, 41, 68–70, 73–4, 102–4, 106–7, 109–11, 134–5, 137–8, 150–1, 155, 159, 164–5, 172, 176–8, 194–5, 201, 204, 210, 217–18, 225, 228, 230, 232, 235, 243, 249; type I organisation 160; *see also* citizens'
Ostrom, E. 14, 15, 23, 35, 46–8, **49–50**, **52**, 54–8, 61, 116, 123, 192, 203, 224, 227, 237–8

outcomes 11, 45, **48**–52, 56, 74, 99, 108–9, 123–4, 127
overuse 1, 53, 96, 131, 148, 149, 150, 224

Pact **32**, 159–60, 188, 201–2; *see also* Pact/LEI
Pact/LEI **30**, 32, 33–4, 159–62, 166–74, 182–**5**, **187**–90, 201
Paris 26, **28**, 61, 63–4, 67, 69, 73, 75, 81, 94–5, 97, 98–9, 109, 114–15, 118, 210, 213
participation 26, 41–**3**, 46, **52**, 54, 56, 67–9, 71, 81, 92, 102–3, 105–9, 113–15, 118–19, 132–5, 139, 145, 150–1, 155–6, 189, 193–4, 199, 216–17, 222, 224–9, 231, 235–6, 238, **242**, 246–50, 252; *see also* citizens'
participation and self-organisation 41, 57, 61, 66, 68–9, 71, 76, 79, 89, 91, 102, 105–8, 111, 115, 119, 122–4, 133, 137, 146, 149, 155–6, 195–6, 198, 220, 222, 224, 235–6, 242, 247, 250–1
"participation paradox" 109
participatory budget 102
partnership 6, 34, **42**, 84, 135, 158–60, 171–3, 184–5, 188–9, 190, 200, 204, 209, 218, 220, 248, 251
'People of Malstadt' 232
PER.KA 235
Perlas, N. 223
PES 32–4, 159–60, 201–2
Piketty, T. 6
place-blind versus place-based policies 200–3; *see also* policy
planetary boundaries *see* boundary
Poland **16**, **18**–**22**, **28**, 122, 142, 161, 208, 213, 217
Polanyi, K. 44, 199
policy: place based 12, 192, 200–3, 212; place blind 12, 192, 200, 203; policy instruments 80, 116–18, 211; *see also* labour market
pollution **24**, 63, 75, 90, 86, 98–9, 108, 125–7, 131–3, 136, 139, 142, 148–50, 194
Polycentric governance 227, 229
population 9–10, 13, 17, **29**, 34, 60, 67, 74, 76, 78, 86, 90–1, 96–7, 131, 135, 139, 142, 147; European population 16, 18, 23–**6**; ever-ageing-population 100; overpopulation 40; world population 3, 60
Porto Alegre 229
Portugal **7**, **21**
Postcommunist 20
"post-democracy" 91, 222
post-growth 98, 239
Poteete, A.R. 15, 46, 48, **49–50**, **52**, 54, 116
Potsdam **28**, 61, 64, 69, 71, 76–9, 82–4, 87, 94, 96, 98, 100, 102, 108, 113–14, 118, 121–2, 215, 234–5
poverty **7**, 9–10, **62**, 65, 104, 111–12, 132, 194, 233–4, 236
power: delegated power **42**, 55, 58, 196–7, 250; power structured 104, 115, 249

Prague **28**, 61–3, 66–7, 74, 78, 81–3, 85, 102, 127–9, 131–3, 135–6, 138–9, 142–3, 145–7, 151, 153
Pratchett, L. 229
principle of connexity 122, 228
privatisation 96, 100, 114, 124, 194–7, 223, 236, 251; *see also* water
process: governance transition process 251; local transition process 73, 122, 208–9, 246; socio ecological transition process 56, 57, 80, 146, 196; sustainability transition process 206, 246; transition process 14–15, 46, 55, 60–1, 63, 65, 76, 78, 89, 143–4, 206, 217, 220, 227, 243–4, 248; water transition process 137
production: energy production 59–60, 69, 92, 125, 194–5, 197–8, 220, 249; *see also* food production
productivity: productivity of the drinking water system 129–30; productivity of the resource system 49, 52–3, 64; regional productivity levels 202
programme: capacity building programme 209; Competitiveness and Innovation Programme CIP 219; designing programme 162–4, 173, 179, 182, 184, 188–90; EU programme 81, 84, 86–7, 120, 167, 212; 7th Framework Programme for Research and Technological Development FP7 219; local action programme 76, 91; OECD LEED programme 200; protection programme Greece 213–14; sustainability programme 66; 2000-Watt-Society strategy 18; *see also* Europe 2020
property rights 10, 19
prosperity 239
protest: citizens' protest 100, 103; Gezi Park protests 104; protest against building or infrastructure development on public green spaces 103; protest movement 41, 104, 195; water protests 139, 145
public sphere 12, 66, 84, 91, 224–**5**
public transport **25**, **62**–3, 73–4, 193

qualitative data 13–14, 34–5, 37, 94, 96, 102, 105, 109, 112, 127, 196, 229
quantitative data 13–14, 26, 33, 37, 94, 97, 101, 104, 112, 119, 121, 127, 196

rainwater 94, 129, 131, 133, 137, 141, 147, 152
Rauschmayer, F. 46
reflexive localisation 222, 227–8
reform 2, 22, 86, 91, 132, 200–2, 208, 213; 'Kallikrati' reform 84–5
Regalia, I. 162
regime: 4, 8, 39, 41, 50, 51, 62, 196, 222, 225, 240; climate-neutral regime 3; welfare regime 9, 13, 17, **19**–20, 22–3, 89, 247
regionalised states **21**–**2**

regional policy 11, 158, 159, 164–5, 167, 173, 176–8, 188–90
renewable energy 3, 10, 53, 59, 60, 64–5, **67**, 71, 79, 83, 86, 88, 132, 141, 154, 193–5, 211, 241–3, 246–50
Rennes **28**, 61, 64, 67, 71, 73–4, 76, 79, 82, 84–6, 92, 127–35, 139–40, 143–6, 148–9, 151, 153, 213, 215, 219
Reputation: reputation 50, 52–4, 56, 58, 109–10, 134, 136, 138, 143, 195, 206, 229; trust and reputation **244**, 248
research design 11, 13–15, 33–36
resilience: 220, 224, 228, 239; city resilience 8, 218; resilience of ecological resource system 3–6, 11, 40, 43, 124, 221
resource: resource management 58, 62, 109, 125, 132, 135, 156, 211; resource units **48**, 56; urban resources 12, 192, 250; *see also* ecological resource system
responsibility: collective responsibility 146; European responsibility 151; human responsibility 1; individual responsibility 72, **244**; irresponsibility 232; responsiveness 172–4, 176, 179, 184, 189–90, 212; self-responsibility 89, 91; shared responsibility 207; socio-ecological responsibility 229
Rifkin, J. 225–6
'Right to the city' 8, 14, 91, 103, 195
'Right to water' 8, 127, 155
ROCSET project 247
Romania 9, **16**, **18**–21, **28**, 117, 122, 130, 142, 213–14, 216
Rome **28**, 61, 65, 67, 69–70, 73–4, 76, 83, 86–7, 94, 98, 100, 103–4, 107–8, 110, 112–13, 115, 117, 120, 127–9, 131, 133–40, 142, 145–6, 153, 213, 230
rules: aggregation rules **51**–**2**, 54, 56, 105, 196; choice rules **51**, 54–7, 196, 203; information rules **51**, 53, 56, 106, 193; payoff rules **51**, 53, 56, 194; position rules **51**, 53–4, 56, 195; scope rules **51**, 54–5, 193; *see also* boundary
rural and urban life difference 215

'Saarbrücken – Edible City' 235
sample creation process **17**
sanctions 53, 56, 118, 127, 148–50, 196; *see also* capability
Savenije, H. H. 156
Scandinavian welfare policies 22
Schäpke, N. 46
Schumpeter, J. 225
Schumpeter, J.A. 5, 225
sealing 103
sector *see* third sector; business
Seibel, W. 226

self organisation *see* participation and self-organisation
Sellers, J. M. 22–3
Sen, A. 239–40
SES 3, 9, 23, 44, 46, **48**, 50–8, 240–1, 247
SES framework 46, 49
SET 3, 6, 8–11, 12, 14–16, 18, 33, 35, 44–7, 49–51, 54–7, 59–61, 63–4, 66, 71, 76–80, 127, 206, 209, 220, 240–1, 246, 251
SET model 55–8
shared responsibility *see* responsibility
Sibiu **28**, 61, 94–9, 102–3, 107, 109, 111, 113, 117, 120–2, 229, 231
Single European Climate Mitigation Bill 82
Slovakia **7, 21**
Slovenia **7, 21**
'Smart City' 64, 219–20, 247; *see also* smart governance
smart governance 8, 60, 64, 131, 197, 211, 219; *see also* smart city
smart inclusion 246
social and ecological innovation 226
social capital **49, 52**, 224, 226–7, 238
social cohesion 64, 73, 98, 220, **245**
social conflicts in urban area 111, 136, 143, 193, 196, 198, 224, 242; *see also* conflict
social dilemma 40, 47–50
social ecological sustainability 65–6, 72, 82, 132, 193–4, 216, 221–2, 224, 226, 231, 233–4, 237, 247, 249–52
social exclusion 62
social inclusion 8, 212, 216, 228, 247, 249
social inequality 6, 9, 226, 232
social innovation 1, 4, 5, 11, 45, 74, 91, 123, 210, 219, 221–6, 230–1, 235–6, 238, 240, 242
social justice: inter-temporal justice 248; social and ecological justice 225; social justice 193; socio-ecological transition justice 247; transition justice 247
social movements 103–4, 112, 195, 209, 243
social rights 19
societal change 209, 226, 232; *see also* change
societal innovation 222, 235
soil pollution 96
soil sealing 93, 97
South Korea 208
space: spatial dimensions 73, 87, 156, 199; spatial limitation 197, **245**; urban spaces 91, 131, 198, 232–4, 249–51
Spain **16, 18, 19–23, 28**, 108, 210
speculation: building speculation 99, 234; land speculation 234; real estate and infrastructure speculation 103
stakeholder engagement 102–3; *see also* participation

stakeholders: stakeholders involvement 164; stakeholder network 176, 179, 182; *see also* network
stakeholders state: stakeholders structure 160, 164, **171**–4, 189
STATA software 33
St. Gallen **29**, 60–1, 63, 69, 73, 76–8, 83–4, 94, 96, 107, 110, 113, 118, 127–8, 131, 134, 146, 151, 153–4, 218
Stocker, G. 230
storage 53, 143; pumped-storage power plants 249
Strasbourg **28**, 61–4, 67, 69, 74, 76–7, 79–80, 86–8, 94, 95–7, 99–100, 106–7, 119, 213, 215, 234–5
strategy: sector strategy 167–**8**, 170, 179, 190 (*see also* sector)
structural change 20, 65, 76, 93, 96, 143
structural funds 176, 204; *see also* funding
subsidiarity 200, 204, 213, 220, 227, 251
support: financial support 82–3, 122, 143, 209, 236; support by ICLEI 29–30; support from public authorities **137**, 152
sustainability: sustainability and education 63–4, 72–4, 76, 80–1, 87, 89–90, 114–15, 128, 208, 244, 247; sustainability and participation capability 75, 113, 203, 240–1; three-pillar model of sustainability 62, 64, 89, 95, 202, **207**; *see also* energy; process; programme; social ecological sustainability; urban sustainability; water
sustainable development 1, 3–6, 8–9, 15–16, 30, **31**, 37, 39, 40, 46, 56–7, 66, 76, 80, 87, 93, 95, 98, 129, 131, 135, 143–4, 152, 155–6, 193–4, 198, 208, 218, 221, 227, 244, 246, 249
Sustainable Development Goals 1, 245–46; *see also* UN Post-2015 Agenda
sustainable governance 4, 8, 14, 15, 40, 51, 55, 60–2, 77–9, 81, 86, 89, 96–7, 100, 108–9, 115, 118–20, 131, 146, 150–1, 193, 195, 198–9, 204–5, 208, 210–12, 215, 218, 227, 229, 232, 243–8, 251–2
Sweden 9, **16, 18**–19, **21**, **23**, **28**, 72, 128, 218, 258
Switzerland **16, 18, 19**, 20, **21**–**3**, 26, **29**, 68, 84, 102, 113, 121
system: ecological system 6, 40, 41, 43, 48, 221; green space ecological system 122; resources and ecological system **207**; resource system 3–6, 8, 12, 14–15, 30, 32–3, 35, **48**–9, 52, 55, 59, 93, 125, 193, 244; *see also* SES

Tampere 210
tangibility 123, 196–7, 244
Tarde, Gabriel de 5
target group 34, 160–91
tax 6, 86–7, 122, 202
taxonomy 19, 22

TEPSIE 42–**3**
theory of Communicative Action 223, 231; see also Habermas, J.
theory of Economic Development 5; see also Schumpeter, J.
theory of Social Capital 226; see also Bourdieu, P.
Thessaloniki **28**, 61, 63, 65, 71, 73–4, 79–80, 85–7, 90, 94, 96, 98, 103, 106–7, 110–13, 115–16, 118, 120, 122, 215, 230–1, 234–5
third sector 6–7, 9–10, 11, 71, 193, 196, 224
time horizon 50, 52, 55, 77–8, 81, 97–9, 127, 132–3, 155, 193, 197, 245–6
Timisoara **28**, 61, 63, 68, 71, 73, 76, 78, 80, 85–7, 94–7, 99–100, 113–15, 117–18, 215
Tocqueville de, A. 228
top-down 108, 115, 143, 188, 229, 235, 248–9; see also bottom up
Tosics, I. 21, **22**
trade off 10, **25**, 60, 210, 242
tragedy of the commons' 40, 47, 49, 156, 193, 251; see also Hardin G.
transdisciplinary strategies 97
transformation 10, 20, 39, 44–6, 73, 89, 91, 112, 114, 116, 192, 207, 211, 213, 235, 237, 246–7, 250; Great Transformation 10, 44, 250; see also Polanyi, K
transition: Joint Transition 248; local transition 35–6, 73, 78, 83, 90, 122, 204, 208–9, 246; multilevel transition 204–19; participatory transition 249; socio ecological transition (*see* SET); transition analysis 39
Transition Cities project 210, 211
transition management see management
transparency 67, 103, 106–7, 135, 139, 143, 153, 155, 231, 247
transport 8, 25, 59–60, 62–3, 69, 73–5, 82, 125, 129, 156–7, 193, 213, 219
transportation 59, 69, 73, 74, 82, 125, 156
triangulation 13
Trieste **28**, 61, 66, 69, 71, 74, 77, 79–80, 83, 127, 129, 131–5, 138–9, 142, 144–6, 153, 214
trust 47–54, 56, 58, 80, 99, 103, 107, 113, 116, 123, **136**, 139, 146, 196, 207, 209, 217
Turkey **16**, **18–19**, 20, 26, **29**, 83, 115, 213
typology of welfare regimes 20

Umea **28**, 61, 63–4, 69, 71, 77–8, 80, 82, 84, 88, 94–8, 118, 127, 129, 133, 136, 138–9, 141, 143, 151, 218
uncontrolled woodcutting 60
unemployment 4, 6, 10, 161, 166, 168, 188, 200–3, 223
unemployment rate disparities 10, 200–3

unitary states 21–2
United Kingdom 9, **16**, **19**, **21–3**, **29**, 89–90
UN Post-2015 Agenda 1, 246
Urban Agenda 8, 195, 251–2; see also City statistics
Urban Audit database Eurostat 23, 26, **29**
urban agriculture 7, 10, 94, 112, 225, 232–3, 235
urban food production *see* food production
urban gardening 100, 104, 195, 234–5
urban heat island effect 93, 124
urbanisation **7**, 9–10, 91, 93, 103, 194
urban planning 32, 84–5, 99, 118, 121, 234
urban sprawl 93, 96, 99, 103, 124
urban sustainability 10, 12, 19, 33, 77, 85, 99, 108–9, 120, 151, 154–5, 204–6, 208, 210–11, 214, 216, 231–2, 241, 243
urgency 44, 59, 95, 97, 99, 110, 132
US. 10
users 9, 40, **48**–54, 60, 119, 127–8, 140, 149, 156–7, 194, 196, 198, 224, 249
utility 239
utility provider 87, 127, 135–7, 148, 156, 195, 199

Valencia **28**, 127–9, 131, 133–5, 138–9, 143–6, 148, 151, 153, 218
variables: context variables 47–8, 50–4
Viederman, S. 221
Vision: long term vision 208, 215–16, 246
Voluntariness 232
Von Carlowitz, H.C. 60

wage bargaining system 202
Walsh, A. 157
waste 8, **25**, 60, 64, 80, 126–7, 129, 156, 216, 242, 248
wastewater **25**, 135, 147–8, 151
water: drinking water 9, 96, 125; water management 8, 41, **62**, 125–7, 134, 138, 141, 143, 146, 148–9, 152, 154–6, 195–6, 219; water market 131–2, 157; water privatisation 127–8, 132–3, 138, 144–5, 147, 152–3, 155, 197, 223, 242; water sustainability 137–9, 150; water system 5, 8, 9, 14, **25**, **30–1**, 39, 53, 55–7, 60, 94–5, 119, 122–3, 125–57, 195–9, 212, 216, 242; see also monitoring
Wealth 5–6, 43, 48, 98, 122, 194, 239
Weber, M. 65
welfare state 6, 19–20, 22, 23, 89, 200, 202, 247
well-being 6, 10, 11, 66, 86, 89, 98, 207, 219, 239, 243
White Paper on Multilevel Governance 204
World Commission on Environment and Development 1, 60